JEWISH BIOMEDICAL LAW

JEWISH BIOMEDICAL LAW

Legal and Extra-legal Dimensions

DANIEL B. SINCLAIR

OXFORD
UNIVERSITY PRESS

This book has been printed digitally and produced in a standard specification in order to ensure its continuing availability

OXFORD
UNIVERSITY PRESS

Great Clarendon Street, Oxford OX2 6DP

Oxford University Press is a department of the University of Oxford.
It furthers the University's objective of excellence in research, scholarship,
and education by publishing worldwide in

Oxford New York

Auckland   Cape Town Dar es Salaam   Hong Kong   Karachi
Kuala Lumpur Madrid Melbourne Mexico City   Nairobi
New Delhi Shanghai Taipei Toronto
With offices in
Argentina Austria Brazil Chile Czech Republic France Greece
Guatemala Hungary Italy Japan South Korea Poland Portugal
Singapore Switzerland Thailand Turkey Ukraine Vietnam

Oxford is a registered trade mark of Oxford University Press
in the UK and in certain other countries

Published in the United States
by Oxford University Press Inc., New York

ISBN 978-0-19-826827-7

Acknowledgements

I would like to express my gratitude to Prof. Bernard S. Jackson for his guidance, and helpful and constructive criticism of my work over a period of many years. Thanks are also due to Prof. Shmuel Shilo, Prof. Amos Shapira, and R. William Novick for providing help and support for my research in the past, and to Prof. Daniel Friedman for his encouragement in the preparation of the book.

I have benefited greatly from the thoughtful and insightful comments of academic and professional colleagues on the ideas discussed in the present work, and my thanks are owed to them.

This work has been a long time in the making. I would like to acknowledge the constant support of my wife, Deborah, for this and other academic projects throughout the years. I have learned much about clarity of thought and expression from her, and for that, as well as for her rigorous proofreading of the entire manuscript, I express my heartfelt thanks.

All errors are the sole responsibility of the author.

March 2003   D.B.S.

Contents

Table of Cases

Table of Statutes

Introduction

1. AIM OF THE PRESENT WORK

The treatment of biomedical matters in Jewish law, or *halakhah*,[1] has been the subject of much keen interest since the middle of the twentieth century, and there is no shortage of works describing the *halakhah* in this field. The literature covers almost every area of contemporary biomedical interest, ranging from issues relating to the beginning of life, such as abortion and cloning, to topics concerning the end of life, such as the refusal of life-support, and cadaver organ donations.[2] The present work does not seek to add yet another volume to the long list of books describing biomedical *halakhah*. Instead, it focuses on three general features of Jewish biomedical law: the influence of morality upon the *halakhah* in this area, patient autonomy, and the role of scientific progress in the shaping of halakhic decisions. The bulk of the book deals with the moral dimension of biomedical *halakhah*. Patient autonomy is dealt with principally in Chapters 4 and 5, and the role of scientific progress in halakhic decisions is the major theme in Chapter 6. In order to discuss and analyse these features in a convincing manner, it will be necessary to outline the major doctrines in most of the major areas of biomedical *halakhah*. We will make an effort to keep these outlines short and succinct, and to concentrate, as far as possible, on the three above-mentioned features.

2. THREE FEATURES OF JEWISH BIOMEDICAL LAW

The first and major feature is the role played by universal, rational morality in the shaping of biomedical *halakhah*. Now, the presence of moral principles in one *halakhah* is a well-established phenomenon in Jewish law,

---

[1] *Halakhah* is the Hebrew term for Jewish law and is derived from a root meaning 'to go'. According to R. Nathan of Rome's classical lexicon of the Talmud and Midrash, the word *halakhah* is used to describe Jewish law, since it is 'the path in which the people of Israel goes' (*Arukh Hashalem*, iii. 208 *s.v. halakh*).

[2] For a partial list of materials in the field, see the Bibliography. In 1998, the final volume of A. Steinberg's six-volume Hebrew Language *Encyclopaedia of Jewish Medical Ethics* was published in Jerusalem. This encyclopaedia contains references to a large amount of both classical and modern halakhic material in over eighty entries on a wide range of biomedical topics. The English version is due to be released in the near future.

constituting one of its hallmarks as a religious legal system.[3] These moral principles are part of the halakhic tradition, and have a long and detailed history in halakhic texts. There is, however, another type of moral principle at work within the halakhic system, and that is one the source of which is traced explicitly to universal, rational morality. Moral principles of this type do not, as a rule, possess a lengthy and detailed halakhic history, nor are they well defined in terms of their application. They are particularly significant in the area of biomedical *halakhah*, and it is with this type of moral principle that the present work is chiefly concerned.

In terms of how they function within the *halakhah*, legal norms are fairly specific in nature, they are not generally dependent on a particular context for their application, and they are almost invariably accompanied by a judicial sanction. Moral principles, on the other hand, are usually very general, and their application often depends upon factors of a contextual nature. They normally lack any form of judicial sanction.[4] The moral component of Jewish biomedical law discussed in the present work possesses an additional characteristic, i.e. a source in universal, rational morality. This characteristic indicates an affinity with natural law in general jurisprudence, an affinity which is explored in detail in Chapter 1.[5] Suffice it to say at this stage that there is an affinity but not an identity, and there is no attempt in the present work to make a case for classifying the universal, rational moral component of biomedical *halakhah* as a full-blown form of classical natural law doctrine.

The word 'halakhah' is used in two senses. The first is a wide one, in which it simply designates the normative position under the Jewish tradition on any particular issue. The second sense is a narrow one, in which it signifies the purely legal—as opposed to moral, aggadic,[6] or any other non-legal aspect of the norm in question. The sense in which the word is used in any particular sentence in this work will normally be evident from the context.

The second feature of Jewish biomedical law treated in the present work is patient autonomy, which is discussed mainly in the second half of the book. In general, the idea of autonomy is not associated with Jewish law, and writers in the field of Jewish biomedical law tend to downplay the need for patient consent in comparison with the significant role it plays in the common law.[7] Nevertheless, there is some evidence that

---

[3] See M. Elon, *Jewish Law* (Philadelphia, 1994), 141; B. Jackson, 'The Concept of Religious Law in Judaism', *Aufsteig und Niedergang der Romischen Welt*, 19 (1979), 33.

[4] See Elon, *Jewish Law*, 141–60; A. Lichtenstein, 'Does Jewish Tradition Recognize an Ethic Independent of *Halakhah*?', in *Contemporary Jewish Ethics*, ed. M. Kellner (New York, 1978), 102.   [5] See text at Ch. 1 nn. 99–105.

[6] The term 'aggadah' is defined in s. 4(b) below.

patient autonomy is gaining recognition as a value in biomedical *halakhah*, especially in the context of treating the terminally ill. In the present work, it will be argued that there has always been a role for such autonomy in this area of Jewish law, although a distinction must be made between the way in which the concept of autonomy is used in contemporary liberal thought, and the way in which it functions in the *halakhah* with respect to decision-making by a patient.[8] Halakhic patient autonomy has a different starting point from the modern liberal form, and is more limited in its legal expression. It is also based, *inter alia*, upon the theological principle that healing is fundamentally a Divine activity. The nature and scope of patient autonomy in biomedical *halakhah* is discussed at length in Chapter 4.

The third feature is the relationship between science and *halakhah*. The tremendous progress made in biomedical science in the modern period has raised legal and moral problems of the most serious kind and continues to do so, and no legal system can avoid the fundamental question of how the law ought to relate to scientific progress per se. In terms of Jewish law, this question has received significant attention in the areas of heart transplants, cadaver organ donations for research purposes, and the allocation of scarce medical resources. These areas are all discussed in Chapter 6, the main focus of which is the issue of the relationship between science and *halakhah* and in particular, the influence of scientific developments upon the process of halakhic decision-making. Other areas in which this relationship features are artificial reproductive techniques and genetics, and the religious validity of human healing, which turns to a great extent upon the definition of sound scientific research.

3. METHODOLOGY

For reasons that will be explained shortly, the method we have chosen to apply in the present work is to begin with a focused study of the major areas of substantive medical *halakhah*—abortion, artificial reproductive techniques, genetics, the obligation to heal and patient autonomy, withdrawing life support from a terminally ill patient, defining death, heart transplants, organ donation, and the allocation of medical resources—and to reserve any general theoretical remarks for the Conclusion, rather than beginning with a chapter on legal and moral theory, and proceeding to a

---

[7] J. D. Bleich, 'Risk Versus Benefits in Treating the Gravely Ill Patient', in *Jewish Values in Bioethics*, ed. L. Meier (New York, 1986), 73; G. Rabinowitz, 'Procedure for a Daughter who has Digressed from the Correct Way' (Heb.), *Halakhah Urefuah*, 1 (1980), 336. See D. Shatz, 'Concepts of Autonomy in Jewish Medical Ethics', *The Jewish Law Annual*, 12 (1997), 5, for a discussion of this issue in Jewish law.   [8] See Shatz, 'Concepts of Autonomy', 24.

study of the substantive law. The focus of this study is, as stated, the three features mentioned above, but only in the Conclusion will any attempt be made to use the results of that study in order to gain a clearer understanding of the way in which biomedical *halakhah* works.

There are two main reasons for choosing this type of methodology. The first is the absence of a rich body of academic legal theory in Jewish law. *Halakhah* has been applied for over three thousand years, but its academic study in terms of any type of sophisticated legal theory is very new,[9] and the existing tools for carrying out a theoretical analysis of an issue such as the relationship between law and morality are scarce. It is not really possible to rely principally upon the theoretical insights of a large number of modern legal scholars, and to apply them directly to the material under discussion in a convincing manner. The only material from which appropriate tools of analysis may be legitimately fashioned in the field of biomedical *halakhah* is the substantive material in the field: there is simply no other source. According to the present writer, therefore, it makes better sense to undertake a general study of biomedical *halakhah*, with a view to gaining a proper understanding of the above-mentioned features in context, before proceeding to a purely theoretical discussion of those features.

Another reason for choosing this approach is in order to avoid the danger of applying contemporary Western tools of legal analysis to Jewish law in an indiscriminate and insensitive manner.[10] Our attempt both to construct the tools of theoretical analysis, and to apply them to biomedical *halakhah* as an organic part of the study of biomedical halakhic texts, will, it is hoped, help us to avoid this pitfall, since the theory will be rooted in the halakhic material itself, rather than in an independent discussion of legal theories drawn mainly from Western jurisprudence.

4. BRIEF INTRODUCTORY REMARKS ON THE STRUCTURE OF JEWISH LAW

(a) Literary Sources

The *halakhah* is the traditional normative framework of the Jewish people. It consists of a vast body of primary and secondary norms governing everything from minute details of religious ritual to complex issues of criminal and civil law. These norms were developed over some three

---

[9] See B. Jackson, B. Lifshitz, A. Gray, and D. Sinclair, 'Halakhah and Law', in *The Oxford Handbook of Jewish Studies*, ed. M. Goodman, J. Cohen, and D. Sorkin (Oxford, 2002), 643.

[10] See H. Ben-Menahem, 'The Judicial Process and the Nature of Jewish Law', *An Introduction to the History and Sources of Jewish Law*, ed. N. Hecht, B. Jackson, S. Passamaneck, D. Piatelli, and A. Rabello (Oxford, 1996), 421.

thousand years, and have been the subject of innumerable commentaries, codes, learned monographs, *responsa* (rabbinic case law) and, more recently, purely academic discussion. The major literary source of the law is the Bible (Torah), and the major corpus of Jewish law is the Talmud, a work compiled some fifteen hundred years ago. The Talmud is an extensive commentary on the Mishnah, an earlier and much more concise halakhic compendium. An important commentary on the Talmud was written by R. Solomon b. Isaac (eleventh century), known by the acronym, Rashi. A group of medieval scholars known as Tosafot wrote important glosses on the textual structure and legal analysis of the Talmud. Rashi's commentary and Tosafot's glosses are regularly printed together with the text of the Talmud. Amongst the other important medieval commentators and glossators on the Talmud are R. Moses b. Nahman (Ramban) and R. Solomon b. Adret (Rashba). The most important codes of Jewish law are Maimonides' *Mishneh Torah* (twelfth century); R. Jacob b. Asher's *Tur* (fourteenth century), and R. Joseph Karo's *Shulhan Arukh* (sixteenth century). These codes have been supplemented over the ages by numerous super-commentaries and glosses aimed at explaining and updating the original material. In addition, halakhic authorities published volumes of their *responsa*, i.e. answers to practical problems. These collections of authoritative answers serve as the case law of the *halakhah*, and for modern issues, especially those with which this book is concerned, the *responsa* literature constitutes an extremely important source of *halakhah*.[11]

(b) *Halakhah* and *Aggadah*

There is a fundamental distinction in Jewish law between *halakhah* (in the narrow sense) and *aggadah*. The word *halakhah* is used to denote binding law, and any material relating directly to such laws. *Aggadah*, on the other hand, is material specifically related to the biblical narratives, moral

---

[11] The leading modern work on Jewish law is M. Elon's four-volume *Jewish Law* (see n. 3) and the third volume of this work is devoted entirely to an account of the literary sources of the *halakhah*. Another useful work dealing with the sources of Jewish law and their history is *An Introduction to the History and Sources of Jewish Law* mentioned in the previous note. It is noteworthy that Elon makes a distinction, based upon general jurisprudence, between the literary and the legal sources of Jewish law, and lists five legal sources of the *halakhah*, i.e. interpretation, legislation, custom, precedent, and legal reasoning. Each of these legal sources is dealt with at length in the first two volumes of his *Jewish Law*. An old, but still relevant book on the legal sources of the *halakhah* is Z. H. Chajes, *The Student's Guide Through the Talmud*, trans. J. Shachter (New York, 1960). The entry on 'Halacha and Law' in *The Oxford Handbook of Jewish Studies* (n. 9) carries an extensive bibliography of the modern scholarship in the field, and reference should also be made to B. Jackson, 'Mishpat Ivri, Halakhah and Legal Philosophy: *Agunah* and the Theory of Legal Sources', *Jewish Studies, an Internet Journal*, 1 (2002), 69, at http://www.biu.ac.il/JS/JSIJ/1-2002/Jackson.pdf, accessed 26 March 2003.

teachings, and the rational, ideological, and mystical underpinnings of Jewish texts and halakhic norms. In common with the *halakhah* it has been the subject of interpretation, literary exposition, commentary, and development for thousands of years. Unlike the *halakhah*, however, it is not considered binding, and it lacks any mechanism for deciding on definitive outcomes to its discussions.[12]

This distinction between *halakhah* and *aggadah* carries normative significance, and the derivation of halakhic norms from aggadic sources was strongly disapproved of by the post-talmudic authorities known as Gaonim (sixth–eleventh centuries),[13] support for whose position may be derived from the Talmud itself.[14] In other periods of Jewish history, however, aggadic elements have been incorporated into the *halakhah*, and it is evident that in practice the line between *halakhah* and *aggadah* is not an easy one to preserve. Halakhists have also felt free to support their arguments on the basis of sources drawn from the *aggadah*.[15] Nevertheless, the basic distinction between *halakhah* and *aggadah* remains an important one in Jewish law, and the general rule is that halakhic decisions are to be based on halakhic sources only. This issue is of particular significance in the biomedical area. As a result of the dearth of specifically halakhic material in relation to many of the novel problems raised by contemporary scientific advances, many a halakhist has been tempted to look to the *aggadah* as a source for providing guidance to these problems. However, the scholars concerned generally remain sensitive to the distinction between the two types of source, and to its ramifications for the binding quality of solutions propounded on the basis of aggadic material. The influence of aggadic sources upon the *halakhah* is especially pronounced in the context of artificial reproductive techniques discussed in Chapter 2, and a special section is devoted to the use of aggadic sources in a halakhic context in that chapter.

(c) The Distinction between Biblical and Rabbinic Law

An important and pervasive distinction in Jewish law is that which is drawn between biblical and rabbinic law. The two types of law are distinguished from each other on the basis of both literary and doctrinal

---

[12] *Yerushalmi Peah*, 2: 4; *Yerushalmi Hagigah*, 1: 8; *Encyclopaedia Talmudit*, ix. 252–3; *Kol Kitvei Maharaz Hayut* (Jerusalem, 1958), 203. Also see the second part of Chajes *Student's Guide*, and Elon, *Jewish Law*, 94–104.

[13] See G. Libson, 'Halakhah and Law in the Period of the Gaonim', in Hecht *et al. An Introduction*, 197.

[14] See *Teshuvot Hagaonim* (Harkavi), nos. 9, 352; *Teshuvot Hagaonim* (*Hemdah Genuzah*), no. 124. See also Rashbam, *Bava Bathra* 130b, *s.v. ad sheyomru*.

[15] See R. Tam, *Sefer Hayashar*, no. 519; *Resp. Shevut Ya'acov*, 2 no. 178; cf. *Resp. Noda Biyehuda*, 2, *Yoreh Deah*, no. 161; *Resp. Havat Yair*, no. 14.

factors, and there are fundamental debates between eminent halakhic authorities with regard to the classification of various types of law.[16] Nevertheless, it is unanimously accepted that the binding quality of biblical law is superior to that of rabbinic law, and that the exercise of rabbinic creativity in terms of modifying the *halakhah* in order to accommodate individual needs or changing objective circumstances, is confined, by and large, to the latter. Noteworthy illustrations of the difference between biblical and rabbinic law in this context are the rule that doubts regarding biblical laws are to be resolved in a stringent manner whereas those regarding rabbinic ones are resolved leniently, and the principle that mitigating factors such as economic loss and the preservation of human dignity are operative in relation to rabbinic laws alone.[17]

The distinction between biblical and rabbinic law is important in all areas of *halakhah*, and the biomedical field is no exception. It crops up in almost every topic discussed in the following chapters, from the classification of the prohibition on non-therapeutic foeticide to the definition of the religious validity of bringing a child into the world using artificial insemination. Its role as a catalyst for rabbinic creativity is one of the hallmarks of modern biomedical *halakhah*.

(d) The Casuistic Nature of the *Halakhah*

The halakhic system is casuistic both in relation to its literary style, and its approach to individual cases. From the Talmud to contemporary halakhic literature, the preferred style of presentation is case analysis rather than generalized rules and principles.[18] There is also a tendency in *halakhah* to allow its vast store of primary and secondary principles to be moulded by the facts of the particular case. The *halakhah* is quite prepared to distinguish cases on their facts, and sometimes, to permit a radical departure from the governing legal norm in order to avoid negative consequences in the case at hand. This aspect of halakhic reasoning is particularly evident in the field of modern biomedical law, and a number of illustrations will be found in the following chapters, especially in relation to abortion and assisted reproduction.[19] The casuistic approach to the resolution of cases in the light of the consequences of the decision for the people concerned is particularly apt in the field of biomedical *halakhah*, since it is often the very lives of those people that are hanging in the halakhic balance.

---

[16] See Elon, *Jewish Law*, 207–12.
[17] See ibid. 212–14; Maimonides, *Hilkhot Kilaim*, 10: 29; *Resp. Rema*, no. 125; *Resp. Divrei Hayyim*, no. 35; N. Rakover, *Gedol Kevod Habriyot* (Jerusalem, 1998).
[18] See Elon, *Jewish Law*, 1072–6.
[19] This type of casuistry is also discussed in the first section of the Conclusion.

5. COMPARATIVE LAW

Jewish biomedical law is of concern not only to Jewish and Israeli law: it is a matter of universal interest. For example, it was cited in the recent decision of the English Court of Appeal permitting the surgical separation of Siamese twins in a case in which not operating meant that neither twin would survive for more than nine months, and operating meant that the weaker one would die immediately upon being separated from the stronger. The Court wrestled with the concept of necessity as a justification for permitting one innocent life to be taken in order that another equally innocent life be spared, even though neither was in immediate danger, and found guidance in the halakhic sources dealing with this type of dilemma.[20] This case, and the relevant halakhic sources, are discussed in detail in Chapter 5.

The comparative approach is also used in this book in order to illuminate various aspects of biomedical *halakhah*, ranging from foetal status and abortion to the withdrawal of life-support from the terminally ill. One topic in which the comparative perspective plays a major role in clarifying the *halakhah* is patient autonomy, and the second half of Chapter 4 is devoted to this issue. In general, this type of explanatory comparison is made between Jewish and common law, although there are instances, as in the case of abortion, where the canon law provides the best comparative perspective for illuminating the halakhic approach.

6. THE INFLUENCE OF BIOMEDICAL *HALAKHAH* ON THE ISRAELI LEGAL SYSTEM

Throughout the book, reference is made to the influence of biomedical *halakhah* on Israeli law. The relationship between *halakhah* and Israeli law in general is a long-standing feature of Israeli jurisprudence,[21] and it is particularly strong in the biomedical field. In order fully to appreciate the many references to biomedical *halakhah* in Israeli law, some insight into the history of this relationship would be helpful.

Matters of personal status, i.e. marriage and divorce, have been within the exclusive jurisdiction of the Rabbinical courts—which are staffed by religious judges applying traditional *halakhah*—since the establishment of the State of Israel in 1948. Religious jurisdiction in this area was a feature of both the legal system under the British Mandate and the Ottoman

---

[20] See *In re A (Children)* (2001) 2 WLR, 480. The case is discussed in detail in Ch. 5, s. 6.
[21] See Elon, *Jewish Law*, 1619–1945. Also see D. Sinclair, 'Jewish Law in the State of Israel', in Hecht *et al.*, *An Introduction*, 397.

system that preceded it, and Israeli law simply took on board the existing legal arrangement. The jurisdiction of the Rabbinical Courts in matters of marriage and divorce is codified in the Rabbinical Courts Jurisdiction (Marriage and Divorce) Law, 5713-1953, the first section of which provides that 'matters relating to the marriage and divorce of Jewish citizens or residents of the State of Israel shall be within the sole jurisdiction of the Rabbinical Courts'. This statute also provides that the law to be applied in these matters is the 'law of the *Torah*' (s. 2).

Other areas of Israeli law are governed by a secular system, the basis of which lies in the common law and equity of the Mandatory period. The majority of judges in Israeli courts are secular, with little expertise in Jewish law, although the Supreme Court always has at least one expert in Jewish law sitting on the bench. Still, it has always been unofficial practice amongst judges and lawyers in the secular system to make use of halakhic language and concepts when these help elucidate the issues at bar. There is also a small number of cases in which Jewish law effectively provided the basis for the court's decision, and this continues to be the case, especially in the biomedical field. In all these cases, the law applied is Israeli law; the halakhic grounds cited in the judgments merely provide justification for a decision under the law of the land.[22]

A major judicial debate over the formal role of Jewish law in the Israeli legal system took place in the wake of the enactment of the Foundations of Law Act, 5740-1980, which dealt with the filling in of lacunae in the law. Prior to 1980, such gaps were filled, in theory at any rate, by rules and principles drawn from English common law and equity. The 1980 law abolished this link between Israeli and English law and provided for the filling in of lacunae: 'Where a court finds that a question requiring a decision cannot be answered by reference to an enactment or a judicial precedent or by way of analogy, it shall decide the same in the light of the principles of freedom, justice, equity and peace of the heritage of Israel.' In relation to the last phrase of the section, it is noteworthy that according to the Declaration of Independence, the State of Israel is 'based upon freedom, justice and peace as envisaged by the prophets of Israel'. Clearly, there is an echo in this Act of both the wording and the spirit of the democratic sentiments articulated in that founding charter.

For a court to be required to turn to the 'heritage of Israel'—and there is no doubt in the mind of the Israeli judiciary that this term applies to the legal heritage of the Jewish people, i.e. Jewish law—there must be a legal issue to which there is absolutely no answer in the existing law, i.e. a lacuna. Such a situation is extremely rare in any developed legal system,

---

[22] See the cases cited in Sinclair, ibid. 410–11, 413–15. Also see the case of *Kurtam* v. *State of Israel*, Cr. A. 480/85, PD 40(3), 637, which is discussed in detail in Ch. 4.

since analogy normally yields answers to virtually all legal questions. Indeed, one of the parliamentarians who proposed the bill that led to the Foundations of Law Act stated quite explicitly that 'it is doubtful whether even half a per cent of the cases before the court would fall into the category of a *lacuna*'. It was also emphasized by the same member of the Israeli parliament that the law 'was not intended to possess any far-reaching practical consequences; its significance was primarily symbolic'.[23]

This approach to the law was challenged by Elon J., then Deputy President of the Supreme Court, in the leading case of *Kupat Am Bank* v. *Hendeles*.[24] According to Elon J., the scope of the Foundations of Law Act is not restricted to the filling in of lacunae in the law, but extends to complex questions of interpretation. In his view, the interpretation of such questions is to be governed by the principles of Jewish law. This approach, however, was rejected by the majority in the Supreme Court on the grounds that there is a clear difference between a lacuna and a question of interpretation, even if the latter is extremely complex, and the Foundations of Law Act is clearly confined to the former. Also, the majority pointed out that the fundamental postulates of Israeli law were quite different from those of Jewish law, and it would be ill-advised to mix the two systems. It was also pointed out by the majority that the Foundations of Law Act was couched in extremely wide terms precisely in order to indicate that the legislature did not intend to make Jewish law systemically binding upon the judiciary, even in relation to genuine lacunae. The use of phrases such as 'heritage of Israel', and the need to ensure that the results of applying it to any novel problem conform to the democratic standards of 'freedom, justice, equity and peace', indicate that the intention of the legislator was merely to point the judges towards Jewish law in a general way, and to give them the option of selecting rules or principles from that system that would lead to a result in conformity with the spirit of democracy. This is not the type of application envisaged by Elon J., who argues for a much more systematic adoption of the *halakhah* under the 1980 Act.

In a Further Hearing devoted specifically to the proper scope of the Foundations of Law Act, the majority view in the Supreme Court was that the interpretation of legal concepts does not fall within the scope of the Foundations of Law Act. It was also emphasized that even when looking to Jewish law for inspiration, Israeli courts should not use rabbinical authorities as expert witnesses in determining the legal position. Rather,

---

[23] See Sinclair, ibid. 412.
[24] FH 13/80, PD 35(2) 785 and see Sinclair, ibid. 412–13.

Israeli judges are to go directly to the sources of the *halakhah* and derive the legal position on the basis of first-hand research.

On the basis of this decision, and in the light of the cases decided after the Act, it is evident that as far as the Israeli judiciary is concerned, the aim of the legislature in passing the Act was not the mandatory imposition of Jewish law upon Israeli judges. The Act simply gave expression to the existing practice of judges and lawyers learned in Jewish law of making use of that system in cases in which it would help the court to arrive at a decision based upon 'freedom, justice, equity and peace'.

In the wake of the *Kupat Am* case, the position regarding the role of Jewish law in the Israeli legal system reverts to what it was prior to the Foundations of Law Act. Israeli judges and lawyers have habitually cited Jewish law in their decisions, arguments, and learned writings. On occasion, they have also used Jewish law in order to help them arrive at a conclusion in a particular case. The citation habit does not seem to be dying out, at least not yet, and it may be concluded that by virtue of long usage alone, Jewish law is a part of the Israeli legal system even in areas other than that of personal status.[25]

It is against this background that the references throughout the present work to the influence of biomedical *halakhah* on Israeli law need to be understood. Contemporary Israeli biomedical law is an area in which the *halakhah* plays a highly significant role in Israeli law, and a prime example is the *Kurtam* case,[26] discussed at the end of Chapter 4, involving coercive life-saving medical treatment. The acceptance of the halakhic position by the court in that case was due in no small measure to the fact that Jewish law has been dealing with the complexities of life and death for thousands of years, and as a result has developed an extremely richly textured approach to these issues. Another example is the recent Draft Law: The Terminally Ill Patient, 2002, which provides a practical medical framework for the contemporary halakhic position in this area—discussed in detail in Chapters 4 and 5—whilst at the same time, taking into account the democratic demand for patient autonomy at the end of life. The Appendix outlines the major provisions of this draft law, and illustrates the influence of the *halakhah* upon its formulation.

The following chapters discuss a number of illustrations of this type, thereby demonstrating the relevance of an ancient religious legal system to the biomedical law of a young, secular democracy.

---

[25] The academic study of Jewish law has flourished in the Israeli legal academic community since the establishment of the State. Notwithstanding a particularly heated debate over legitimacy of the movement in academic circles to prepare parts of Jewish law for large-scale adoption by Israeli law (see Elon, *Jewish Law*, 1906–17), Jewish law continues to thrive as an academic discipline, and is a required subject in Israeli law degrees.

[26] See n. 22.

1

Abortion

1. FOETAL STATUS AND ABORTION

The killing of a foetus is not an act of homicide[1] in Jewish law. Hence, abortion is permitted for the sake of saving the mother's life, or preventing serious damage to her health. This mishnah is the major halakhic source for such a position:

If a woman is in hard travail,[2] one cuts up the offspring in her womb and brings it forth member by member,[3] because her life comes before the life of her foetus. But if the greater part[4] has proceeded forth, one may not set aside one person for the sake of saving another.[5]

The mishnah deals with the prioritization of the claims to life of the mother and the foetus respectively. Prior to birth, both are living beings, but, as is evident from the end of the mishnah, the mother is a person whereas the foetus is not, and therefore 'her life comes before the life of her foetus'. Once the major part of the foetus has emerged, however, the foetus is also a person, and the general rule is that one person may not be killed in order to save the life of another.

The use of the word 'life' in relation to foetal existence inside the womb indicates that the mishnah does, indeed, recognize the foetus as a living

---

[1] A foetus is excluded from the scope of culpable homicide in Jewish law on the grounds that it is not a person, and the death penalty, which is the hallmark of the crime of homicide in Jewish law, is not meted out to a non-person (*Sifra, Emor*, 20: 1; *Mekhilta, Mishpatim*, 4). It ought to be pointed out that in general, the word 'homicide' in the present work refers to the killing of a human being, and not to the distinction between intentional and unintentional killing.

[2] The Hebrew for 'hard travail' is *mekashah*. By using this word, the mishnah is clearly referring to the biblical passage describing the death of Rachel in the course of giving birth to Benjamin (Gen. 35: 16–17). Although the Hebrew root *kashah* does, indeed, mean 'hard', the biblical context indicates that it is not merely a hard birth that is under discussion, but a life-threatening one.

[3] In terms of late-term or 'partial birth' abortion, little has changed since mishnaic times. The same process, i.e. the dismemberment of the foetus inside its mother's body, is used today, see *Stenberg v. Carhart* 530 US 914 (2000) for a Supreme Court decision on the constitutionality of a Nebraska statute banning this procedure.

[4] This definition is amplified in *Niddah*, 3: 5, according to which it means the forehead. On the question of how much of the forehead must emerge in order to render the foetus a legal person, see Maimonides, *Hilkhot Rozeah*, 1: 9; Tur, *Yoreh Deah*, 194; *Shulhan Arukh, Yoreh Deah*, 194: 10; *Resp. Melamed Lehoil, Yoreh Deah*, no. 69.   [5] *Oholoth*, 7: 8.

being prior to its attainment of personhood. The view that the biological life of the foetus commences at conception is found in the Talmud, in an aggadic passage that records the opinion of Antoninus, a Roman emperor who appears in a number of passages in the company of R. Judah the Prince, to the effect that a foetus would not be capable of surviving without an animating spirit or 'biological soul'. His proof is an empirical one, i.e. since even a piece of meat will not remain fresh for more than three days unless it has been salted, a foetus cannot live and grow inside its mother's womb unless it has a biological soul. R. Judah the Prince accepts Antoninus' view, and even finds scriptural support for it.[6] This recognition of a foetus as a living being in biological terms is not, however, translated into legal doctrine with regard to abortion. In keeping with its aggadic nature, the notion of life at conception does not figure in a single halakhic source on the question of abortion for the sake of saving maternal life.[7]

Personhood for purposes of the law of homicide is only achieved by born individuals, and the mother's life takes precedence over that of her foetus precisely because she is such a legal person, whereas the foetus is not. The Hebrew word used by the mishnah to indicate legal personhood is *nefesh*. This word includes both biological and legal personhood, but it is used in the mishnah to indicate legal personhood only. In biblical criminal law, *nefesh* is used with reference to the mandatory death penalty imposed upon any person found guilty of the crime of homicide, i.e. 'You shall give a *nefesh* for a *nefesh*.'[8] The nexus between biology and law implicit in the word '*nefesh*' is expressed in the talmudic rule that the death penalty applies only if the victim of the homicide was a physically viable individual. There is, therefore, no mandatory death penalty for the killing of a foetus, or a person suffering from a fatal organic defect, since they both lack physical viability.[9]

In this context, it is noteworthy that according to the *halakhah*, a person will not be executed for homicide unless the victim, in addition to being born, also enjoys a presumption of viability, which is obtained by either a full nine-month pregnancy or survival for thirty days.[10] Accordingly, the rule that foetal life does not override that of the mother will only apply if the foetus is born and enjoys a presumption of viability.

---

[6] Job 10: 12. The source of the discussion is *Sanhedrin*, 91a. For the historical identity of the talmudic Antoninus, see *Encyclopaedia Judaica*, iii. 165. There is, of course, abundant aggadic material dealing with the spiritual life of the foetus and its development *in utero*, see A. Steinberg, *Encyclopaedia of Jewish Medical Ethics* (Heb.), v (Jerusalem, 1996), 115–21.

[7] See I. Jakobovits, *Jewish Medical Ethics* (New York, 1975), 182–3, and J. D. Bleich, 'Abortion in Halakhic Literature', in F. Rosner and J. D. Bleich (eds.), *Jewish Bioethics* (New York, 1979), 147.   [8] Lev. 24: 17. Also see n. 27.

[9] *Sanhedrin*, 84b, and see Ch. 5, s. 5(b).   [10] See Maimonides, *Hilkhot Rozeah*, 2: 6.

Halakhic authorities have consistently maintained that foeticide is not an act of full-blown homicide, and the fact that it is not subject to the death penalty is a significant factor underlying this position. In criminal matters in particular, there is a strong connection between the provision of a penalty and the existence of an offence.[11]

The analysis underlying the mishnaic ruling is now clear, and Rashi spells it out: 'as long as the foetus has not emerged into the air, it is not a person and [it] may be killed in order to save the mother'.[12]

It ought to be noted that some modern halakhic authorities adopt the view that in relation to the theoretical analysis of abortion law, a foetus ought to be defined as a potential person, whilst others suggest that there is a category of quasi-personhood that is applicable to a foetus in this context.[13] However, the ruling that the mother's life takes precedence over that of the foetus remains unaffected by both of these analyses. In a situation of conflict, maternal life carries greater normative weight than that of the foetus, even if the latter is defined as a potential or a quasi-person.

A different analysis of the mishnah is offered by Maimonides, the effect of which is to upgrade the status of the foetus and restrict therapeutic abortion to cases of a direct threat to the mother's life. His analysis, and the numerous conceptual difficulties to which it is subject, are discussed below. It ought to be emphasized that Maimonides' approach is not adopted by other authorities; notwithstanding his major role in the codification of Jewish law, his view remains that of only one—albeit highly influential—authority, whereas the non-personhood of the foetus is the explanation for the mishnaic ruling given by the majority of classical commentators.[14] It is on this basis of both its inherent difficulties and its

---

[11] The absence of a positive criminal sanction for a particular act of homicide indicates that it is permissible, in morally complex situations, to carry out that act without incurring any legal liability, see Ch. 5, s. 5 (c).

[12] *Sanhedrin*, 72b, *s.v. yaza*. A similar formulation is employed by other classical authorities, see Ramban, *Niddah*, 44b, *s.v. veha*; Meiri, *Sanhedrin*, 72b, *s.v. ubarah*; *Resp. Radbaz*, 1 no. 695.

[13] See R. Isser Yehuda Unterman, *Shevet Miyehudah*, i (Jerusalem, 1959), 10. The basis for R. Unterman's approach is the potential of the foetus for attaining viable life. Foeticide is, therefore, a lesser form of homicide. It is not a full-blown form of the crime. Consequently, a person is not obliged to choose martyrdom rather than commit foeticide, which would be the case if it had fallen into the category of full murder (*Sanhedrin*, 74a). See also the analysis of R. Hayyim Soloveitchik (*Hiddushei R. Hayyim Halevi, Hilkhot Rozeah*, 1: 9) and R. Moses Sternbuch's suggestion that a foetus is a 'half-measure' for purposes of punishment (*Yoma*, 74a, cited in *Resp. Seridei Esh*, 3 no. 127).

[14] It is noteworthy that in formulating the law mandating the destruction of the foetus in order to save the mother's life, R. Joseph Caro adopts Maimonides' language verbatim (*Shulhan Arukh, Hoshen Mishpat*, 425: 2). The adoption of Maimonides' approach to the rationale of a ruling in the *Shulhan Arukh* is not, however, that halakhically significant, since the authority of the *Shulhan Arukh* lies in its practical rulings rather than their rationales: see M. Elon, *Jewish Law* (Philadelphia, 1994), 1319–41. Note in particular Elon's remark that: 'The *Shulhan Arukh* presents only the normative rule; in contrast to Maimonides . . . it includes neither rationales for the law nor any philosophic considerations.'

minority status that Maimonides' analysis is disregarded by R. Yehiel Weinberg in a case in which he feels that the majority view is the more appropriate one for the situation at hand.[15]

Foetal status is also discussed in other areas of Jewish law, e.g. ritual purity and some aspects of civil law. In some of these areas, the foetus is endowed with legal status at certain stages of its development, i.e. forty days[16] and three months.[17] These stages however, are specific to these areas of *halakhah*,[18] and there is no indication in the Talmud that they also apply to abortion. Nevertheless, halakhic authorities do invoke the stages of foetal development as supporting arguments in abortion decisions. In fact, this makes perfect sense on purely medical grounds, since the earlier an abortion is performed, the less risky it is to the mother's life and reproductive health. In doctrinal terms, however, it must be emphasized that the stages of foetal development never supplant the fundamental criterion in abortion *halakhah*, namely, the preservation of the mother's life.[19] The purely supporting role of these stages of foetal development in the abortion context is clearly articulated by R. Yair Bachrach, who characterizes both the forty-day and the three-month stages as criteria based upon 'the inclination of the mind and reasoning of the stomach'.[20] In R. Bachrach's view, the halakhic decision to abort turns solely upon the type of threat posed by the foetus to its mother's life. The stages of foetal development are not an integral part of the legal doctrine of foeticide in the *halakhah*, and R. Bachrach emphasizes the non-doctrinal origin of these criteria in

[15] See *Resp. Seridei Esh*, 3 no.127.

[16] *Niddah*, 30a; *Yevamot*, 69b. According to these sources, a foetus that has not reached its fortieth day is 'mere water' for the purposes of ritual purity and the eating of tithes. Post-talmudic halakhists extend this limit to civil law, and maintain that a father may pass title to property to his foetus after the fortieth day (*Siftei Kohen, Hoshen Mishpat*, 210: 2). It is noteworthy that Aristotle (*History of Animals*, 7:3) maintains that a male foetus receives its rational form forty days after conception. This period corresponds to the forty-day period of 'pure blood' specified by the Bible, which follow the birth of a male child (Lev. 12: 2–4).

[17] *Niddah*, 8b.

[18] See *Yevamot*, 78a–b; *Gittin*, 23b; *Sanhedrin*, 80b; *Hullin*, 58a, and *Bava Kamma*, 78b; *Tur, Hoshen Mishpat*, 350; *Siftei Kohen, Yoreh Deah*, 79: 8; *Mishneh Lemelekh, Hilkhot Tumat Met*, 3: 1; *Ma'adanei Yom Tov, Niddah*, 1: 3; *Sidrei Taharah, Yoreh Deah*, 194: 7. Also see A. Aptowitzer, 'The Status of the Embryo in Jewish Law', *Jewish Quarterly Review*, 15 (1924), 85, and G. Ellinson, 'The Foetus in the Halakhah' (Heb.), *Sinai*, 66 (1970), 20.

[19] See *Resp. Torat Hesed, Even Haezer*, no. 42; *Resp. Seridei Esh*, 3 no. 127. The purely secondary role of the stages of foetal development is demonstrated by the fact that they are almost entirely ignored in the *responsa* on the abortion of a Tay-Sachs foetus discussed at length in s. 5 below. In that debate, R. Waldenberg extends his permission to abort a foetus stricken with Tay-Sachs to the seventh month, whereas his protagonist, R. Feinstein, insists that no Tay-Sachs foetus of any age whatsoever may be aborted. R. Feinstein only mentions the 3-month stage in passing at the end of the *responsum*, as part of a general critique of R. Waldenberg.

[20] *Resp. Havat Yair*, no. 31; cf. *Resp. Pri Hasadeh*, 4 no. 50; *Resp. Yabia Omer*, 4, *Even Haezer*, no. 1.

his remark that they are found in 'medical science and conventional morality'. R. Bachrach does not, of course, intend to disqualify the use of the stages of foetal development as supporting arguments in abortion decisions. His sole concern is to ensure that they are not treated as primary arguments in this area of the law. The use of these stages in a secondary role is, indeed, a pervasive feature of abortion *halakhah* in the modern period.[21]

An argument often encountered in *responsa* adopting a stringent approach to abortion is that foetal life must possess significant legal, and not merely biological, status, since the Sabbath may be broken for the sake of saving it.[22] Breaking the Sabbath on behalf of a born individual needs a legal justification, thereby indicating that it is not a step to be taken lightly. It may, therefore, be assumed that by qualifying for life-saving activity on the Sabbath, a foetus must also be legally significant.[23]

In fact, the legal position with regard to violating the Sabbath in order to save a foetus is far from clear. Many authorities explain that the Sabbath is broken on the basis of a concern for the life of the foetus only because a threat to the life of the foetus is, by definition, also a threat to the life of the mother. Accordingly, it is not the saving of foetal life that overrides the Sabbath, but the saving of the life of the mother.[24] This understanding of the law regarding Sabbath-breaking in the case of a sick foetus undoubtedly reflects the fact that in the past, the scope for diagnosing foetal problems independently of those of the mother was virtually non-existent. The law regarding the breaking of the Sabbath for the sake of a distressed foetus is not, therefore, conclusive proof of its status as a legal person.

---

[21] See *Resp. Beth Shlomoh, Hoshen Mishpat*, no. 132; *Resp. Seridei Esh*, 3 no. 127. Also see *Resp. Rav Pa'alim*, 4, *Yoreh Deah*, no. 14; *Resp. Ahiezer*, 3 no. 65; the sources cited in n. 14 above, and A. Lichtenstein, 'A Halakhic Perspective on Abortion' (Heb.), *Tehumin*, 21 (1991), 93.

[22] See e.g. *Resp. Torat Hesed, Even Haezer*, no. 42; *Shevet Miyehudah* (n. 13); *Resp. Iggrot Moshe, Hoshen Mishpat*, 2 no. 102.

[23] See *Encyclopaedia Judaica*, xiii. 509–10, for a concise summary of the principle that saving human life (*pikuah nefesh*) overrides the sanctity of the Sabbath.

[24] Rosh, *Yoma*, 8, no. 13; *Magen Avraham, Orah Hayyim*, 330: 15; Nahmanides, *Torat Ha'adam, Inyan Hasakanah, s.v. midekamar mitaker; Korban Netanel, Yoma*, 8 no. 20. In the case of a pregnant woman who dies in childbirth on the Sabbath, the Talmud provides that the mother may be cut open and the baby removed, even though a breach of the Sabbath laws is involved (*Arakhin*, 7a–b). This does not, however, constitute conclusive evidence that the Sabbath is to be desecrated for the sake of foetal life since, as Tosafot explain, permission to break the Sabbath in order to save the foetus is based upon the fact that had the mother not died, the foetus would already have been born. Hence, its status is that of a full legal person, whom the mother's death has prevented from leaving her womb (*Niddah*, 44a, *s.v. ihu*). R. Moses Isserles points out that care must be taken in order to ensure that the mother is indeed dead before taking any action to remove the foetus from her body (Rema, *Orah Hayyim*, 330: 5). Also see the final section of the present chapter for the relevance of this discussion to modern Israeli law (n. 186).

Another reason for casting doubt on the argument that the rule permitting violation of the Sabbath for the sake of a foetus constitutes proof that foetal life is legally significant, is that the rationale behind the rule that human life overrides the sanctity of the Sabbath is that 'it is better to break one Sabbath in order that the person whose life is saved may keep many more Sabbaths'.[25] Permission to set aside the Sabbath when human life is at stake is based upon potential for future Sabbath observance, and it says very little, if anything, about the present legal status of the life being saved. Even on the view that the *halakhah* permits the Sabbath to be broken for the sake of a foetus, irrespective of its connection with its mother, we would still not know that the foetus was a legal person. All we would know is that it has a potential for legal personhood at some time in the future. In relation to therapeutic abortion, the issue is the status of the foetus at the present time. As long as the foetus is threatening its mother's life, its potential, as we have already observed, is not taken into account, and the mother's life comes first. In the clash between the competing claims of maternal life and foetal existence, the foetus loses out precisely because it is not a legal person until it emerges from the womb. The concept of the foetus as potential life is irrelevant to the law relating to life-saving abortion; in the latter context, the mother always comes first.[26]

In any case, none of the authorities who base their stringent abortion rulings on permission to break the Sabbath in order to save foetal life adopt the view that the foetus has the same status as a full person and that its life is to be preferred to that of the mother. As far as halakhic doctrine is concerned, it is unanimously accepted that a direct threat to the mother's life justifies the destruction of the foetus at any stage of its development, including the process of childbirth itself.

In addition to the mishnaic ruling cited at the beginning of the chapter, there is also biblical support for the principle that a foetus is not a legal person for the purposes of the law of homicide. This support is derived from a passage in the book of Exodus dealing with the consequences of striking a pregnant woman and causing her to miscarry the fruit of her womb. In such a case, biblical law provides that the striker must make monetary compensation to the husband, provided that the only damage done to the woman is the loss of her foetus. If, however, the woman dies as a result of the blow, the biblical principle of 'a *nefesh* for a *nefesh*' is invoked.[27] The link between this biblical passage and the concept of foetal

---

[25] *Shabbat*, 151b; *Hiddushei Ramban, Niddah*, 44b, s.v. *veha ditnan*.

[26] *Resp. Ziz Eliezer*, 13, no. 102. According to R. Jakobovits: 'None of these regulations necessarily prove that the foetus enjoys human inviolability', (*Jewish Medical Ethics*, 183).

[27] Exod. 21: 22–3. This passage is open to interpretation, and is the subject of an ancient debate between Jewish and Christian views, which is outlined in s. 2 below. The present analysis is based upon the halakhic interpretation of the passage, according to which the

non-personhood expressed in the mishnah is stated by R. Joshua Falk, in his commentary on the *Shulhan Arukh*:

And it is permitted [in a case of danger to the mother's life] to dismember the foetus in its mother's womb, even though it is a living being, since as long as it has not emerged into the atmosphere of the world, it is not called a *nefesh*, i.e. a person. The proof for this is that [according to the Bible] one who strikes a pregnant woman and causes her to miscarry pays monetary compensation, but he is not called a killer, nor is he liable to the death penalty.[28]

According to R. Falk, the fact that the penalty for foeticide in the Bible is strictly financial serves as an indication that a foetus is not a legal person and that foeticide is not a matter of homicide. Those authorities who maintain a liberal approach to abortion make extensive use of this passage in their decisions.[29]

R. Falk's formulation indicates that the biblical passage does not, by itself, exhaust the issue of foeticide in Jewish law. He begins by citing the mishnaic ruling with which we began the present chapter, and then proceeds to provide support for it from the Bible. There are various reasons for not using the biblical ruling regarding the striking of a pregnant woman as the primary source for the position on abortion under Jewish law, its biblical pedigree notwithstanding. First, it is open to an interpretation that would make the killing of a foetus that is capable of movement into a capital crime. This interpretation was adopted by the canon law, and will be discussed in the following section. Applying this interpretation would yield the result that the welfare of the mother is no longer the major issue in abortion law. This is clearly incompatible with the ruling in the Mishnah, according to which the mother's welfare is the fundamental issue in the halakhic position on abortion. Secondly, from the way in which the biblical law is presented, i.e. 'if two men brawl and strike a pregnant woman', it is arguable that there was no intention on the part of the attacker to cause the death of the foetus. The foetus's death could have been the result of a pure accident: one of the men might have aimed

killing of the woman is the sole situation in which capital punishment is mandated. It has already been observed that when the Bible wishes to indicate the operation of the *talionic* principle in relation to capital punishment, it uses the phrase *'nefesh tahat nefesh'* (see M. Elon (ed.), *The Principles of Jewish Law* (Jerusalem, 1974)), 525–6, and n. 8 above), and this is, indeed, the phrase used in the present passage, in accordance with the halakhic interpretation, to indicate the penalty that is to be meted out to the striker if the woman dies. In practice, however, talmudic law rules that monetary compensation applies even in the case in which the mother dies (n. 30).

[28] *Sefer Meirat Einayim, Hoshen Mishpat*, 425: 8. This link is also found in earlier sources, see *Yad Remah, Sanhedrin*, 57b, *s.v. ketiv*; R. Nissim, *Hullin*, 58a, *s.v. uleinyan*; *Resp. Radbaz Mikhtav Yad*, no. 22.   [29] See especially *Resp. Ziz Eliezer*, 9 no. 51; 13 no. 102.

badly, missed his opponent and hit a pregnant passer-by.[30] This passage does not, therefore, provide clear evidence that a deliberate attack on a foetus would carry a financial penalty only, and, more importantly, it does not absolutely exclude foeticide from the category of homicide. Finally, the analysis of this passage in such a way that foeticide, whether accidental or deliberate, is never more than a tort against the woman's husband is unacceptable, since the operative scope of foetal non-personhood is confined to life-saving abortions only. As a result of these and other complications, the force of the biblical law with regard to abortion is limited, and halakhic authorities generally use the biblical passage as a support for the position articulated in the Mishnah, rather than as the primary source for the position on abortion in Jewish law.

Our lengthy argument regarding the legal non-personhood of the foetus raises a serious question: is it wrong to kill a foetus in Jewish law? In order to answer this question, we return to the mishnah from which the principle of foetal non-personhood was derived. Since the mishnah applies this principle in relation to a threat to maternal life, it may be inferred that this is the appropriate context for its practical application. Accordingly, the principle of foetal non-personhood is not to be understood as a basis for permission to kill foetuses in general, but rather, it is limited to the therapeutic context. Indeed, this view is a unanimous one: no halakhic authority permits non-therapeutic foeticide on the basis of the argument that a foetus is not a person.[31]

A positive inference does not, however, constitute an unequivocal prohibition. There is no strictly logical basis in the mishnah for limiting the doctrine of foetal non-personhood to the therapeutic context, and despite the above mentioned halakhic consensus, it is certainly arguable that all the mishnah really does is to indicate the preferred context in which abortion is an acceptable, or even recommended course in Jewish law. It does not act as a source for prohibiting it in other contexts. Indeed, once foeticide is removed from the category of homicide and its capital derivatives[32] there is no obvious prohibition under which it may be neatly subsumed. The question that then arises is whether there is any definitive legal source for prohibiting non-therapeutic abortion in the *halakhah*. This question is significant in both moral and legal terms. If the answer is in the negative, Jewish law would appear to suffer from a serious moral

---

[30] It is for this reason that the Talmud provides that even if the mother dies, there is no capital punishment in this case since the striker did not intend to kill the pregnant woman but only to hit his assailant in the brawl (*Sanhedrin*, 79a–b). For a critical biblical law perspective, see B. Jackson, *Essays in Jewish and Comparative Legal History* (Leiden, 1975), 75.

[31] *Resp. Havat Yair*, no. 31. Also see Bleich, 'Abortion in Halakhic Literature', 136.

[32] See Unterman, *Shevet Miyehudah*, 28.

lacuna, especially in the light of comparison with other religious legal systems.

In fact, halakhic authorities throughout the ages have compensated for the lack of any clearly defined prohibition on non-therapeutic abortion in Jewish law in a number of different ways, ranging from the invocation of a general rabbinic ban on the practice to the requirement that the Sabbath be desecrated in order to save the life of a foetus trapped inside the body of its mother who died between the onset of the birth process and the emergence of her baby. These and other approaches to this question are discussed at length in section 3, where the argument is made that the halakhic approach to abortion consists of both a legal and a moral dimension, the two of which are necessary for understanding the richness and complexity of the position on this issue in Jewish law.

It is important to observe that the moral challenge of the doctrine of foetal non-personhood is particularly significant when Jewish law is compared with canon law. In order to highlight this challenge, the following section is devoted to a comparison of the basic position on foeticide and abortion in Jewish law with that in early Christian thought and the canon law. It also traces the influence of the Christian position regarding abortion on the common law. In the light of the fact that both Judaism and Christianity share the same Scripture, this is also a convenient point for such an exercise in comparative law, since the two religious traditions differ significantly in their interpretation of the seminal biblical passage cited above regarding the striking of a pregnant woman and the destruction of her foetus. In terms of the moral challenge, the question that arises is that if the Christian position on abortion is a stringent one, how can the *halakhah* fall behind this apparently superior moral position by failing to provide a clear prohibition on non-therapeutic abortion?

The tension between the principle of foetal non-personhood, which supports a very liberal approach to abortion, and the view that this principle is limited to the strictly therapeutic context, manifests itself in practice as well as theory. The precise scope of therapeutic abortion is a much-discussed matter in the *responsa* literature, and almost every type of situation is a matter of debate. Halakhic authorities and commentators deal with a wide range of questions and, as a rule, there are as many liberal answers as there are stringent ones. One major question is whether therapeutic abortion is limited to direct threats to the mother's life. According to some authorities, permission to abort also extends to threats of an indirect nature, such as the exacerbation of a serious heart or kidney condition as a result of the pregnancy running to term. Others disagree.[33]

---

[33] *Resp. Beth Shlomoh, Hoshen Mishpat*, no. 132; *Resp. Zofnat Paneah*, 1 no. 59; *Resp. Yabia Omer*, 4, *Even Haezer*, no 1.

Whereas some authorities permit abortion in cases in which the mother's life may be endangered at a later stage of the pregnancy, even if she is not under immediate threat, others permit it only in cases of present danger to her life.[34] The question of abortion for the purpose of slowing down the progress of a fatal condition is also a matter of dispute, especially amongst modern authorities.[35] Abortion for the purpose of preserving the mother's sight is discussed in halakhic sources,[36] as is the permissibility of aborting a foetus in order to prevent the mother from becoming mentally ill.[37] It is generally agreed that a woman who has been raped is permitted to take action to destroy her foetus.[38] The question of aborting a *mamzer* foetus, i.e. the product of an adulterous or an incestuous union,[39] or a deformed or defective foetus, is debated by halakhic authorities, and will be discussed in detail below. Clearly, the parameters of therapeutic abortion are by no means set in stone, and it is evident from even a cursory glance at the halakhic literature in this field that many authorities are prepared to extend the rubric of therapeutic abortion to cases in which there is no direct and immediate threat to the mother's life. The pervasiveness of these debates is ongoing testimony to the tension between

[34] *Hemdat Yisrael, Maftehot Vehosafot*, 16b; *Resp. Mahazeh Avraham*, 2, *Yoreh Deah*, no. 19.

[35] *She'elat Yeshurun*, 1 no. 39; *Nishmat Avraham, Hoshen Mishpat*, no. 425.

[36] *Resp. Torat Hesed, Even Haezer*, no. 42; *Resp. Mishpetei Uziel*, 3, *Hoshen Mishpat*, no. 46; *Resp. Mishneh Halakhot*, 9, no. 386; *Nishmat Avraham, Hoshen Mishpat*, no. 425.

[37] *Resp. Koah Shor*, no. 20; *Resp. Pri Ha'aretz, Yoreh Deah*, no. 2. A noteworthy decision in this context is that of R. Ben Zion Uziel, the first Sephardic Chief Rabbi of the State of Israel, permitting a pregnant woman to seriously endanger her foetus in order to save her hearing. The woman was, in fact, already deaf in one ear, and the treatment for saving her other ear would almost certainly cause the death of her foetus. R. Uziel permitted the woman to undergo the treatment in reliance upon the mishnaic ruling in *Arakhin*, 1: 4, that a pregnant woman upon whom a death sentence has been passed is executed as long as she has not yet commenced labour, notwithstanding her pregnant condition. This ruling is explained on the basis of the need to avoid causing the mother mental suffering by making her wait for the child to be born before taking her out to be executed (Ran, *Hullin*, 3, *s.v. uleinyan havalad*). R. Uziel argued that loss of hearing is as traumatic, from a mental point of view, as having to anticipate one's execution for a lengthy period of time (*Resp. Mishpetei Uziel, Hoshen Mishpat*, no. 4). As far as the apparent contradiction between the onset of labour as a criterion for birth in *Arakhin* and the classical definition of the emergence of the major part of the foetus in *Oholoth* is concerned, it may be explained in terms of the context. In *Oholoth*, where the mother's life is at stake, birth is fixed at the latest possible point in order to ensure that maternal life remains the paramount consideration until the existence of the foetus as an independent person is clearly established. In *Arakhin*, however, the mother will die in any case; hence the only life at stake is that of the foetus. In such circumstances, birth is fixed at the earliest possible point in time, i.e. the onset of labour, in order to maximize the possibility of saving the potentially viable foetus.

[38] *Resp. Ziz Eliezer*, 9 no. 51: 3; *Nishmat Avraham, Hoshen Mishpat*, no. 425.

[39] A *mamzer* is a Jew for all purposes, including the prohibition on intermarriage. However, a *mamzer* may not marry another Jew. The only person a *mamzer* may marry is another *mamzer* or a convert, and in both cases the product of the union is also a *mamzer*; see Elon (ed.), *Principles of Jewish Law*, 435–8. The Hebrew word for the state of being a *mamzer* is *mamzerut*.

the principle of foetal non-personhood and the view that its practical application is restricted to the therapeutic context. The following sections attempt to deepen our understanding of this tension, and to analyse the way in which it is played out in halakhic literature from the Middle Ages down to the present.

2. FOETICIDE AND ABORTION IN EARLY CHRISTIAN WRITINGS, CANON LAW, AND THE COMMON LAW

Early Christian teachers, similarly to halakhic authorities, used the biblical passage dealing with the striking of a pregnant woman and the death of her foetus in order to fashion their approach to abortion. Their reading of the passage was quite different, however, to that of the rabbis, and they also reached different legal conclusions. The story begins with the Greek versions of this passage. According to the Septuagint—the classical Greek translation of the Bible—a penalty is to be paid if the stillborn foetus is imperfectly formed. If, however, 'the [stillborn] child is perfectly formed, then he shall give life for life', i.e. the striker of the pregnant woman is to be put to death.[40] The dramatic difference between this translation and the Hebrew version as understood by the rabbis is that the death penalty is meted out to the attacker if the foetus has reached the stage of formation *in utero*. There is no reference, in the Greek version, to the death of the mother. The passage deals only with the foetus, and it provides that causing the death of a formed foetus is a full-blown act of homicide. If the foetus has not yet reached the stage of formation inside the womb, however, the penalty is merely financial.

Philo, the Greek-speaking, Alexandrian Jewish scholar who lived in the first century, presents the biblical law governing the causing of a miscarriage along the same lines and in almost lyrical terms:

If one has contest with a woman who is pregnant and strike a blow on the belly, and she miscarry: if the child which was conceived within her is still unfashioned and unformed, he shall be punished by such a fine...But if the child which was conceived has assumed a distinctive shape in all its parts, he shall die. For such a creature as that is a man, who he has slain while still in the workshop of nature, which had not thought it as yet a proper time to produce him to the light...[41]

---

[40] Exod. 21: 22–3. Also see G. Alon, *Mehkarim Betoldot Yisrael* (Tel-Aviv, 1967), i. 280 n. 32; Jakobovits, *Jewish Medical Ethics*, 372 n. 43.

[41] *The Special Laws*, 2: 19. Also see S. Belkin, *Philo and the Oral Law* (Harvard, 1940), 129–30. Cf. Philo's description of the formed foetus with the phrase, 'placed in a box' (*munah bekufsa*) used by Tosafot in *Niddah*, 44a, *s.v. ihu*.

Philo's formulation clearly reflects the idea that a foetus becomes a legal person for the purposes of the law of homicide while still in its mother's womb.

The idea that biblical law treats foeticide as a form of homicide also appears in the writings of Philo's younger contemporary, Flavius Josephus,[42] although it ought to be noted that Josephus' position is not consistent, and elsewhere in his writings, he refers to the halakhic doctrine that a foetus does not become a legal person until birth.[43]

The distinction between the formed and the unformed foetus is developed by Aristotle in his work on natural science,[44] and the moral significance of formation finds expression in his directive regarding foetuses conceived in defiance of Greek laws limiting the number of children in a family. In such cases, Aristotle recommends that 'abortion should be procured before [the foetuses] acquire sensation or life; for the morality or immorality of such action depends upon whether the child has or has not obtained sensation and life'.[45] There is an explicit connection between morality and biology in this passage, and it is illustrative of a significant school of Greek thought on the status of the foetus, which undoubtedly influenced the Septuagint, Philo, and Josephus in their formulations of the biblical position on foeticide.[46] These writers were addressing audiences steeped in Greek culture and morality, and it is arguable that they would have looked askance at a sacred text that deviated from the accepted idea that a formed foetus *in utero* is a full person, entitled to the protection of the criminal law and whose deliberate killing constitutes a serious moral offence.[47]

The Greek distinction between the formed and the unformed foetus was widely accepted in early Christian circles, together with many other Greek ideas.[48] The Septuagint version of the law of miscarriage undoubtedly played an important role in acceptance of this distinction.[49] Early

---

[42] *Contra Apion*, 2: 25.   [43] *Antiquities of the Jews*, 4: 8.

[44] *History of Animals*, 7: 3. Also see Jakobovits, *Jewish Medical Ethics*, 174.

[45] *Politics*, 4: 16.

[46] Both writers also deviate from the *halakhic* tradition regarding the issue of sexual relations with a single woman. Philo equates such intercourse with adultery (*The Special Laws*, 3: 65; Belkin, *Philo*, 258) and Josephus maintains that there is a firm biblical prohibition on such intercourse (*Contra Apion*, 2: 24).

[47] See Aptowitzer, 'Status of the Embryo', 102–11, 37; Jakobovits, *Jewish Medical Ethics*, 179.

[48] See *Library of Christian Classics*, ed. C. C. Richardson (London, 1955) i. 172; ii. 17; Clement *Pedagogus*, 3: 10; Tertullian, *Apologeticum ad Nationes*, 1: 15.

[49] Jakobovits, *Jewish Medical Ethics*, 173–4. It is noteworthy that the Vulgate translation is in accordance with the halakhic interpretation. If the mother is still alive—*sed ipsa vixerit*—then a fine is to be paid. However, if the mother also died as a result of the blow—*si autem mors eius fuerit subsecuta*—then the striker is to be put to death. For a list of translations of this passage in classical Jewish and non-Jewish sources, see Aptowitzer, 'Status of the Embryo', n. 116.

teachers such as Augustine combined it with a spiritual conception of foetal life, expressed in terms of the possession of a soul.[50] Thomas Aquinas maintained that there is a direct relationship between physical formation and ensoulment, and added that the only practical test for the entrance of the soul into the body of the foetus is sensation and movement.[51] This combination of physical formation and ensoulment also meant that an unbaptized but formed foetus would be condemned to perdition in the same way as a born person who dies without baptism. This is undoubtedly a factor in the restrictive attitude of the Catholic Church towards therapeutic abortion, since an aborted foetus may not be baptized and as a result, its soul is condemned to eternal suffering.[52] The distinction between the formed and the unformed foetus became part of the medieval canon law, and the killing of an ensouled foetus was defined as an act of murder.[53]

From a historical perspective, therefore, it is possible to distinguish between the Greek-Christian approach to abortion and the rabbinic approach. The former regards the foetus as a full legal person for the purposes of the law of homicide once it has reached the stage of bio-spiritual formation inside the womb. The latter does not accept that legal personality can be achieved *in utero*, and only confers this status at birth, when the foetus achieves an existence independent of its mother.[54]

The distinction between formed and unformed foetuses was officially abolished by the Catholic Church in 1869.[55] It has, however, since been invoked by liberal theologians, especially in the United States, in support of greater leniency in the current Catholic position on this issue.[56] An analysis of the process leading from the very liberal view of the highly influential sixteenth-century Jesuit scholar, Thomas Sanchez, according to whom the abortion of an unformed foetus is permitted in order to save the mother's life or reputation,[57] to the current position under which the ban on abortion is almost absolute, is clearly beyond the scope of this

---

[50] *Questions on the Heptateuch*, no. 80.   [51] *Libros Politicorum*, 8. 9. 11.
[52] W. Lecky, *History of the Rise and Influence of the Spirit of Rationalism in Europe* (London, 1870), 360.
[53] *Concordia Discordentium Canonum*, 2. 32. 2.
[54] This is the view generally adopted in the ancient Near Eastern codes, see Hammurabi's Code, nos. 209–10, and M. Weinfeld, 'The Genuine Jewish Attitude towards Abortion' (Heb.), *Zion*, 42 (1977), 142. Also see Aptowitzer, 'Status of the Embryo', 85–90.
[55] See *The Human Embryo*, ed. G. Dunstan (Exeter, 1990), 4; P. Simmons, 'Religious Approaches to Abortion', in J. Butler and D. Walbert (eds.), *Abortion, Medicine and the Law* (New York, 1992), 713. The abolition was part of the official rejection of Aristotelian science by the Catholic Church.   [56] Simmons, 'Religious Approaches', 714.
[57] *De Sancto Matrimoni Sacramento*, 3. 20.

work.[58] For present purposes, we wish merely to highlight the contrast between the position prior to 1869 and the one adopted after that date.

Although the stages of foetal development are no longer of any great significance in relation to abortion in contemporary Catholic thinking, the link between the biological state of the foetus and its legal status passed into the common law. Naturally, the canon law distinction between the formed and the unformed foetus figures in the law of medieval England.[59] At that time, England was a Catholic country and the canon law was the only law in the area of abortion. It remained a part of English common law even after the triumph of Protestantism and the Civil War, and was incorporated into the works of such seminal writers as Edward Coke and William Hawkins. Coke's position was also adopted by William Blackstone in his *Commentaries on the Laws of England* (1765). There is, however, a significant difference between the position under the canon law, and that adopted by these writers on the common law. Neither Coke nor Hawkins regard the killing of a formed foetus as an act of homicide. In his magisterial compilation of the common law, Coke classifies such an abortion as a 'great misprision', i.e. serious offence, but not as an act of homicide. The term actually used by Coke to distinguish between the formed and the unformed foetus is 'quickening', by which he means to indicate the capacity of the foetus to move within the womb.[60] This concept follows on from Aristotelian thought and Aquinas's definition of ensoulment in terms of movement and sensation, and it preserves the Greek-Christian link between biology and law with regard to abortion. William Hawkins, another writer from this period on the common law, points out that 'in this respect, the common law seems to be agreeable to the Mosaical' in that killing a foetus, even if already formed, is not murder, but 'a great misdemeanour'. In effect, both Coke and Hawkins adopt the Jewish law approach to foeticide in the sense that neither of them regards it as homicide. Indeed, Hawkins specifically cites the 'Mosaical law' in support of this argument.[61] In the light of his remark concerning the 'Mosaical law', it is tempting to link the rejection of the canon law position defining the killing of a formed foetus as homicide, with a return to the Hebrew version of the biblical text, as opposed to the Greek. Any attempt to elaborate this point would, however, take us well beyond the scope of the present work, and the temptation must, therefore, be resisted.

---

[58] See J. T. Noonan (ed.), *The Morality of Abortion* (Harvard, 1971), 29, n. 149, and G. Grisez, *Abortion: The Myths, the Realities and the Arguments* (New York, 1970), 117.

[59] Bracton, *De Corona*, iv. s. 121. Also see P. Winfield, 'The Unborn Child', *Cambridge Law Journal*, 3 (1944), 76.

[60] *Institutes of the Laws of England* (London, 1648), iii. s. 50. Also see I. Kennedy and A. Grubb, *Medical Law* (London, 1994), 860–4.

[61] William Hawkins, *A Treatise on the Pleas of the Crown* (London, 1762), 80.

It is noteworthy that the idea that the killing of a formed foetus is a capital offence briefly reasserted itself in English law in Lord Ellenborough's Act, 1803, according to which, 'procuring the miscarriage of any woman, then being quick with child' was defined as a felony and carried the death penalty. Under this Act, the abortion of a formed foetus constituted a capital crime, whereas the abortion of an unformed foetus was defined as a felony but was not subject to the death penalty.[62] The major Victorian codification of English criminal law, the Offences Against the Person Act, 1861, dropped both the death penalty for killing 'quick' foetuses, and the distinction between the formed and the unformed foetus. The distinction did not, however, totally disappear from the statute book until 1931, when the Sentence of Death (Expectant Mothers) Act provided that the commuting of a pregnant woman's death sentence to life imprisonment no longer depended upon a decision by a 'quickening jury' as to whether the foetus had moved.[63]

Nevertheless, the connection between the biological development of a foetus and its legal status remained a part of English law, and it is manifested in the Infant Life Preservation Act, 1929, which defines the crime of child destruction during late pregnancy and childbirth.[64] Under that Act, the crime consists of the destruction of the life 'of a child capable of being born alive'. The definition of the capacity to be born alive has exercised the courts on a number of occasions, and the definition that has emerged is that stage at which the foetus is capable of breathing on its own.[65] More recently, the Human Fertilization and Embryology Act, 1990 amended the provision in the Abortion Act, 1967, permitting abortion if the risk of running the pregnancy to term is greater than that of abortion, in terms of the mother's physical or mental health or the health of her existing children. The new law, which was prompted by dramatic improvements in abortion technology since 1967 resulting in the procedure becoming significantly less risky than birth until the very final stage of pregnancy, limits the

---

[62] Under the Act, the penalty for aborting the foetus of a woman 'not quick with child' was a fine, imprisonment, whipping, or transportation for up to fourteen years.

[63] See Hawkins, *Pleas of the Crown*, 657. The oath administered to the female quickening jury was as follows: 'I, as a fore-matron or a matron of this jury, swear by Almighty God that I will search and try the prisoner at the bar, whether she be with child of a quick child, and thereof a true verdict give, according to my skill and understanding'.

[64] The purpose of this law was, in fact, to protect doctors who needed to destroy the foetus for the sake of saving the mother's life, just prior to or during birth. Strictly speaking, such an act would have constituted criminal abortion under the 1861 Act which made no allowance for killing a foetus in the course of a difficult birth. Presumably, the 1929 law was confined to the very last stage of foetal existence because it was assumed that no respectable doctor would ever abort a foetus unless he was assisting at a birth, and needed to destroy the foetus in order to preserve the mother's life.

[65] *C* v. *S* [1987] 1 All ER 1230. Also see *Rance* v. *Mid-Downs Hospital Authority* (1991) 1 All ER 801.

application of the greater risk provision to pregnancies under twenty-four weeks. If the pregnancy has exceeded twenty-four weeks, this provision no longer applies.[66] The imposition of the twenty-four week limit indicates that English law is still concerned with the link between biology and law in the context of abortion law.

The link between foetal development and abortion law is even more pronounced in American jurisprudence than in English law. In the leading 1973 case of *Roe* v. *Wade*,[67] the United States Supreme Court held that the constitutionality of state abortion laws turned on the age of the foetus, and in particular, upon the stage at which it reached the point of viability *in utero*. The *Roe* Court laid down a scheme for measuring the legal status of a foetus for abortion law purposes in accordance with the trimesters of the pregnancy, with viability being fixed at the beginning of the third trimester. The very close link between biology and law in this decision was the subject of much critical discussion in both subsequent case law and academic writings, and the trimester scheme was officially discarded by the Supreme Court in 1992, on the grounds that progress in medical science had rendered it obsolete. States are now entitled to insist that a doctor perform an abortion test for the viability of the individual foetus before carrying out the procedure. Also, the strength of the woman's right to abort her foetus was reduced from a fundamental right to a liberty interest, with the result that it is now much easier for a State to regulate abortion than it was under the decision in *Roe*.[68] The retreat from *Roe* v. *Wade* in general, and from the trimester system in particular, raises a serious question as to the wisdom of maintaining the ancient link between foetal development and the law of abortion in modern times.

Under the Jewish approach, the stages of foetal development are not of major significance in abortion law. The main focus of the halakhic position on abortion is the mother, and this focus is reflected in the rabbinic interpretation of the biblical verse with which we began this section. In the Greek-Christian understanding of the verse, however, the mother is absent, and as a result, the canon law, and to a lesser degree, the common law, struggle with the question of defining the legal status of the foetus

---

[66] Human Fertilization and Embryology Act, 1990 section 37. Note that the twenty-four week limit does not apply if there is a risk of grave permanent injury to the mother's physical or mental health, or of the birth of a severely handicapped child. In both these situations the balance of risks may be applied even after the twenty-fourth week.

[67] 410 US 113 (1973).

[68] See *Webster* v. *Reproductive Health Services*, 492 US 490 (1989); *Planned Parenthood* v. *Casey* 112 S. Ct. 2791 (1992). It is noteworthy that under the *Casey* decision, only the 'essential holdings' of *Roe* v. *Wade* still apply. Also see G. Annas, 'Four-One-Four', *Hastings Center Report* (September/October, 1989) 27–9, and R. Dworkin, *Limits: The Role of Law in Bioethical Decision Making* (Indiana, 1996), 29, 36–49.

in utero. In these systems, the welfare of the pregnant woman is not the sole significant issue, as it is in Jewish law.

In conclusion, the parting of ways of the Jewish and Christian views on abortion is an ancient one. In its wake the two systems developed along very different lines. Nevertheless, Jewish thinkers such as Philo and Josephus were influenced by the Greek environment in which they lived, and reflect that influence in their Jewish writings. Whether or not halakhists operating in Christian countries and exposed to the significantly stricter view of foeticide adopted by the Christian Church were influenced by that view and translated that influence into halakhic terms, is one of the questions that will be explored in the following section.

3. THE RELATIONSHIP BETWEEN LAW AND MORALITY IN THE *HALAKHAH* ON ABORTION

The above account of the development of the canon and common law position on abortion sharpens the question posed at the end of the first section, i.e. does the fact that there seems to be no clear prohibition on non-therapeutic abortion in Jewish law give rise to a moral lacuna in that system? As pointed out briefly at the end of that section, there are a number of ways in which halakhic authorities deal with this question. Some argue that Jewish law does, in fact prohibit non-therapeutic abortion, but the basis for so doing lies either in prohibitions such as assaulting the mother or frustrating the procreative process. Others maintain that non-therapeutic abortion is prohibited on the basis of a general, unspecific prohibition of a rabbinic nature. Another approach is that of Maimonides, who goes beyond the generally accepted understanding of the mishnah dealing with therapeutic abortion, and finds a way to limit its scope to a direct and immediate threat to maternal life. A fourth method is to distinguish between law and morality, and to define halakhic opposition to non-therapeutic abortion in moral rather than legal terms.[69]

Attempts to identify a legal source for prohibiting non-therapeutic abortion began in the sixteenth century with R. Joseph Trani, and continued with R. Yair Bachrach in the seventeenth century. R. Trani identified this source as the offence of assaulting the mother,[70] and R. Bachrach found it in the prohibition on deliberately frustrating the process of

---

[69] A similar situation arises in relation to defining a legal prohibition on sexual relations with a single woman. In the absence of any clear legal prohibition on this type of sexual intercourse, the emphasis is shifted to, *inter alia*, the moral wrongfulness of such conduct, see. E. Ellinson, *Nissuin Shelo Kedat Moshe Veyisrael* (Jerusalem, 1980), ch. 1.

[70] *Resp. Maharit*, no. 97.

procreation.[71] The exclusion of non-therapeutic homicide from the prohibition on homicide was so well established that neither authority was even tempted to look in the direction of that offence for a legal source. In this respect, it is noteworthy that there are modern authorities who do, nevertheless, seek to read non-therapeutic foeticide into the biblical prohibition on homicide,[72] and in the fourth section of this chapter it will be argued that this development has come about as the result of a strongly felt moral need on the part of these authorities to rule strictly on abortion in an increasingly morally relativist world. Neither R. Trani's nor R. Bachrach's suggestions are, however, entirely satisfactory. R. Trani's maternal assault theory is open to the objection that on the view that the offence of assault does not extend to voluntary self-injury, all consensual abortion would be permitted.[73] R. Bachrach's argument from the prohibition on frustrating the procreative process suffers from two major difficulties. The first is that, prima facie, this prohibition applies to males only. As a result, non-therapeutic abortion would be permitted to women. The second is that there is no definitive legal prohibition on a procreation-frustrating act, if it is done in order to achieve a halakhically justifiable end, e.g. the production of male semen for purposes of fertility testing.[74] An abortion carried out in order to save the mother from an unwanted pregnancy might also be justified on the grounds that the purpose is not to frustrate procreation but to achieve a halakhically positive result, namely, the preservation of maternal well-being.[75] In other words, both of these suggestions are more convincing at a general rather than a specific level. Non-therapeutic abortion clearly contains conceptual elements of both the crime of assault and the prohibition on frustrating procreation. In terms of a definitive prohibition specific to abortion, however, the quest is still ongoing.

The second approach mentioned above, i.e. the existence of a non-specific prohibition on non-therapeutic abortion, is found in a number of halakhic sources. A striking formulation of this approach is that of R. Yehiel Weinberg, in a *responsum* on the abortion of the foetus of a mother stricken with German measles during her pregnancy: 'Although foeticide is clearly not a form of homicide, it is nevertheless prohibited, but we are simply unaware of the precise nature of the prohibition.'[76]

R. Weinberg clearly admits that there is no specific prohibition. Most authorities are far less frank in their approach than R. Weinberg, and

---

[71] *Resp. Havat Yair*, no. 31.   [72] See *Resp. Iggrot Moshe, Hoshen Mishpat*, 2 no. 69.
[73] See *Resp. Seridei Esh*, 3 no. 127.   [74] See Ch. 2 s. 1.
[75] The broad scope of the criterion of maternal welfare was outlined at the end of s. 1 above.   [76] *Resp. Seridei Esh*, 3 no. 127.

attempt to flesh out this unknown prohibition somewhat. Many authorities classify it as a 'rabbinic' prohibition, without further elaboration.[77] R. Eliezer Waldenberg adds the appellation 'weak prohibition'[78] to the prohibition's rabbinic pedigree, but provides no further detail. The absence of any specific source for this 'weak rabbinic prohibition' tends to support R. Weinberg's position that it is more a question of needing to have a legal prohibition on non-therapeutic abortion, than actually having one. Once again, the impression is one of a general prohibition without any specific legal source.

Another method used by halakhic authorities to compensate for the lack of any definitive prohibition on non-therapeutic foeticide is to restrict the scope of therapeutic abortion to situations in which abortion is the only way of saving the mother from a direct and immediate threat to her life. This is done by relying upon Maimonides' analysis of the mishnaic permission to carry out therapeutic abortions in Jewish law. As observed in the first section, Maimonides presents a different analysis of the mishnah than the foetal non-personhood explanation offered by the majority of commentators. According to Maimonides, the mishnaic ruling regarding life-saving foeticide is based upon the pursuer principle in Jewish criminal law.[79] This principle provides that a bystander is permitted to kill a person who is pursuing another individual with intent to kill the latter, provided that there is no other way of preventing the pursuer from carrying out his evil designs. It is important to note that in order for the pursuer principle to come into effect, the threat to the pursued person must be both immediate and direct.[80] Maimonides applies this principle to the therapeutic abortion situation, and explains that the foetus is 'like a pursuer threatening its mother's life'. Thus, therapeutic abortion comes within the ambit of the pursuer principle. By adopting this explanation of the mishnah and defining the foetus as a pursuer, Maimonides seems to imply that the principle that a foetus is not a legal person is not, by itself, sufficient to ground the mishnaic permission to kill it in order to save the mother's life. He also effectively limits therapeutic abortion to those cases in which there is a direct and immediate threat to the life of the mother, since only such a threat is sufficient to justify killing the pursuer in a case involving born persons. The application of Maimonides' explanation of

---

[77] *Resp. Emunat Shmuel*, no. 14; *Resp. Hayyim Veshalom*, 1 no. 40; *Resp. Zeluta Deavraham*, no. 60; *Resp. Maharash Engel*, 5 no. 89; *Resp. Mishpetei Uziel*, *Hoshen Mishpat*, no. 46; *Resp. Ziz Eliezer*, 9 no. 51; *Nishmat Avraham, Hoshen Mishpat*, 425: 1; Bleich, 'Abortion in Halakhic Literature', 137.   [78] *Resp. Ziz Eliezer*, 9 no. 51; 13 no. 102.

[79] *Hilkhot Rozeah*, 1: 9.

[80] Deut. 25: 12; *Sanhedrin*, 8: 7; 72b; Maimonides, *Hilkhot Rozeah*, 1: 6; Elon (ed.), *Principles of Jewish Law*, 474.

the mishnah leads, therefore, to a fairly restrictive view of the scope of justifiable abortion in Jewish law.[81] Adoption of the Maimonidean position would, for example, almost certainly militate against aborting a foetus suffering from mental or physical defects, since in the majority of such cases, the threat to the mother's life is neither immediate nor direct.

Maimonides' approach raises a number of conceptual problems. As pointed out above, the adult pursuer may be killed because of his intent to kill the person he is pursuing. A foetus has no such intent *vis-à vis* its mother and ought not, therefore, to be subject to the law of the pursuer. Indeed, the Talmud specifically rejects the application of the pursuer principle to a foetus on the grounds that in striving to be born, it is merely obeying a natural urge and 'it is nature rather than the foetus which is the true pursuer'.[82] Moreover, Maimonides follows the mishnah in prohibiting the destruction of the foetus for the sake of the mother once the head of the foetus has emerged. Now, if the operative principle in therapeutic abortion is indeed the pursuer principle, then there should be no such limit on sacrificing the foetus for the sake of its mother. The emergence of the foetus from the womb should make no difference to its categorization as a pursuer: once a pursuer, always a pursuer!

One of the better-known attempts to deal with these problems is based upon the concept of objective pursuit.[83] As already observed, it is the pursuer's evil intent that makes him liable to the death penalty, administered in effect by the bystander who intervenes in order to save the life of the pursued individual.[84] If the pursuer is not a legal person, however, killing him does not constitute a fully-blown act of homicide, and the presence of evil intention is no longer a necessary element in the pursuer law. The pursuer who is less than a legal person may be killed solely because he poses a threat to the pursued person. This type of pursuer is known as an objective pursuer and obviously includes the foetus which must be killed in order to save its mother. There are, however, very few other cases to which the concept of objective pursuit would apply in the human context.[85] As a result, its explanatory power is rather limited. All this answer

---

[81] See *Resp. Seridei Esh*, 3 no. 127, and D. Sinclair, 'The Legal Basis for the Prohibition on Abortion in Jewish Law', *Israel Law Review*, 15 (1980), 121–2.

[82] See *Sanhedrin*, 72b.   [83] See *Hiddushei R. Hayyim Halevi, Hilkhot Rozeah*, 1: 9.

[84] *Sanhedrin*, 74a. See also Ch. 5 s. 5, and D. Frimer, 'On the Element of Intention in the Law of the Pursuer' (Heb.), *Or Hamizrah*, 22 (1984), 309.

[85] It is also applicable to a Siamese twin with a defective heart whose survival depends upon the healthy heart of her twin, with the result that both will die once the shared heart becomes too weak to sustain both twins. This case is discussed in detail in Ch. 5 s. 61. In the non-human context, the pursuer principle is applied by Maimonides in order to free a person who jettisons maritime freight to save a ship from capsizing from any obligation to compensate the owner (*Hilkhot Hovel Umazik*, 8: 15).

really does is to expand the concept of the pursuer in Jewish law; it does not really account for the need on Maimonides' part to employ the principle of pursuit in explaining the mishnah as opposed to simply stating, together with Rashi and the other commentaries, that the foetus is not a *nefesh*. At the end of the day, even Maimonides relies upon the lesser status of the foetus in order to provide the ultimate justification for therapeutic abortion in Jewish law.

Similar weaknesses emerge in relation to the many other attempts to explain why Maimonides forbids the killing of a foetus whose head has emerged from the mother's body, notwithstanding the fact that it is still pursuing her, albeit in an objective fashion.[86]

It ought to be pointed out that Maimonides himself is careful to state that the foetus is 'like' a pursuer. The choice of the analogical expression surely indicates that he is quite aware that the case of the adult pursuer is not fully congruent with that of the foetus. The question still remains as to why he needs the pursuer principle in the first place, and to this question there is no satisfactory answer.

Notwithstanding these difficulties, the Maimonidean position holds much appeal for modern authorities seeking to ground a restrictive approach to therapeutic abortion. It is the most stringent medieval approach to the scope of such abortion, and Maimonides' halakhic status is such that it is difficult to ignore his views, even if they raise a host of unanswered conceptual problems. A good illustration of the influence of Maimonides' position is the fact that even when it is rejected, care is taken to explain why the rejection is justified. In his above-mentioned *responsum*, R. Weinberg permits the abortion of a foetus whose mother contracted German measles during pregnancy. This ruling is clearly not in line with Maimonides' stringent approach. Nevertheless, R. Weinberg takes the trouble to state that he is deviating from the Maimonidean approach and to explain the reasons behind that deviation. He begins by pointing out that his ruling is based upon 'those authorities who maintain that the mishnaic permission to kill the foetus turns on its non-personhood'. He goes on to point out that this view and the ruling to which it gives rise

---

[86] A partial list of sources dealing with these problems in Maimonides' use of the pursuer principle in relation to therapeutic abortion includes the following: *Tosafot R. Akiva Eiger, Oholoth*, 7: 6; *Resp. Noda Biyehuda*, 2, *Hoshen Mishpat*, no. 59; *Resp. Avnei Zedek; Hoshen Mishpat*, no. 19; *Resp. Ahiezer*, 3 no. 72; *Resp. Beth Yizhak, Yoreh Deah*, 2 no. 162; *Resp. Koah Shor*, no. 20; *Resp. Torat Hesed, Even Haezer*, no. 42; *Resp Mishpetei Uziel, Hoshen Mishpat*, 3 no. 47; *Resp. Tiferet Zvi; Orah Hayyim*, no. 14; *Hiddushei R. Hayyim Halevi, Hilkhot Rozeah*, 1: 9; *Resp. Geonei Batrai*, no. 45; *Resp. Seridei Esh*, 3 no. 127; *Untesman, Shevet Miyehuda*, 26; *Resp. Yabia Omer*, 4, *Even Haezer*, no. 1; *Resp. Ziz Eliezer*, 14 no. 100; *Resp. Iggrot Moshe, Hoshen Mishpat*, 2 no. 69; *Resp. Shevet Halevi*, 5 no. 193. See also D. Feldman, *Marital Relations, Birth Control and Abortion in Jewish Law* (New York, 1974), 276; Bleich, 'Abortion in Halakhic Literature' 147–52, and D. Sinclair, *Tradition and the Biological Revolution* (Edinburgh, 1989), 29.

in the present case are not compatible with Maimonides' explanation of the mishnah, since the pursuer principle applies only in the case of a direct threat to the mother's life; in relation to German measles, the problem is only the high likelihood of giving birth to a severely defective baby. As such, the mother's life is not at stake in any direct fashion, and Maimonides would not, therefore, permit the abortion. R. Weinberg nevertheless deviates from the Maimonidean position. He justifies his action in the light of the many difficulties associated with Maimonides' view, and the fact that it is a minority one. As a result, he is not bound by the latter's approach, and is free to rule permissively on the basis of the foetal non-personhood explanation of the mishnah, together with the many lenient precedents in this area.[87]

The fourth approach is based upon a distinction between law and morality in relation to questions of life and death in the *halakhah*. Its origin lies in a statement of Tosafot that non-therapeutic abortions are 'not allowed'.[88] This statement is used by many authorities to justify the existence of a general, unspecified legal bar on non-therapeutic abortion referred to above. In the present writer's opinion, this statement is of a moral, rather than a legal nature. It will be argued below that it is made in the context of a halakhic tradition of compensating for the lack of legal prohibitions on morally objectionable practices by invoking universal, rational norms in order to condemn them. It thus becomes unnecessary to seek any form of legal prohibition on foeticide, since there is a moral condemnation already in place. One important feature of this approach is that it allows for a reasonable measure of flexibility with respect to defining therapeutic abortion, without granting approval to the non-therapeutic form. As long as there is no strictly legal bar on non-therapeutic abortion, the scope of the therapeutic form may be extended quite significantly in morally justifiable circumstances. The nature and scope of the moral condemnation on non-therapeutic abortion and the universal, rational norm from which it is derived, are the subjects of the remainder of this section.

Tosafot's approach to foeticide and abortion is rather complex, and the best place to begin is their discussion of a talmudic passage dealing with the saving of foetal life at the cost of breaking the Sabbath.[89] Tosafot observe quite simply that 'even though it is permitted (*mutar*) to kill a foetus', the Sabbath ought, nevertheless, to be broken in order to save its

---

[87] See *Resp. Seridei Esh*, 3 no. 127.

[88] *Sanhedrin*, 59b, *s.v. leka medam*; *Hullin*, 33a, *s.v. ehad*.

[89] *Niddah*, 44b; *s.v. ihu*. After having explained that it is permitted to break the Sabbath in order to release a baby from the womb of its mother who died in childbirth, Tosafot suggest that even prior to that stage, the Sabbath may be broken on behalf of a foetus, since the rubric of the obligation to preserve life is wide enough to include a foetus: 'In any case, the foetus is saved on the basis of *pikuah nefesh*.'

life. Taken at its face value, this sentence means that there are no negative legal consequences arising out of the destruction of a foetus. Several commentators are unhappy with this formulation, and suggest an alternative reading with a view to softening this permission to kill a foetus. In their view, the word 'permitted' should be replaced with the word 'exempt', and the line should read: 'even though the killer of a foetus is exempt from criminal liability', the Sabbath may be broken in order to save foetal life.[90] Now, the concept of 'prohibited but exempt from any sanction' is found in various areas of Jewish law, and it occurs frequently in relation to the laws of the Sabbath. However, it does not normally feature in relation to matters of a moral nature. In that context, the preferred course is to invoke a sanction on the basis of moral concepts such as Divine punishment, the extra-legal authority of the monarch to preserve the social order, and the universal laws of the Noahide code, all of which are discussed at length in the following paragraphs, and again in Chapter 5. The reason for this is that moral concepts are not relevant to the laws of the Sabbath. Either something is legally prohibited on the Sabbath, or it is not. The Sabbath is not a moral matter; its existence is grounded in revealed law, not morals. As a result, the preferred method of fortifying a legally weak prohibition in the context of the Sabbath laws is to declare the act prohibited in principle, but exempt from punishment. Since foeticide is a moral matter, the natural method for blunting the effect of Tosafot's permission to kill foetuses is to declare non-therapeutic abortion morally wrong. To call it a legally prohibited offence merely lacking a positive sanction—especially when there is little evidence that such an offence exists—does not seem to be the most appropriate way of dealing with the issue. Also, it involves a completely different reading of the words used by Tosafot. At the end of the day, the word used in their text is 'permitted' and not 'exempt'.

In fact, there is no need to change Tosafot's language at all. They themselves qualify their permission to commit foeticide in the context of breaking the Sabbath for the sake of foetal life, in their other statement, that non-therapeutic foeticide is 'not allowed' (*lo shari*).[91] This phrase implies that although there is no legal prohibition on foeticide, it is not allowed because it is immoral. If it were illegal, the word 'forbidden' (*asur*) would be used.[92]

---

[90] *Hagahot Mahari Ya'avez, Niddah*, 44b, *s.v. veim tomar; Resp. Beth Yizhak, Yoreh Deah*, 2 no. 162; *Resp. Iggrot Moshe, Hoshen Mishpat*, 2 no. 69; cf. *Hiddushei Maharaz Hayut, Niddah*, 44b, *s.v. ihu; Resp. Ziz Eliezer*, 14 no. 100.

[91] *Sanhedrin*, 59b, *s.v. leka medam; Hullin* 33a, *s.v. ehad.*

[92] For the point about the use of different phrases to indicate different levels of wrongfulness in *halakhah*, see L. Roth, 'Moralization and Demoralization in Jewish Ethics', *Judaism*, 11 (1962), 294, in which he suggests that in rabbinic usage, the type of term used by Tosafot as opposed to the standard form of *asur*, i.e. prohibited, indicates the lack of any formal prohibition and a shift from a legal doctrine to a moral principle.

Also, in the light of the fact that Tosafot make this statement in a context that, as we shall shortly explain, is informed by universal, rational moral norms, the claim that the limit they place on this form of abortion is a moral one is highly suggestive. Assuming that this approach is correct, there is no problem with the fact that on purely legal grounds, Tosafot maintain, in their first statement, that foeticide is always permitted. This is because it is condemned on moral grounds, in all but the context of saving the mother's life.

It is, in fact, unnecessary to blunt the legal force of Tosafot's statement in relation to saving foetal life on the Sabbath. In that context, Tosafot seek to establish the existence of an obligation to break the Sabbath in order to save foetal life, which is totally independent of the position with regard to killing the foetus for the sake of saving its mother. In order to highlight the absence of any connection whatsoever between saving foetal life on the Sabbath and therapeutic abortion, Tosafot emphasize that in purely legal terms, there is no prohibition on killing a foetus in any situation, even a non-therapeutic one, i.e. killing a foetus 'is permitted'. There is, nevertheless, an obligation to save its life on the Sabbath, and the sanctity of the holy day is to be disregarded in order to achieve this purpose. The provision that it is permitted to kill a foetus does, indeed, accurately reflect the legal position, which is put in the strongest form possible, in order to make the argument as a whole more powerful and dramatic.

In their statement providing that non-therapeutic foeticide is 'not allowed', Tosafot seek to demonstrate why it is morally forbidden to Jews as well as Noahides. In this context, the use of the phrase 'not allowed' is highly appropriate. It is, therefore, unnecessary to tinker with Tosafot's language in their first statement in order to solve the problem of what appears to be a blanket permission to kill foetuses. Their view is that there is, in fact, no legal prohibition on foeticide. The immoral quality of the act, however, is sufficient to render it out of bounds to any Jew.

4. MORALITY, THE NOAHIDE LAWS, AND A LIMITED FORM OF NATURAL LAW IN ABORTION *HALAKHAH*

We have referred several times to the moral context of Tosafot's statement about non-therapeutic abortion not being allowed; it is now time to provide detailed backing for this claim. The statement is actually made in the context of a discussion of the link between the *halakhah* and the Noahide laws, a group of norms named after Noah who is, of course, the ancestor of the whole post-diluvian human race, and designated by the *halakhah* as being binding upon all humanity, with the exception of the Jewish people, who received the Torah.[93] Nevertheless, these laws do have an impact upon the *halakhah*, since they serve as a moral benchmark for the halakhic system, especially with regard to matters of life and death. It is on the basis of this moral benchmark role of the Noahide prohibition on bloodshed that Tosafot reach their conclusion that non-therapeutic abortion is 'not allowed'. Hence our claim that Tosafot's statement is a moral rather than a strictly legal one.

Before proceeding to a detailed analysis of the impact of the Noahide laws on the *halakhah* something more must be said about the nature of these laws in general. Their biblical source is a passage in Genesis in which God makes a covenant with Noah and his family based upon the acceptance of two prohibitions. The first is on homicide: 'Whoever shall shed man's blood, by man shall his blood be shed.' The second is on tearing a limb from a living creature: 'Nevertheless flesh with the soul thereof, and the blood thereof, you shall not eat.'[94] Both prohibitions reflect a basic moral intuition to the effect that the taking of human life must be severely punished, and that the humane treatment of animals, even when their flesh is being used for human consumption, is a necessary prerequisite for a civilized society. These two Noahide laws constitute the biblical framework of the system as a whole and express its fundamental ethos. The Talmud expands on these two laws and concludes that there are, in fact, seven Noahide laws altogether, i.e. the offences of idolatry, blasphemy, bloodshed, forbidden sexual relations, theft, tearing of a limb from a living animal, and the positive obligation to set up a system of justice.[95] It is noteworthy that according to an aggadic tradition cited in the Talmud, six of these laws were given to Adam, the first human being in the Bible. Only the seventh law, i.e. the prohibition on tearing a limb from a living creature, was given to Noah, since meat-eating originated with him; Adam was a vegetarian.[96] These seven laws are further elaborated in the Talmud, and it is noteworthy that in this elaboration the Noahide offence of bloodshed is wider in scope than the halakhic prohibition on murder, extending to the killing of foetuses, which carries the death penalty under Noahide law. This extension reflects the biblical framework of the entire Noahide system, i.e. respect for, and preservation of human life as the basic cornerstone of civilized society.[97]

---

[93] See Elon (ed.), *Principles of Jewish Law*, 708–10; *Talmudic Encyclopaedia* (Heb.), iii. 346–62.
[94] *Hilkhot Melakhim*, 9: 1–7.   [95] *Sanhedrin*, 57a; Maimonides, *Hilkhot Melakhim*, 9: 1.
[96] *Sanhedrin*, 56b.
[97] It also extends to the case of killing a fatally ill individual; a topic discussed at length in Ch. 5, and hiring an agent in order to carry out a homicide. In both of these cases, no capital punishment is provided by the *halakhah*. There are also fundamental distinctions in the law of evidence between Noahides and Israelites in the area of bloodshed: see *Talmudic Encyclopaedia* (Heb.) iii. 351. Also see A. Lichtenstein, *The Seven Laws of Noah* (New York, 1981).

In order to understand better the moral nature of the Noahide prohibition on bloodshed upon which Tosafot base themselves in order to establish a source for condemning non-therapeutic abortion, it will be useful to examine the link made by a number of modern commentators between the Noahide system and the concept of natural law. This concept has a long and complex history in Western jurisprudence, but it is basically the belief in the existence of a universally valid rational morality, which requires us to adhere to certain laws if we wish to ensure the survival of civilized society.[98] It must be emphasized that the object here is not to engage in a detailed study of the concept of natural law, but only to explore, in a very general way, its significance for understanding the moral nature of the Noahide prohibition on bloodshed.

A number of thinkers have seen in the Noahide system a weak form of natural law, particularly in its prohibitions on bloodshed, immorality, and theft and in the obligation to set up a judicial system.[99] This view is based upon the fact that the basic premise of natural law theory, i.e. that its norms are derivable from universal, rational morality, also underlies the Noahide system. Now, at first glance, the idea that human reason may provide the ultimate validating criterion for any form of law would not seem to rest well with the concept of a revelation-based religion such as Judaism. Indeed, the term 'natural law' is hardly found in rabbinic writings.[100] Upon further reflection, however, there would appear to be a valid parallel between the way in which the *halakhah* in general, as we will

[98] See J. Maritain, *Man and the State* (Chicago, 1951); L. Fuller, *The Morality of Law* (Yale, 1964); A. d'Entrèves, *Natural Law* (London, 1970); J. Finnis, *Natural Law and Natural Rights* (Oxford, 1980).

[99] The link between the Noahide code and the concept of natural law in the Western philosophical tradition was made by Hugo Grotius as early as the 17th cent.: see I. Husik, 'The Law of Nature, Hugo Grotius and the Bible', *Hebrew Union College Annual*, 2 (1925), 406. Later literature includes S. Atlas, *Netivim Bemishpat Ivri* (New York, (1978), 17; N. Lamm and A. Kirschenbaum, 'Freedom and Constraint in the Jewish Judicial Process', *Cardozo Law Review*, 1 (1979), 110; O. Leaman, 'Maimonides and Natural Law', *Jewish Law Annual*, 6 (1987), 78; S. Schwarzschild, 'Do Noahides Have to Believe in Revelation?' in M. Kellner (ed.), *The Pursuit of the Ideal: Jewish Writings of Steven Schwarzschild* (New York, 1990), 29. For the most recent works in this area, see n. 105. For a rejection of any but the thinnest form of natural-law thinking in Judaism, see M. Fox, 'Maimonides and Aquinas on Natural Law', *Dine Israel*, 5 (1972), 1; J. Faur, *Iyyunim Bemishneh Torah* (Jerusalem, 1978), 151; J. D. Bleich, 'Natural Law', *Jewish Law Annual*, 7 (1988), 6–7. This approach is criticized in D. Novak, *Jewish Social Ethics* (New York, 1992). For a fuller argument than the one made below in favour of the Noahide laws as a Hartian form of minimal natural law in the Jewish legal heritage, see D. Sinclair, 'Maimonides and Natural Law Theory', in M. Golding (ed.), *Jewish Law and Legal Theory* (Dartmouth, 1994), 123–8, and S. Stone, 'Sinaitic and Noahide Law: Legal Pluralism in Jewish Law', *Cardozo Law Review*, 12 (1991), 1157.

[100] See R. Abraham Isaiah Karelitz, *Inyanei Emunah Uvitahon* (Tel-Aviv, 1984), 21; Bleich, 'Natural Law', and Schwarzschild, 'Do Noahides Have to Believe in Revelation?'.

see shortly, manifests a deep revulsion towards bloodshed on the basis of rational morality alone, and the weak notion of natural law found in the writings of H. Hart. According to Hart—a legal positivist, not a natural lawyer—there are certain aspects of universal, conventional morality that embrace various 'rules of conduct which any social organisation must contain if it is to be viable'. These rules constitute the 'minimum content of natural law' and have their basis in 'elementary truths concerning human beings and their natural environment and aims'.[101] Rationally based revulsion towards bloodshed is a striking feature of Jewish criminal law, and is found, for example, in Maimonides' ruling that killers who are exempt from the death penalty for purely formal reasons are, nevertheless to be put to death in order 'to preserve civilised society'.[102] It is also significant that rationality (*sevarah*), as distinct from revealed doctrine, is cited by the Talmud as the source for important principles in Jewish criminal law relating to the preservation of human life.[103] The link between the rational nature of the halakhic approach to homicide and the Noahide offence of bloodshed is discussed at length in Chapter 5 and in the Conclusion. For present purposes, it is sufficient to note that in relation to questions of life and death, rational morality is not foreign to the halakhic system and, hence, the concept of a Noahide offence of bloodshed validated by such a form of morality is not as unacceptable as it may have seemed at first glance.

It is also noteworthy that from the perspective of natural law doctrine, there is no problem with the fact that the Noahide laws constitute part of the written halakhic tradition. Written form is not fatal to natural law, nor does it negate its underlying rationality. The salient point is that natural law would be valid even if it were not written. This feature of natural law theory is nicely illustrated by the talmudic statement that even if the Torah had not been given, 'we would have learned modesty from the cat, aversion to robbery from the ant and chastity from the dove'.[104]

The aspect of natural law theory that is important for our purposes is the idea that it is legitimate to criticize the moral standard of formally valid Jewish law in the area of life and death on the basis of rational moral criteria. The rest of this section is a sustained effort to demonstrate that this idea is borne out by the *halakhah* relating to abortion. The question of natural law in Judaism in general is a complex one and has been analysed

---

[101] *The Concept of Law* (Oxford 1964), 188.
[102] Maimonides, *Hilkhot Rozeah*, 4: 9. For further discussion of this source, see nn. 118–120.
[103] See Conclusion, s. 2.
[104] *Eruvin*, 100b. For a discussion of this remark see B. Jackson, 'The Jewish View of Natural Law', *Journal of Jewish Studies*, 52 (2001), 136.

in depth in a number of recent works.[105] Various questions are discussed in these works, including the origin of natural law thinking in the Jewish tradition, the dynamics of the relationship between natural law and the *halakhah*, and the way in which Jewish natural law impacts upon relations between Jews and non-Jews. These general issues are beyond both the province and the scope of the present work. In any case, it would appear that in the final analysis the common theme in most of the recent works on Jewish law and natural law is precisely the underlying concept in the present chapter, i.e. the notion that rational morality is a necessary and perpetual critique of the revealed law.

To return to the main theme, there is a well-known source for demonstrating the validity of a rational approach to the Noahide system. This source is Maimonides' ruling on the question of granting Noahides the right of residence in the land of Israel. Under Jewish law, only a non-Jew who accepts the Noahide laws is entitled to the right of residence in a sovereign Jewish state. According to Maimonides, it is not necessary for the non-Jew wishing to qualify as resident in the land of Israel to accept these laws because they are part of the Bible or the *halakhah*; it is sufficient that his acceptance be based upon the rational nature of the Noahide laws. It ought to be pointed out that, according to Maimonides, rational acceptance of these laws is not sufficient to entitle a non-Jew to a share in the Hereafter. In order to qualify for spiritual eternity, the non-Jew is required to accept the Divine origin of the Noahide laws and their basis in the Torah. In relation to the formal acceptance of the Noahide laws in relation to right of residency in the land of Israel, Maimonides states, in the manuscript versions of his code of *halakhah*, that acceptance on the basis of the 'inclination of human reason' is sufficient to make of that person 'a wise individual although not a pious one'. This reading is to be preferred to the one in the definitive printed version[106] which denies the attribute of wisdom to a rationally-motivated Noahide. Not only does the manuscript version constitute the more authentic text, it also provides a better fit in terms of Maimonides' general philosophical approach.[107] This Maimonidean

---

[105] See *Jewish Law Annual*, 6 (1987); 7 (1988); D. Novak, *Natural Law in Judaism* (Cambridge, 1998); A. Sagi, 'Natural Law and *Halakhah*—A Critical Analysis', *Jewish Law Annual*, 13 (2000), 149. Novak makes a sustained argument for natural law in Judaism claiming, *inter alia*, that it is an integral part of the biblical tradition, and that it ought to be understood in a dynamic fashion, i.e. both influencing the *halakhah* and being influenced by it. He also claims that it is the best way for the resolution of disputes amongst different groups in humankind, and also within Jewish society itself.

[106] The first and principal printed edition of the *Mishneh Torah* was published in Rome in 1480.

[107] Maimonides refers to the rational nature of the Noahide laws in *Hilkhot Melakhim*, 9: 1. In *Hilkhot Melakhim*, 8: 11, he states that acceptance of the Noahide laws on the basis of reason alone endows an individual with the status of a wise person, albeit not that of a pious

position provides strong support for the view that the Noahide laws are valid on the basis of their rationality alone and may, therefore, be classified as a form of natural law along the lines referred to above.[108]

Another important aspect of natural law theory is its universal applicability. In this respect, there is an exact fit with the Noahide laws, the paramount feature of which, as indicated by their attribution to Noah, the biblical progenitor of humanity following the biblical Flood, is their universal scope. The one apparent exception to this universality is the Jewish people who, after having received the Torah, are bound exclusively by its norms and not those of the Noahide system. It may, however, be argued that the Torah simply develops the Noahide system further, rather than replacing it.[109] Also, it will be demonstrated in the following paragraphs that Jews are indeed bound by the Noahide laws, but in a moral rather than a legal sense. The Noahide laws are, therefore, of universal application, but the sanctions for breaking them vary from the positive in the case of Noahides to the moral in relation to the Jewish people.

This leads us to the nature of the influence of the Noahide system upon the *halakhah*. Clearly, the Noahide laws do not override those of the *halakhah*. This is not only a legal fact: it is also a systemic one. The essence of the *halakhah* is the concept of a Divinely revealed written law, interpreted by authorized interpreters throughout the ages.[110] In these terms there is certainly no room for endowing the rationally driven, universal Noahide system with the authority to override halakhic norms. Such a system may, however, act as a moral threshold below which the *halakhah* ought not to be allowed to fall. It is important to emphasize that the nature of the Noahide law in this respect is moral rather than legal, and it might, therefore, be more appropriate to refer to natural morality than to natural law. We will, however, continue to use the term 'natural law',

---

one. In fact, the reading in the first printed edition of the *Mishneh Torah* is that such an individual is 'not one of their pious ones nor is he wise'. The reading referred to in the present text, i.e. 'not of their pious ones but of their wise ones' is found in the majority of manuscript versions: see J. Dienstag, 'Natural Law in Maimonidean Thought and Scholarship', *Jewish Law Annual*, 6 (1987), 75. It also appears in the 15th-cent. philosophical commentaries of Profiat Duran and Joseph b. Shem Tov (ibid.). R. Moses Alashkar cites this version in his *responsa* (*Resp. Maharam Alashkar*, no. 117). R. Abraham Kook also cites the manuscript version (*Iggrot Harayah*, 1 no. 89) and explains at length that in the Maimonidean scheme of things, a sage is indeed on a higher plane than a pious person. Together with the philosophical approach outlined in nn. 98–9, there would appear to be a very strong case for adopting the manuscript version and endowing a rationally motivated Noahide with the status of a sage.

[108] See the sources in n. 99 and in particular, E. Benamozegh, *Israël et l'humanité* (Paris, 1914), 688, and D. Novak, *The Image of the Non-Jew in Judaism* (New York, 1983), 290.

[109] *Sefer Haikkarim*, i. ch. 25: R. Joseph Engel, *Beth Haozar, Ma'arekhet*, 1–2, *Ot Zayin*; R. Meir Simha Hacohen, *Or Sameah, Hilkhot Issurei Biah*, 3: 2.

[110] See J. D. Bleich, *Contemporary Halakhic Problems* (New York, 1977), 1, Introduction.

since the source of the moral principles lies in a system of law, i.e. the Noahide code. In any case, it is widely accepted that the norms of the *halakhah* do not exhaust the moral standards of Judaism, and that it is always possible to improve moral conduct by aiming higher and not taking advantage of halakhic permissions, as in the case of foeticide.[111] It is in this form that natural law theory has a role to play in the halakhic system.

The role of the Noahide prohibition on bloodshed as a moral regulator of Jewish law in the sense of non-reliance upon halakhic permissions, is exemplified in the talmudic rule that 'there is nothing allowed (*shari*) to an Israelite yet prohibited to a Noahide'.[112] As already observed in relation to the second comment of the Tosafot discussed above, the phrase 'not allowed', as opposed to the more technically legal term 'forbidden' (*asur*) probably signifies a moral rather than a legal limitation on a person's freedom of action. What this rule is saying is that all Israelites are required to take note of the Noahide prohibitions on moral grounds, even if they are not specifically incorporated into the Jewish law.[113]

A good illustration of the manner in which Jewish criminal jurisprudence responds to the demands of the Noahide prohibition on bloodshed is the discussion in the Midrash *Halakhah*[114] regarding the culpability of an Israelite who murders a non-Jew. The discussion begins with the proposition that the killer in such a case is not liable to the death penalty—the mandatory punishment for murder—since that sanction is reserved for someone who murders 'his neighbour',[115] and a Gentile is not included in that category. Absence of a criminal sanction would seem to imply that there is no prohibition upon the act in question. The following objection is then raised: 'Issi b. Akabyah says: Before the giving of the Torah, we had been warned against shedding blood, After the giving of the Torah, whereby laws were made stricter, shall they be considered lighter?'[116] Issi b. Akabyah bases his objection to the proposition that the Israelite murderer of a non-Jew is not considered a shedder of blood upon an assumption that the laws of the Torah must be more stringent than those of the Noahides. Since the Noahide prohibition on bloodshed does not

---

[111] See A. Lichtenstein, 'Does Jewish Tradition Recognize an Ethic Independent of *Halakhah?'*, in M. Kellner (ed.), *Contemporary Jewish Ethics* (New York, 1978), 102.

[112] *Sanhedrin*, 59a.

[113] The relationship between the Noahide laws and the provisions of the *halakhah* is a multifaceted and complex issue: see *Shabbat*, 153a; *Resp. Rashbash*, no. 543; *Beth Haozar*, 1: 1: 7; M. Potolsky, 'The Rabbinic Rule "No Rules are Derived From Before Sinai"' (Heb.), *Dine Israel*, 6 (1967), 195; N. Rakover, 'Law as a Universal Value' (Heb.), *Sidrat Mehkarim Usekirot*, 58 (Jerusalem, 1987), 15; D. Frimer, 'Israel, the Noahide Laws and Maimonides', *Jewish Law Association Studies*, 2 (1986), 89–102.

[114] This term refers to the compilations of halakhic interpretations of Scripture connected to the verses upon which they were based, see Elon, *Jewish Law*, 1047–9.

[115] Exod. 21: 14.   [116] *Mekhilta Derabbi Yishmael, Masekhta Dinezikin*, 4: 263.

distinguish between Jews and non-Jews, any attempt to do so in relation to Torah law would result in weakening the prohibition. Issi b. Akabyah gives no formal reason for his rejection of the inference that the murderer of a non-Jew is not considered a shedder of blood; rather, he bases it on a moral intuition that if homicide is evil, the religious affiliation of the victim must surely be irrelevant. Implicit in his formulation is the idea that the intention of the Torah was to build upon the existing moral framework of the Noahide system, and not to allow individuals to adopt a lower moral standard as a result of exegetical deductions. It is wrong to rule that an Israelite who murders a non-Jew is not culpable, notwithstanding the argument to the contrary derived from the interpretation of the biblical text. The implied permission to kill non-Jews inherent in the absence of culpability must, therefore, be rejected solely on the strength of the rational morality inherent in the Noahide code, and its role as the moral benchmark of the *halakhah*.

Issi b. Akabyah's argument is accepted by the sages, who, in the same passage, go on to rule that one who kills a non-Jew is 'free from judgment by the human court, but his judgment is left to Heaven'. This penalty is typically invoked when it is necessary to place a particular activity beyond the pale of acceptable conduct despite the absence of any specific halakhic prohibition. The phrase 'is left to Heaven' recalls the Divine warning in the biblical source for the Noahide offence of bloodshed, that God will 'seek the blood' of the innocent victims of homicide; moreover, as will be pointed out below, it is also used by Maimonides to indicate that certain forms of killing are morally condemned, notwithstanding the killer's exemption from any form of criminal sanction. The sages respond to the moral basis of Issi b. Akabyah's critique and formulate an appropriate sanction. This is also the definitive halakhic position on this matter.[117]

Another example of the regulatory role of rational morality in relation to the prevention of bloodshed in Jewish criminal jurisprudence is Maimonides' argument that the talmudic provision that a murderer who is not executed for his crime on technical grounds, e.g. the witnesses did not witness the crime simultaneously or the accused was not officially warned of the penalty for the crime, is nevertheless executed in an indirect manner, on the orders of the court. The murderer is incarcerated in a confined space and put on a special diet, which eventually results in death.[118] Maimonides explains this provision as follows:

This, however, is not done to other persons guilty of crimes involving the death penalty at the hands of the court...for, although there are worse crimes than

---

[117] See *Sefer Ra'avan*, *Bava Kamma*, 113b; *Sefer Yereim*, 175; *Meshekh Hokhmah*, Exodus 21: 14.

[118] 'He is placed in a cell...and fed with bread of adversity and water of affliction until his stomach bursts' (*Sanhedrin*, 9: 5). Also see B. Jackson, *Essays in Jewish and Comparative Legal History* (Leiden, 1975), 187.

bloodshed, none causes such destruction to civilised society as bloodshed. Not even idolatry, nor immorality nor the desecration of the Sabbath is the equal of bloodshed. For these are crimes between man and God, while bloodshed is a crime between man and man. If one has committed this crime, he is wholly wicked, and all the meritorious deeds he has performed during his lifetime cannot outweigh this crime or save him from judgement, as it is said:[119] 'A man that is laden with the blood of any person shall hasten his steps to the pit; none will support him'.[120]

Maimonides uses the argument that the principle of steps having to be taken in order to preserve civilized society lies at the core of the Noahide prohibition on bloodshed in order to justify the severe measures taken against killers who escape the death penalty on a technicality, but are clearly guilty on the basis of all the available evidence. Such killers are legally exempt from capital punishment, and strictly speaking, they ought to be set free. However, it is highly immoral for such killers to go free, since such a course of action would imperil the fabric of civilized society. The concept of the preservation of civilized society is the essence and the spirit of the limited type of natural law doctrine under discussion. Bloodshed is the single most powerful threat to the social fabric, and a way must be found to visit condign punishment upon those technically exempt killers who constitute such a serious threat to the social order. The way is the drastic diet mentioned above.

Maimonides is not content with merely overriding the legal exemption of the technically innocent murderer and bringing about his death by incarceration and special diet. He goes on to characterize bloodshed as a more severe offence than all the other capital offences in the *halakhah*. This is a bold statement, which may be understood in moral and theological terms as well as strictly legal ones.[121] Clearly, Maimonides feels very strongly about this issue, and he is prepared to allow a very wide gap to open up between the provisions of the law and the principles of universal, rational morality. There is no legal mandate for this punishment: it is the fruit of a highly sensitized concern for the moral well-being of society or, in Maimonides' own words, 'the preservation of civilized society'. Indeed, Maimonides goes on to give further vent to his feelings on the

---

[119] Prov. 28: 17.   [120] *Hilkhot Rozeah*, 4: 9.

[121] Some commentators understand it as referring to the fact that, unlike the other offences, which are punishable by stoning, bloodshed is punishable by decapitation, which in legal terms is the more severe punishment. The whole passage, however, is too striking and effusive for such a narrow approach and there is undoubtedly a theological and moral thrust to Maimonides' comment on the relative severity of bloodshed.

gravity of the offence of bloodshed by incorporating a mini-sermon into this particular halakhic ruling.[122]

This concludes our discussion of the role of the Noahide laws as a natural law component in the halakhic system. We have argued that the universally compelling, rational principle of the need to preserve society underlying the Noahide laws sets a moral threshold below which the *halakhah* ought not to fall. In that sense, the Noahide laws, especially the offence of bloodshed, constitute a form of natural law in the Jewish tradition. In particular, the Noahide laws serve to prevent Jews from relying upon halakhic permissions that offend against universally accepted moral principles. Examples of this role are the effective abolition of the distinction between Jews and non-Jews in relation to the crime of homicide, and the effective neutralization of the halakhic rules of evidence in murder cases where the murderer escapes on a technicality. In this respect, the effect of the Noahide prohibition is also to make the *halakhah* more realistic in terms of the need for basic social control in society. This aspect of the role of the Noahide law on bloodshed is discussed further in Chapter 5.[123]

The impact of the Noahide system upon the *halakhah* is moral rather than legal. Legality in the area of the criminal law, is defined in terms of specific offences and their penalties at human hands. Foeticide is not the subject of such a specific prohibition, and the penalties for breaching it are Divine and extra-legal in nature. For Jews subject to the *halakhah*, the Noahide norms are of moral significance only.

We are now in a position fully to appreciate the moral force of Tosafot's statement that Israelites are 'not allowed' to carry out non-therapeutic abortions. As observed above, Tosafot make this statement in the context of the talmudic discussion of the Noahide laws. In the course of that discussion, the Talmud cites the opinion of R. Yishmael that foeticide falls within the Noahide prohibition on bloodshed.[124] Tosafot respond to

---

[122] In fact, he follows the above-mentioned extract with a mini-sermon on the biblical episode of Naboth's vineyard (1 Kings 21) in order to provide homiletical support for his statement regarding the ranking of bloodshed over all the other offences, including idolatry; see I. Twersky, *Introduction to the Code of Maimonides* (Yale, 1980), 148.   [123] See Ch. 5, s. 5(b).

[124] R. Yishmael bases his ruling that the Noahide prohibition on bloodshed includes foeticide upon an exegetical interpretation of the passage in Gen. 9: 6, which deals with the covenant between God and Noah and the commandment not to spill blood. Both the exegesis itself and the background to it have stimulated scholarly commentary. According to I. Weiss, *Dor Dor Vedorshav* (Berlin, 1923), ii. 23, R. Yishmael used the device of the Noahide laws in order to express his revulsion at the widespread practice of abortion in Roman society, cf. Aptowitzer, 'Status of the Embryo', 113. Others maintain that R. Yishmael's exegesis indicates an early, non-rabbinic school of thought closer to the Greek approach outlined in s. 2 above (A. Geiger, *Hamikrah Vetirgumav* (Jerusalem, 1948), 280; Alon, *Mehkarim Betoldot Yisrael*. It is also possible that R. Yishmael extended the prohibition on bloodshed to foeticide on the basis of the theory of rational morality outlined in the present section.

R. Yishmael's categorization of foeticide as a Noahide offence by citing the above-mentioned talmudic dictum that 'there is nothing permitted to an Israelite yet prohibited to a Noahide', and raising the following question: if R. Yishmael is correct, then the dictum requires that foeticide be prohibited to Israelites as well as to Noahides. There is, however, no such prohibition! In order to reconcile R. Yishmael's position with the talmudic dictum, Tosafot claim that Israelites, too, are 'not allowed' to engage in non-therapeutic foeticide. The moral nature of this statement emerges from its context, i.e. the Noahide prohibition on bloodshed and its role as a moral regulator of the *halakhah*. As demonstrated above, the basis for the interaction of Noahide law with the halakhic system is the moral imperative articulated by Issi b. Akabyah. In deriving their conclusion that Jews are 'not allowed' to carry out non-therapeutic abortions from the Noahide offence of bloodshed, they are, in effect, declaring that the basis for making such abortions off-limits to Jews is the limited natural law doctrine discussed above. Non-therapeutic abortions are unacceptable in terms of universal, rational morality, and it is their immorality that places them beyond the pale for halakhically observant Jews.

It is noteworthy that Tosafot imply that by the same token that it is permitted to Jews, therapeutic abortion is also permitted to Noahides. This fits in with the rational morality underlying the Noahide offence, which would not penalize foeticide when performed for the sake of saving maternal life.

In the light of this analysis, it is evident that the *halakhah* in the area of foeticide is shaped by a combination of legal doctrine and moral principle. The legal doctrine comprises the elements of foetal non-personhood and the permission to perform therapeutic abortion. The moral principle is based upon the Noahide offence of bloodshed, and comes into play whenever it is necessary to ensure that abortion law does not fall below the standard of universal, rational morality.

In the following section, it will be argued that this moral principle is not fixed in time, but extends to those aspects of general morality that are acceptable to Jews and non-Jews alike, in any particular period of history. It will be claimed that the tension between the legal and moral positions on foeticide, together with the awareness that both these positions seem to fall below the accepted moral standard, especially in Christian countries, is endemic to the *responsa* in this area, especially since the eighteenth century. These *responsa* have even, on rare occasions, made this tension explicit. The authors of these *responsa* deal with the tension on both the legal and the moral levels. In legal terms, they often seek out arguments to justify prohibiting abortion, except in the most compelling of therapeutic cases. Often they will rely upon the minority opinion of Maimonides. On the moral level, they effectively incorporate principles

drawn from general morality in order to bring the *halakhah* up to what is
generally regarded as being an acceptable moral standard in society at
large. Sometimes these principles are made explicit, and sometimes they
are presented without any reference to their source. Explicit references to
the moral input into the *halakhah* is most often found in the writings of
those specifically concerned with halakhic jurisprudence,[125] although, as
we will see, they also occur in the practically oriented *responsa* literature.
In relation to abortion, Tosafot provide the key source for this moral input,
and it is in the light of the tension between the legal and the moral
elements involved in foeticide and abortion that much of the recent
halakhah on abortion may be best understood.[126]

A final point in this discussion of the relationship between legal and
moral elements in the *halakhah* on abortion arises out of the distinction
made in the sources between the different sanctions for bloodshed in the
Noahide code and the halakhic system. The pattern that emerges, both in
relation to the killing of a Gentile and to bringing about the deaths of
those guilty of homicide but legally exempt from the death penalty, is to
distinguish between the penalties meted out to Israelites and Noahides.[127]
Penalties under the Noahide code involve capital punishment. The same
offences in the *halakhah*, once they have been morally condemned on the
basis of the Noahide laws, carry only Divine or extra-legal penalties. In
this respect, it is important to observe that there is a view that the penalty

---

[125] See *Or Sameah, Hilkhot Melakhim*, 3: 10; R. Meir Dan Plotzki, *Hemdat Yisrael, Kuntres Ner
Mizvah*, no. 288, 75; Sinclair, 'Maimonides and Natural Law Theory', 124–7. See also Ch. 5,
s. 5(b).

[126] The drawing of any hard and fast distinction between law and morality in the context
of *halakhah* is well-nigh impossible, and care must be taken to avoid reading Western categories into Jewish law; see H. Ben Menahem, 'The Judicial Process and the Nature of Law',
in N. Hecht *et al.* (eds.), *An Introduction to the History and Sources of the Jewish Law* (Oxford,
1996), 421–36. However, the present argument is simply that the concern with the limits of
halakhic doctrine and the legitimacy of general moral input is so pervasive in the halakhic
literature on abortion, that the distinction seems to arise out of the texts themselves in a natural and organic fashion, rather than it being the result of a forced synthesis between theoretical Western categories and halakhic reasoning.

[127] The sages' reply to Issi b. Akabyah in the above-mentioned *Mekhilta* (n. 116) is that
while they accept the force of his argument on the level of the prohibition against homicide,
they maintain that the killer's 'judgment is left in the hands of Heaven'. A historical
approach to this disparity is adopted by Novak, *Image of the Non-Jew*, 290, who suggests that
it is an expression of the rejection of the generally cruel and barbaric modes of punishment
practised in the ancient world. On a conceptual level, it is arguable that the difference in
penalties is based upon an a priori assumption that Israelite society functions at a high level
of morality, and breaches of basic norms such as bloodshed will simply not occur. The same
thing cannot be assumed in relation to general society; therefore, positive criminal sanctions
are required in that society: see D. Sinclair, 'The Right to Life: Defending the Lives of the
Terminally Ill, Foetuses and Non-Jews in Jewish Law' (Heb.), in G. Frishtik (ed.), *Human
Rights in Jewish Law* (Jerusalem, 1992), 40–1. Clearly, this argument is made solely on a conceptual level and has nothing to do with real life. In reality, the Israelite King is empowered
to execute Israelites who break the Noahide laws: see Ch. 5, s. 5(b).

for unjustified foeticide is also 'death at the hands of Heaven';[128] thus, non-therapeutic foeticide also follows this pattern.

It ought, however, to be pointed out that human intervention in the process of divine retribution is not unknown; in this area in particular, it is even required. The authority of the court to bring about the death of killers exempt from capital punishment was referred to above. The Israelite monarch is also empowered to put his subjects to death on the basis of offences committed against the Noahide prohibition. Indeed, the monarch's jurisdiction to deal with offenders against the moral order as manifested in the Noahide laws is fairly draconian. It is spelled out by Maimonides[129] and R. Nissim,[130] and will be discussed at length in the discussion on the treatment of the terminally ill in Chapter 5. The short point is that the distinction between Israelites and Noahides in terms of the penalties imposed for transgressions under the Noahide Code may be less pronounced than it would first appear, even though the element of discretion that applies to the extra-legal jurisdiction of both Israelite king and court, will, of course, always remain an important difference between the two systems.

5. THE MORAL ELEMENT IN THE *RESPONSA* LITERATURE ON ABORTION

The moral element in abortion *halakhah* outlined above plays an important role in reducing the tension between the fundamentally liberal approach of the *halakhah* to abortion, and the often highly negative attitude towards it in many of the societies in which halakhic authorities live and write their *responsa* on real-life problems. *Responsa* on abortion penned in Christian countries often betray the influence of the moral element in the way in which they deal, for example, with the question of the existence of a prohibition on non-therapeutic abortion, and a number of examples of this influence were given in the course of the discussion in the previous section. The aim of the present section is to focus specifically on these *responsa*, and to cite clear examples of the influence of the moral element on the halakhic decisions contained therein. Since halakhists generally choose to express this type of influence in as legal a manner as possible,

---

[128] R. Meir Simha, *Meshekh Hokhmah, Exodus* 35: 2. For a general treatment of the role of Divine penalties in Jewish law, see Elon (ed.), *Principles of Jewish Law*, 522–4.
[129] *Hilkhot Rozeah*, 2: 4–5; *Hilkhot Melakhim*, 3: 10; *Guide for the Perplexed*, 3: 40; D. Sinclair, 'The Interaction between Law and Morality in Jewish Law', *Criminal Justice Ethics*, 11 (1992), 79–80. [130] *Derashot Haran*, no. 11; Sinclair, 'Maimonides and Natural Law Theory', 80.

the existence of very clear examples indicates that in this area in particular, morality has an important role to play in shaping the *halakhah*.

An unusually lucid example of the role of morality in abortion *halakhah* is a *responsum* of R. Yair Bachrach, who lived in Germany in the late seventeenth and early eighteenth centuries. The question before R. Bachrach was whether an adulterous woman could take a potion in order to kill the *mamzer*[131] foetus in her womb. In ruling against the abortion, R. Bachrach concludes his discussion of the classical halakhic approach to the issue of foeticide with this striking statement: 'Abortion would, therefore, be perfectly permissible on the basis of Torah law. There is, however, a widespread custom amongst Jews and non-Jews alike to prohibit it in order to prevent promiscuity and immorality'.[132] According to R. Bachrach, the basis for forbidding the abortion in this case is purely moral. Banning abortions constituted an important deterrent to adulterous relationships, especially in an era in which effective contraception was not available. It was the only way in which the evidence of adultery could be destroyed. In strictly legal terms, there is no basis for prohibiting the abortion. R. Bachrach makes no attempt to conceal the fact that his ruling is motivated by purely moral considerations, which he points out are common to Jews and non-Jews alike. In support of his approach, he cites the opinion of the Tosafot to the effect that foeticide is 'not allowed', thereby strengthening our point made above regarding the fundamentally moral thrust of Tosafot's position, and in particular, the universal nature of that morality which flows from its natural law background.

Now, it is true that R. Bachrach also advances a strictly legal argument for prohibiting unjustified foeticide. He suggests that since there is ample evidence that *halakhah* prohibits the vain emission of male seed,[133] it may be assumed that it would also prohibit foeticide on the basis of an a fortiori argument: if vain emission of seed is prohibited, how much more ought foeticide to be banned. At the same time, however, he is clearly aware that this argument is far from definitive. R. Bachrach admits that most authorities maintain that the prohibition on seed destruction does not apply to females, since they are not subject to the commandment to 'be fruitful and multiply'.[134] In order to avoid the somewhat bizarre conclusion that foeticide is prohibited to males only, he cites a view of Tosafot that women are included in the general directive to populate the world

---

[131] See n. 39 for the definition and general legal position with regard to the *mamzer* in Jewish law.   [132] *Resp. Havat Yair*, no. 31.

[133] *Yevamot*, 34b; *Niddah*, 13a; *Shulhan Arukh, Even Haezer*, 23: 2. Also see Feldman, *Marital Relations*, 109–31.

[134] *Tosafot, Yevamot*, 12b, s.v. *shalosh*; *Ketubot*, 39a, s.v. *shalosh*; Feldman, *Marital Relations*, 123–8.

and as such, they are bound to preserve human seed, even though they are exempt from the halakhic obligation to procreate.[135]

R. Bachrach's case is also the subject of a *responsum* by an eighteenth-century authority, R. Jacob Emden, who reaches the conclusion that it is permitted to destroy the *mamzer* foetus.[136] In the course of his discussion, R. Emden observes that the prohibition on seed destruction used by R. Bachrach as the basis for prohibiting the abortion is probably based on mystical rather than legal sources. Hence, if the abortion is legally justified, it would not be appropriate to override it on the basis of a mystical prohibition. R. Emden also points out that even the mystical prohibition is only on the 'vain' emission of the seed. It would not apply to a case in which the foetus was being destroyed for a valid reason, even if that reason was not the immediate and direct saving of maternal life, but a threat of a less severe nature. R. Emden defines such a threat as 'a great need', and in the present case, it consists of the shame and disgrace accruing to the mother as a result of bringing a *mamzer* child into the world. According to R. Emden, 'even in relation to a regular foetus, it is possible to rule leniently, prior to the onset of labour, for the sake of great need and to permit an abortion, even if the mother's life is not in danger, but the foetus is causing her great suffering'.[137] R. Emden is clearly not persuaded by R. Bachrach's concern for the prevention of promiscuity, and consequently permits the abortion of the foetus.

---

[135] *Tosafot, Gittin,* 41b, *s.v. lo tohu; Bava Bathra,* 13a, *s.v. shenemar; Resp. Radakh,* 2 no. 17. See also *Resp. Haran,* no. 27; *Beth Shmuel Even Haezer* 1: 2.

[136] R. Emden's first argument is that since the mother of a *mamzer* foetus is liable to the death penalty for the sinful act of intercourse that resulted in its conception, and under talmudic law the execution of a pregnant woman is not delayed on account of her foetus (*Arakhin,* 1: 4), the foetus may be regarded, from a purely legal standpoint, as if it were already dead. This argument is hardly a convincing one, and it is on the criterion of 'great need', which is R. Emden's second argument, that the legal force of the *responsum* is based (see *Resp. Ziz Eliezer,* 13 no. 102). It is also noteworthy that R. Emden indicates that the destruction of a *mamzer* foetus may very well constitute a meritorious deed since it is 'cursed seed' inside the mother's womb. This approach is in direct contrast with that of R. Bachrach, and the clash between the two authorities may serve to indicate the existence of a specifically Sephardic lenient approach to the abortion issue—R. Emden was a Sephardi—as opposed to a more stringent Askenazic one, typified by R. Bachrach. For another example of the Sephardic approach, see *Resp. Mishpetei Uziel, Hoshen Mishpat,* no. 47. The strong moral opposition to abortion typical of Christian countries would not be a feature of Islamic society, since the position on foeticide and abortion in Islamic law is much less severe than it is in Catholicism; see V. Rispler-Chaim, *Islamic Medical Ethics in the Twentieth Century* (Leiden, 1993), 12–18.

[137] *Resp. She'elat Ya'avez,* no. 43. The evils of seed destruction are strongly emphasized in the *Zohar* (*Vayeshev,* 188a; *Vaheyi,* 219b) and it is noteworthy that R. Emden criticizes the mystical doctrine of seed destruction on the grounds that it constitutes a departure from the Talmudic position on this issue; see *Mitpahat Sefarim* (Altona, 1768), 1: 20. For the influence of the *Zohar* on the *Shulhan Arukh,* see J. Katz, *Halakhah Vekabbalah* (Jerusalem, 1984), 67–9. Also, see Ch. 2 n. 5 for the influence of kabbalistic doctrines on the *halakhah* in relation to artificial reproductive techniques.

A recent illustration of the direct influence of the Catholic position towards abortion on a halakhic authority, is a remark by R. Moses Zweig of Antwerp in a *responsum* written at the time of the thalidomide trial in Belgium in the mid-1960s. Thalidomide was a drug taken for the purpose of easing the unpleasant side effects of pregnancy, especially morning sickness. Unfortunately, it also caused terrible damage to the foetus, and many mothers who took the drug gave birth to children with severe deformities. R. Zweig ruled strictly on the question of aborting a deformed thalidomide foetus, observing that this decision was necessary in order to ensure that the Divine Name would not be profaned by a lenient ruling 'when...the Church has unequivocally expressed its opposition to killing the foetus in this context'.[138] Although R. Zweig does not articulate the tension between his ruling and the classical rabbinic position in as stark a manner as R. Bachrach, it is evident that his halakhic reasoning is also driven by the moral imperative in this area of *halakhah*. It is also clear that he is concerned with the moral image of the Jewish law, which to his mind means that its position on abortion must conform to the strict stance of the Church of Rome and of the many Catholic jurists and physicians in Belgium who were vehemently opposed to the abortion option at the time of the trial.

The moral imperative in abortion *halakhah* makes itself felt not only in European countries and against the backdrop of Christian moral values, it is also found in *responsa* written in Moslem countries, where abortion was much less morally problematic. A very clear example is a *responsum* written by R. Joseph Hayyim, the leading halakhic authority in Baghdad at the turn of the twentieth century. R. Joseph Hayyim was asked concerning an adulterous woman who was five months pregnant when she requested permission to abort her *mamzer* foetus. R. Joseph Hayyim begins his *responsum* with the remark that 'he did not wish to give a definitive answer in terms of either prohibition or permission'. All he was prepared to do was to 'copy the *responsa* of the earlier authorities on this matter', amongst which that of R. Yair Bachrach was cited at length. In his concluding sentence, R. Joseph Hayyim reiterates his intention not 'to reveal any opinion on the case', and the questioner is told to take the review of precedents to a local rabbi, who will then instruct him as to how to proceed.[139] R. Joseph Hayyim's approach is highly uncharacteristic, both of his own halakhic writings and of the *responsa* genre in general. Indeed, it is precisely the provision of a definitive reply to a given factual situation that endows the rabbinic *responsum* with its unique normative

---

[138] 'Regarding Abortion' (Heb.), *Noam*, 7 (1964), 45.
[139] *Resp. Rav Pa'alim, Even Haezer*, 1 no. 4.

status.[140] Presumably, the reason for R. Joseph Hayyim's deviation from generally accepted methods of *responsa* writing lies in a felt need to express the tension between halakhic doctrine and the moral issue of preserving foetal life, especially when the mother is not in any direct physical danger. Indeed, in his brief reference to R. Bachrach's *responsum*, R. Joseph Hayyim cites his remark regarding the conflict between Torah law and conventional morality. It may, therefore, be assumed that in R. Joseph Hayyim's eyes, it must have been evident that the best solution for this type of tension was to desist from writing a definitive legal *responsum*, and to leave the actual decision in the hands of the local rabbi. The latter will be in a position to assess the moral aspects of the case on a first-hand basis, and reach an appropriate conclusion based upon all the relevant legal and moral elements. R. Joseph Hayyim, unlike R. Bachrach, does not explicitly cite external moral influences as a reason for his decision. Nevertheless, his concern with the tension between the legal and the moral is palpable. It is no simple step, morally speaking, to sanction the abortion of a 5-month foetus in the absence of any direct threat to the mother's life. He deals with this tension by taking the unusual step of simply recording precedents and leaving the actual decision to the local authority.

The obvious difference between R. Joseph Hayyim on the one hand and R. Bachrach and R. Zweig on the other is the fact that the former lived in a Moslem society whereas the two latter authorities operated in a Christian milieu. Abortion was, and still is, morally problematic in Christian societies, and it is natural that rabbinic authorities in such societies would take a moral cue from the general environment. The moral imperative within the halakhic tradition regarding non-therapeutic abortion links up easily with the Christian position. As already observed,[141] the position under Islamic law is much closer to that of Jewish law, and halakhic authorities working in a Moslem environment would not find the same unequivocal moral resonance in their surroundings as did their Ashkenazic brethren. There is nevertheless, a tension between morality and law in the context of abortion, and in R. Joseph Hayyim's case it is evinced by the unusual methodology employed in the *responsum*.

The most recent illustration of the tension between legal abortion doctrine and the moral imperative in this area is undoubtedly the debate that took place in the late 1970s between R. Eliezer Waldenberg of Jerusalem and R. Moses Feinstein of New York, regarding the abortion of a foetus afflicted with Tay-Sachs disease. In the present author's view, R. Feinstein's *responsum* forbidding the abortion provides a good illustration of the

---

[140] See Elon, *Jewish Law*, 1457–9.   [141] See n. 136.

ways in which the moral imperative is worked into a halakhic ruling on abortion.

Tay-Sachs is a genetic disorder affecting Jews of East European ancestry. The genetic defect results in a deficiency of the enzyme hexosaminidase A and, in the absence of this enzyme, fatty deposits build up on the nerve cells of the newborn baby. Within the first four or five months of life, the baby becomes afflicted by mental retardation, blindness, paralysis, and dementia. Nearly all affected children die by the age of 4; none survive beyond their fifth year. Since the disease is genetic, there is 25 per cent chance that the offspring of two carriers of the defective gene will suffer from the disease. It is possible to test for Tay-Sachs during pregnancy, since normal cells contain the enzyme hexosaminidase A, whereas those of a Tay-Sachs foetus do not.

In 1975, R. Eliezer Waldenberg replied to the director of the Shaarei Zedek Hospital in Jerusalem, Israel, concerning the abortion of a Tay-Sachs foetus.[142] R. Waldenberg was prepared to permit abortion in such cases until the seventh month of pregnancy. In his opinion, the danger to the mother of an abortion after that stage would outweigh any benefit that would accrue to her by preventing the birth of a Tay-Sachs child.[143] His decision was based upon the classical legal doctrine of foetal nonpersonhood and its application on behalf of the mother's welfare, as outlined in the first section of this chapter. In particular, R. Waldenberg relied upon the lenient approach of R. Jacob Emden in the *mamzer* foetus case cited above. In that case, R. Emden was prepared to permit the abortion of a regular, non-*mamzer* foetus prior to the onset of labour 'for the sake of great need and . . . even if the mother's life is not in danger but the foetus is causing her great suffering'.[144] R. Waldenberg points out that in the light of the mental and emotional suffering in store for the mother as a result of the birth of a Tay-Sachs child, this is a classical case for the application of the 'great need' principle. His remark that 'the eyes of both parents must witness the child's agony without being able to provide any relief', indicates that he is prepared to take into account the suffering of the father as well as the mother, and that the baby's own suffering is also a factor to be considered. R. Waldenberg states quite categorically that the fact that the suffering involved is primarily of a mental rather than a physical nature does not detract from the 'great need' principle, since mental distress is often more acute than physical pain.

R. Waldenberg's argument is built to a great extent upon factors relating to the course a Tay-Sachs child's life will take after its birth.

---

[142] *Resp. Ziz Eliezer*, 13 no. 102. It is important to note that this hospital is run in accordance with the *halakhah*.

[143] Whether or not this is still the case today is open to question, see nn. 3 and 66.

[144] *Resp. She'elat Ya'avez*, no. 43.

The emphasis throughout is on the future suffering of the mother, the child and 'the parents'—both mother and father. There are references throughout the *responsum* to the permissive rulings on the abortion of a *mamzer* foetus. In those cases, the future-oriented nature of the suffering is spelled out in the halakhic sources, i.e. bringing the bastardy and the sin which caused it into the public eye and, in the words of R. Joseph Hayyim, 'causing shame, disgrace and profanation of the Divine Name' as the matter becomes public knowledge. The force of these references is that defects that will cause suffering only after birth are valid grounds for abortion in Jewish law. Evidently, R. Waldenberg regards the *mamzer* foetus cases as precedents for the abortion of physically defective foetuses whose condition is brought to light by modern genetic techniques. The mental suffering attendant upon the birth of a *mamzer* foetus is paralleled by the mainly mental, but sometimes also physical, anguish of the parents of a Tay-Sachs foetus. Presumably, the same argument would apply in relation to any serious genetic or other type of defect that could be established during pregnancy. In this respect, R. Waldenberg's *responsum* merely extends the scope of the general principle of non-life-threatening maternal suffering defined by R. Emden in his *responsum* on the *mamzer* foetus case.

Some two years later, R. Moses Feinstein, a leading North American halakhic authority, wrote a *responsum* in which he adopted a severely critical approach towards R. Waldenberg's decision. In R. Feinstein's view, foeticide does, indeed, fall into the halakhic category of homicide, and the only difference between an adult victim and a foetus is that there is no capital punishment for killing the latter. Moreover, foetal life may not be sacrificed for the sake of saving any person other than the mother. R. Feinstein is prepared to sanction abortion only in a case of a direct and immediate threat to the mother's life.[145]

Amongst the grounds cited by R. Feinstein in support of his decision is the talmudic law regarding the violation of the Sabbath for the purposes of rescuing a foetus trapped inside a dead mother,[146] and Maimonides' justification of therapeutic abortion in terms of the pursuer principle.[147] R. Feinstein presents his arguments in the strongest possible terms. Not only does he insist that foeticide falls within the category of homicide in Jewish law,[148] with the sole reservation that it does not carry the death penalty, but he dismisses two major sources for the lenient position as forgeries by

---

[145] *Resp. Iggrot Moshe, Hoshen Mishpat*, 2 no. 69.   [146] See n. 24.
[147] See nn. 79–81.
[148] As already observed, this approach is adopted by several modern authorities and in our view reflects the moral element in abortion *halakhah*. The majority of these opinions, especially those of R. Unterman, *Shevet Miyehudah; Resp. Yabia Omer*, 4, *Even Haezer*, no. 1; and *Resp. Mishneh Halakhot*, 9 nos. 328–30 are based upon the seminal statement of Tosafot

an errant disciple.[149] He dismisses two others[150] on equally slim grounds: lack of library resources in one case, and a highly unconvincing reading of the *responsum* in question in the other. In terms of substantive halakhic analysis, R. Feinstein relies mainly upon the Maimonidean position, according to which the life of the foetus may be terminated only if there is a direct and immediate threat to that of the mother. Notwithstanding the apparent logical inconsistencies in this position,[151] R. Feinstein insists that Maimonides' words are not to be questioned, and that any attempt to blunt their literal meaning is tantamount to 'bringing all of Maimonides' rulings throughout the entire *Mishneh Torah* into disrepute'. According to R. Feinstein, the classical critical commentators on the *Mishneh Torah* do not record any difficulty in relation to Maimonides' ruling on therapeutic abortion; the problems of more recent authorities with this ruling are to be attributed to their weak intellects and deficient understanding, rather than to any logical deficiency on Maimonides' part.

In the final section of his *responsum*, R. Feinstein makes the remark:

I have written all this in the light of the fact that many governments, including that of the State of Israel, have sanctioned foeticide and as a result, countless foetuses have already been destroyed. At such a time, it is most necessary to erect a fence around the Torah and to avoid issuing lenient rulings in an area as serious as that of homicide.

This concern with universal moral standards relating to abortion clearly reflects the universal moral element in the *halakhah* on foeticide discussed at length above. It also helps to explain R. Feinstein's harsh and, in some respects, legally simplistic critique of R. Waldenberg's *responsum*, expressed both in the charges of forgery made against some of R. Waldenberg's sources and in a remark concerning the ill-advised nature of the decision as a whole: 'And I was therefore amazed to see a *responsum* by an Israeli scholar written to the director of the *Shaarei Zedek* Hospital...permitting the abortion of foetuses diagnosed as Tay-Sachs victims beyond the third month of pregnancy.'[152] R. Feinstein concludes

---

cited above at n. 91, which imports the distinction made in the present text between law and morality into the formulation of the halakhic basis for prohibiting foeticide. It goes without saying that no authority extends the homicide argument to a life-saving abortion. In the case of a direct and immediate threat to the mother's life, there is no question that the foetus is to be destroyed, if necessary, right up until birth (n. 5).

[149] Tosafot, *Niddah*, 44b, *s.v. ihu*, and *Resp. Maharit*, nos. 97, 99.

[150] *Resp. Rav Pa'alim, Even Haezer*, 1 no. 4, and *Resp. She'elat Ya'avez*, no. 43.

[151] See nn. 82–5.

[152] It is noteworthy that R. Feinstein alludes to the three-month stage of pregnancy as a possible basis for ruling leniently, in this passage at the very end of the *responsum*. It does not figure in his substantive discussion and in this respect the *responsum* reiterates the claim made in the first section, that the stages of foetal development are not of primary significance in this area.

his *responsum* by totally rejecting R. Waldenberg's understanding of the classical rabbinic doctrine of foeticide, ruling that 'it is an act of homicide to kill any foetus, regular or *mamzer*, healthy or known to be suffering from Tay-Sachs'. In his view, R. Waldenberg's *responsum* is not to be relied upon, and ought never to have been written.

The bulk of R. Feinstein's *responsum* is couched in purely legal terms. It is, however, replete with formal and substantive indications of the workings of the moral imperative in this area. Each one of these is picked up by R. Waldenberg, who was not slow to come to his own defence. In a *responsum* published the following year,[153] R. Waldenberg reiterated his opinion concerning the authentic legal position with regard to foeticide. He also criticized R. Feinstein's use of the forgery argument, which he condemned as being both simplistic and a radical departure from the accepted approach to the analysis of halakhic topics over the ages.[154] The general point is that R. Feinstein's approach, with its heavy reliance on forgery charges and charges of missing sources, is not acceptable to R. Waldenberg: 'With all great respect, this is not the way. We follow the method of the luminaries of previous generations...none of whom would even have thought of solving conceptual problems with the simplistic device of the ascription of scribal error.' Amongst the several examples of the clash of methodologies between R. Feinstein and R. Waldenberg is the treatment of the above-mentioned *responsum* of R. Joseph Hayyim, who desisted from giving a definitive ruling on the issue of aborting a *mamzer* foetus, and instead, simply presented a number of leading opinions and recommended that a local rabbi make the final decision. In our discussion of this *responsum*, we suggested that R. Joseph Hayyim's approach reflected the tension between legal doctrine and moral concerns in this area. It would also appear that R. Waldenberg opts for this analysis of the *responsum*. R. Feinstein, however, disagrees. In addition to criticizing R. Joseph Hayyim's apparent lack of objectivity in citing sources,[155] R. Feinstein opines that R. Joseph Hayyim's hesitation

---

[153] *Resp. Ziz Eliezer*, 14 no. 100.

[154] For a detailed analysis of the disagreements between R. Waldenberg and R. Feinstein, see Sinclair, 'Legal Basis for Prohibition of Abortion', 93–8.

[155] R. Feinstein writes that R. Joseph Hayyim cited only the lenient *responsum* of R. Joseph Trani (*Resp. Maharit*, no. 99) according to which there is 'not even a trace of homicide attached to the act of foeticide', but does not mention the stricter ruling in *Resp. Maharit*, no. 97. In fact, R. Joseph Hayyim does write 'and see that which R. Trani wrote further in *Resp. Maharit*, no. 97'. His emphasis on the lenient *responsum* is simply an indication of his preference for a source in accordance with the classical rabbinic doctrine on foeticide. It is noteworthy that the resolution of the two apparently contradictory *responsa* of R. Trani has exercised a number of authorities. It is by no means clear that the two *responsa* are dealing with the same issue; it is very likely that they are not. The strict one is concerned with the issue of a Jewish physician dealing with a non-Jewish patient, whereas the lenient one is concerned with the halakhic approach to foeticide. Also, the fact that both *responsa* are cited by

in reaching a final ruling was a result of his 'not having had sufficient books available to him'. R. Waldenberg takes R. Feinstein to task on this point, saying that this charge is not borne out by any evidence whatsoever and is totally unwarranted.[156] Even a cursory acquaintance with R. Joseph Hayyim's *responsa* and other halakhic works proves beyond any doubt that his library did not suffer from a dearth of halakhic literature.

In terms of the argument made above regarding the significant role of morality in abortion *halakhah*, and the observation that many authorities prefer to elide the difference between morality and law in this area and present their rulings in as purely legal a style as possible, it is not difficult to understand R. Feinstein's deviations from classical legal reasoning in this *responsum*. Indeed, both the forgery charges and those relating to lack of library facilities may be more rhetorical than realistic: they serve to indicate a fundamental disagreement with the opposing viewpoint, rather than an unorthodox form of legal reasoning.[157] In any case, the heart of the debate is not about the nature of legal reasoning; it is about the morality of abortion. R. Waldenberg believes that his decision in the Tay-Sachs case is perfectly moral, whereas R. Feinstein disagrees vehemently with this position. The two widely divergent perspectives are understandable if it is borne in mind that R. Feinstein was not actually responding to a specific case, but rather to R. Waldenberg's permissive position. Since his major concern in the *responsum* was with the moral image of the *halakhah*, R. Feinstein may very well have felt the need to adopt a particularly strict anti-abortion stand, in order to emphasize that foeticide is beyond the pale for Jews, unless there is a very strong

---

R. Hayyim Benveniste (*Sheirei Knesset Hagedolah, Yoreh Deah,* 154) who was one of R. Trani's major disciples, is evidence of the authenticity of them both (see *Resp. Ziz Eliezer,* 9 no. 51; 13 no. 102). In R. Waldenberg's opinion, R. Feinstein's critique is a misguided one, resulting from his 'not having read the actual *responsum* of R. Joseph Hayyim'.

[156] R. Feinstein's claim that R. Joseph Hayyim's reluctance to rule in a definitive manner was a result of 'lack of books' is quite baseless. R. Joseph Hayyim begins his *responsum* with the statement that he 'does not wish to give a definitive ruling, neither to prohibit nor to permit', but he will 'copy what I have found in the *responsa* of the later scholars on this issue'. R. Joseph Hayyim's words speak for themselves. Not only is his decision to avoid making a decision a principled one, but his entire methodology in the *responsum* is premised upon adequate library facilities. R. Waldenberg's point is, therefore, well taken. It might be noted in passing that R. Feinstein's own library might not have been that well stocked. In one of his *responsa* on the issue of dubiously motivated conversions to Judaism, he deals with the views of a fairly prominent early 20th-cent. German authority, R. David Zvi Hoffman, but states that R. Hoffman's volume of *responsa*—*Melamed Lehoil*—'is not in my possession and I am, therefore, unable to examine his views' (*Resp. Iggrot Moshe, Even Haezer,* 2 no. 4).

[157] The forgery charge is used elsewhere by R. Feinstein, see *Resp. Iggrot Moshe, Even Haezer,* 2 no.11, in relation to a comment of Nahmanides concerning the definition of adultery in the context of AID (Ch. 2, n. 55). This technique is not unique to R. Feinstein. It was used to good effect by R. Ezekiel Landau in a *responsum* on the *kashrut* of the sterlet (*Resp. Noda Biyehudah* 2, *Yoreh Deah,* no. 28; and see Ch. 4 n. 19).

therapeutic justification for the abortion. It is possible to surmise that his response to an actual case may have been both truer to the classical halakhic doctrine, and more liberal than the *responsum* reacting to R. Waldenberg's ruling.

It is also possible to surmise that R. Feinstein's *responsum* reflects the strength of the debate with regard to abortion in North America, his country of residence. In that country, abortion is a morally, socially, legally, and politically explosive issue of national proportions[158] and must, therefore, be dealt with cautiously by halakhists. Any formulation of the Jewish position on abortion may very well have moral significance for the national abortion debate. In such a climate, R. Feinstein may have felt that any statement on abortion *halakhah* should emphasize its moral as well as its legal aspects. In R. Feinstein's view, the position adopted by R. Waldenberg undoubtedly failed to do justice to the moral gravity of non-therapeutic abortion in the Jewish tradition, and this could well be the background to R. Feinstein's sharp criticism of R. Waldenberg's *responsum*. R. Waldenberg, on the other hand, was writing in Israel, where there are many morally explosive issues in the public arena, but abortion is not one of them. R. Waldenberg, therefore, rests content with a purely legal exposition of the *halakhah* as he sees it in relation to the case of a Tay-Sachs foetus and evidently, does not feel the need to grapple with the moral image of the *halakhah* in terms of its approach to foeticide and abortion.

Now, there may be more than one dimension to R. Feintein's moral concerns. He may also have had his eye on the eugenic aspects of abortion. Indeed, it may be surmised that the stringency of R. Feinstein's approach is a result of his concern with the whole question of testing foetuses for genetic defects and using abortion as a means of dealing with these defects. There are undoubtedly many situations in which the gap between therapeutic and eugenic abortions becomes dangerously narrow and the spectre of a slippery slope looms large. The human genome project, genetic testing and research, and gene therapy all raise profound problems of both a moral and a halakhic nature.[159] R. Feinstein's ruling may be an indication of these dangers and the need to combat the widespread use of abortion as a means of improving the race. Of course, it is eminently arguable that adopting an extremely stringent approach to the abortion of

---

[158] In an article in *Time* (9 March 1998, 165), Everett Koop, the former Surgeon General of the United States, likens the abortion controversy to 'the precursor of a civil war, if not a civil war itself'. He is also quoted as saying that 'nothing like it has separated our society since the days of slavery'. For an analysis of the abortion debate in the social context and religious contexts of society in the United States, see E. Mensch and A. Freeman, *The Politics of Virtue* (Durham, NC, 1995).   [159] See Ch. 3.

a Tay-Sachs foetus is not really the best way of dealing with these problems. The eugenic argument is, nevertheless, a possible justification for R. Feinstein's strong moral position in the Tay-Sachs *responsum*.

The final point with regard to R. Feinstein's reasoning in the Tay-Sachs case is that he ignores the fact that the certain death of a Tay-Sachs baby may bring it into the category of a human *terefah*, i.e. a person suffering from a fatal condition for which there is no cure known to medicine and from which he will die within a year. The killer of such a person is exempt from the death penalty,[160] and the significance of this exemption is that in certain morally complex situations, the life of a *terefah* may, indeed, be sacrificed in a worthy cause, i.e. to save the life of a viable individual.[161] The combination of the classical doctrine of foetal non-personhood and the law of the *terefah* would seem to make a strong case for permitting the abortion of a Tay-Sachs foetus. Since we are dealing with a foetus, certain aspects of the law of the *terefah*, such as the twelve-month limit and the idea that the life of a *terefah* may only be sacrificed in order to save a viable life, may no longer be relevant. This is precisely the line of reasoning adopted by R. Aryeh Grossnass, another modern authority, in order to permit the abortion in this case.[162] R. Feinstein, however, makes no reference to the absolutely fatal nature of Tay-Sachs, and concentrates solely upon the issue of foeticide. His one concern throughout the *responsum* is to emphasize the severity of the prohibition on killing a foetus in Jewish law. Indeed, the *responsum* opens with the phrase, 'and with regard to the killing of a foetus in its mother's womb'.

To return to the main theme, it is evident that R. Feinstein's treatment of the Tay-Sachs issue is a powerful example of the moral input into abortion *halakhah*. However, it goes much further than Tosafot's statement that non-therapeutic abortion in general is 'not allowed', and R. Joseph Hayyim's strategy of presenting a range of views in relation to what he clearly regarded as a doubtful case, leaving the final decision in the hands of a local authority. Unlike R. Bachrach, R. Feinstein does not make a clear distinction between the application of legal doctrine and the influence of morality. He does not make any explicit reference to a felt need not to be less moral than Catholicism, as does R. Zweig, although this need may be present, even if it is not articulated. Moreover, in categorizing foeticide as a form of homicide, R. Feinstein deviates dramatically from the classical legal doctrine and from the position of most authorities, including modern ones. The extent to which he deviates from legal doctrine raises the question of the preservation of the boundary between law and morality

---

[160] *Sanhedrin*, 78a; Maimonides, *Hilkhot Rozeah*, 2: 8.   [161] See Ch. 5 s. 5(c).
[162] *Resp. Lev Aryeh*, 2 no. 32 (end-notes), 204–5.

within the *halakhah*. This question is a systemic one affecting Jewish law as a whole, and will be discussed further in the Conclusion, which deals with the general nature of the relationship between law and morality in biomedical *halakhah*.

A final reflection on the moral element in abortion *halakhah* concerns the influence of general morality, including that of other faiths, upon the *halakhah*. The question here is whether the Noahide prohibition on bloodshed, upon which this moral element is based, is to be derived from the dominant religious position of the time, or from a more critically refined body of universal, rational norms. From the examples cited in this section it is evident that halakhic authorities tend to follow the actual religious morality of the time in a relatively uncritical fashion. Whether this ought to be the pattern of the future will be discussed in the following section.

6. FUTURE TRENDS IN ABORTION *HALAKHAH*

The major elements in abortion law throughout the ages have been the doctrine of foetal non-personhood and the influence of morality. In the modern period, the issue of the abortion of genetically defective or eugenically disadvantaged foetuses is likely to become a prominent feature of this area.

In order to begin to explore the question of defective foetuses, it must be noted that the scope of the doctrine of foetal non-personhood was confined by the mishnah to maternal welfare,[163] and the question traditionally raised in abortion law is the nature of the danger posed by the foetus, or by its birth, to the life or health of the mother.[164] Even in the *mamzer* foetus cases, the main rationale behind the permissive rulings was the saving of the mother from the adverse effects, both psychological and physical, of giving birth to tainted progeny.[165] Abortion for the sole purpose of preventing the birth of a child, without any material reference to the mother's life or health, is not a part of the legal tradition in abortion *halakhah*.

It is wise to avoid stating any case too strongly, and it is certainly arguable that the abortion of a *mamzer* foetus has as much to do with prevention of *mamzerim* being born[166] as it does with the mental and

---

[163] *Oholoth*, 7: 8. [164] The broad scope of therapeutic abortion was referred to at nn. 33–9.

[165] See *Resp. She'elat Ya'avez*, no. 43; *Resp. Rav Pa'alim, Even Haezer*, 1: 4.

[166] See *Resp. She'elat Ya'avez*, no. 43 for a reference to the *mamzer* foetus as 'cursed seed'. In this *responsum*, R. Emden points out that 'it is obvious that in the present case, the foetus may be aborted even in the first instance, and it is possibly a *mitzvah* to do so'. Also see *Resp. Mishpetei Uziel, Hoshen Mishpat*, no. 47; cf. *Resp. Havat Yair*, no. 31.

physical welfare of the mother. Nevertheless, the general trend has always been to emphasize the welfare of the mother, and to preserve a close link between the doctrine of foetal non-personhood and abortion for the sake of maternal life or health. Recently, however, this link has been called into question by our newfound ability to test for genetic defects in foetuses.

Another context in which a wedge has been driven between foetal non-personhood and the saving of maternal life and health, is that of multi-foetal pregnancy reduction and the disposal of embryos obtained in the course of artificial reproductive technology but not transplanted into a womb. Modern infertility treatment typically involves super-ovulation, whereby the female releases a large number of eggs, as opposed to the sole egg normally released in the natural female reproductive cycle. Multiple embryos in the womb are likely to cause the pregnancy to terminate early, with the result that the babies, if they survive, may be physically and mentally damaged. When fertilization takes place *in vitro*, successful implantation into the womb often requires the fertilization of many embryos, and the selection of a limited number of healthy ones for transfer into the woman who is bringing them to term. Some modern authorities have solved this problem using the pursuer principle,[167] arguing that the reduced embryos are threatening the survival of the unreduced ones, and hence may be eliminated in order to prevent the deaths of the potentially viable foetuses.[168] Other authorities permit both foetal reduction and the disposal of excess embryos in reliance upon the concept of foetal non-personhood, together with the procreative rationale underlying infertility treatment in general. According to R. Hayyim David Halevy,[169] the fact that the majority of halakhic authorities accept the doctrine of foetal non-personhood provides the basis for ruling that it is permissible to destroy some embryos in order that the rest will proceed to term and enjoy a much better chance of developing into healthy individuals. He also makes the point that embryos *in vitro* are not susceptible to any form of prohibition on foeticide, since, as a result of their artificial environment, 'they have no standing as foetuses'. The same point about the non-uterine environment of the *in vitro* embryos is made by R. Mordekhai Eliyahu, who permits reduction *in vitro*, stating that 'eggs which have not been chosen for implantation may be discarded'.[170]

---

[167] See nn. 79–80.

[168] Y. Silberstein, 'Foetal Reduction' (Heb.), *Assia*, 45–6 (1989), 62; *Nishmat Avraham Hoshen Mishpat*, 234. The precise nature of the form of pursuer principle being applied in this case is discussed at length in Ch. 5 s. 6 in relation to the separation of Siamese twins in Jewish law.

[169] 'On Foetal Reduction' (Heb.), *Assia*, 46–7 (1990), 14–17.

[170] 'Discarding Fertilised Eggs and Foetal Reduction' (Heb.), *Tehumin*, 11 (1991), 272–4.

It is evident, therefore, that in modern times, the legal doctrine of foetal non-personhood in relation to embryo reduction has been disassociated from that of maternal therapy and recombined with the halakhic mandate to propagate. In other words, some embryos may be eliminated solely in order that others may survive. Now, it is arguable that the mother might suffer both physically and mentally if, as a result of not eliminating some of the embryos produced in IVF, she gives birth to defective foetuses, or she suffers a miscarriage and continues to be infertile. A miscarriage in these circumstances, although undoubtedly tragic, does not normally constitute a serious threat to maternal life or health. Infertility also falls short of a threat to life or health. The driving principle here may, therefore, be the avoidance of infertility rather than a threat to the mother in the traditional sense.

An interesting question is that of the halakhic position where it is not the life or health of the mother that is at stake, but that of another, such as a close relative. For example, is a mother permitted to undergo a bone-marrow transplant to save her husband's life, even if there is a chance that the transplant procedure may result in the death of her foetus? On the one hand, it is arguable that the mental suffering of the mother as a result of knowing that she could have saved her husband's life but did not do so is sufficient to override the life of the unborn child. On the other hand, there is no direct threat to her person. The serious actual threat in this case is to the life of the husband. As in other cases involving hard choices in life and death matters,[171] the *halakhah* may, in fact, give the mother the choice.

A more drastic form of this question is the scenario in which a mother is struggling with the question of sacrificing her foetus in order to use its stem cells for the purpose of saving the life of someone very dear to her. What would the halakhic position be in such a case, if the science in this area progresses dramatically, and the procedure has become standard? This question is more difficult than the previous one, since it involves a deliberate decision to kill the foetus in order to save the life of an individual other than the mother. Her welfare is implicated, but the major threat to adult life is directed at someone other than herself. An even more morally problematic question is that of a woman who initiates a pregnancy solely for the purpose of using foetal tissue for the life of another person, including herself. These problems are becoming ever more real with the progress in stem-cell research and its possible therapeutic benefits.[172] The halakhic response to these questions has yet to be crafted. It clearly involves moral as well as legal issues, and the halakhic approach

---

[171] See Ch. 4, s. 5. [172] C. Gorman, ' "Brave New Cells" ', *Time*, 8 May 2000, 54.

to this type of scenario is bound to become one of the major features of
Jewish abortion law in the coming years.

It is noteworthy that if the stem cells had been taken without prior consultation, and the sole question was the ethics of using them for therapeutic purposes, the halakhic response would probably be a positive one.
Neither the obligation to bury a foetus nor the prohibition on deriving
benefit from its corpse are strong enough to override the therapeutic
benefits likely to arise from the results of the research.[173] The moral issues
surrounding deliberate decisions to use foetal cells or tissue have not,
however, been addressed in a direct manner.

Another important issue in the abortion *halakhah* of the future must
surely be the precise content of its moral element. As demonstrated in the
previous section, this element is often determined by the conservative
religious opinions of the era, with the result that lenient rulings on abortion are often viewed as constituting 'profanations of the Divine Name' in
that they tend to suggest an inferior morality of Jewish law *vis-à-vis* these
opinions.[174] The natural-law approach with which the Noahide laws were
identified earlier is much more elementary, consisting of the principle of
the preservation of society and its defence against attacks on the bodies
and property of its citizens.[175] It is rooted in the very basis of social life
and, as such, answers as closely as possible to the notion of a universal
code, which is intrinsic to the whole idea of Noahide law.[176] The more
basic the morality, the more universal will its scope be. This lesson is well
known in natural-law thinking, and lies at the root of those theories of
natural law, that have succeeded in gaining adherents even amongst the
ranks of the positivists.[177] The almost automatic identification of abortion
morality in a halakhic context with the dominant religious morality of the
time is, therefore, open to question.

The problem of defining specific content is not, however, unique to
abortion *halakhah*. It is also endemic to natural-law thinking in general.
Natural-law theory has always been strong on the basic principle of the
preservation of society but fairly weak on specific content. To resolve this
problem in the context of abortion *halakhah*, a concerted effort is required
to develop a set of substantive moral principles to which halakhists may
turn in order to test the conclusions of their doctrinal reasoning in a
particular case. The establishment of such a body of principles will

---

[173] See J. D. Bleich, 'Foetal Tissue Research', *Tradition*, 24 (1989), 69–75.
[174] Zweig, 'Regarding Abortion', 45.   [175] See n. 99.
[176] See the sources cited in nn. 98–9.
[177] See in particular Hart, *Concept of Law*, 188 n. 76.

undoubtedly be on the agenda of those concerned with abortion *halakhah* in the future.

The pressing need for such a body of moral principles rapidly emerges in the course of any examination of the problem of aborting genetically defective foetuses in Jewish law, the starting point for which is the Tay-Sachs foetus debate discussed above. R. Feinstein's position on Tay-Sachs is certainly an extremely strict one and might well be diagnosed as suffering from an overdose of moral concern. R. Waldenberg's decision, on the other hand, may strike a liberal as being perfectly humane, and since its halakhic methodology appears to be in order, that liberal might be tempted to argue that in the area of abortion there is no need for any moral input, and halakhic positivism should carry the day. However, a slightly deeper examination reveals that this conclusion is rather superficial. In the same volume as that in which his second *responsum* on Tay-Sachs appears, R. Waldenberg deals with the question of a foetus suffering from Down Syndrome. Now, it is possible that the same liberal who was fully supportive of R. Waldenberg's permissive ruling on Tay-Sachs might be less comfortable with a similarly permissive ruling in the case of Down Syndrome. The differences between the two cases are clear, and they include both physical factors, such as the span and quality of life of a Down Syndrome victim as opposed to that of a Tay-Sachs baby, and psychological elements such as the capacity of Down Syndrome sufferers to enter into emotional relationships with those to whom they are close. In terms of pure halakhic doctrine, however, there is little to distinguish between the two cases and, indeed, R. Waldenberg observes that 'on the basis of my *responsa* on Tay-Sachs, there are more than adequate grounds to use the same sources in order to permit the abortion of a Down Syndrome foetus'.[178] Although his permissive ruling in relation to Down Syndrome is expressed in a much more equivocal manner than in the Tay-Sachs case, the logical force of halakhic doctrine impels him to permit the abortion in this case as well.

The liberal halakhic positivist may become even more uneasy at the prospect of permissive decisions in cases involving genetic diseases that manifest themselves only much later in life, mere genetic predispositions as opposed to actual diseases, or genetic conditions that are of a much lower order of magnitude than Tay-Sachs or even Down Syndrome. What would his reaction be if the strong doctrine of foetal non-personhood were to be extended to genetic predispositions such as heart conditions or cancer, rather than actual genetic diseases per se? Would the correct approach in such circumstances be to develop a formula for balancing the

---

[178] *Resp. Ziz Eliezer*, 14 no. 101.

risk of contracting a debilitating disease later in life against the chance of living until that stage is reached? At this point, even the liberal halakhic positivist may become dissatisfied with pure doctrine and call for a method of limiting its operative scope. Tosafot's remark about there being no legal sanction on foeticide, but it not being allowed in situations of a non-therapeutic nature, then becomes highly relevant, and the Noahide principle of the preservation of the moral fabric of civilized society combines with pure legal doctrine in search of a solution to the problem that is both halakhically valid and morally sound.

In other words, it is easy to criticize those halakhists who adopt conventional morality in its various forms, or those who deliberately legalize these moral positions in defiance of the systemic principles of Jewish law. The difficult issue is the nature of the morality that ought to be applied in this area and the crafting of an acceptable set of practical principles for its application.

There can be little doubt that one of the greatest challenges of the future to Jewish biomedical law in general, and abortion *halakhah* in particular, will be mounted by developments in genetic science. As the knowledge of the human genome is applied, so the problems of eugenic selection will dominate this area of bioethics. Halakhists concerned with abortion must ensure that there is a suitable body of moral principles available for directing the application of their legal doctrine in this complex field of Jewish law. A little more will be said on this issue in Chapter 3, which is devoted to the topic of genetics and the *halakhah*.

7. FOETUSES AND CRITICALLY ILL MOTHERS IN JEWISH AND ISRAELI LAW

The final section of this chapter returns to the question of deciding the fate of the foetus in cases involving conflict between maternal well-being and foetal life. As already observed, the *halakhah* always prefers the mother over the foetus, and although the stages of foetal development and the legal status of the foetus in the context of the laws of the Sabbath are taken into account, they do not determine the outcome in a situation where the mother's welfare is under threat. It has also been shown that the underlying approach of the common law is rooted in the attempt to define the stage at which a foetus becomes a full, legal person and the final word in any conflict situation is, therefore, delivered on the basis of foetal status at the time of the decision. The difference between the two legal systems emerges rather neatly in an Israeli case dealing with the question of non-consensual surgery on an incompetent mother in order to improve the chances of her foetus being born alive.

In *Attorney General* v. *B*,[179] the respondent's wife was being treated in an intensive care unit as a result of severe respiratory problems caused by the lupus disease from which she was suffering. She was also in the twenty-eighth week of pregnancy. In view of the seriousness of her condition, and the feeling that she would probably not survive, the gynaecological staff at the hospital wished to carry out a Caesarean section in order to preserve the life of the foetus. The hospital approached the respondent in order to receive his consent to the surgery, since his wife was incapable of providing it herself. Upon being informed that there was a 40 per cent chance of the foetus being defective, he declined to give his consent, on the grounds that should his wife die as a result of the lupus, it would not be practical for him to bring up a handicapped child by himself. This view was shared by the respondent's parents as well as his father-in-law. His mother-in-law, on the other hand, felt that the operation ought to be carried out since her daughter would want to be survived by a child, even if it was defective.

In the absence of unanimous consent on the part of the family, the hospital summoned the duty judge of the Jerusalem District Court, with a view to obtaining authorization for the Caesarean. Bazak J. observed that there appeared to be no source in Israeli or common law for acting on behalf of a foetus in this type of situation, since there is no provision in section 68 of the Capacity and Guardianship Law, 5722-1962, for appointing a legal guardian for a foetus.[180] This omission had provided the basis for an earlier decision by another District Court judge not to intervene under similar circumstances. In that case, both mother and foetus died.[181]

In the present case, Bazak J. invoked Jewish law as the basis for issuing an order to operate on the mother, once her brain stem became irreversibly dysfunctional.[182] In Bazak's view, the omission of a foetus from the list of wards in the Capacity and Guardianship Law constituted a gap in the Israeli legal system which, under the Foundations of Law Act, 5740-1980, could be filled by turning to the Jewish legal heritage.[183]

---

[179] PS 103/92. See J. Bazak, 'Caesarian Section After Brain Death' (Heb.), *Assia*, 65–6 (1999), 13–19.

[180] For the Common law background to this issue see J. Phillips, 'Wardship and Abortion Prevention', *Law Quarterly Review*, 95 (1979), 332. On the influence of the Common Law on Israeli law in this area, see *A* v. *B*, CA 413/80, PD 35 (3) 60.

[181] *A* v. *B*, PS 38/93 (unpublished).

[182] This definition of death is accepted by the Israeli Chief Rabbinate and many contemporary halakhic authorities; see Ch. 6 s. 2.

[183] On the origin, nature, and scope of this law, see the Introduction; Elon, *Jewish Law*, 1827–97; D. Sinclair, 'Jewish Law in the State of Israel', in *An Introduction to the History and Sources of Jewish Law*, 409–15.

The rule in the Talmud,[184] as codified in the *Mishneh Torah*[185] and the *Shulhan Arukh*,[186] is that the Sabbath may be desecrated in order to remove a baby from the body of a woman who died in childbirth. The implication of this rule is that a foetus does have a right to life, as long as its continued existence is not in conflict with the health or life of its mother.[187] It is therefore arguable that under such circumstances the foetus ought to fall under the rubric of section 68 of the Capacity and Guardianship Law, and the judge is empowered under Israeli law to act on its behalf and issue an order for the Caesarean section to be performed. Bazak J. also pointed out that the definition of death for the purposes of this case was that of irreversible dysfunction of the brain stem, which was itself derived, *inter alia*, from the sources of Jewish law, including the 1987 decision of the Israeli Chief Rabbinate to authorize cardiac transplants in Israeli hospitals.[188]

The significance of this decision is that it demonstrates the flexibility of Jewish law in a situation in which the mother's life is no longer an issue but her body still constitutes a threat to the survival of her foetus. The *halakhah* yields a ready and intuitively acceptable solution in terms of its rule that, in the absence of the mother, the foetus benefits from the status afforded to it by the laws of the Sabbath and it may, therefore, be taken out of the dead woman's body without the consent of her legal guardians. The common law approach, as manifested in Israeli law, provides a much more rigid framework, in which the issue of foetal status is central, and in the absence of any clear-cut right on the part of the foetus, nothing can be done to save its life in this particular case.

In a somewhat oblique way, this case takes us back to the ancient parting of ways between Judaism and Christianity with regard to abortion. The major doctrinal element of the *halakhah* is the welfare of the mother. Hence, as soon as she is no longer in the picture, the welfare of the foetus is paramount. The Greek-Christian approach adopts the notion of foetal status as its basic doctrinal element. The common law follows in the Greek-Christian tradition with the result that in the present case there is

---

[184] *Arakhin*, 7a–b.   [185] *Hilkhot Shabbat*, 2: 15.

[186] *Orah Hayyim*, 330: 5. As mentioned above (see n. 24), R. Moses Isserles states that care ought to be taken in order to ensure that the mother is actually dead before taking any action to 'cut her open' and remove the foetus from her womb. Also see *Resp. Ziz Eliezer*, 18: 31 for the halakhic position regarding the removal of a 7-month foetus from the womb of a brain-stem dead mother.

[187] The desecration of the Sabbath for the sake of saving a foetus that does not yet possess a presumption of viability is discussed by several halakhic authorities and is eventually resolved in favour of breaking the Sabbath laws on the basis of the rational principle of the overriding value of human life; see *Mishnah Berurah, Orah Hayyim*, 330: 18.

[188] This entire topic is discussed at length in Ch. 6.

no legal basis for acting on behalf of the foetus, even if the mother is brain-stem dead.

We will conclude with a brief summary of abortion in Israeli law. Under Israeli criminal law, abortion is legal when performed in order to avoid danger to the mother, foetal defects, and pregnancy arising as a result of crime, incest, or extramarital intercourse.[189] A woman's decision to abort must be approved by a committee consisting of two physicians and one social worker. Under a 1980 amendment, at least one member of the committee must be a woman. An outstanding feature of Israeli abortion law is that there is no reference to the stages of foetal development, and the question of timing is a purely medical decision. In this respect, Israeli law follows the *halakhah*.[190] Finally, it is noteworthy that abortion is not a highly controversial issue in Israel as it is in the United States. The reason for this is undoubtedly the traditionally lenient halakhic approach to abortion outlined in this chapter.[191]

---

[189] *Penal Law*, 1977, section 316. The original law contained a section permitting account to be taken of any serious harm that might be caused to the mother or her existing children by the continuation of the pregnancy as a result of the mother's familial or social environment. This section is similar to section 1 (2) of the English Abortion Act, 1967, which provides that 'account may be taken of the pregnant woman's actual or reasonably foreseeable environment' in making a decision on abortion under the Act. This section, however, was repealed in 1980.

[190] The abolition of the so-called 'social clause' referred to in n. 189 was in response to the halakhically rooted objections of the religious parties, who claimed that familial and environmental factors were not directly related to the mother's welfare and ought not, therefore, to be taken into account in abortion decisions. The idea that a threat to existing children as a result of the continuation of the pregnancy would provide the basis for an abortion was also objected to on halakhic grounds. The section was duly abolished.

[191] Israeli courts have refused to give the father of a foetus any standing before an abortion committee (*A* v. *B*, CA 413/80, PD 35 (3) 57) notwithstanding any financial interest he may have in his foetus under biblical law (n. 27). In this respect, the common law approach reigns supreme (see *Paton* v. *British Pregnancy Advisory Service Trustees* [1978] 2 All ER 987; *Planned Parenthood of Central Missouri* v. *Danforth* 428 US (1976) 52).

2

Assisted Reproduction

1. MORALITY, NATURALISM AND ARTIFICIAL INSEMINATION USING THE HUSBAND'S SPERM (AIH)

As in the case of abortion, the moral aspects of assisted reproduction find expression in the *halakhah* governing this area of Jewish law. There is, however, an important distinction between assisted reproduction and abortion. In relation to abortion, the fundamental moral issue, i.e. the taking of human life, albeit at the very earliest stage of its existence, lies at the very heart of our system of morality. Few would argue that the major occupation of assisted reproduction, which is the manipulation and disposal of sperm and eggs and the use of surrogate mothers, is of the same order of gravity, or that it implicates the taking of human life in the same way.[1] Nevertheless, important moral issues do arise in the area of assisted reproduction, including the value of natural procreation, and the ramifications of the technology for the institution of the family and its legal framework. It is with these issues and their effect upon the *halakhah* that the bulk of this chapter is concerned.

In passing, it might be noted that although these moral issues may not, at present, seem as serious as those relating to abortion, this perception may change with the passage of time. Indeed, it is not inconceivable that in the long run scientific developments will make the moral ramifications of some of these questions as controversial as those of abortion, if not more so. They do, after all, concern the very foundations of our biological and social make-up, and their impact is only just beginning to make itself felt upon society at large.

It ought also to be pointed out that the moral imprint on the *halakhah* governing modern assisted reproduction is much less clearly visible than it is in relation to abortion, since the field is much younger and the moral

---

[1] One possible exception is the destruction of excess foetuses implanted in the womb as a result of using *in vitro* fertilization (IVF). This procedure is often referred to as 'foetal reduction'. Although foetal reduction is sometimes discussed in the context of assisted reproduction (see s. 5 below), it is strictly speaking, an abortion issue, and the concepts that halakhists use in order to deal with foetal reduction are drawn from abortion *halakhah*. It was, therefore, discussed in Ch. 1 (see nn. 168–70). It is noteworthy that in English law, foetal reduction is governed by section 37 of the Human Fertilization and Embryology Act, 1990, which amends the relevant provisions of the Abortion Act, 1967.

issues are far less clearly defined. As a result, we are not likely to be in a position to draw up a complex theoretical model governing the relationship between law and morality in this area, as we did in the context of abortion. Indeed, because of the relative novelty of this technology, even the basic legal doctrines are still in their infancy and are often surrounded by controversy. Two examples, with which we will deal at length below, are artificial insemination using donor sperm and the establishment of maternity. Since the legal doctrine is still fluid, it is not practical to look for a well-defined model for the relationship between law and morality. Accordingly, our conclusions as to this relationship will be more tentative than they were in relation to abortion. The aim in the present chapter is merely to cull such evidence of the influence of morality upon the *halakhah* as may be gathered from the material, and to present it in conjunction with the legal material.

The novelty of assisted reproduction and the fluid nature of the legal doctrines involved also dictate the order of discussion of this subject. The halakhic responses to moral issues occur in the interstices of the legal discussion, and the chapter is, therefore, divided up in accordance with the legal responses to each emerging technology—artificial insemination using the husband's sperm (AIH), artificial insemination using a donor's sperm (AID), *in vitro* fertilization (IVF), and surrogacy. Unlike abortion, it is not yet possible to isolate the legal doctrine and deal with the relationship between that doctrine and moral issues in a thematic way.

Our analysis of assisted reproduction begins with AIH, in which a married woman is artificially fertilized with her husband's semen. Artificial insemination has been carried out successfully since the eighteenth century,[2] and its most halakhically non-controversial application is AIH. It is noteworthy that today only a small proportion of artificial insemination cases involve AIH, which is generally recommended in situations where the husband suffers from anatomical defects in his sexual organ or from severe psychological impotence. It is also used, although rarely, in cases of low sperm count. Occasionally, AIH is relevant where the husband is about to undergo a medical treatment that will render him infertile or carries a high risk of doing so.

AIH is permitted by a majority of halakhists.[3] Part of the minority opposition to AIH is based upon the prohibition on seed destruction.[4]

---

[2] The technique was used successfully for fish in 1742 and for mammals in 1780. The first successful human insemination took place in 1785, see A. Steinberg, *Encyclopaedia of Jewish Medical Ethics* (Heb.), 6 vols. (Jerusalem, 1988–98), i. 149. IVF dates from the middle of the 20th cent., and surrogacy is even more recent.   [3] Ibid. i. 151.

[4] *Niddah*, 13b; Maimonides, *Hilkhot Issurei Biah*, 21: 18; *Shulhan Arukh, Even Haezer*, 23: 3. Also see D. Feldman, *Marital Relations, Birth Control and Abortion in Jewish Law* (New York, 1974), 109.

In accordance with a strictly objective definition of this prohibition, any situation in which the husband does not ejaculate his semen directly into the wife's genital tract must be avoided.[5] Clearly, the collection of semen for artificial insemination purposes falls foul of this prohibition.

Another argument against AIH is the fear that the husband's sperm might be replaced, either inadvertently or by design, with that of a stranger, with the result that the legal status of the child may be seriously compromised.[6] It is important to emphasize that there is no specific mention amongst the majority of prohibitionists of any opposition to AIH on the grounds that it offends against the natural order of things, or that a child produced in such a manner is morally or spiritually deficient.

Those who permit AIH do not find it difficult to overcome these objections. As far as the argument from the strictly objective definition of seed destruction is concerned, the permissive scholars maintain that the

---

[5] Those authorities who prohibit AIH define seed destruction as any unnatural break between the production of semen and its entry into the female reproductive organ. Their view is that any such break constitutes seed destruction even if it is the husband's intention to use the seed in order to establish a family (*Resp. Divrei Malkiel*, 4 nos. 107–8; *Resp. Yaskil Avdi*, 5, *Even Haezer*, no. 10; *Resp. Ziz Eliezer*, 9 no. 51). It ought to be pointed out that there is a strong mystical input in the decisions of a minority of prohibitionist authorities. A case in point is R. Ovadyah Hadaya who, besides being a leading prohibitionist in relation to AIH, was also a noted kabbalist. His approach is directly influenced by the mystical belief that any semen that does not travel directly into the female reproductive organ gives rise to 'demons of the night', which remain in existence to plague the semen-emitter right up until the moment of death (*Resp. Yaskil Avdi* ibid.). This mystical belief also underlies his strong opposition to the use of AIH as a means of overcoming the very specific problem of infertility caused by early ovulation. Under Jewish law, sexual relations are prohibited during the menstrual period and for some time later (see the entry on menstruation in Steinberg, *Encyclopaedia of Jewish Medical Ethics*, iv. 300), so that if a woman ovulates during the time that the *halakhah* prohibits sexual relations, she will be unable to conceive. In order to overcome this difficulty, a number of authorities suggest the use of AIH. The prohibition on relations with a menstruant is limited to the physical realm and does not include conception using assisted reproductive techniques. Moreover, those authorities who do recommend the use of AIH in order to overcome this problem generally confine their permission to that part of the period in which regular intercourse is forbidden under rabbinic law only. Nevertheless, R. Hadaya maintains that in such a case, 'the child would suffer from a great burden of mystical impurity, which is not easily removable', and bans the use of AIH as a means of solving the problem of early ovulation (*Resp. Yaskil Avdi*, 5, *Even Haezer*, no. 10). Some of the other authorities who prohibit AIH also base their opinions on kabbalistic prohibitions associated with seed destruction (D. Lasker, 'Kabbalah, Halakhah and Modern Medicine', *Modern Judaism*, 8 (1988) 1–14). Now, although there is a relatively long-standing relationship between *halakhah* and *kabbalah* in Jewish law, it is also a feature of halakhic reasoning that the literary pedigree of a particular source is taken into account when dealing with practical questions, and the solution is generally shaped by the normative ranking of the sources involved. The majority of halakhists, therefore, do not accept the binding quality of the kabbalistic doctrines regarding seed destruction and conduct the debate regarding AIH in terms of purely halakhic considerations (see Ch. 1, n. 137).

[6] The legal ramifications of donor insemination in the context of adultery and *mamzerut* are discussed in s. 2.

definition is misguided, since it is inconceivable that there should not be a subjective element in this prohibition. The proof for this is the fact that some semen always goes to waste, even in the course of natural sexual relations. If the strictly objective approach were correct, even natural intercourse should be prohibited! The correct approach, therefore, is the subjective one, which takes the intention of the sperm producer into account. If the goal of any particular procedure is to bring a child into the world, it is halakhically irrelevant that in the course of achieving that goal, there is a break between the ejaculation of the semen and its entry into the female reproductive organ. AIH does not, therefore, constitute a breach of the prohibition on seed destruction.

In terms of the fear of deliberate or accidental sperm replacement, it is well established, on the basis of general halakhic principles, that the mere fear of such a mix-up is not sufficient to prohibit an otherwise halakhically permitted procedure, especially when the object of the procedure is as worthy as the establishment of a family.[7] Moreover, it is possible to take measures in order to ensure that, as far as possible, no mix-ups occur. To this end, there are now trained supervisors available in a number of clinics used by observant Jews, whose job it is to ensure that no donor semen is used in the procedure.[8]

On the assumption that AIH is permitted, especially in relation to a couple for whom it is the only hope for having children, the most acceptable method for collecting the semen would need to be worked out in consultation with a halakhic authority.[9] The same goes for the possibility that in order to achieve pregnancy, the insemination must take place during the wife's menstrual period, during which intercourse between the couple would be forbidden under Jewish law.[10]

Another legal issue that arises in relation to AIH is whether it constitutes fulfilment of the biblical commandment to 'be fruitful and multiply'.[11] Some authorities maintain that sexual intercourse is a vital ingredient in the performance of this commandment (*mitzvah*); hence, having an AIH child does not constitute fulfilment of the obligation.[12] The competing view is that the essence of the obligation lies in the production

---

[7] *She'elat Ya'avez*, no. 43; *Resp. Maharsham*, 3 no. 268; *Resp. Zekan Aharon*, 2 no. 97; *Resp. Pri Hasadeh*, 3 no. 53; *Resp. Seridei Esh*, 3 no. 5; *Resp. Minhat Yitzhak*, 1 no. 50; *Resp. Yabia Omer*, 2, *Even Haezer*, no 1; *Resp. Iggrot Moshe, Even Haezer*, 1 no. 71; 2 nos. 11, 18; 4 no. 32.

[8] See 'Kosher Conception', *The Jewish Week*, 11 July, 1997, 10.

[9] *Resp. Iggrot Moshe, Even Haezer*, 1 no. 70. It would appear to be noteworthy that R. Aaron Walkin forbids the extraction of semen for any purpose other than the insemination of a wife in the context of marriage (*Resp. Zekan Aharon*, 2 no. 97).

[10] See *Encyclopaedia of Jewish Medical Ethics*, i. 152–3.

[11] Gen. 1: 28; 9: 1, 7; 35: 11; *Yevamot*, 6: 6; *Yevamot*, 61b–64a; Feldman, *Marital Relations*, 46.

[12] *Turei Zahav, Even Haezer*, 1: 8; *Resp. Mishpetei Uziel, Even Haezer*, no. 19; *Resp. Yaskil Avdi*, 5, *Even Haezer*, no. 10.

of live progeny, and the process is irrelevant. On this view, the biblical commandment to procreate is, indeed, carried out by a father who inseminates his wife in an artificial manner.[13] A compromise position is adopted by R. Shlomo Zalman Auerbach, who suggests that although AIH does not constitute performance of the full-blown biblical commandment to be fruitful and multiply, it does qualify for the fulfilment of the rabbinic obligations to populate the earth and not to leave it desolate.[14] By downgrading the commandment to the rabbinic level, R. Auerbach ensures that AIH is still endowed with religious significance, even though it is not invested with the full normative force of a biblical precept.

To sum up, not only is AIH permitted by the majority of halakhists; it also constitutes the fulfilment of a *mitzvah*, albeit of a rabbinic rather than a biblical nature.[15] Undoubtedly, this permissive approach also reflects the social consequences of infertility in observant circles. In these circles, children are a supremely important focus of religious, and hence social, practice. Sensitivity to the social as well as the halakhic pressures on observant Jewish married couples to have children undoubtedly contributes to the trend amongst halakhic authorities to find ways of resolving fertility problems.[16]

As already observed, even those authorities opposed to AIH do not, in general, base their opposition upon any ideological objection to assisted reproductive technology. They do not believe that it is morally wrong to bring children into the world using any method other than the natural one. The underlying assumption made by Jewish law in this area is that as long as a new procedure is not prohibited, it is permitted.[17] This position would appear to be in stark contrast to that of the Catholic Church, which rejects all assisted reproduction on the grounds that children born using unnatural reproductive technology suffer from a grave moral handicap. In this sense, naturalism is endowed with moral significance and acts as a moral principle in relation to all new forms of reproductive technology. Whereas the Catholic form of naturalism is a very strong one, there are weaker forms that emerge in the context of Jewish law every time moral qualms regarding new reproductive technology are expressed by halakhic authorities. Since the debate over

---

[13] *Resp. Minhat Yitzhak*, 1 no. 50; *Resp. Yabia Omer*, 2, *Even Haezer*, no. 1; *Resp. Ziz Eliezer*, 3 no. 27.

[14] See Isa. 45: 18; *Eduyyot*, 1: 13; *Yevamot*, 62a; Feldman, *Marital Relations*, 48; R. Auerbach cited in *Nishmat Avraham, Even Haezer*, 1: 9.

[15] See *Encyclopaedia of Jewish Medical Ethics*, i. 153.

[16] See Y. Jakobovits, 'The Longing for Children in a Traditional Jewish Family', in R. Grazi (ed.), *Be Fruitful and Multiply* (Jerusalem, 1994), 5–11.

[17] This is the attitude of the *halakhah* towards new technologies in general. A leading source in this context is the statement of R. Israel Lifschitz that anything that the Torah, does not explicitly forbid is presumed permitted (*Tiferet Yisrael, Yadaim*, 4: 3).

naturalism is one of the major moral problems in this area, and the difference between the *halakhah* and Catholicism with regard to AIH brings the debate out nicely, we will now turn to a brief survey of the Catholic view on this topic.

According to the Catholic position, any intrusion of technology into human reproduction is absolutely forbidden. AIH is not a viable option for a Catholic married couple struggling with an infertility problem. According to the Catholic doctrine, as laid down in the 1987 *Instruction on Respect for Human Life in its Origins and on the Dignity of Procreation (Donum Vitae)*,[18] it is forbidden to separate procreation from marital sex. This provision, which is often referred to as the 'inseparability principle', insists that children must come into being only as a result of marital intercourse, and that any reproductive method that replaces intercourse as the cause of human generation is immoral.[19] The inseparability principle is based upon the idea that children born in any other context than that of marital love will be adversely affected in terms of their own capacities to love and be loved. The status of marriage as a sacrament is also relevant in this context. Also, there is the concern that artificial reproductive techniques can be easily abused.[20] In sum, the Catholic approach is a naturalist one; *Donum Vitae* gives strong expression to this idea, and the dominant Catholic view is that AIH is forbidden.

Mention should be made of a minority Catholic view that regards the total ban on assisted conception in *Donum Vitae* as being too strong an application of the inseparability principle. According to this view, if a married couple is desperate to have their own child and looks to assisted reproduction as the means for achieving this end, the act of reproduction is imbued with the same ingredient of marital love as that which suffuses the act of marital intercourse, and AIH ought to be permitted.[21] As far as the fear of abuse is concerned, the argument offered by the liberal Catholic minority is that this concern can be met by a combination of religious sanctions and practical precautionary measures. It should not, in and of itself, provide the basis for a universal ban on artificial reproduction in all circumstances.[22]

It is noteworthy that Islamic law in this area resembles Jewish law, in that it, too, has no principled opposition to the use of artificial reproductive

---

[18] *Origins*, 16 (1987), 697.

[19] See R. McCormick, *The Critical Calling: Reflections on Moral Dilemmas Since Vatican II* (Washington, 1989), 333; P. Hannam, 'In Vitro Fertilisation', *Irish Theological Quarterly*, 55 (1989), 14.

[20] See McCormick, *Critical Calling*, 347–9. An example of abuse is the replacement of the husband's sperm with that of a donor.

[21] See T. Shannon and L. Cahill, *Religion and Artificial Reproduction* (New York, 1988), 111–15, 127–39. See also McCormick, *Critical Calling*, 348.

[22] See McCormick, ibid. 348.

techniques in order to overcome a fertility problem within a marriage. AIH is permitted, with certain safeguards, under Islamic law.[23]

As stated above, the halakhic position would appear to be in stark contrast with that of the Catholic Church, with the emphasis on the word 'appear'. The case against naturalism in the *halakhah* must not be made too strongly. Just as there is a significant moral element in abortion *halakhah*, the halakhic position on artificial reproduction is also informed by moral factors, one of which is the principle of naturalism. As a result, although the naturalist approach is never actually articulated as a fundamental principle in this area of Jewish law, the arguments used by a number of modern halakhic authorities to cast doubt on the acceptability of AIH, as well as other methods of assisted reproduction, seem to reflect the naturalist approach. There are two main arguments in favour of this weaker form of naturalism.

The first argument is that although AIH is not halakhically prohibited, it is not on a par with natural procreation as far as the fulfilment of the *mitzvah* of procreation on a biblical level is concerned. This downgrading of the religious validity of AIH may serve as evidence of 'back-door' naturalism in Jewish law.

The second is the existence of a few rare instances of explicit naturalist ideology expressed in the halakhic literature on this area. One such instance is found in the writings of R. Immanuel Jakobovits in relation to artificial insemination by a donor (AID). Of course, both the legal and moral ramifications of AID are far more serious than those of AIH and as a result, legal permission to undergo AID, if and when granted, is often qualified by reservations of a moral nature. Nevertheless, for purposes of the naturalism issue, the fact that R. Jakobovits' point is made in the context of AID is not critical, since its force is equally applicable to AIH. R. Jakobovits begins his discussion by noting that although there is nothing intrinsically illegal about AID, it is, nevertheless, opposed by the majority of halakhic authorities on moral grounds. According to R. Jakobovits, the basis for this opposition is the belief that the use of artificial reproductive techniques turns childbearing into a 'mechanical' act, bereft of 'those mystical and intimately human qualities which make man a partner with God in the creative propagation of the race'.[24] The reference to the

---

[23] See V. Rispler-Chaim, *Islamic Medical Ethics in the Twentieth Century* (Leiden, 1993), 18–27. Islamic law does insist that safeguards are adopted in order to prevent any donor semen entering the picture and destroying the purity of the husband's line.

[24] *Jewish Medical Ethics* (New York, 1975), 248–9. The use of naturalist discourse would undoubtedly have spoken to the general readership of this English language path-breaking book on Jewish medical ethics. In this respect, it may be significant that the book was written in London and in Dublin and contains numerous references of a comparative nature to both Catholic and Protestant positions.

'mechanical' nature of AID is highly reminiscent of the naturalist theory underlying the inseparability doctrine of the Catholic Church. In using these terms to describe the moral reservations on the part of halakhists towards AID, R. Jakobovits uses naturalist discourse, thereby exemplifying its use in a Jewish context.

It is noteworthy that according to one contemporary authority in Islamic law, which, as already mentioned, is very similar to Jewish law in its underlying position on artificial reproductive techniques, a child born using artificial techniques lacks 'feelings and human warmth'. According to this minority view, all artificial reproduction is prohibited.[25]

Neither of these arguments, however, supports the presence of a strong form of naturalism in the *halakhah*. In terms of the argument from the *mitzvah* of procreation, it must be pointed out that there is a significant difference between the manifestation of 'back-door' naturalism in the form of downgrading AIH reproduction to the level of a rabbinic precept, and the full-blown form of naturalism manifested in the fundamental objection to the use of reproductive techniques in the Catholic tradition. The halakhic form of naturalism is certainly not an invitation to a blanket prohibition on all forms of assisted reproduction.

In effect, the naturalist element in the *halakhah* may be understood as an attempt to introduce a note of caution into the use of assisted reproduction, rather than as a clarion call to total rejection. In fact, this form of weak or 'back-door' naturalism may not be an unwise course at all, since it does not close off the technological option to couples desperately seeking help in order to compensate for nature's shortcomings, and at the same time, it leaves the door open to serious debate about their moral status. At the end of the day, even serious misgivings about the negative moral effect of a particular technology upon society as a whole are not strong enough to prohibit an otherwise legally acceptable method.

Weak naturalism also has a practical advantage in that the downgrading of the *mitzvah* status of AIH has an important role to play in ensuring that the new technology will not become a tool of abuse in the hands of an unscrupulous spouse. One of the halakhic ramifications of the downgrading is that if one or both parties to an infertile marriage do not wish to pursue assisted reproduction for valid personal reasons, they are not obliged to do so, and may even claim that in the absence of any possibility of fulfilling a biblical commandment by means of AIH, they are adopting the most virtuous course by refraining from it. In other words, AIH may not be used by one party to a marriage as a means of obtaining a divorce on the grounds that the spouse's refusal to use assisted reproduction is tantamount to nullifying the biblical commandment to propagate,

---

[25] See Rispler-Chaim, *Islamic Medical Ethics*, 24.

which is an undisputed grounds for divorce in Jewish law.[26] By the same token, a couple struggling hard to overcome a fertility problem are not only permitted to engage in AIH; with the production of a child they will even have a rabbinic *mitzvah* to their credit. The rabbinic status of procreation achieved by means of AIH provides the basis for an element of choice in this area, which might not be the case if it were held to be a valid means for fulfilling the biblical obligation to procreate.[27] In this respect, the downgrading ensures that a technology of hope is not turned into a tool of abuse.

As far as the second argument is concerned, naturalist discourse in halakhic sources is either employed in a secondary role, as in the case of R. Jakobovits' remarks concerning the legal ban on AID, or as part of a clearly labelled moral argument against both AID and *in vitro* fertilization. It is absent from all definitive legal discussions, and is probably best explained as a cautionary measure, in the same way that we explained the downgrading of the commandment to procreate using AIH from the biblical to the rabbinic level.

To sum up, a naturalist element is present in the *halakhah*, but it is certainly not the full-blown theory expressed in the Catholic tradition. It reflects a degree of moral uneasiness in relation to assisted reproduction, and a fear that its untrammelled use may lead society down a path to moral chaos. Nevertheless, it is not translated into actual law, and is not even quoted as a direct source for the moral condemnation of assisted reproduction by those authorities whose prohibitionist views are cited in section 4. At the end of the day, moral judgement is left suspended, and determined halakhic Jews are entitled to use assisted reproduction provided that they do not violate any specific legal norms in the process.

2. ARTIFICIAL INSEMINATION USING DONOR SPERM (AID) AND THE ISSUES OF ADULTERY AND *MAMZERUT*[28]

AID is the most widely practised form of artificial insemination, and it is often the only solution for a wide range of fertility problems including total male infertility, very low sperm counts, complications due to incompatibility between a couple's blood types, especially the Rh factor, and problems relating to the immune system in the reproductive organs. AID is also used as a last resort in cases in which there does not seem to be any reason for the existence of an infertility problem. It has been estimated

[26] See M. Elon (ed.), *The Principles of Jewish Law* (Jerusalem, 1974), 418.
[27] J. D. Bleich, *Bioethical Dilemmas* (Hoboken, NJ, 1998), 207–8, 241.
[28] See Elon (ed.), *The Principles of Jewish Law* and Ch. 1, n. 39.

that about 30 per cent of infertility cases are due to deficiencies in the male reproductive system.[29] AID is, therefore, often the only hope for an infertile couple desiring a child who is genetically related to the mother, and whom she can carry in her womb through a full pregnancy culminating in birth. The tragedy of infertility and its special significance for traditional Jewish families was referred to in relation to AIH, and it is no less relevant in the present context.

From a legal point of view, AID poses many more problems than insemination carried out using the husband's sperm (AIH). These include adultery (*mamzerut*), the possibility of incest between the sperm donor's children and those of the inseminated woman, and a whole range of problems in the areas of family and succession law resulting from the fact that the origin of the AID child might not be a matter of public knowledge.

The gravest legal issue relating to AID is that of adultery, and its consequences for the children of the adulterous union. The halakhic answer to the question of whether AID constitutes adultery turns, *inter alia*, on a talmudic passage dealing with the permissibility of a marriage between a high priest and a pregnant virgin. Under biblical law, a high priest is required to marry a virgin.[30] The Talmud poses the following question: Is a virgin who happens to be pregnant permitted to a high priest? In attempting to provide this scenario with some factual basis, the Talmud suggests that a virgin may become pregnant as a result of entering a bath into which a man had recently discharged his semen.[31] For our purposes, the significance of the discussion clearly lies in the light it seeks to shed on the legal definition of sexual offences in Jewish law, and not in the history or physiology of virgin conception. The question that the Talmud is seeking to answer is whether in relation to the issue of marriage to a high priest, a woman ceases to be a virgin only as a result of having had intercourse with a man, or whether becoming pregnant is sufficient to deprive her of her virginal status, even in the absence of any act of intercourse.

If the answer is that virgin status is lost only as a result of intercourse, the pregnant virgin would be permitted to the high priest, and more importantly, a general rule may be derived to the effect that in all prohibited sexual relationships, the physical element of the prohibition is intercourse and not impregnation. A married Jewish woman who is impregnated by the semen of a Jewish man other than her husband without having had sexual relations with him is not, therefore, an adulteress.

---

[29] See *Encyclopaedia of Jewish Medical Ethics*, i. 149.   [30] Lev. 21: 13.

[31] *Hagigah*, 14b–15a. Although some earlier authorities believed in the possibility of bathtub conception (R. Hananel, *Commentary to the Talmud*, Hagigah, 15a; *Tashbez*, 3 no. 263) the majority of halakhists deny the possibility of conception taking place in such circumstances (*Ozar Haposkim*, 1 no. 42).

If, on the other hand, the answer is that pregnancy is incompatible with virginity, then the virgin is prohibited to the high priest, and more significantly, the general rule that suggests itself is that impregnation alone is sufficient to constitute the physical element of prohibited sexual relationships such as adultery and incest.

Both Rashi and Tosafot conclude from the passage that intercourse rather than pregnancy renders a virgin unsuitable for marriage with a high priest.[32] The majority of halakhic authorities would also appear to adopt this view of the passage, accepting the conclusion that a high priest is permitted to marry a pregnant virgin. The principle that emerges from this ruling, therefore, is that sexual intercourse alone, not impregnation, constitutes the physical element in the definition of sexual offences such as adultery and incest in Jewish law.[33]

Another important halakhic source for this issue is a discussion by R. Perez of Corbeil, a French Tosafist, in relation to a woman who becomes pregnant during her menstrual period. Under Jewish law, sexual relations between a husband and wife are forbidden during menstruation.[34] R. Perez deals with the scenario of a married menstruant who becomes pregnant as a result of lying on her husband's sheets shortly after he ejaculated onto them. According to R. Perez, there is no question of any breach of Jewish law here, since no actual intercourse has taken place. The status of a child born as a result of insemination in such circumstances is completely free of any taint, including that of 'the child of a menstruant'.[35]

---

[32] Rashi, *Shabbat*, 151, *s.v. ushmuel amar*; Tosafot, *Ketubot*, 6b, *s.v. rov beki'in*; *Niddah* 64b, *s.v. sha'ani Shmuel*. Also see B. Firrer, 'Regarding Artificial Procreation' (Heb.) *Noam*, 3 (1964), 295–9 for a discussion of the opinion of the Tosafot in *Hagigah*, 14b, *s.v. betulah sheibrah*, and the way in which it is in line with the other two Tosafot cited in this note. R. Firrer bases his view upon a textual emendation proposed by R. Joel Sirkes in his *Hagahot Habah* on *Hagigah*.

[33] See *Tashbez*, 3 no. 263; *She'elat Ya'avez*, no. 96; *Helkat Mehokek, Even Haezer*, 1: 6; *Beth Shmuel, Even Haezer*, 1: 10; *Resp. Seridei Esh*, 3 no. 5; *Resp. Yabia Omer, Even Haezer*, 1 no. 6. For different views, see *Mishneh Lemelekh, Hilkhot Ishut*, 16: 4; *Turei Zahav, Even Haezer*, 1: 18; *Resp. Ziz Eliezer*, 3 no. 27. See also F. Rosner, 'Artificial Insemination in Jewish Law', in F. Rosner and J. D. Bleich (eds.), *Jewish Bioethics* (New York, 1979), 111.

[34] The offspring of such intercourse are not, however, subject to any purely legal disqualification, see *Encyclopaedia Judaica*, xii. 1141–8.

[35] In the course of the gloss as cited in *Bayit Hadash, Yoreh Deah*, 195, reference is made to a legend with regard to the conception of Ben Sira, whose book is to be found in the Apocrypha. According to this legend, the prophet Jeremiah was forced into an act of onanism in a bath, after which his daughter was compelled to enter the bath and become pregnant as a result of her father's semen entering her body (*Midrash Alef Beth Deben Sira*, ed. Y. Eisenstein (New York, 1928), 43). The legend supports the notion that bathtub conception cannot give rise to *mamzerut* since Ben Sira, notwithstanding his origin, was considered a 'perfectly legitimate Jew' (*kasher hayah*). This legend appears in various halakhic works and is cited in support of the view that the child of a married Jewish woman who underwent AID using Jewish sperm is not a *mamzer* (see *Likkutei Maharil*, no. 5; *Tashbez*, 3 no. 263; *Helkat Mehokek, Even Haezer*, 1: 18; *Birkei Yosef, Even Haezer*, 1: 14; *Pahad Yizhak, s.v. ben bito*;

However, he goes on to say that a married woman must avoid lying on the semen-covered sheet of a man other than her husband. The reason for this is that if she does become pregnant and give birth, the resulting child may, unwittingly, marry the progeny of his biological father, thereby committing incest. Any child of this marriage will be a *mamzer*.[36] R. Perez's ruling that a married woman must not lie on the sheet of another man is based solely upon the fear of possible incest. There is no indication that becoming pregnant with a stranger's semen, without any act of intercourse with him, constitutes adultery. Indeed, in the absence of any such indication, it may be assumed that intercourse alone, and not impregnation, constitutes the defining physical element in the offence of adultery in Jewish law.

R. Perez reiterates the principle implicit in the talmudic discussion of the high priest and the pregnant virgin, i.e. impregnation alone does not constitute the defining physical element of sexual prohibitions under Jewish law. He also emphasizes that the progeny of a married woman conceived as a result of lying on a sheet covered with the semen of a man other than her husband is not a *mamzer*: 'Since no act of intercourse is involved, the child is completely free of the taint of *mamzerut*'. R. Perez's opinion is cited by all the major commentators on the *Shulhan Arukh*,[37] and provides the main supporting source for the many authorities who rule that in the absence of sexual intercourse, the insemination of a married woman with donor sperm does not constitute adultery, and the offspring is free of any taint whatsoever.[38]

There is no indication that R. Perez's discussion was related to an actual case, and it would appear to have remained a purely theoretical issue for many centuries. Indeed, the idea that pregnancy could be brought about other than by means of sexual intercourse was simply not accepted by most medieval halakhists as a practical possibility.[39] In the mid-twentieth

---

Resp. Yabia Omer, Even Haezer, 8 no. 21). Some recent authorities, however, deny that it carries any legal weight whatsoever (*Resp. Ziz Eliezer*, 9 no. 51; Jakobovits, *Jewish Medical Ethics*, 247–8).

[36] Classical Jewish law recognizes only natural parenthood, hence the father of an artificially inseminated child is always the sperm donor; see M. Broyde, 'The Establishment of Maternity and Paternity in Jewish and American Law', *National Jewish Law Review*, 3 (1988), 118–9. R. Perez's ruling is cited in the *Bayit Hadash, Yoreh Deah*, 195; *Shiltei Hagiborim, Shevuot*, ch. 2, and *Birkei Yosef, Even Haezer*, 1: 14. See also Maimonides, *Commentary to the Mishnah, Sanhedrin*, 7: 4. *Mamzerut* is established even if the parents were unaware that their relationship was an incestuous one.

[37] *Turei Zahav, Even Haezer*, 1: 5; *Helkat Mehokek, Even Haezer*, 1: 8; *Beth Shmuel, Even Haezer*, 1: 10.

[38] *Resp. Shoel Umeshiv*, 3 no. 132; *Resp. Mishpetei Uziel, Even Haezer*, no. 19; *Resp. Seridei Esh*, 3 no. 5; *Resp. Menahem Meshiv*, no. 26; *Resp. Iggrot Moshe, Even Haezer*, 1 no. 71;. Auerbach, cited in *Nishmat Avraham, Even Haezer*, 1: 9.　　　　　　　　　　　　　[39] See n. 31.

century, however, things changed. With the advent of artificial insemination, the issue of conception without intercourse became a highly relevant
halakhic topic, and the subject of a heated debate between two prominent
North American authorities, R. Moses Feinstein and R. Yoel Teitelbaum.
The debate began with a question posed to R. Feinstein concerning an
infertile couple who were desperate to have a child. The problem clearly
lay in the husband's lack of viable sperm. R. Feinstein, following the position in the Talmud and R. Perez, concluded that there was no issue of adultery in relation to donor sperm, and permitted them to undergo AID in a
local fertility clinic.[40] In order to overcome the problem of potential incest,
upon which R. Perez's strict ruling regarding a married woman lying on
another man's sheets is based, R. Feinstein confines his permissive ruling
to a non-Jewish sperm donor. The reason for this is that non-Jewish paternity is legally irrelevant under the *halakhah*. Jewish children fathered by a
non-Jew share no legally significant relationship with each other on the
paternal side, and therefore, if they are born to different mothers, they are
free to marry each other without fear of transgressing the prohibition on
incest.[41] Indeed, even if the non-Jew were to convert to Judaism, his child
conceived with a Jewish woman prior to his conversion may marry his
child conceived with a different Jewish woman after his conversion, and
no act of incest will have been committed. These principles governing
non-Jewish paternity will also apply if the conception of the child is the
result of AID. In R. Feinstein's view, it is safe to assume that the majority
of sperm in North American sperm banks and fertility clinics is of non-
Jewish origin. Hence, the couple in question may use the services of any
sperm bank in order to help solve their fertility problem and avoid the
breakdown of their marriage.

In R. Feinstein's view, therefore, there is no question of adultery or
mamzerut in relation to AID, even if the sperm comes from a Jewish donor.
However, because of the fear of possible incest between the AID child and
other children of the donor, his permissive ruling is confined to non-
Jewish sperm.

R. Feinstein's ruling came under heavy attack from a number of rabbinic colleagues,[42] although most of them disagreed with his ruling on

---

[40] *Resp. Iggrot Moshe, Even Haezer*, 1 no. 71. It is noteworthy that R. Feinstein refers to a
view cited in the *Ozar Haposkim*, 1: 42, that 'AID using Jewish sperm constitutes adultery
and any children will be *mamzerim*', but dismisses it on the grounds that 'it is clearly not
possessed of any halakhic weight'.

[41] *Yevamot*, 45b; Maimonides, *Hilkhot Issurei Biah*, 15: 3; *Tur, Even Haezer*, 16; *Shulhan Arukh,
Even Haezer*, 4: 1.

[42] The American halakhic journal *Hamaor* published numerous articles between 1961 and
1965 heaping criticism upon R. Feinstein in both halakhic and personal terms. Indeed, the
author of the journal saw fit to state that R. Feinstein's strict rulings in other areas were
undoubtedly to be relied upon, since if even he could not permit, then the matter under

purely moral grounds. A notable exception is R. Yoel Teitelbaum, a staunch traditionalist, who became R. Feinstein's major critic on this matter. According to R. Teitelbaum,[43] the halakhic prohibition on adultery is defined in terms of causing lineage confusion, i.e. uncertainty with regard to the father, as well as forbidden intercourse. This idea is derived from a point made by Nahmanides in his *Commentary on the Torah* on the verse defining the prohibition of adultery: 'And you shall not lie carnally to seed (*lezara*) with your neighbour's wife.'[44] According to Nahmanides, the word 'to seed' in the biblical prohibition on adultery implies that the offence also involves the children of the adulterous relationship in the sense that they are unaware of their true ancestry. Adultery is, therefore, wrong because it leads to a situation in which lineage becomes confused.[45] This idea is also cited by the author of the *Sefer Hahinukh* as a reason for the prohibition on adultery.[46] In R. Teitelbaum's view, donor insemination, even without intercourse, constitutes adultery under biblical law, since it raises doubts as to the paternity of the child. The doubt is not capable of resolution in an empirical way, such as by keeping a register of insemination donors, since the issue is a matter of principle, not of practice. No method of reproduction may be used, the effect of which is to blur the identity of the father. Any such method constitutes adultery in Jewish law.

As far as R. Perez's ruling is concerned, R. Teitelbaum distinguishes between a case in which the impregnation was purely accidental, as in the case of a woman lying upon sheets containing semen, and a planned pregnancy, as in the case of AID. In R. Teitelbaum's view, R. Perez's statement that 'since no act of intercourse is involved, the child is completely free of the taint of *mamzerut*', is based upon the fact that the semen ejaculator did not intend to impregnate the woman in question, and she did not intend to become pregnant as a result of lying on his sheets. The pregnancy came about in a totally unplanned way, and it is for this reason alone that it is not considered adultery, and the child is not a *mamzer*.

discussion was surely prohibited beyond a shadow of doubt! His lenient rulings, however, needed to be treated most circumspectly since 'his capacity for leniency exceeds that of the most lenient authorities in Israel' (M. Amsel, 'Further Important Details Regarding Artificial Insemination' (Heb.), *Hamaor*, 16/1 (1965), 147).

[43] *Resp. Divrei Yoel, Even Haezer*, nos. 107–10. All the citations in the body of the text are taken from these *responsa*. Also see *Resp. Ziz Eliezer*, 9 no. 51.   [44] Lev. 18: 20.

[45] Nahmanides observes that the word *lezara* might be used 'in order to mention the reason for the prohibition i.e. it will not be known to whom the child belongs, and as a result, great and wicked abominations might be done by both father and child'. Note that this is only raised as a possibility by Nahmanides. He goes on to say that 'the right interpretation in my view' of the word is to define the sin as not merely lying with a forbidden woman, but lying with her in such a way that it is an act of sexual intercourse. It is also evident that this prohibition applies to men only (Maimonides, *Sefer Hamitzvot, Mitzvat Aseh*, no. 347).

[46] *Yitro*, no. 5.

R. Perez's ruling may not, therefore, be used to free the product of deliberate donor insemination from the taint of *mamzerut*; it extends only to chance insemination.[47]

The problem with this argument is that nothing in R. Perez's text indicates that the crucial issue with which he is dealing is the intention of the parties, and not the physical definitions of the offences of sexual relations with a menstruant and a married woman. Indeed, he states quite clearly that 'since no act of intercourse is involved, the child is completely free of the taint of *mamzerut*'. If the real reason for avoiding the taint of *mamzerut* in this case was lack of intention to transfer the semen from the man to the married woman by means of the sperm-covered sheet, this should have been indicated in the text. Also, the role of intention in relation to the law of *mamzerut* is unclear. It is established law that the child of a woman who mistakenly believed her husband to have died, and on that basis was permitted to remarry by a rabbinical court, will, upon the reappearance of her first husband, be declared an adulteress and have her children from the second marriage declared *mamzerim*.[48] This law suggests that *mamzerut* is defined solely in physical terms and that mental intention is irrelevant.

Perhaps sensing the weakness of the argument from lack of intention, R. Teitelbaum goes on to claim that the offence of adultery must be understood on many levels, some of which are comprehensible only to the mystics: 'And, in truth, there are many more hidden reasons than revealed ones and they are only known to the mystics. Indeed, there are such lofty matters involved in the commandments that no human being is capable of fathoming their entire significance.' It is, therefore, dangerous to rely upon a purely rational understanding of *halakhah*, especially in relation to as serious an offence as adultery. In R. Teitelbaum's view, 'the correct approach is to exercise great caution before permitting any course of action which might even conceivably constitute the crime of adultery'.

R. Teitelbaum also finds room to criticize R. Feinstein in terms of the theory of halakhic decision-making. R. Feinstein's halakhic decisions are almost always based upon talmudic sources, early medieval commentators, and the major codes of Jewish law. He does not generally pay much attention to later commentators or mystical works on the *halakhah*. R. Teitelbaum cites the ancient debate between those authorities who arrive at their decisions on the basis of the Talmud alone, and those who base themselves upon the post-talmudic gaonic sources.[49] He prefers the view of R. Joseph ibn Migash, the principal spokesman of the second

---

[47] A similar explanation is provided by R. Teitelbaum for the finding that Ben Sira was perfectly legitimate notwithstanding his highly dubious origin (see n. 35).

[48] See Elon (ed.), *Principles of Jewish Law*, 412.

[49] See M. Elon, *Jewish Law* (Philadelphia, 1994), 1229–31.

of the above-mentioned schools of thought, who maintains that it is more appropriate to arrive at halakhic rulings with the aid of later gaonic *responsa* than to rely upon the Talmud alone, since 'there is no scholar in our times who is able to fathom the true meaning of the Talmud without the aid of gaonic commentaries'.[50] In R. Teitelbaum's view, R. Joseph ibn Migash's opinion that a true understanding of talmudic law is only available to those who follow the entire chain of traditional interpretation of the Talmud, applies even more strongly in contemporary times, 'when halakhic knowledge in general is at a high premium and a profound understanding of all its levels is virtually non-existent'. It is therefore to be regretted that there are 'contemporary authors who, on the basis of vain and unsubstantiated inferences from the Talmud itself, produce terrible leniencies in areas requiring extreme care such as adultery and *mamzerut*'.[51]

R. Teitelbaum's conclusion is that AID constitutes adultery and any resulting children will be *mamzerim*.

R. Feinstein responds to the entire range of R. Teitelbaum's criticisms in his second *responsum* on AID in Jewish law.[52] As far as the definition of adultery is concerned, R. Feinstein insists that a strict separation must be made between sexual intercourse, which is the physical element in the offence of adultery, and lineage confusion, the avoidance of which may or may not be an extra-halakhic, peripheral dimension of the prohibition. R. Feinstein makes his point by observing that acceptance of lineage confusion as a core legal element in the offence of adultery may well lead to the patently false argument that adultery with an infertile woman is not illegal, since there is no danger of lineage confusion in such a case![53] Clearly, sexual intercourse constitutes the sole core element in the offence of adultery; lineage confusion is at best a peripheral, extra-halakhic dimension of the offence. R. Feinstein also argues that the major source used by R. Teitelbaum for the idea that lineage confusion constitutes an integral part of the offence of adultery, i.e. Nahmanides' *Commentary on the Torah*, is not, strictly speaking, a halakhically authoritative work. As such, there is no genuinely normative basis for R. Teitelbaum's major legal argument in favour of including lineage confusion in the biblical offence of adultery.[54] Moreover, argues R. Feinstein, the remark about lineage

---

[50] *Resp. Ri Migash*, no. 114. The Gaonim were post-talmudic authorities located mainly in Babylon who originated the halakhic literary genres of codes and *responsa* in an effort to summarize and consolidate the vast body of talmudic law, see Elon, *Jewish Law*, 42–3, 1150–67; 1468–73.   [51] *Resp. Divrei Yoel, Even Haezer*, no. 110.

[52] *Resp. Iggrot Moshe, Even Haezar*, 2 no. 11. All the citations in the body of the text are from this *responsum* unless indicated to the contrary.

[53] See Abraham ibn Ezra, Lev. 18: 20.

[54] The halakhic status of Nahmanides' *Commentary on the Torah* is a matter for debate, see *Resp. Noda Biyehuda*, 2, *Yoreh Deah*, no. 28; D. Sinclair, 'The Status of Human Healing and

confusion constituting a core element in the offence of adultery may be the addition of an errant disciple to the text of Nahmanides' commentary. It may never have been penned by Nahmanides himself.[55]

In terms of the process of halakhic decision-making, R. Feinstein turns the tables on R. Teitelbaum and other critics who share the same view, by claiming that whereas his own ruling is based upon purely objective halakhic analysis, their rulings are, in fact, influenced by 'external opinions'. As a result, it is R. Feinstein's opponents who 'prohibit the permitted, and permit the prohibited'. He is most insistent that halakhic rulings be evaluated according to objective legal criteria, and that lenient decisions are not refuted purely on the grounds of their leniency:

All my opinions are based solely upon the knowledge of the *Torah* and are completely free of any external ideas. For the laws of the *Torah* are true whether their effect is to be strict or to be lenient. There is no halakhic validity whatsoever in external ideas or inclinations of the mind, even if they lead to a strict ruling. The idea that a strict result is necessarily purer and more holy than a lenient one is false.

R. Feinstein does not elaborate the 'external ideas' upon which his opponents in the contemporary debate rely, but these ideas may be easily established on the basis of their written criticisms of him. One 'external idea', which is cited by a number of critics, is that it is always better to err on the side of strictness when confronting a novel situation as in the case of AID.[56] Another is the claim that AID is wrong on mystical and moral grounds.[57] However, it is not so much the content of these criticisms as their lack of formal halakhic pedigree that raises R. Feinstein's ire. He takes pains to point out that until the advent of this debate, no significant halakhic authority had adopted the view that a child produced by AID might be a *mamzer*. The one or two who had done so represented a tiny minority and their views were at best, of a tentative nature only: 'They are, in fact, completely irrelevant, since they do not possess the normative authority of the more classical sources, and their opinions are formed entirely on the basis of external factors, which are at odds with the very

Coercive Medical Treatment in Jewish Law' (Heb.), *Shenaton Hamishpat Haivri*, 18–19 (1992–4), 270.

[55] The 'errant disciple' or 'forger' is a not uncommon theme in R. Feinstein's *responsa*; see Ch. 1 n. 157 in relation to abortion. It may be safely assumed that these claims are not based upon historical research, but are a formal device used in order to remove the tension between R. Feinstein's conclusions regarding any particular halakhic matter, and the opposite view taken by less than leading authorities in that area. In the present case, the method is used with regard to Nahmanides' *Commentary on the* Torah which, as pointed out in the sources mentioned in the above note, is not a primary halakhic source. Similarly, the sources dismissed on the basis of this argument in the context of abortion are not front rank authorities as far as R. Feinstein and his classical approach to halakhic decision-making is concerned.

[56] See n. 42.   [57] See s. 4.

fundamentals of the laws governing forbidden sexual relations as laid down in the Torah and the Talmud.' R. Feinstein is clearly of the opinion that a strictly legal approach is to be adopted in this area, and it should not be compromised by extra-legal principles.

R. Feinstein's opinion, therefore, remains unchanged, and in his view, there is no halakhic bar to AID provided that use is made of non-Jewish sperm.[58] Moreover, if the resulting child is female, there will not even be any restriction on her marrying a *kohen* (priest).[59]

In 1965, a book appeared in Brooklyn purporting to carry a retraction by R. Feinstein. He is reported in that book to have stated that his lenient decision is not to be relied upon in practice, since he permitted the use of AID with non-Jewish sperm only in the gravest of cases, and the discretion to decide whether a particular case falls into this category is, in fact, beyond the capacity of even the most experienced halakhic authority.[60] However, some twenty years after his original debate with R. Teitelbaum, R. Feinstein obviously felt the need to reiterate his position on AID, and in another *responsum* on the topic, he emphasizes that everything he had written in his two earlier *responsa* is 'true and clear law and there is absolutely no basis for any retraction'.[61] He does, however, add that he did not always give practical rulings in accordance with his view of the *halakhah*, but used his discretion in line with considerations of a pastoral nature. It is important to realize, explains R. Feinstein, that rather than bringing a couple together, AID may, in fact, drive them apart. In particular, without proper counselling there is no guarantee that the child will be accepted by the husband of the inseminated woman. Now, as already observed, there are no halakhic grounds for regarding AID as a compulsory procedure, since artificial insemination per se may not be a valid method for carrying out the biblical, as opposed to the rabbinic, commandment to procreate.[62] Therefore, it ought to be recommended only to a couple who are properly prepared for receiving a child resulting from AID. In situations in which this is not the case, R. Feinstein would not recommend AID. Nevertheless, as far as its halakhic status is concerned, R. Feinstein reiterates his earlier position and states quite categorically that if a couple proceeds with AID using non-Jewish sperm, 'the child is perfectly legitimate and may even marry a *kohen*'.

---

[58] There is an issue of the couple waiting three months before resuming sexual relations in order to distinguish between the child born from AID and one born from natural intercourse, see: *Talmudic Encyclopaedia* (Heb.), viii. 102.

[59] Priests are restricted in the type of women they are allowed to marry and the daughter of a non-Jew falls within these restrictions, see Elon (ed.), *Principles of Jewish Law*, 361.

[60] Z. Freidman, *Zvi Hemed* (Brooklyn, 1965), *kuntresim*, 41–3. This retraction is also cited in *Resp. Ziz Eliezer*, 9 no. 51, and *Resp. Helkat Yaacov*, 3 no. 47.

[61] *Resp. Iggrot Moshe, Even Haezer*, 4 no. 32.   [62] See n. 14.

It is interesting to note that in an essay published in an Israeli halakhic journal at the same time as publication of R. Feinstein's original *responsum*, R. Shlomo Zalman Auerbach, a prominent Israeli authority, also argued that since the product of AID using non-Jewish sperm would be free of all legal impediments, the use of the technique may well be permitted to a couple 'in dire need'.[63] This essay did not attract the same type of heavily negative criticism as was levelled at R. Feinstein's *responsum*. Presumably, the fact that R. Auerbach's view was expressed in the form of a theoretical insight rather than a practical ruling, and that it was accompanied by a stern warning to the effect that his words were not to be treated as binding *halakhah*, but merely as a basis for experienced authorities to use in their future rulings on this matter, saved it from becoming the focus of controversy. R. Auerbach also took care to attach to his halakhic opinion strong moral reservations regarding the use of non-Jewish sperm.

As far as the practical question of establishing the non-Jewish origin of sperm obtained from a sperm bank is concerned, R. Feinstein relies upon the fact that the majority of donors in a country such as the United States are non-Jewish. Hence, it may be assumed that the sperm in any particular case will originate from the majority, and will be that of a non-Jewish donor; the problem of potential incest is thus avoided.[64] R. Teitelbaum, however, insists that a higher standard than normal must be applied with regard to lineage determination. Hence, even if he were to accept R. Feinstein's argument regarding the definition of adultery, he would still be unable to accept his lenient ruling, since the possibility of incest amongst the various children of the sperm donor may only be discounted if it is known for a fact that the donor sperm is from a non-Jew. Since this is not the type of information generally given to infertile couples requesting AID, the procedure may not be used even in R. Feinstein's own terms.[65]

Another authority who supports R. Feinstein's approach in relation to the use of non-Jewish sperm is R. Weinberg, who also maintains that sperm obtained from a sperm bank outside Israel is considered non-Jewish by virtue of the simple majority principle.[66]

In purely legal terms, R. Feinstein's solution appears to be free of complications, and is, in fact, accepted by the majority of authorities.[67]

---

[63] 'Artificial Insemination' (Heb.), *Noam*, 1 (1958), 145.

[64] *Resp. Iggrot Moshe, Even Haezer*, 2 no. 11.

[65] *Resp. Divrei Yoel, Even Haezer*, nos. 107–10.   [66] *Resp. Seridei Esh*, 3 no. 5.

[67] See *Encyclopaedia of Jewish Medical Ethics*, i. 157. As far as the issue of *mamzerut* is concerned, R. Auerbach, 'Artificial Insemination', maintains that the product of AID using Jewish sperm is a doubtful *mamzer*, whereas according to R. Yehiel Weinberg, (*Resp. Seridei Esh*, 3 no. 5) its status is that of a *shetuki*, i.e. one whose father is unknown (*Kiddushin*, 74a;

On moral grounds, however, it was rejected by the majority of prominent halakhists of his day. The nature of these grounds and their practical significance, if any, for the practice of AID by observant Jews will be discussed in section 4.

The final point in this section concerns R. Feinstein's halakhic methodology. The contrast between his *responsum* on AID and the one on the abortion of a Tay-Sachs foetus, discussed in the previous chapter, is quite striking. In the AID *responsum*, he adopts a lenient position based upon his 'pure' legal methodology, whereas in relation to Tay-Sachs, he apparently adopts a strongly moral approach that is at odds with the purely legal doctrine and, as a result, reaches an extremely stringent conclusion. In fact, the two debates are distinguishable, and it is worthwhile attempting to spell out the difference between them. In the context of AID, R. Feinstein takes his critics to task for basing practical halakhic decisions on 'external ideas', such as a policy of strictness with regard to new situations, or aggadic, kabbalistic, and other non-binding sources. His analysis is based upon purely legal sources and principles, and in the absence of any well-established tradition of introducing a moral element into this area of *halakhah*, he reaches his decision on the basis of the binding sources only. In the Tay-Sachs decision, however, there is a well-established moral tradition and, as pointed out in Chapter 1, halakhists have often sought to elide the distinction between law and morality in this area by absorbing morality into law in an apparently seamless manner. R. Feinstein follows this pattern of the direct absorption of the moral aspect of abortion *halakhah* into the legal sources, and although his method of so doing, and the extent to which he dismisses halakhic sources on the basis of charges of forgery and poor bibliographical facilities,[68] may be a little strong for our taste, he is following a well-established course in this area.

Of course, there is always the possibility that things might change in the future, and it could transpire that AID indeed poses a significant threat to morality, as does non-therapeutic abortion. At present, however, it is not clear that it poses such a threat. This lack of clarity may account for the fact that most authorities do not agree with R. Teitelbaum on the adultery and *mamzerut* issues; instead, they confine their misgivings regarding the use of AID to quasi-legal or moral grounds, as we will see in the following section.

In terms of halakhic methodology, both R. Feinstein in relation to AID, and R. Waldenberg in the context of Tay-Sachs, achieved their respective

---

Maimonides, *Hilkhot Issurei Biah*, 15: 12; *Shulhan Arukh, Even Haezer*, 4–26; Elon (ed.), *Principles of Jewish Law*, 437). A *shetuki* is treated as a doubtful *mamzer*, but unlike the latter, its status may be resolved by the mother's statement regarding the identity of the father or by a statistical analysis of the semen donors at the clinic attended by the mother.

[68] See Ch. 1, nn. 156–7.

lenient results by limiting the legally binding material to a small number of sources all carrying an impeccable talmudic pedigree. It is interesting to note that this formal approach allows for much greater flexibility in responding to new issues than the competing one—exemplified by R. Teitelbaum in relation to AID—which requires that all the traditional sources, including blatantly non-talmudic ones, are satisfied before any ruling is produced.

The methodology adopted by R. Feinstein and R. Waldenberg in relation to modern biomedical issues was, in fact, used by liberal halakhists during the eighteenth century in order to bridge the gap between Jewish law and modernity. An outstanding example is R. Ezekiel Landau, who, in the latter part of that century, developed a highly formal approach that he used to good effect in integrating various aspects of modern life within the *halakhah*.[69] The link between legal formalism and leniency is an interesting feature of *halakhah* in general, and it is the subject of further comment in the Conclusion.

Of course, it is also arguable that R. Feinstein's *responsum* on Tay-Sachs is the exception to the rule, and that it is his ruling on AID which is typical of his halakhic methodology. The Tay-Sachs opinion may have been written in the light of a moral position on abortion about which R. Feinstein felt strongly enough to justify a radical departure from his normal methodology. It is not unheard of for a judge, even on a secular bench, to depart from a previously consistent juristic line of thought in a particular case in which the subject is especially controversial from a moral standpoint.[70]

3. OTHER HALAKHIC PROBLEMS ASSOCIATED WITH AID

The present section is concerned with cases in which reliance is placed both upon R. Feinstein's basic position that AID, even if carried out with Jewish sperm, does not constitute adultery, and upon the assumption that the possibility of incest between children of the sperm donor is either entirely insignificant, or fundamentally preventable by legal or medical means. In such cases, a number of problems may yet arise[71] including the fear that the wife of a childless man might remarry upon her husband's death without first obtaining *halitzah* from her brother-in-law, even though

---

[69] See D. Sinclair, 'Halakhic Methodology in the Post-Emancipation Period: Case Studies in the Responsa of R. Yechezkel Landau', *Le'ela* (April 1998), 16.

[70] See R. Cover, *Justice Accused* (Yale, 1975) for several illustrations of this phenomenon in relation to American judges dealing with the legal status of fugitive slaves in the period shortly before the Civil War.

[71] See *Encyclopaedia of Jewish Medical Ethics*, i. 155, for a detailed list of problems.

she had produced a child by AID. Under biblical law, the widow of a man who died without issue is required to marry his brother in order to continue the line of her dead husband. The brother of the dead husband may, however, release her from the levirate marriage in a ceremony called *halitzah*,[72] and she will then be free to marry whomever she pleases. Today, *halitzah* is the norm, and if the dead brother's wife does not go through with it, she may not remarry; if she does so, her second husband is required to divorce her.[73] Clearly, if AID is permitted, a woman who gave birth after being artificially inseminated with donor sperm will, on the death of her husband, be in a position to avoid *halitzah* by concealing the fact of her child's AID origin. Some authorities consider this possibility serious enough to provide a basis for banning AID entirely.[74] Others, such as R. Feinstein, argue that the problem may be avoided by identifying AID children to the rabbinic authorities in charge of registering marriages. Indeed, lack of secrecy as to the halakhic identity of sperm donors and their offspring is an essential element in R. Feinstein's liberal approach to AID.[75]

The possibility of concealing the fact that a particular child was born as a result of AID is also disturbing in relation to those areas of Jewish law in which male lineage is a legally constitutive element. In this context, it is important to note that Jewish law defines paternity in natural terms only:[76] it does not recognize adoption as a substitute for natural parenthood.[77] One area in which the establishment of natural paternity is legally significant is the establishment of priestly identity. Priestly status passes on only to the male descendants of a priest; hence, if the sperm donor is a non-priest, and the donee's husband is a priest, the male child is not entitled to priestly status. The danger exists that the husband may be tempted to conceal his son's origins and bring him up as a priest. Similarly, if the sperm donor is a priest, his son will also be a priest, and if the donee's husband is a non-priest, he may be tempted to conceal the priestly identity of the child in order to avoid the need to make the nature of the conception public knowledge. In this case as well, modern halakhic authorities are divided over the ramifications of this problem. Some see it as a serious objection to the use of AID in general,[78] whereas others claim that it is easily overcome by requiring complete openness with regard to the origin of the child in question.[79]

---

[72] Deut. 25: 5–6.

[73] Her children from the second marriage, however, will not be *mamzerim* (*Yevamot*, 13b; Maimonides, *Hilkhot Ishut*, 4: 14; Elon (ed.), *Principles of Jewish Law*, 403–9).

[74] *Resp. Zekan Aharon*, 2 no. 97; *Resp. Ziz Eliezer*, 3 no. 27.

[75] *Resp. Iggrot Moshe, Even Haezer*, 2 no. 11.

[76] See Broyde 'Establishment of Maternity and Paternity', 118–19.

[77] See Elon (ed.), *Principles of Jewish Law*, 440.   [78] *Resp. Minhat Yizhak*, 6 no. 140.

[79] The Israeli Rabbinate has recently raised the controversial issue of establishing the identity of sperm donors in order to ensure that marriages involving their AID children

Another problematic area is that of inheritance. Here the problem is the possible concealment of AID in order to allow the child to inherit that which rightly belongs to the deceased man's relatives. Views are also divided on this issue.[80]

Problems may arise with respect to the establishment of the paternity of an AID child. According to the majority of authorities, the sperm donor, provided that he is Jewish, is the father in all respects, including priestly status and inheritance.[81] Other authorities, however, argue that he is only the father as far as prohibitions such as the ban on sibling marriage are concerned. In all other respects, e.g. inheritance rights, paternity is not established, and the child's lineage follows that of its mother or maternal grandfather. The reasoning behind this approach is the very unlikely possibility that the sperm donor is not actually the father. It may be the husband or another man entirely.[82]

All these problems may be resolved by means of adequate record-keeping. In most jurisdictions in the world today the sperm donor is anonymous, and only under Swedish law is an AID child entitled to learn the identity of his or her sperm donor upon achieving the age of majority.[83] Information necessary to prevent AID children from marrying other children of their sperm donor is, however, always available, as is information in relation to the donor's ethnic type and genetic health. In order to introduce a halakhic register of AID donor information in a modern society, a balance needs to be struck between the sperm donor's right to anonymity, and the need to make his identity known to those parties for whom this information is vital in order to prevent the problems outlined above. Any such halakhic register would be valid for halakhic purposes only, and would not affect the civil rights of either donor or child.

As the use of artificial reproductive technology increases, the problems associated with AID are liable to present themselves in more sophisticated forms. In relation to the laws of the levirate marriage referred to above, the following problem may be posed. A childless married couple prepare pre-embryos using the wife's eggs and the husband's sperm and then freeze them. The husband then dies. Is it arguable that the pre-embryos

---

conform to halakhic requirements, e.g. that the son of a priestly donor does not marry a divorcee, see A. Pheffer, 'Sperm Donors Are Liable to Lose their Anonymity Due to Demands by Dayanim' (Heb.), *Ha'aretz* (2 April 2002).

[80] See *Encyclopaedia of Jewish Medical Ethics*, i. 156.

[81] *Tashbetz*, 3 no. 263; *Beth Shmuel*, *Even Haezer*, 1: 10; *Helkat Mehokek*, *Even Haezer*, 1: 8; R. Auerbach, 'Artifical Inseminatioin', 156.

[82] *Turei Zahav*, *Even Haezer*, 1: 8; *Resp. Mishpetei Uziel*, *Even Haezer*, no. 19; *Resp. Zekan Aharon*, 2 no. 97; cf. Broyde, 'Establishment of Maternity and Paternity', 120 n. 23.

[83] See J. Mason and R. McCall Smith, *Law and Medical Ethics* (London, 1999), 66–7.

constitute issue for the purpose of releasing the wife from the need to obtain *halitzah* upon her husband's death? Now, the question of the need for *halitzah* in the case of a widow in the first trimester of pregnancy at the time of her husband's death is debated by eighteenth-century authorities. According to one view, the first trimester is too early to establish the existence of issue, and the widow requires *halitzah* before she may remarry. According to another view, the widow may be freed from the need for *halitzah* at the onset of pregnancy. One of the arguments cited in support of the latter view, is that a woman whose husband died leaving behind a child is not required to undergo *halitzah* when that child dies, even though she is now the widow of a childless man. It may, therefore, be assumed that according to the second view, it is the potential for issue, rather than the issue itself, that provides the legal basis for dispensing with *halitzah*.[84] In his above-mentioned essay, written in the mid-twentieth century, R. Shlomo Zalman Auerbach disagrees with the concept that potential issue is issue for the purpose of the laws of *halitzah*.[85] In his view, it is the existence of actual, not potential, issue at the time of the husband's death that frees his widow from the levirate bond. Nevertheless, he concludes that the very onset of pregnancy constitutes valid grounds for freeing the widow from *halitzah*. Presumably, the reason for this is a purely practical one, i.e. the improvement in women's health in general has resulted in the chances of a pregnancy running to term being much higher today than they were in the eighteenth century. It is, therefore, no longer necessary to wait for three months to elapse in order for the pregnancy to become established in order to release the mother from the need to obtain *halitzah*. On purely pragmatic grounds, the onset of pregnancy is sufficient for the establishment of the existence of issue at the time of the husband's death in relation to the levirate marriage laws. A question that may now be posed in the light of modern technology is whether there is a significant difference, with respect to relieving the widow of the need to perform *halitzah*, between the onset of pregnancy and the freezing of a fertilized egg for the purpose of future implantation. As the technology improves and the success rate of IVF rises, it is possible that implanting frozen pre-embryos will be as sure an indication of the birth of a child as the onset of pregnancy itself. To what extent would R. Auerbach's position be affected by this improvement in the technology? The answers to these and other questions lie partly in the debate regarding the halakhic relevance of scientific progress, which is discussed at length in Chapter 6 in relation to heart transplants.[86]

---

[84] *Resp. Noda Biyehuda*, 1, *Even Haezer*, no. 69; *Keren Orah*, *Yevamot*, ch. 9, end.
[85] R. Auerbach, 'Artificial Insemination', 145.
[86] See Ch. 6 s. 2 on heart transplants, and the Conclusion.

4. MORAL OBJECTIONS TO AID

As already observed, the majority of halakhic authorities tend to agree with R. Feinstein that AID does not constitute full-blown adultery for the purposes of Jewish law. They are, nevertheless, opposed to the practice on moral grounds.[87] This point was made by R. Jakobovits whose naturalist argument against AID was cited above.[88] According to him the major objection to AID is that it is a mechanical act bereft of the human qualities associated with the act of marital love. Underlying this view is undoubtedly a profound moral discomfort in relation to the use of artificial reproductive techniques. It is to this moral discomfort that the present section is devoted.

R. Yehiel Weinberg touches on a wide range of possible halakhic objections to AID in his *responsum* on artificial insemination, but bases his main opposition on the notion that the introduction of a stranger's semen, including that of a non-Jew, into the womb of a married woman constitutes 'an ugly act and an abomination of Egypt'.[89] The reference to 'an abomination of Egypt' is biblical in origin, and the source is in the moral prologue to the chapter in Leviticus dealing with the laws of forbidden sexual relations. These laws are introduced with a general warning not to follow in the ways of the Egyptians and the Canaanites, and not to practise any of their abominations.[90] By including AID in this general warning, and not in any of the specific prohibitions in the chapter, R. Weinberg indicates that there is no major halakhic prohibition on AID: it is forbidden mainly on moral grounds, constituting an offence against sexual morals rather than sex laws.

A similar approach is adopted by R. Jacob Breisch, with whom R. Weinberg corresponded on this matter. Both rabbis lived in Switzerland in the period after the Second World War, and R. Breisch belongs to the same school of Hungarian Orthodoxy as R. Yoel Teitelbaum, whose stringent approach to AID was discussed at length above. In common with the majority view, R. Breisch does not agree with R. Teitelbaum's view that AID constitutes adultery and that the issue is *mamzer*, but he does maintain that 'from the perspective of our religion, it is clearly forbidden to do such ugly things which are comparable to the deeds of the lands of Egypt and Canaan and their abominations'. R. Breisch adds that AID is contrary to 'religious sensibility in general'.[91]

---

[87] See *Encyclopaedia of Jewish Medical Ethics*, i. 154–5.
[88] *Jewish Medical Ethics*, 248–9.   [89] *Resp. Seridei Esh*, 3 no. 5.
[90] Lev. 18: 3. See also Lev. 18: 26–30, 20: 13; Ezek. 23: 19; *Encyclopaedia Mikrait*, viii. 466–8.
[91] *Resp. Helkhat Ya'akov*, 1 no. 24. R. Breisch also argues that to condone a practice 'condemned by the Catholic church and its leader' brings Judaism into disrepute, and constitutes a profanation of the Divine Name. The same argument was used, *inter alia*, by R. Zweig

In this respect, he goes a little further than R. Weinberg, and suggests that when the morality of AID is tested against the standard of 'religious sensibility' in general, it is found to be lacking. R. Breish also maintains that AID is contrary to the 'spirit of Judaism'. Presumably, his point here is that artificial insemination offends against the traditional Jewish value of modesty in matters of sex and reproduction by making public that which ought to remain private. This value is central to the Jewish ethos, especially in its biblical setting, and plays a highly significant role in distinguishing the Israelites from the other nations—Egypt and Canaan—and in shaping their identity as a chosen people.[92]

A more specific interpretation of the category of 'Egyptian and Canaanite abominations' is advanced by R. Waldenberg, who maintains that it refers to the issue of lineage confusion.[93] According to R. Waldenberg, it is a 'great abomination' to introduce another man's semen into a married woman's womb since, according to the Talmud, the Divine Presence rests only on offspring who are certain of their lineage.[94] This concept is an aggadic one and R. Waldenberg does not classify lineage-confusion as a legal element in the biblical offence of adultery. He does not, therefore, adopt R. Teitelbaum's stringent approach to the legal consequences of AID. As far as he is concerned, it is a purely moral offence, falling into the general rubric of the 'abominations of Egypt and Canaan'.

The moral opposition on the part of many modern halakhic authorities to AID also focuses on R. Feinstein's suggestion that non-Jewish sperm be used in order to avoid the problem of possible incest. In addition to the claim that it offends against a whole range of concepts relating to the bio-spiritual disadvantages of non-Jewish sperm, it is also accused of opening a back door to assimilation.[95] Indeed, there is something odd about the fact that marrying a non-Jew is regarded as anathema by many sections of the Jewish community, whereas the use of his sperm for solving an infertility problem is perfectly acceptable.

The widespread moral opposition of many halakhic authorities to AID is not, however, translated into quasi-legal form, as it is in the case of abortion. The impression gained from many of the modern *responsa* is that there is no principled halakhic objection to the practice but it should be

---

in justifying his opposition, to the abortion of a thalidomide foetus ('Regarding Abortion', *Noam*, 7(1964), 45).

[92] For an anthropological-phenomenological study of this point see S. Stern, *Jewish Identity in Early Rabbinic Writings* (Leiden, 1994), ch. 5.

[93] *Resp. Ziz Eliezer*, 3 no. 27.   [94] *Yevamot*, 42a.

[95] See *Resp. Ziz Eliezer*, 3 no. 27; *Resp. Yaskil Avdi, Even Haezer*, no. 10; *Resp. Divrei Yoel*, nos. 107–10.

avoided on ideological and moral grounds. In practice, therefore, a couple resorting to AID know in advance that there will be no serious halakhic consequences as a result of using the procedure. Indeed, even R. Breisch, who condemns AID using non-Jewish sperm in very strong moral terms, takes pains to point out that legally speaking, sperm from a sperm-bank outside Israel may be assumed to be non-Jewish, and the resulting child will, therefore, be free of any serious halakhic stigma.[96] In this respect, it is noteworthy that the option of using R. Feinstein's approach is presented in a recent handbook on fertility issues aimed at observant Jews in the United States.[97] In Israel, the availability of batches of non-Jewish sperm is a special feature of many Israeli fertility clinics.[98] Another recent development is the use in Israel of Jewish sperm for AID purposes by couples who are, presumably, not only concerned with the halakhic niceties of the process. As a result the Rabbinical courts have begun to request the details of sperm donors before issuing certificates regarding the fitness of children conceived using AID to marry. The reason for this is the desire to avoid the problems outlined above.

The reason for this difference between the approaches of many modern authorities to AID and abortion respectively was referred to at the beginning of the chapter. Whereas abortion involves the taking of a human life, albeit at an early stage of its development, the use of artificial reproduction to aid childbirth is fundamentally a life-affirming practice, albeit one that raises a whole gamut of legal and moral problems. Assisted reproduction is therefore less morally problematic than abortion. Moreover, many of the problems associated with assisted reproduction are of a speculative nature, and only time will tell whether they will provide as powerful a moral challenge as presented by abortion. This difference manifests itself both in relation to the extent to which moral disapproval is translated into halakhic form, and in social attitudes to the two practices. In the present section we have seen that the majority of authorities admit that, legally speaking, there are no insurmountable difficulties with regard to AID. Almost all the legal difficulties can be overcome by removing the veil of secrecy surrounding the use of donor sperm. There are moral problems, but these are presented as such, and no attempt is made

---

[96] *Resp. Helkat Ya'akov*, no. 24. This assumption is based upon the majority principle, see *Resp. Iggrot Moshe, Even Haezer*, 1 no. 71.

[97] See R. Grazi and J. Wolowelsky, 'New Ethical Issues', in Grazi (ed.), *Be Fruitful and Multiply*, 202–3. According to these writers: 'a Jewish couple who is sensitive to halakhic concerns should insist on obtaining donor semen from a non-Jew. Not all couples are aware of this, and the physician should bring up in his or her counseling session the fact that, halakhically, it is preferable to choose a non-Jew as the sperm donor.' It is noteworthy that the volume carries an Introduction by R. Jakobovits.

[98] See D. Ross, 'Artificial Insemination for a Single Woman' (Heb.), in M. Halpern and C. Safrai (eds.), *Jewish Legal Writings by Women* (Jerusalem, 1998), 46.

to obscure the boundary between law and morality in relation to AID in the same way that that it is obscured in the context of abortion. In terms of social attitudes, it was pointed out above that observant Jews are voting with their feet, relying upon R. Feinstein's permissive ruling in order to solve particularly pressing fertility problems. These same Jews regard abortion as a matter for serious rabbinical consultation, and even if it is approved, they approach it with anguish and despair. They are not doing the same in relation to AID.

For the present, the *halakhah* seems content to utter a general warning with regard to artificial reproduction, while at the same time, it effectively permits those who are desperate to have children to avail themselves of the most advanced modern technology in this area. Provided that the moral and legal ramifications of assisted reproduction do not change drastically in the near future, the halakhic response will probably continue to be a muted one.

A final point is the effect of assisted reproduction upon the traditional structure of the family. The fear that techniques such as AID will destroy this structure is one of the other arguments against AID raised by R. Jakobovits.[99] Here too, much will depend upon future developments; at the present time, the halakhic attitude to this potential problem is to express moral discomfort rather than articulating a legal ban.

5. *IN VITRO* FERTILIZATION (IVF)

Certain cases of female infertility may be overcome by using IVF, a process in which egg production is stimulated hormonally, and a number of eggs are fertilized with sperm in a petri dish. At the point of six- to twelve-cell separation, which usually occurs between twenty-four and seventy-two hours after the union of egg and sperm, three to four fertilized eggs are implanted in a uterus, in the hope that one at least will be successfully brought to term. The success rate of IVF varies between 10 and 30 per cent, with factors such as age, drug use, congenital deformities, and the relatively high spontaneous abortion rate associated with IVF all impacting upon the chances of success. Any excess fertilized eggs are normally frozen for future use by the couple undergoing IVF, or for purposes of donation.[100]

Amongst the older generation of modern authorities, R. Waldenberg is most strongly opposed to IVF, even for a married couple using the wife's eggs, the husband's sperm, and implanting the embryo into the wife's womb and not that of a surrogate.[101] He raises a whole host of objections

---

[99] *Jewish Medical Ethics*, 248–9.   [100] *Encyclopaedia of Jewish Medical Ethics*, ii. 118–23.
[101] *Resp. Ziz Eliezer*, 15 no. 5.

to the procedure, the first of which relates to the offence of seed destruction, which was discussed in section 1 above in the context of AIH. According to R. Waldenberg, the argument used by those authorities who permit AIH in the face of the prohibition on seed destruction is that this is the only way in which the husband is able to overcome his infertility problem and fulfil the religious obligation to reproduce.[102] This argument fails in relation to IVF, which is designed to deal exclusively with female infertility. Since the obligation to propagate does not apply to a woman,[103] her husband is not justified in 'destroying his seed' in order to facilitate IVF.

Another objection raised by R. Waldenberg is that that the grounds for concern over the possibility of a sperm or embryo mix-up are more serious in relation to IVF than they are in the case of artificial insemination. This is because in IVF, both semen and egg are initially placed in a glass dish, where they remain for two to three days in the hope that fertilization will take place. Only at the end of this period is a fertilized egg implanted into a uterus. During the period in which both the egg and the sperm are *in vitro*, mix-ups of sperm, eggs, or embryos are possible. Such mix-ups may occur either by accident or by design. In artificial insemination, the only cause for concern is the source of the sperm. Since it is injected directly into the woman, there is less scope for mix-ups. Hence, R. Waldenberg's practical misgivings in relation to IVF.

Finally, R. Waldenberg argues that because fertilization in IVF takes place in a glass dish and not in a womb, the resulting child has no mother under Jewish law. The source for this novel idea lies in the explanation given by R. Menahem Azariah of Fano for the well-known ruling in Jewish law that a child born as the result of a union between a Jewish woman and a non-Jewish father is, nevertheless, Jewish by virtue of its birth to a Jewish mother.[104] According to R. Menahem, the sinfulness of this union ought to result in the foetus losing its maternal lineage since it is a 'bizarre combination' of Jewish and non-Jewish gametes. However, since the foetus is physically part of the mother, it is treated as her child in the same way as a limb or any other physical appendage. Womb occupancy endows the child of this union with a Jewish mother, and hence, a Jewish identity.[105] In applying R. Menahem's argument to IVF, R. Waldenberg maintains that every IVF child is a 'bizarre combination'—in the literal sense of the word—since it is conceived in an unnatural way. There is, however, no womb occupancy at the time of conception to justify the

---

[102] See n. 7.   [103] Maimonides, *Hilkhot Ishut*, 15: 2.

[104] *Yevamot*, 45b. As already observed, Jewish law does not recognize non-Jewish paternity, hence, it is taken for granted that the child of such a union has no father as far as the *halakhah* is concerned. Indeed, it is precisely because non-Jewish paternity is not recognized in Jewish law that R. Feinstein recommends using non-Jewish sperm in AID (s. 2 above).

[105] *Resp. Rema Mifano*, no. 116.

endowment of this particular 'bizarre combination' with maternal lineage, since conception takes place in a dish. Hence, R. Waldenberg arrives at his rather startling conclusion that an IVF child has no mother.

R. Waldenberg also seems to maintain that an IVF child has no father, simply on the basis of the non-natural method of conception. In this respect, he follows the minority view of R. Malkiel Tennenbaum, according to whom, 'once the semen has been emitted and has warmth only because of the ministration of the physician and his skill with the pipette', the resulting child is not considered to be that of the sperm donor.[106]

R. Waldenberg's ruling prompted a firm rebuttal on the part of R. Avigdor Nebenzahl, the rabbi of the Jewish Quarter of the Old City of Jerusalem.[107] As far as the issue of seed destruction is concerned, R. Nebenzahl repeats the claim made by the permissive school in relation to AIH, i.e. that the prohibition on vain emission of seed is inapplicable in the context of fertility treatment involving a married couple. Since the sole intention behind every act of seed emission in this context is to bring about the birth of a child, the concept of seed destruction is simply irrelevant. He also emphasizes the human cost of prohibiting IVF to a couple desperate to conceive their own child using the husband's sperm and the wife's own eggs and womb. Such a course of action may lead to divorce and 'the destruction of the family unit in relation to the preservation of which, the Torah permitted the holy Name of God to be washed away'.[108]

As far as R. Waldenberg's argument regarding the adulteration of the eggs and sperm is concerned, R. Nebenzahl maintains that whilst 'the potential for such abuse always exists, it would hardly seem right for the future of a Jewish couple to be determined on the basis of a concern over a purely potential abuse'. He points out that practical measures may be taken in order to ensure that mix-ups of sperm and eggs do not occur. In the light of these measures, the chances of sperm or egg being replaced are extremely small, and do not justify outlawing the procedure as a whole.

Finally, R. Waldenberg's application of R. Menahem's concept of a 'strange combination' to the IVF offspring of a Jewish couple is also disputed by R. Nebenzahl. The two cases are entirely different. R. Menahem deals with a forbidden relationship under Jewish law, i.e. a Jewish woman made pregnant by a non-Jewish man. IVF involving a Jewish married

---

[106] *Resp. Divrei Malkiel*, 4 no. 107.

[107] 'Observations on In Vitro Fertilization' (Heb.), in *Sefer Assia*, 5, ed. M. Halperin (1987), 92–3.

[108] A reference to the ritual of the *sotah*, i.e. a wife suspected of adultery who was compelled to swallow a drink containing a parchment slip with God's Name written on it. Clearly, the liquid would erase the Divine Name, nevertheless, in order to restore peace between a man and his wife by proving that the woman had not committed adultery, the erasure of God's Name was permitted; see Num. 5: 11–31; *Shabbat*, 116a.

couple poses no such legal problem and there is, therefore, no question of the child being a 'bizarre combination'.

In a direct attack on the blatant naturalism underlying R. Waldenberg's ruling that the artificiality of artificial reproductive techniques per se deprives the resulting offspring of all lineage, R. Nebenzahl points out that 'we ought not to follow external form, but ought to focus on inner content', and as long as the aim is the fertilization of the egg, the mode of fertilization ought to be irrelevant. Citing a kabbalistic doctrine, the effect of which is to characterize the present millennium as 'the age of technical wisdom',[109] R. Nebenzahl argues that there ought to be no distinction between the acceptance of modern technology with regard to, say, the mending of severed limbs, and its application in relation to reproduction. In the same way that no one would suggest that the 'artificiality' of artificial limbs offends against the halakhic mandate to heal, so too, modern reproductive technologies ought not to be stripped of their therapeutic significance merely as a result of their artificial nature. R. Nebenzahl concludes by noting that 'both the husband and the wife in the case of IVF are potentially capable of producing their own biological child; all they need is a little help'.[110]

R. Waldenberg's strong naturalist position is the most striking feature of his *responsum*. In terms of the argument regarding maternity attributed to R. Menahem Mifano, it is clearly evident, as pointed out by R. Nebenzahl, that the foetus of a Jewish woman and a non-Jewish man is a 'bizarre combination' only because of the legal prohibition involved in the union of a Jew and a non-Jew, and not as a result of the method of conception. It is only R. Waldenberg who reads the phrase 'bizarre combination' in a naturalist vein; it is certainly not part of R. Menahem's theory of Jewish maternity in mixed unions. Moreover, it is not at all evident that R. Menahem subscribes to the view that maternity is established at conception. Perhaps he would agree that any time spent in a Jewish womb makes a foetus the child of the womb-owner, even if entry into the womb took place after conception. After all, in that case too, the foetus becomes part of the mother's body. Since a foetus conceived *in vitro* must be placed in a womb within a short time of conception, R. Menahem may very well

---

[109] See *Resp. Ziz Eliezer*, 14 no. 101, in which R. Waldenberg relies upon this very source in order to reject the argument that it is necessary to 'accept the Heavenly decree' in a passive manner in the context of the abortion of a Down Syndrome foetus. According to R. Waldenberg, the availability of modern techniques for detecting the genetic disorder associated with Down Syndrome makes it possible to consider performing an abortion in those cases in which the parents are completely incapable of facing the prospect of giving birth to, and coping with the rearing of, such a child. The existence of modern biotechnology is, therefore, to be welcomed as a potentially positive feature of contemporary times provided, of course, that it is used solely for therapeutic purposes.

[110] R. Nebenzahl, 'Observations', 92–3.

agrée that womb occupancy, even if it only began after conception, is sufficient to establish maternity; it is not necessary for that occupancy to begin at the time of conception. Indeed, it is arguable that R. Waldenberg's additional claim that it is important for the egg to be 'attached' to the mother's body during fertilization in order to establish maternity, is made precisely in order to rebut any such interpretation of R. Menahem's approach to the establishment of Jewish maternity in a mixed marriage. However, he does not offer any proof for this claim, and it remains as tentative as the rest of his theory regarding the application of R. Menahem's approach to the question of establishing maternity in the context of IVF.

In the course of his *responsum*, R. Waldenberg adds a third unsupported naturalist argument against maternity, i.e. that IVF is 'unnatural' because it takes place through the agency of a 'third power', namely the petri dish, and, therefore, the child has neither a mother nor a father. The whole *responsum* is, in fact, shot through with naturalist arguments, all of which are devoid of any firm halakhic basis.[111]

It is also worthwhile mentioning that as far as the above-mentioned claim that an IVF child has no paternity is concerned, R. Tennenbaum admits that his view is unique and, most significantly, he himself did not rule in accordance with it in practice.[112]

R. Waldenberg's view of IVF is rejected by the majority of halakhists and remains firmly in the minority. His full-blown naturalism is not a part of reproductive *halakhah*; it is only the 'back-door' form which, as pointed out at the end of section 1, is granted a background role in mainstream halakhic discourse in this area.

In any case, it would appear that as far as the establishment of maternity is concerned, the whole notion that any artificiality in the course of fertilizing the mother's egg destroys the maternal link with the child is not a well-founded one since, as we will demonstrate in the following section on donor eggs and surrogate mothers, the maternal link in Jewish law is established by birth, not gestation. In this light, the fact that the sperm and the egg met in a glass dish is legally irrelevant to the establishment of maternity.

R. Waldenberg reiterated his position in spite of R. Nebenzahl's challenge and other critical reactions to his strongly prohibitive stance on IVF.[113] It is noteworthy that R. Waldenberg's position on IVF is in stark contrast to his position in relation to the abortion of a Tay-Sachs foetus. The combination of strict halakhic formalism and a generous measure of

---

[111] See J. D. Bleich, *Contemporary Halakhic Problems*, 4 vols. (New York, 1977–95), iv. 238–42.

[112] *Resp. Divrei Malkiel*, 4 no. 107. See also Bleich, *Contemporary Halakhic Problems*, iv. 239.

[113] 'Editorial Comment', *Sefer Assia*, 5 (1987) 93.

sympathy for the individuals involved, which was so striking a feature in the Tay-Sachs case, seem to be in rather short supply in relation to IVF. It is also worth recalling that there is almost no support for R. Waldenberg's approach to the denial of maternity to an IVF child in contemporary halakhic literature.[114] Of course, part of the reason for the apparent contrast may lie in the fact that the case for leniency with regard to abortion has a long history in the *halakhah*, and reflects legal doctrine built up over the ages. This is not the case in relation to IVF, which is a new procedure, both medically and legally. The moral uncertainty with which such procedures are shrouded may have found its strongest expression in R. Waldenberg's approach. Other authorities prefer to leave room for legal manœuvre and, as in the case of AID, express their reservations in moral and quasi-legal terms only.

Another point that emerges from this comparison is that there is a tendency amongst halakhic authorities to balance lenient rulings with strict ones. It may be surmised that in order to preserve a certain equilibrium between strictness and leniency, R. Waldenberg may have followed up his permissive Tay-Sachs ruling with a particularly stringent one on IVF.[115] The stark contrast between R. Feinstein's *responsa* on AID and on the abortion of a Tay-Sachs foetus may be explained on similar grounds.

Two of the issues in the debate between R. Waldenberg and R. Nebenzahl merited special attention in the entry on IVF in A. Steinberg's *Encyclopaedia of Jewish Medical Ethics*.[116] The first is the virtue of naturalism so strongly espoused by R. Waldenberg. Following a lengthy review of numerous sources, Steinberg concludes that 'Judaism does not accept the view that nature is supreme and that technology ought not to be allowed to intervene in natural processes. On the contrary, man is a partner with God and his role is to improve the world in all its aspects.' Steinberg goes further, and echoing R. Nebenzahl's remaks on IVF, states that in the context of medical therapy, there is a halakhic obligation to develop new technologies in order to conquer all manner of physical disability, especially in an area in which the disability in question also threatens the survival of a marriage.[117]

---

[114] See *Encyclopaedia of Jewish Medical Ethics*, ii. 129 n. 48.

[115] The *responsa* on Tay-Sachs are dated 1977 and 1978 respectively. The *responsum* on IVF is dated 1982. Now, it is true that in his original, lengthy *responsum* on contraception, abortion, and artificial reproductive techniques (*Resp. Ziz Eliezer*, 9 no. 51), R. Waldenberg also takes a rather dim view of AIH and restricts its scope to a case in which the couple have been infertile for ten years, or where there is medical evidence that natural intercourse will never result in a pregnancy. He does, nevertheless, permit it provided that all precautions are taken in order to avoid any form of AID. In the 1982 *responsum* he prohibits IVF for a married couple under all circumstances.   [116] *Encyclopaedia of Jewish Medical Ethics*, ii. 125.

[117] Ibid. 126–7. Steinberg also refers, in this context, to the talmudic statement regarding the erasure of the Divine Name for the purpose of bringing about peace between a man and his wife (n. 108).

The second issue concerns the fear of abuse in the course of the procedure and in particular, the introduction of donor sperm and the possibility of mixing gametes *in vitro*. As observed above, R. Nebenzahl rejects the view that the existence of such a fear, even if it is justifiable in a particular situation, ought to result in a blanket prohibition on the use of modern reproductive technology. Steinberg deals with this issue separately in a special appendix to the entry on IVF.[118] In a general survey of precautionary rabbinic legislation in Jewish law, Steinberg concludes that there is no power in contemporary times to make the entire Jewish people subject to new prohibitions aimed at protecting either biblical or rabbinic laws. This power ceased with the Talmud, and any subsequent protective legislation is, perforce, local in its scope.[119] There is also a principle that local protective legislation ought not to be enacted, unless it is considered vitally necessary by all the authorities in that particular place.[120] As far as the halakhic approach to protective legislation in cases where the fear of breaching the law is based upon considerations of a purely practical nature, such as in relation to the fear of gamete and embryo mix-ups in AID and IVF, is concerned, Steinberg concludes that there is no principled halakhic basis for rabbinic legislation in this area.[121] From an institutional perspective, therefore, R. Nebenzahl's point about the lack of any legal basis for prohibiting IVF because of a practical fear of mix-ups is fully justified.

Steinberg also makes the eminently cogent claim that a necessary prerequisite for any such legislation, assuming that it was justified, is that the halakhic authorities promulgating it possess a high degree of scientific and medical expertise. Such expertise is necessary in order that the legislation proposed be well based in scientific and medical terms. After all, it is because of doubts concerning scientific and medical matters that the legislation is proposed in the first place. Often, halakhic authorities in this area adopt a 'strict is best' policy because they lack the necessary knowledge and understanding of the empirical context of the *halakhah* in question. The authority to ban assisted reproduction technology ought, therefore, to be used very sparingly, if at all.[122]

In conclusion, the debate between R. Waldenberg and R. Nebenzahl focuses on the position that *halakhah* ought to adopt *vis-à-vis* new, morally unsettling technology. R. Waldenberg argues strenuously for a stringent,

---

[118] Ibid. 150.

[119] See Rosh, *Shabbat*, 2 no. 15; *Sedei Hemed, Maarekhet Gimmel*, no. 11.

[120] See *Resp. Rivash*, no. 271; *Resp. Rashba*, 3 no. 411; *Resp. Maharil*, no. 121. On the topic of communal enactments in general, see Elon (ed.), *Principles of Jewish Law*, 679–779.

[121] See *Yadaim*, 4: 3; *Berakhot*, 60a; Rashi, *Bezah*, 2b, *s.v. deheterah*; *Sedei Hemed, Ma'arekhet Kaf*, no. 19.   [122] See *Encyclopaedia of Jewish Medical Ethics*, ii. 158–66.

non-permissive approach based upon fears for the future, and especially for the principle of naturalism in the way in which children are brought into the world. R. Nebenzahl sees no principled halakhic objection to the use of modern reproductive technology in a reproductive context, when the sole motivation of all concerned is to enable a married couple to have a child of their own, and to avoid the possibility of the break-up of a marriage as a result of infertility-related stress.[123]

In several respects, there is a parallel between this exchange and the exchange between R. Feinstein and R. Teitelbaum over the issue of AID using non-Jewish sperm. In both cases, the permissive position is based upon a formalist approach to halakhic decision-making, together with the rejection of the view that any deviation from natural procreation is morally and religiously wrong. The prohibitionist position relies upon a deeply naturalist ideology and seeks to read it into the halakhic sources.

6. HALAKHIC PROBLEMS IN RELATION TO IVF USING DONOR EGGS OR A SURROGATE MOTHER

In the above section, the discussion centred on IVF using the couple's own gametes. Many forms of female infertility, however, are only treatable using donor eggs and a surrogate mother. These are very new technologies, and it is significant that they are dealt with mainly by a new generation of native Israeli and American rabbis in articles published in the halakhic periodical literature. The more established techniques discussed— AIH, AID, and IVF using the couple's own eggs and sperm—feature in the *responsa* of the late nineteenth- or twentieth-century authorities, many of whom were born in Eastern Europe, making their way to Israel, the Unites States, and Western Europe during the early or mid-twentieth century. One of the interesting features of the current writing on donor eggs and surrogacy is the absence of the strong legal and moral reservations characteristic of the more established literature. The recent writers tend to take the use of the technology for granted and concentrate on specific legal problems such as the establishment of maternity in a surrogacy situation, or the Jewish identity of a child born from a Jewish egg and a non-Jewish womb. Of course, it is also true that the new technologies do not involve issues of the same order of legal significance as abortion and AID. There are, however, significant moral issues, and authorities such as R. Waldenberg were undoubtedly prompted by those issues to raise a

---

[123] On the high social motivation underlying the trend to seek infertility treatment amongst Orthodox Jews, see S. Barris and J. Comet, 'Infertility: Issues From the Heart', in Grazi (ed.), *Be Fruitful and Multiply*, 19–37.

whole battery of problems in relation to IVF. Modern commentators do not appear to share such reservations, and it may be surmised that what we are witnessing is the halakhic approach to assisted reproduction passing from moral rejection to qualified legal acceptance.

The focus in the present section is on the uncertainty surrounding both maternity and Jewish identity generated by the use of donor eggs and surrogate mothers; we are not concerned with actual prohibitions as we were in relation to the discussions of AIH and AID in the first four sections of this chapter.[124] Still, the problems generated by this uncertainty are serious, for unlike the secondary issues raised in relation to AID, such as the concerns regarding the laws of *halitzah* and the establishment of priestly lineage, they are not resolvable in purely practical terms.[125] Maternity and Jewish identity are substantive legal issues that require principled halakhic solutions.

The question of maternal identity—which is important for the halakhic issues of incest, Jewish identity, and some aspects of civil law—arises with regard to IVF in a case in which the genetic mother and the birth mother are two different people, i.e. a surrogacy situation.[126] One widely accepted view amongst halakhic authorities and commentators is that the birth mother alone is considered to be the halakhic mother of a child born as a result of this type of process.[127] The leading talmudic precedent for this view is the ruling that twin brothers whose mother converted to Judaism during pregnancy are not included in the law of levirate marriage and *halitzah*, but are nevertheless forbidden to marry each other's wives.[128] The reason for the non-applicability of the levirate law is that the brothers are not related on their father's side, since non-Jewish paternity is not recognized under Jewish law, and the levirate law applies only to brothers from the same father.[129] They are forbidden to each other's wives because the prohibition on sisters-in-law is defined in terms of the maternal relationship.[130] The question then posed by the Talmud is that since conversion to Judaism severs all pre-existing legal links between members of the same biological family,[131] why are the two brothers considered related on their

---

[124] See *Encyclopaedia of Jewish Medical Ethics*, i. 129.   [125] See s. 3.

[126] See M. Hirshler, 'Test Tube Babies According to the Halakhah' (Heb.), *Halakhah Urefah*, 1 (1980), 313–20; N. Goldberg, 'Establishing Maternity in the Case of Foetal Implants' (Heb.), *Tehumin*, 5 (1984), 249; A. Kilav, 'Is Maternity Established by Conception or Birth?' (Heb.) *Tehumin*, 5 (1984), 260–7; Y. Ben-Meir, 'The Lineage of a Child Born to a Surrogate Mother and an Egg Donor' (Heb.), *Assia*, 41 (1986), 25–40; E. Bick, 'Foetal Implants' (Heb.), *Tehumin*, 7 (1986), 260; 'Ovum Donations: A Rabbinic Conceptual Model of Maternity', *Tradition*, 28 (1993), 28–45.

[127] See Broyde, 'Establishment of Maternity and Paternity', 131–40.

[128] *Yevamot*, 97b. For levirate marriage and *halitzah*, see nn. 72–3.

[129] Deut 25: 5–6.   [130] Lev. 18: 16.

[131] *Yevamot*, 22a; Maimonides, *Hilkhot Issurei Biah*, 14: 12.

mother's side? Since they are both converts to Judaism by virtue of their mother's conversion, they ought to be considered total strangers. Proof that conversion does indeed cut all legal links between members of the same biological family is found in the halakhic ruling that, in principle, a convert is permitted to marry any converted relative, including a sister. The basis for this ruling is the principle that following conversion, all family members are considered as if they were born anew.[132] It ought to be pointed out that under rabbinic law, such marriages between biological relatives are forbidden, since they offend against universally accepted moral conventions.[133] The answer to the question posed by the Talmud is that the fact that the brothers come out of a Jewish womb recreates the maternal link severed by the conversion that took place during pregnancy. This point is made by Rashi who comments that, as far as the issue of marrying sisters-in-law is concerned, the link between the brothers is established by their birth, since their converted mother 'is like any other Jewish woman who gives birth'.[134] Maternity is thus established at birth,[135] and not at conception, or even pregnancy. Hence, the rule in surrogacy situations is that the woman who gives birth to the child, and not the egg donor, is the legal mother.

A variation on this view is that the mother who carries the foetus for the last two trimesters of pregnancy is the halakhic mother.[136] This position is derived from an analogy made by R. Akiva Eiger between paternity, which he believes is established at the end of the first trimester,[137] and maternity.[138]

One recent writer opines that a foetus removed from a womb after forty days is considered to have been born.[139] On this view, a foetus conceived in one womb and then transferred to another after a forty-day occupancy of the first one, would be the child of the first mother, even if the second one gave birth to it. This view is derived from the talmudic discussion of the case of a foetus which is removed from one mother's womb and thrust into the womb of another for the duration of the pregnancy.[140] The outcome of the halakhic discussion of this case would appear to be that the first mother alone is the halakhic mother.[141] At the present time, there

---

[132] *Shulhan Arukh, Yoreh Deah*, 269: 1. There is undoubtedly room for speculation as to the relationship, if any, between this halakhic principle and the Christian idea of a convert as someone who is 'born again'.   [133] *Tur, Yoreh Deah*, 269.

[134] Rashi, *Yevamot* 97b, s.v. *aval hayavin*.

[135] See also Tosafot, *Ketubot*, 11a, s.v. *matbilin oto*.

[136] See Goldberg, 'Establishing Maternity', 249.   [137] See *Sanhedrin*, 69a.

[138] *Hiddushei R. Akiva Eiger, Yoreh Deah*, 87: 6; cf. R. Joseph Engel, *Beth Haozar; Ma'arekhet*, 1–2, *erekh av*; R. Isaac Rabinowitz, *Zekher Yizhak*, 1 no. 4.

[139] Bick, 'Foetal Implants', 260. The basis for this position is the talmudic discussion of embryo transfer from one womb into another in *Hullin*, 70a, and Maimonides' ruling on that case (*Hilkhot Bekhorot*, 4: 18).   [140] *Hullin*, 70a.

[141] Maimonides, *Hilkhot Bekhorot*, 4: 18.

is no practical difference between this view and the view based upon the criterion of birth, since the implantation of IVF pre-embryos into the birth mother's womb takes place no later than three to four days after fertilization. The birth mother, therefore, is also the one who carries the foetus at the completion of the first forty days of pregnancy. A practical difference may emerge if, in the course of time, implantation into a human womb is delayed until the beginning of the second trimester or even later. On the basis of the forty day criterion, it will no longer be evident that the birth mother is also the halakhic one.

All these writers espouse one form or other of the birth mother criterion. Although this is the dominant view, there is a minority opinion according to which the egg donor is the halakhic mother.[142] This view is based primarily on aggadic sources,[143] and has not been accepted by the majority of halakhic authorities.[144] Notwithstanding its weak normative basis, the egg donor approach is, nevertheless, very much in keeping with the temper of a genetic age. It makes sense, therefore, to find a way of incorporating the egg donor approach into the contemporary halakhic definition of maternity. This insight lends support to R. Bleich's double maternity theory, which we will now proceed to discuss.

The existence of two definitions of maternity—the birth mother and the egg donor—prompted R. David Bleich to suggest that in the absence of any definitive criterion for determining the identity of the mother in a surrogacy situation, the child born to a surrogate ought to have two mothers for legal purposes.[145] Citing a number of examples drawn from the laws of agriculture, R. Bleich develops a general theory that a case in which the status of a plant transplant is in doubt is best resolved by adopting a stringent approach, and treating the transplant, for the purpose of all relevant prohibitions, as being an organic part of the plant onto which it has been grafted. In the same way, the product of a surrogate mother would be forbidden to marry two sets of relatives: those of the egg donor and those of the surrogate.

---

[142] S. Goren, 'Embroyo Transplantation According to the Halakhah' (Heb.), *Hazofeh*, 17 December 1984; I. Warhaftig, 'An Addendum to the Test Tube Babies Debate' (Heb.), *Tehumin*, 5 (1984), 268–9 (editorial comment).

[143] The first is the discussion in *Sanhedrin*, 91b (see Ch. 1 n. 6) regarding the time of ensoulment, which would appear to take place at conception. Hence, it is logical to assume that maternity is also fixed at conception. The second is the talmudic statement that there are three partners in a person, i.e. father, mother, and God. Each partner makes his or her contribution at the time of conception, hence, that is the moment at which maternity must be established (see *Niddah*, 31a). Another source cited by the proponents of this view is the passage in Exod. 21: 22 in which the Bible describes a miscarriage as 'the loss by a woman of her offspring' (*yeladehah*). The word 'offspring' implies the existence of the maternal link during pregnancy. Maternity is, therefore, relevant to the foetal stage and does not arise only at birth. [144] See R. Bleich, *Contemporary Halakhik Problems*, iv. 238.

[145] Ibid. 237–72.

In fact, the analogy with agricultural laws is not new in this area of the *halakhah*. These laws were used by R. Yekutiel Kamelhar in a halakhic journal published in Warsaw in 1932, in order to tease out some of the legal implications of the halakhic status of a child born as a result of an ovarian transplant. On the question of its maternal lineage, R. Kamelhar held that it was determined by the birth mother since upon implantation, the ovary became an integral part of her body. As a result, any child born from an egg produced by that ovary was hers. His reasoning was based, *inter alia*, upon the law of *orlah*, the prohibition upon eating the fruit of a newly planted tree during the first three years after planting.[146] According to a plain reading of the Talmud, the fruit of an *orlah* branch grafted on to a tree that is older than three years may be eaten, since the transplant has become an integral part of the tree onto which it was grafted.[147] R. Kamelhar applies this principle directly to the case of an ovarian transplant, and decides in favour of the birth mother.[148]

R. Bleich undertakes an extensive analysis of the sources dealing with plant transplants,[149] and reaches the conclusion that in all of them, the final status of the transplant remains unresolved both in the Talmud and in later halakhic works. Consequently, any legal ramifications of the transplant are to be dealt with by applying the strictures relating both to the transplant and the recipient of the transplant. In other words, the transplant should, 'for safety's sake', be treated as if it were the product of both the donor and the donee.[150] In the same way, a child born to a surrogate mother using a donor egg is halakhically bound to refrain from marrying into the families of both the egg donor and the birth mother.

This notion of double maternity is not without its critics. R. Auerbach, for example, objects to the idea that any useful analogy can be made between agricultural laws and the *halakhah* governing the assisted conception of human beings.[151] A similar objection is raised by

---

[146] See *Encyclopaedia Judaica*, 1467–8.   [147] *Sotah*, 43b; *Menahot*, 69b.

[148] The article was reprinted in R. Kamelhar's *Hatalmud Umadei Hatevel*, 44–5, and is cited by R. Yekutiel Greenwald, *Kol Bo Al Avelut*, i. 306. R. Kamelhar also makes the point that it is the womb rather than the egg that nurtures the foetus, and he cites another talmudic rule, this time in the area of animal husbandry (*Hullin*, 79a), to indicate that nurturing plays an important role in arriving at a definition of maternity. Also, see Bleich, *Contemporary Halakhic Problems*, i. 106–9.

[149] See Z. Low, 'Concerning the Children of Surrogate Mothers' (Heb.), *Or Hamizrach*, 133 (1989), 150–60, who is cited by Bleich and whose analysis of maternity from the standpoint of laws concerning agriculture and animal husbandry provides the setting for R. Bleich's argument.

[150] Clearly, R. Bleich reads the talmudic discussion in *Menahot*, 69b, in a more complex manner than did R. Kamelhar and he also analyses other cases ranging from the status of produce reaching growth prior to the offering of the *Omer* sacrifice (*Encyclopaedia Judaica*, xii. 1282–4) to the prohibition on planting mixed agricultural species in a vineyard (see *Encyclopaedia Judaica*, xii. 169–72).   [151] See Low, 'Children of Surrogate Mothers', 158.

R. Nebenzahl,[152] whose permissive approach to IVF was referred to above.

There is also an important analytical distinction between the issue of doubtful maternity generated by IVF, and that of the agricultural hybrids referred to above. In the agricultural context, the question of the status of the hybrid remains unresolved in the Talmud, and there is no attempt by later authorities to forge a majority view on the issue. This is not the case with regard to the establishment of maternity. There is considerable talmudic support for defining maternity according to the birth mother, and the majority of contemporary authorities accept this definition. Moreover, the only talmudic support for defining maternity in terms of the egg donor is of an aggadic nature, and it is only a minority of modern authorities who accept that the egg donor is the halakhic mother. As such, there is much less of a legal doubt in the case of defining maternity in a human surrogacy situation than in relation to agricultural hybrids. From an analytical perspective, R. Bleich's view that there is a genuine doubt in relation to establishing maternal identity in a surrogacy situation, which is best resolved by adopting the stringency rule governing doubtful situations in Jewish law, is not entirely convincing.

It is also questionable whether the best course for dealing with doubts generated by new technologies is to adopt the most stringent approach, thereby covering all possible bases. This point was raised by Steinberg in his critique of R. Waldenberg's stringent approach to IVF cited above.[153]

In terms of the genetic approach to maternal lineage, however, R. Bleich's double maternity theory may be regarded as an interesting development, if it is understood as an expression of contemporary halakhic uncertainty with regard to the negation of genetics as a factor in determining the maternal link. The birth mother criterion is certainly counter-intuitive in the light of modern genetics, which obviously provide the basis for a much stronger argument in favour of the egg donor than of the birth mother. An argument on the part of a prominent contemporary scholar in the field of Jewish bioethics indicating that the claim of the genetic mother is serious enough to require the adoption of the double maternity definition is, therefore, encouraging. In other words, R. Bleich's theory could be read as a response to the challenge to the traditional approach raised by modern genetics.

From this perspective, the double maternity approach is part of the much more general issue of the role of science in the *halakhah*, which is addressed in Chapters 3 and 6 of the present work. For present purposes, it is sufficient to observe that in general, the relationship between scientific

---

[152] Ibid. See also Kilav, 'Conception or Birth?', 267.
[153] *Encyclopaedia of Jewish Medical Ethics*, ii. 125.

theory and halakhic decision-making is a dynamic one, and there are examples from the past of scientific concepts being taken on board by halakhists, notwithstanding the perceived initial lack of fit between these concepts and the traditional halakhic precedents.[154] This may also be the case in relation to the definition of maternity, although only the future will tell whether the *halakhah* will move towards a more genetically friendly definition or not.

Another major problem associated with egg donation and surrogacy is the establishment of Jewish identity. As already observed, Jewish identity in the *halakhah* is determined by birth to a Jewish mother.[155] Now, it might have been assumed that since birth determines maternity, the identity of the egg donor is irrelevant as long as the surrogate is Jewish. However, things are not so simple. Some modern authorities insist that the product of a non-Jewish egg and a Jewish womb must undergo immersion in a ritual bath—one of the main prerequisites of conversion to Judaism—before he or she is qualified to enter into the 'sanctity of Israel'. This immersion is a form of conversion applicable to cases in which there is Jewish maternal lineage, but full affinity with the Jewish people has not yet been achieved.[156] According to this view, both birth and conception must take place in the body of a Jewish woman in order that her child be considered fully Jewish. The source for this view is the talmudic ruling[157] that a child born to a woman who converted during her pregnancy is Jewish because it was in her womb when she underwent the conversion ceremony. During that ceremony, the foetus was also converted to Judaism.[158] If the child is male, the circumcision that takes place after birth doubles as a conversion circumcision, as well as the regular circumcision required for every Jewish boy under biblical law.[159] In order to

---

[154] See D. Frimer, 'Jewish Law and Science in the Writings of R. Isaac Halevy Herzog', *Jewish Law Association Studies*, 5 (1991), 33; D. Sinclair, 'Torah and Scientific Methodology in Maimonides Halakhic Writings', *Le'ela* 39 (April 1995), 30. In general, the fit between traditional notions of parenthood and the reproductive options available as a result of modern technology is coming into question, and the possibility that the very concept of parenthood itself will need to be defined in an entirely new way is a very real one; see Y. Weiler, 'Surrogacy and Changes in the Concept of Parenthood' (Heb.), *Assia*, 57–8 (1966), 141–72.

[155] *Yevamot*, 45b.

[156] *Hiddushei Hagranat, Nashim Unezikin* 11a, *s.v. vehanireh bazeh*; M. Sternbuch, 'On Test Tube Babies' (Heb.), *Bishvilei Harefuah*, 8 (1978), 29–36;. Bleich, *Contemporary Halakhic Problems*, iv. 258–62.   [157] *Yevamot*, 78a.

[158] This would, indeed, seem to be the essence of the ruling since the Talmud goes on to establish that the mother's body does not constitute a barrier between the foetus and the waters of the ritual bath in which the immersion is performed. The reason for this is that being inside its mother is 'part of its natural growth' and natural barriers do not render the immersion invalid; see Nahmanides cited by Rashba, *Yevamot*, 47b–48a; *Nimmukei Yosef*, *Yevamot*, 16a; *Beth Yosef*, *Yoreh Deah*, 268; *Dagul Merevaveh*, *Yoreh Deah*, 268: 6.

[159] See *Encyclopaedia Judaica*, v. 567.

reconcile this view with the principle that birth is determinant of identity, a distinction is made between Jewish maternal lineage and the act of conversion necessary for endowing an individual with the holiness of an Israelite. A child conceived by a non-Jewish woman who converted during pregnancy is born to a Jewish mother and hence, possesses Jewish identity. Conception by a non-Jewish mother, however, constitutes a flaw as far as the 'holiness of Israel' is concerned, and the product of such a conception, even if born to a Jewish mother, requires conversion. It follows from this position that if a fertilized non-Jewish egg is transplanted into a Jewish surrogate, the resulting child still requires conversion.[160]

Not all commentators adopt this understanding of the talmudic ruling in question: some maintain that the child of a convert is fully Jewish merely by virtue of being born to a Jewish mother,[161] and modern authorities argue over this point. R. Shlomo Zalman Auerbach maintains that a child born from a non-Jewish egg and a Jewish surrogate requires conversion.[162] R. Nehemiah Zalman Goldberg, however, is of the view that a fertilized non-Jewish egg implanted into a Jewish surrogate results in a Jewish child, without any act of conversion being required, provided that the implantation took place in the very early stages of foetal development. The basis for this view is the talmudic principle that a foetus is considered to be a part of its mother's body, and hence, partakes in her Jewish identity.[163]

A similar approach is adopted by R. Aaron Soloveitchik, who maintains that an embryo implanted prior to the fortieth day of gestation gains the religious and national identity of its mother by virtue of birth alone.[164] Since implantation in current IVF procedures takes place within three days of fertilization, it is clear that the surrogate mother will determine the Jewish identity of the child.

The different approaches to the case of the Jewish status of the pregnant convert also impact upon the halakhic outcome in a case involving a Jewish egg donor and a non-Jewish surrogate. According to the view that conversion is required, it might conceivably be argued that the child is Jewish on the grounds that it was 'conceived in holiness'. Once conceived in holiness, there is no going back, even if the pregnancy is brought to term by a non-Jewish surrogate.[165]

---

[160] See Bleich, *Contemporary Halakhic Problems*, iv. 258–62.

[161] *Biurei Hagra, Yoreh Deah*, 268: 5; Broyde 'Establishment of Maternity and Paternity', 136–8.

[162] See Low, 'Children of Surrogate Mothers', 170, who also cites R. Nebenzahl in support of his view.   [163] See Goldberg, 'Establishing Maternity'.

[164] M. Soloveitchik, citing his father, A. Soloveitchik, in 'Test-Tube Baby' (Heb.), *Or Hamizrah*, 100 (1981), 127–8.

[165] See Kilav, 'Conception or Birth?', 262. See also Bleich, *Contemporary Halakhic Problems*, 269–70.

7. THE ROLE OF *AGGADAH* IN DETERMINING MATERNITY

As explained in the Introduction, *aggadah* is the term used to indicate Jewish teachings specifically relating to biblical narratives, moral theory, and the rational, ideological, and mystical underpinnings of halakhic norms. Unlike *halakhah*, *aggadah* is not generally binding, although it does, occasionally, play a role in the shaping of legal principles and the creation of binding practices. Furthermore, in areas in which there is not an abundance of legal material—and artificial reproductive technology is one such area—halakhists tend to use aggadic sources in order to support their legal opinions. Since the traditional distinction between the two categories cannot be entirely ignored, the status of this support, and that of the arguments adduced on its basis, is a matter of debate.

The modern halakhic literature on assisted conception frequently refers to two aggadic sources in support of the establishment of maternity at birth rather than conception. The first concerns the biblical account in Genesis of the birth of Dinah, the only recorded daughter of Jacob.[166] Her birth is juxtaposed to the birth of Joseph, the eleventh of Jacob's sons and firstborn of his beloved wife, Rachel. Dinah's mother was Leah, who had already borne six sons to Jacob. Leah and Rachel were sisters, and it was Rachel whom Jacob loved. From the juxtaposition of the births, it is evident that both sisters were pregnant during the same period. The *aggadah* interweaves what was obviously a complex relationship between the sisters, and the births of Dinah and Joseph in the following fashion. Leah knew that the Divine plan provided for twelve sons only, each of whom was destined to found one of the twelve tribes of Israel. Since Leah had already produced six sons, and Jacob's handmaids two each, Leah calculated[167] that if she had a seventh son, Rachel would not be able to produce the two sons needed in order not to suffer the indignity of falling below the level of a handmaid in terms of her contribution to the founding family. Knowing that she was pregnant with a male and that Rachel was carrying a female, Leah overcame any feelings of resentment she may have had for her better-loved sister; she prayed that the foetuses be switched *in utero*, and that she give birth to a girl, and Rachel to a boy. Her prayer was answered and an angel did, indeed, perform an intrauterine foetal transfer. Leah gave birth to a daughter, Dinah, and Rachel bore her first son, Joseph, to Jacob.[168] Now, since the Bible clearly attributes the

---

[166] Gen. 30: 21–3.

[167] Hence the name Dinah, the root of which is *din-*, which normally signifies judgement, but is also used to mean reckoning or calculation.

[168] *Targum Yonatan*, Gen. 30: 21. Also see Maharsha, *Niddah*, 31a, *s.v. ve'et Dinah*; *Daat Zekenim Miba'alei Hatosafot*, Gen. 30: 21. *Targum Yonatan* is wrongly attributed to Yonatan b. Uzziel, a student of Hillel; see *Torah Shelemah*, 24: 5; *Encyclopaedia Judaica*, x. 188.

maternity of Dinah to Leah, and that of Joseph to Rachel, it is evident that birth, and not conception, determines maternity. [169]

This source was first cited in relation to the issue of the halakhic definition of maternity in relation to assisted conception in 1924, and it has figured in the literature ever since that time.[170] Modern commentators who cite it in support of their halakhic conclusions deal with the issue of its aggadic status by insisting that they are only using it as a supporting argument. The main legal source for establishing birth as the definition of maternity lies in the talmudic source discussed in the previous section.[171] The aggadic account of Dinah's birth simply provides extra support for this definition. They also point out that the use of aggadic material is a feature of new areas of Jewish law in which there is not a great deal of definitive legal material available.[172]

The second widely used aggadic source in this area is a talmudic passage[173] discussing the verse in the Book of Esther in which it is written that Mordekhai had cared for Esther 'upon the death of her father and mother', and that 'she had no father or mother'.[174] According to the Talmud, the apparently redundant phrase 'she had no mother or father' serves to indicate that not only was Esther an orphan from a very early age, but her parents died before either of them had a chance to become a fully legal parent under Jewish law. Since it is assumed that Esther's mother did give birth to her, it is evident she died in the course of childbirth, i.e. prior to the establishment of legal maternity. Birth, and not conception, defines maternity.[175] This source, too, is subject to the qualification that its pedigree is aggadic, and it is adduced only as supporting evidence of the birth mother's status as sole mother in discussions of surrogacy in Jewish law.[176]

The issue of aggadic influence on Jewish biomedical law is the subject of much discussion in contemporary halakhic literature.[177] A novel approach, advanced by R. Ezra Bick,[178] is that the formal distinction between *halakhah*

---

[169] According to a talmudic version of this *aggadah*, the foetuses underwent sex changes *in utero*, rather than switching wombs (*Berakhot, 60a; Yerushalmi Berakhot,* 9: 3).This is also the version adopted in *Bereshith Rabbah,* 72: 6 and *Midrash Tanhuma, Vayeze,* no. 8.

[170] See Bleich, *Contemporary Halakhic Problems,* 247, n. 18.   [171] *Yevamot,* 97b.

[172] This is the position adopted by Hirshler, 'Test Tube Babies', 320, who summarizes: 'For even though halakhic principles are not derived from aggadic sources, the latter may be used as supportive evidence.' See also Bleich, *Contemporary Halakhic Problems,* 248.

[173] *Megillah,* 13a.   [174] Esther 2: 7.

[175] See R. Joseph Engel, *Beth Haozar, erekh av.* See also n. 138 in which reference is made to the view of R. Akiva Eiger that legal paternity is established once the pregnancy becomes recognized, i.e. at the beginning of the first trimester. This view is supported by a parallel inference from the verse in Esther i.e. her father died before he became a legal parent, and the assumption is that this took place at the time that the pregnancy became recognized.

[176] See Bleich, *Contemporary Halakhic Problems,* 250.

[177] See sources cited in *Encyclopaedia of Jewish Medical Ethics,* ii. 135 n. 63.

[178] See the sources cited in n. 126.

and *aggadah* should be deliberately blurred, and aggadic sources should be used without any reservation in the area of biomedical *halakhah*. This approach is based upon the theory that all *halakhah* is ultimately derived from underlying moral and theological concepts, which invariably find expression in the texts of the *aggadah*. Biomedical *halakhah* has its roots in concepts relating to the nature of family relationships and procreation. In most areas of Jewish law, there is a sufficiently rich corpus of strictly legal material upon which to base halakhic decisions, and the underlying concepts merely serve in an explanatory role, or on rare occasions, as guides in particularly complex cases. In the biomedical context, however, the fast pace of scientific and technological development has produced a situation in which there is simply not enough purely legal material upon which to base halakhic decisions. It therefore makes sense to go directly to the relevant aggadic sources in order to cull the underlying concepts and use them as the basis for practical decisions. In the course of time it is to be expected that a body of definitive law will emerge in this area that will contain sufficient legal material for decision-making, obviating the need to refer to aggadic sources for this purpose. Until then, *aggadah* ought to play an important role in providing solutions for practical problems such as the definition of maternity. In fact, R. Bick opts for an original approach to the establishment of maternity, since he favours conception rather than birth. His solution is based upon traditional moral, philosophical, and mystical notions of family life, all of which find their expression in texts of an aggadic, as opposed to a halakhic nature.

R. Bleich disagrees with the idea that *aggadah* should be used as the basis for halakhic decisions in this area, and maintains that there is sufficient halakhic material for dealing with issues such as maternity in a genetic age without having recourse to 'inappropriate analogies, construction of conceptual models and derivations of halakhic norms from philosophical or aggadic notions'.[179] The answer, according to his view, is to apply the normal canons of halakhic decision-making, and especially its wide range of secondary principles, which are specifically aimed at areas characterized by a paucity of normative material. As an example of such a principle, he offers his double maternity approach, discussed above. Since there is a genuine legal doubt as to maternity, the secondary principle of maximum stringency comes into play, and for the purposes of consanguinity and other prohibitions, the product of a surrogacy procedure has two mothers—the egg donor and the birth mother. In R. Bleich's view, therefore, there is no need to depart from the strict separation between *halakhah* and *aggadah*, which is one of the classical doctrines of Jewish law.

[179] J. D. Bleich, 'Maternal Identity Revisited', *Tradition*, 28 (1993), 56.

Upon reflection, there would appear to be some truth in both positions. Even if it is possible, as R. Bleich maintains, to resolve every problem using secondary, if not primary principles, the fact is that the halakhic authorities of the past have always been sensitive to the extra-legal aspects of their decisions in these areas, and this sensitivity has always shaped those decisions. At the same time, however, forsaking the legal approach in favour of a purely extra-legal one, as R. Bick appears to be suggesting, may provide more immediate satisfaction, but it will surely result in the loss of the element of certainty, which is so vital for the existence of any legal system, including the *halakhah*. The approach adopted by the majority of authorities, as we have seen throughout the present chapter, is to seek to establish the legal foundations of any particular issue, and then to proceed to the extra-legal elements, where relevant. A similar approach emerged from our discussion of abortion *halakhah* in Chapter 1. Evidently, all biomedical *halakhah* requires both legal rigour and extra-legal sensibility—in that order.

8. PROCREATIVE OBLIGATION AND PROCREATIVE AUTONOMY IN JEWISH AND ISRAELI LAW

As we have seen in the course of this chapter, procreation is a halakhic obligation, and the restrictions imposed upon the use of assisted procreation are couched in terms of halakhic concerns ranging from the fear of adultery and incest to problems of maternal and Jewish identity. This does not mean that halakhic authorities are not sensitive to the powerful human desire to have a child, or that their decisions may not have been influenced by a recognition of this desire. Indeed, authorities such as R. Feinstein and R. Nebenzahl explicitly mention the distress of the infertile parents as factors in their lenient decisions. Nevertheless, it is within the framework of the interlocking halakhic obligations affecting procreation and its various consequences that these authorities arrive at their rulings. They achieve their results within the system, not outside it. Put in somewhat different terminology, procreative autonomy is not an independent goal within the halakhic system, and halakhic rules are not subordinated to the desire of people to give birth. This is in contrast to the majority of modern, liberal legal systems, in which procreative autonomy is regarded as an independent value to which the law should give expression wherever possible, and rights discourse is extensive in relation to legal problems in this area. Jewish law may be said to recognize a limited principle of autonomy, in the sense that like morality, autonomy flourishes at the periphery rather than at the heart of the *halakhah*. A full discussion of the nature of this limited autonomy will be found in Chapter 4 in relation to the halakhically mandated right of a patient to refuse life-saving medical treatment, and the topic is revisited in the Conclusion.

In this final section, we will describe an Israeli case involving a dispute between biological parents as to the fate of their frozen embryos. In dealing with this dispute, one of the Supreme Court justices adverted to the underlying obligatory approach to procreation in Jewish law and the contrast between this approach and that of modern, secular rights-driven jurisprudence. The present section concludes our discussion of assisted reproduction in Jewish law, and places it in a wider, comparative context.

Ruthy and Danny Nahmani were married in Haifa in 1984. Three years later, Ruthy had a hysterectomy in the course of surgery for the treatment of cancer. Prior to the operation, a number of her eggs were removed and fertilized with Danny's sperm. The embryos were then frozen, and since it was not permitted under Israeli law in 1987 to implant an embryo in a woman other than the egg donor,[180] the Nahmanis applied to the High Court for permission to send the embryos to California for implantation into a surrogate mother. Eventually, the High Court gave its permission to proceed,[181] but by that time, the Nahmanis had separated, and Danny was living with another woman who had given birth naturally to a baby girl. He had also initiated divorce proceedings in the Rabbinical courts. Upon Danny's formal withdrawal of consent to the dispatch of the embryos to the United States, Ruthy petitioned the Haifa District Court to recognize her right to have the embryos implanted in a surrogate mother, despite her husband's withdrawal of consent.

In the Haifa District Court,[182] Ariel J. found in favour of Ruthy Nahmani. This finding was based upon the view that Danny Nahmani's original consent to the fertilization and storage of his wife's eggs covered

---

[180] Public Health Ordinance (In Vitro Fertilization), 5747–1987. The position has now changed and surrogacy is legal under the new Surrogacy Law, 5756–1996. According to this law, a fertilized egg may be placed in a woman for the purpose of transferring the child born to her to the adoptive parents at birth. Amongst the salient features of the new law are the provision that, in the first instance, the surrogate ought to be a single woman and a member of the same faith as the adoptive parents (section 2). The provision regarding the single status of the surrogate is aimed at ensuring that even according to R. Teitelbaum's minority position according to which the introduction of donor sperm (or, in this case, a sperm which has already fertilized an egg) into the womb of a married woman constitutes adultery, the child of a surrogate will not be a *mamzer*. However, this provision applies in the first instance only. If the adoptive parents have made every effort to find a single surrogate, but are unable to do so, then the Surrogacy Committee may permit the use of a married surrogate in accordance with the liberal view of R. Feinstein (for the debate between these two authorities, see s. 2 above). The range of adoptive parents is restricted to heterosexual couples (section 1). The surrogate mother may not be related to the adoptive parents; the sperm for the *in vitro* fertilization must be that of the adoptive father and the egg must not come from the surrogate mother (section 2). The Law also provides for the setting up of a committee consisting of medical social and religious personnel to supervise surrogacies (section 3).

[181] *Nahmani v. Minister of Health*, HC 1237/90.

[182] *Nahmani v. Nahmani* PM 599/92.

the entire reproductive process, including implantation in a surrogate. Although the relationship between the Nahmanis had changed drastically since the original agreement, it was Danny who was responsible for the change. He was therefore estopped[183] from arguing the fact of changed circumstances as justification for withdrawing his permission to implant the embryos. The Court also held, following the common law tradition in abortion cases, that it was the mother's right to determine the fate of an embryo, not that of the father.[184] It was also argued by the Court that allowing Danny to block the implantation process might provide him with an unfair advantage in divorce proceedings.

The Supreme Court decision in *Nahmani* v. *Nahmani*,[185] on the other hand, went in favour of Danny Nahmani. The majority opinion was written by Strassberg-Cohen J., who began by pointing out that in modern legal thinking, parenthood was a right and not an obligation, and therefore, no individual could be forced to become a parent against his or her will. Even under Jewish law, a woman who refuses to have sexual relations with her husband is not compelled to do so in order to help him fulfil the commandment of procreation, although she may be divorced as a result of her refusal.[186] In modern, liberal jurisprudence, procreative autonomy, which includes the right not to procreate, is an integral part of the right to be a parent.[187]

Strassberg-Cohen J. accepted the view that under Israeli law, a father enjoys the same rights in relation to an artificially fertilized embryo, as does a mother in relation to the foetus she carries in her womb. The superior legal status of the mother *vis-à-vis* her foetus in the common law tradition on abortion is a reflection of the fact that she alone carries the foetus inside her body. This fact is irrelevant in the case of IVF, since the foetus is in a test tube. Thus, just as the father may not veto his wife's decision to abort her foetus in legally justifiable circumstances, so a mother cannot proceed in defiance of the father's refusal to become a parent in an *in vitro* fertilization situation.[188]

A survey of different legislative and judicial approaches to artificial reproduction also strengthens Danny's case. The general principle in

---

[183] For this doctrine of English equity, see *Central London Property Trust Ltd.* v. *High Trees House Ltd.*, [1947] KB 130; *Amalgamated Property Co. Ltd.* v. *Texas Bank Ltd.* [1982] QB 84.

[184] *Paton* v. *Trustees of British Pregnancy Advisory Services* (1978) 2 All ER 987; *Planned Parenthood of Central Missouri* v. *Danforth* 428 US (1976) 52. This principle was also applied in the Israeli case of *A* v. *B*, CA 413/80, PD 35 (3) 60.

[185] *Nahmani* v. *Nahmani*, CA 5587/93, PD 49 (1) 485.

[186] In certain cases, she will also lose her *ketubah* (Maimonides, *Hilkhot Ishut*, 15: 5; *Shulhan Arukh, Even Haezer*, 154: 4).

[187] See *Davis* v. *Davis*, 842 SW 2d 588 (Tenn. Sup. Ct., 1992) 601.

[188] This view was advanced in *A.* v. *B.*, CA 413/80, PD 35 (3) 57. Also see: C. Shalev, 'A Man's Right to be Equal: The Abortion Issue', *Israel Law Review*, 18 (1984), 381; C. Ganz, 'The Frozen Embryos of the Nahmani Couple' (Heb.), *Iyyunei Mishpat*, 18 (1994), 83 ff.

English, American, Australian, and Canadian law is that consent to implantation of the embryo in a surrogate mother may be revoked by either party to the surrogacy arrangement prior to the actual implantation.[189] Moreover, there is a provision in some legislatures for the destruction of the embryos in such circumstances. In Israeli law, there is no clear proof that the absence of any reference in the 1987 Public Health Ordinance to revocation of consent prior to implantation was intended to restrict the requirement of consent to the beginning of the whole process; in any case, the 1991 Aloni Committee on surrogacy clearly recommended that the principle of the revocability of consent be adopted right up until implantation.[190]

In a detailed discussion of the applicability of the principles of contract law to IVF agreements, Strassberg-Cohen J. tended to the view that doctrines such as frustration of contract, specific performance, incomplete contracts, and estoppel were not suitable for application in the area of personal status. Agreements or promises to marry are probably the closest type of contract to the agreement between the Nahmanis, and it is abundantly clear that even in jurisdictions in which such promises still have legal force, their breach entails the payment of damages for injuries caused, not decrees for specific performance, which was in effect what Ruthy was asking from the Court.[191]

On the issue of the status of the fertilized eggs, the Court preferred the term 'pre-embryo' used in the American case of *Davis* v. *Davis*,[192] and followed the general approach of a number of modern common law jurisdictions, according to which no independent status is granted to a pre-embryo.[193] In this context, it is noteworthy that Jewish law draws a basic distinction between biological status and legal personality,[194] and the general consensus amongst contemporary halakhic authorities is that no foetus is fully alive for legal purposes until a much later stage of pregnancy than that at which the freezing of fertilized eggs takes place.[195]

---

[189] See Human Fertilization and Embryology Act, 1990 section 12, schedule 3, sec. 4; C. Corns, 'Deciding the Fate of Frozen Embryos', *Law Institute Journal*, 64 (1990) 273; B. Dickens, 'The Ontario Law Reform Commission Project on Human Artificial Reproduction' in S. McLean (ed.), *Law Reform and Human Reproduction* (Dartmouth 1992), 69.

[190] Report on In Vitro Fertilization (Ministry of Justice, Jerusalem, 1994), 36. This is the approach adopted in the new Surrogacy Law 5756-1996, section 5(c). Under this law, withdrawal of consent must be authorized by the supervisory committee.

[191] For the relevant Israeli law on estoppel, see D. Friedman and N. Cohen, *Contracts* (Tel Aviv, 1991), 1–93, 220, 368–9, 532–3, 642–57.

[192] See *Davis* v. *Davis*, 842 SW 2d 588 (Tenn. Sup. Ct., 1992), 601.

[193] See n. 189. For another view, according to which some status is given to fertilized eggs; see L. Waller, 'The Law and Infertility—The Victorian Experience', in McLead (ed.), *Law, Reform and Human Reproduction*, 25.   [194] See pp. 12–13.

[195] Steinberg, *Encyclopaedia of Jewish Medical Ethics* v. 122–8.

Strassberg-Cohen J. concluded her judgment with a remark on the issue of the welfare of the child. In her view, the widespread phenomenon of single-parent families, together with the eminent suitability of Ruthy Nahmani for motherhood, meant that the welfare of the child was not a major issue in the present case. Ruthy's petition was, nevertheless, rejected for the reasons outlined above.

In the course of her decision, Strassberg-Cohen J. referred to a halakhic decision on this case by R. Saul Yisraeli, a member of the Rabbinical Court of Appeals in Jerusalem. According to R. Yisraeli, the major issues in this case are the ownership of the foetus, the rules governing a partnership in Jewish law, and the halakhic position with regard to IVF and surrogacy. Under biblical law, it is evident that a husband possesses ownership rights in his foetus, since a person who causes his wife to miscarry is obliged to pay him monetary compensation.[196] Now, although there is a dispute amongst the medieval authorities as to whether the compensation is paid to the husband because he owns the foetus, or in his role as receiver of his wife's income,[197] it is generally agreed that the husband's consent is necessary in order to decide the fate of a foetus; indeed, this requirement is cited in the *responsa* literature in relation to situations that do not fall squarely within the rubric of abortion performed for the sake of saving maternal life.[198] It thus appears that it is the father, rather than the mother, who owns the foetus in Jewish law.

R. Yisraeli's primary argument is drawn from the rules governing partnerships in the *halakhah*. Under talmudic law, a valid partnership exists if two parties agree to enter into a common enterprise and both donate material to it. Unilateral dissolution of a partnership is, prima facie, illegal.[199] Nevertheless, there is provision for withdrawing as a result of duress, e.g. sickness, death, or any other factor constituting a significant change in the circumstances of the defaulting partner.[200] R. Yisraeli concludes that the surrogacy agreement between the Nahmanis constituted a valid partnership in Jewish law. However, the separation between Ruthy and Danny was such a significant change in the circumstances of the original agreement that it amounted to the level of duress required for the

---

[196] Exod. 21: 22. This argument was discussed by Elon J. in *A* v. *B* (see n. 188) and provided the basis for his minority opinion that the father of the foetus ought to be heard by the abortion board, although he has no right of standing and certainly no veto.

[197] Tosafot, *Bava Kamma*, 43a, *s.v. gerushah*; *Piskei Harosh, Bava Kamma*, 5 no. 5; Maimonides, *Hilkhot Hovel Umazzik*, 4: 1–4.

[198] Resp. *Ziz Eliezer*, 9 no. 51; no. 101; Resp. *She'elat Yeshurun*, no. 39.

[199] *Bava Mezia*, 68a; Maimonides, *Hilkhot Shekhenim*, 8: 1; *Shulhan Arukh, Hoshen Mishpat*, 176: 2. [200] *Shulhan Arukh, Hoshen Mishpat*, 333: 5.

dissolution of the partnership. In the final analysis, therefore, Danny Nahmani is not bound by his original agreement with Ruthy:

The circumstances of the Nahmani case constitute duress under the *halakhah* governing partnership and hence, the husband who is, in effect, a partner with ownership rights in the assets of the partnership may not be forced to accede to the wishes of his wife. The proper course is either to destroy the material in question, or, if the wife objects, to preserve it in its present frozen form.[201]

R. Yisraeli also raises the question of the halakhic propriety of surrogacy arrangements in the first instance, and expresses strong reservations with regard to their halakhic status, especially in the light of the doubts with regard to the establishment of maternity that were outlined in section 6. In the present case, however, the fertilization of the eggs is a *fait accomplit*, and the question arises only with regard to their implantation into a surrogate. In such a case, the major issue is whether or not the original agreement is still binding; according to R. Yisraeli, the answer is in the negative.

The conclusion reached by R. Yisraeli in his *responsum* was cited with approval in the majority decision in *Nahmani*, and a similar conclusion was reached in an essay written by the Head of the Haifa District Rabbinical Court at the time the dispute between the Nahmanis became public knowledge.[202]

In his minority decision in *Nahmani v. Nahmani*, Tal J. reached a different conclusion and ruled in favour of Ruthy. In his opinion, justice requires that Ruthy, and not only Danny, be given a chance to build up a family. Danny Nahmani left his legally wedded wife, and now wishes to extinguish her last hope of becoming a genetic mother, while he is enjoying his new family. In these circumstances, it would be unjust for the Court to lend its support to Danny; the only just solution is one which also gives Ruthy the chance to have her own child.

In terms of the issue of the balance of rights between the Nahmanis, Tal J. argued that since Ruthy Nahmani had borne the brunt—both physical and emotional—of the IVF procedure, her right to have a child was superior to Danny's right to avoid fatherhood. In this context, he cited the talmudic rule that 'the side which changes the situation is always at a disadvantage'.[203] According to Tal J., the doctrine of estoppel is applicable to the present case, and since Danny Nahmani himself produced the changed circumstances, he must 'always be at a disadvantage'.

---

[201] 'The Ownership of Fertilized Embryos' (Heb.), in *Encyclopaedia of Jewish Medical Ethics*, iv. 41–2.

[202] S. Shelush, 'The Use of Host Mothers' (Heb.), *Bitaon Hamoezah Hadati Haifa*, 39 (1992), 31.   [203] *Bava Mezia*, 6: 1.

Tal J. wrote that in his view, enforced fatherhood is a lesser evil than enforced childlessness. He also used halakhic sources to argue that Danny Nahmani was obliged to provide his wife with a child, even if their ways were to part and their relationship was to come to an end. Under talmudic law, a woman is entitled to a divorce if, after ten years, her husband is not able to provide her with a child. Indeed, according to R. Nahman, the husband is to be compelled to divorce his wife in such a case, in order that she may marry another man and receive the support of children in her old age.[204] The *halakhah* thus recognizes a woman's need to have a child and legitimates the use of compulsion in order to clear the way for her to be released from a childless marriage in order to remarry.[205] Pressure may, therefore, be used against Danny in order to clear the way for Ruthy to have her child.

Tal J. recognized the conflicting opinion of R. Yisraeli as to the halakhic position in the present case, and simply pointed out that the problem was a new one and it was to be expected that there would be different halakhic approaches to it. It is noteworthy that R. Yisraeli also voiced his disapproval of surrogacy arrangements in general, and it is not inconceivable that his decision to rule in favour of Danny by applying the *halakhah* governing partnership may have been influenced in part by this disapproval. In any case, Tal J.'s emphasis on the concept of obligation, which is the major systemic feature of Jewish reproductive law and the fundamental difference between the *halakhah* and modern, liberal legal systems in this area, constitutes the pivotal point in his decision.

Support for Tal J.'s contention that the halakhic position on this matter is still being formulated and is, therefore, open to debate may be found in the fact that the two Chief Rabbis of Israel were divided in their opinions on the *Nahmani* case, with the Ashkenazi Chief Rabbi upholding Ruthy's right to be a mother, and the Sephardi Chief Rabbi maintaining that it is the father's right to determine the fate of embryos fertilized with his sperm. Had there been a definitive halakhic position, one may have expected the Chief Rabbinate to have issued a single, uncontroversial ruling.

A further hearing of the case was held before an expanded bench of the Supreme Court, and on 12 September 1996, this bench found in favour of Ruthy Nahmani.[206] Most of the majority judges held that since there was no clear law applicable to the case at hand, the correct course was to turn to the demands of individual justice which, in this particular case, favoured Ruthy over Danny. Others held that Ruthy's right to be a mother in this case was superior to Danny's right not to be a father. It was also suggested by two members of the majority that the potential for life in the fertilized eggs

---

[204] *Yevamot*, 65b.   [205] *Shulhan Arukh, Even Haezer*, 154: 3.
[206] *Nahmani v. Nahmani* FH 2401/95, PD 50 (4) 661.

shifted the balance in favour of Ruthy Nahmani. The minority urged caution in forsaking the dictates of the law for the highly nebulous concept of individual justice, and their decisions focused on the issues of contract and consent, with a de-emphasis of the question of parental rights.

Tal J. reiterated the obligatory nature of procreation according to Jewish law, and the argument that in the present case, a decision in favour of Ruthy represents the demands of justice as well as of law.

Tal. J.'s judgment in the *Nahmani* case brings out, *inter alia*, the difference between the concept of procreation as an obligation in Jewish law, and the rights-oriented approach to procreation adopted by general jurisprudence. Jewish law looks with favour upon the use of medical technology to help people achieve their desire to have children; it does not view it as a right. Parental desires must be fitted into the halakhic grid, not superimposed upon it. The most important lesson to be learned from the halakhic approach is probably that procreative responsibility is as important, if not more so, than procreative autonomy. Without adequate education in the responsibilities of procreation, as well as its privileges, a technology of hope may be transformed into a tool of abuse. It might not be a bad thing if general bioethics also leavened its strong rights discourse with a good dose of procreative responsibility.

3
Genetics

1. INTRODUCTORY REMARKS

The major developments to have taken place in medical science in recent years are in the field of genetics,[1] promising to usher in a dramatic new era in which disease, as we know it, will be overcome and the human body will be programmed to resist most of the conditions that currently bring about decline and premature death.[2] At the same time, genetics is regarded by some as a perilous science, the results of which will be loss of human dignity and the development of a society divided between a genetic aristocracy and a genetic underclass.[3] Presumably, not all the medical benefits promised will come to pass, nor will all the worst fears of the critics be realized. The full extent of the therapeutic impact of the new genetics has yet to be established with any certainty, and the same may be said of its moral, legal, and social implications. It is, therefore, necessary to proceed with caution in attempting to outline the halakhic position in this area.

Steinberg's point about the need for halakhic authorities to be experts in science as well as law[4] is particularly apt in relation to genetics. The novelty of the field and the tremendously fast rate of new discoveries within it mean that a great deal of scientific expertise is needed in order to understand fully the potential legal and moral implications of any proposed procedure or treatment. Snap judgements based on insufficient scientific evidence bring the *halakhah* into disrepute, and eventually need to be reversed. The wiser course is to proceed gradually, on the basis of sound science.

There would appear to be no principled halakhic opposition to genetic therapy, provided that it answers to the criterion applicable to all forms of medical treatment, i.e. it is a 'well-tried cure'.[5] As already observed, the

---

[1] See *Our Genetic Future* (British Medical Association, Oxford, 1992); *Human Genetics: The Science and its Consequences* (Science and Technology Committee of the House of Commons, HMSS, London, 1995). For an overview of genetics and *halakhah* see A. Steinberg, *Encyclopaedia of Jewish Medical Ethics*, 6 vols. (Jerusalem, 1988–98), vi. 545 ff.

[2] See 'The Future of Drugs', *Time*, 15 January 2001, 33.

[3] See T. Wilkie, *Perilous Knowledge* (London, 1994).

[4] See *Encyclopaedia of Jewish Medical Ethics*, ii. 158–66.   [5] See Ch. 4 nn. 65–7.

onus of proving that a particular therapy is not permitted is upon the prohibitionist,[6] and until a procedure is found to be contrary to a specific halakhic norm, it may be assumed that it is permitted.

The aim of the present chapter is to sketch the outline of a general halakhic approach to modern genetics, and to address a number of issues in somewhat greater detail. These issues include the abortion of genetically defective foetuses, the preservation of genetic privacy, the theological issue of genetic determinism, and cloning.

2. HEREDITY AND GENETICS IN THE *HALAKHAH*

Awareness of the role of heredity in determining health goes back to ancient times.[7] The talmudic prohibition on marrying into a family of established lepers or epileptics is based upon the understanding that these diseases may be passed on by parents to their children.[8] A similar understanding underlies the prohibition on circumcising the third son in a family in which two boys have already died of blood loss resulting from the procedure.[9] The deaths of two boys indicate the existence of a hereditary

---

[6] See Ch. 2 n. 17.

[7] It has been suggested that the earliest reference to modern genetics in Jewish sources is the biblical passage describing the methods used by Jacob to receive his wages for his many years of faithful service as a shepherd tending the sheep of Laban, his father-in-law (Gen. 30: 31–43; 31: 7–12). Jacob, fearing that Laban would not reward him fairly for his services, asked for payment in the form of all the 'streaked, spotted and grizzled' lambs born to the monochromatic ewes in his charge. In terms of the existing ratio between monochromatic and streaked ewes at the time of the request, this seemed to be a very modest demand on Jacob's part and even the miserly Laban would have no problem in accepting it. In order to obtain a much larger number of lambs, however, the Bible begins by recording that Jacob placed streaked rods in front of Laban's ewes when they were in heat, with the result that an unusually large number of streaked lambs were born over a number of lambing seasons. This strategy accords with the now discredited theory of Lamarck on the influence of the environment on hereditary characteristics. Further on in the passage, however, we are told that God provided Jacob with a vision to the effect that all the rams impregnating the ewes were of the streaked variety. On the assumption that it was this knowledge, rather than the Lamarckian method exemplified in the streaked-rods ploy that constituted the key to Jacob's success, it is arguable that the purpose of the vision was to point out to Jacob one of the cardinal tenets of Mendelian genetics, i.e. the concept of the recessive gene. God showed Jacob that many of the monochromatic ewes carried streaked genes and as a result, when mated with streaked rams, the streaked genes would express themselves in the colouring of the offspring. This did indeed happen and Jacob ended up owning a significant proportion of Laban's flocks (W. Etkin, 'Jacob's Cattle and Modern Genetics', *Tradition*, 7 (1965), 5; *Encyclopaedia Judaica*, iv. 1024–6).

[8] *Yevamot*, 64b; *Bekhorot*, 45b; *Shulhan Arukh, Even Haezer*, 2: 7. On heredity in the *halakhah*, see R. Shlomo Zevin, *Leor Hahalakhah*, 188.

[9] *Yevamot*, 64b; *Shulhan Arukh, Yoreh Deah*, 263: 2–3. The rule also applies to siblings, i.e. if two sisters each lose a boy to circumcision-induced exsanguination, then the third sister's son is not circumcised.

blood disease in the family which, it is assumed, will also cause the death of the third son if he is circumcised. Since the preservation of human life overrides the obligation to circumcise, the third boy is left uncircumcised. Presumably, the hereditary blood disease mentioned by the Talmud is haemophilia, which we now know to be a sex-linked genetic disease passed on by the mother.[10] Both the Talmud[11] and Maimonides[12] imply that the disease is restricted to the maternal line, a position that accords with the modern, genetic understanding of the way in which haemophilia is transferred.

A firm ruling confining the prohibition on circumcising the third son to the offspring of the same mother was made by R. Alexander Susslin Hacohen: 'I was asked concerning a man who had lost two sons as a result of circumcision, and then his wife died. He married another woman and when she gave birth to a son, I ruled that he should be circumcised...and this was done, and the boy lived.'[13] R. Hacohen based his decision upon the Talmud and Maimonides. He also cites an aggadic source according to which a person's blood is supplied by the mother, not the father. According to this source, the embryo receives its blood from the mother, hence, she must be the one who passes on blood diseases.[14]

Not all authorities are as adamant as R. Hacohen with regard to the restriction of the prohibition on circumcision to the sons of the same mother. R. Joseph Karo extends the prohibition to the third son of either the mother or the father.[15] In his glosses to the *Shulhan Arukh*, R. Moses Isserles cites R. Hacohen's opinion, but dismisses it as a minority view on the grounds that in relation to questions of life and death, it is always best to err on the side of life.[16] Now, it is certainly true that in matters of health, the *halakhah* is often more zealous in its protection of human life than is warranted by scientific and medical knowledge. A classical example of this tendency is the ruling that a person who claims that his life is in danger unless he eats on the Day of Atonement is permitted to take nourishment, notwithstanding expert medical opinion to the effect that fasting will do him no harm.[17] There is, however, a distinction between this example and the case of haemophilia. In relation to the Day of Atonement,

---

[10] See F. Rosner, *Medicine in the Bible and the Talmud* (Hoboken, NJ, 1997), 43–9.
[11] See n. 9.   [12] *Hilkhot Milah*, 1: 18.
[13] *Sefer Ha'agudah, Perek Rabbi Eliezer*, no. 164.
[14] *Niddah*, 31a. The Talmud opines that a child receives its white substances, e.g. bones and the white of the eye from its father, and its red substances, e.g. blood and the black of the eye from the mother. Also see *Turei Zahav, Yoreh Deah*, 263: 2.
[15] *Shulhan Arukh, Yoreh Deah*, 263: 2. His source is a ruling by R. Manoah, a 13th-cent. Narbonese scholar, cited in *Beth Yosef, Yoreh Deah*, 263, s.v. *vekatav R. Manoah*.
[16] *Yoreh Deah*, 263: 2.   [17] *Shulhan Arukh, Orah Hayyim*, 328: 10.

the issue is the definitive nature of a medical diagnosis regarding the patient's ability to fast. Since most doctors would not lay claim—even today—to infallibility in this type of situation, it is not unreasonable to err on the side of caution. By contrast, restriction of the gene responsible for haemophilia to the maternal line is a part of contemporary science, and as such, the rule about erring on the side of life in situations of doubt is irrelevant. The law, therefore, ought to be in accordance with R. Hacohen.[18] In fact, contemporary *halakhah* accepts that all decisions with regard to delaying or suspending circumcision are made on the basis of medical evidence, which means that, in effect, R. Hacohen's position is followed in practice.[19]

The above sources display an understanding of heredity and take it into account in the eugenic and medical contexts. Unlike heredity, the science of genetics is very modern. It began in the mid-nineteenth century with the Moravian monk, Gregor Mendel, who succeeded in demonstrating that inherited characteristics are determined by units of hereditary material passed down through the generations. In 1909, the Danish biologist Wilhelm Johannsen gave the name 'genes' to these units of hereditary material. The *halakhah* has also confronted issues raised by modern genetics. An early example is the question of continuing the traditional practice of a man marrying his niece in the genetic age. According to the Talmud, it is a virtuous act to marry a niece[20] and the proof-text is the biblical exhortation 'not to hide from your own flesh'.[21] The reason underlying this 'commandment of the sages'[22] is, apparently, to provide the financial support ensuing from marriage to family members rather than strangers. It has also been suggested that niece-marriages combine similarity of background with romantic love, thereby constituting an ideal basis for a successful marriage.[23] In the Middle Ages, the practice of niece-marriage was disapproved of by R. Judah the Hasid, the leading figure in the thirteenth-century Ashkenazi pietist movement, *Hasidei Ashkenaz*.[24] In his ethical will, known as *Zava'at Rabbi Yehuda Hehasid*,[25] R. Judah expresses

---

[18] On the effect of scientific progress on halakhic rulings, see Ch. 6 s. 2, on heart transplants.

[19] *Resp. Divrei Malkiel*, 3 no. 74. Also see *Nishmat Avraham, Yoreh Deah*, 263: 4; S. Rapoport, 'Defining Danger to Life in the Context of Circumcision' (Heb.), *Halakhah Urefuah*, 1 (1980), 283–91.					[20] *Yevamot*, 62b–63a; *Sanhedrin*, 76b.

[21] Isa. 58: 7.

[22] This is the term used by Maimonides to describe the obligation to marry a niece, which he extends to the daughters of both sisters and brothers (*Hilkhot Issurei Biah*, 2: 14). R. Moses Isserles incorporates this ruling into his glosses on the *Shulhan Arukh, Even Haezer*, 2: 6, 15: 25, although the question of a niece on the side of a brother is left open.

[23] *Maggid Mishneh, Hilkhot Issurei Biah*, 2: 14.

[24] See *Encyclopaedia Judaica*, xiii. 1377, and the sources cited in Ch. 5, n. 9.

[25] *Zava'at Rabbi Yehuda Hehasid*, no. 22.

strong disapproval of this practice, together with a whole range of unions that only the teachings of the *Hasidei Ashkenaz* pronounce unsuitable.[26] Although the will became part of the Ashkenazi religious tradition, it does not, of itself, possess normative halakhic status; consequently, any clash between it and the Talmud ought to be resolved in favour of the latter.[27]

By the beginning of the twentieth century, it was accepted medical knowledge that inbreeding, including marriages between uncles and nieces, caused a wide variety of genetically derived congenital defects and illnesses. In the light of this evidence, R. Elijah Klatzkin of Jerusalem was asked about the possibility of deviating from the talmudic position in order to prevent the birth of defective and diseased children. R. Klatzkin accepted the genetic findings, and cites the position adopted by R. Judah the Hasid as a basis for deviating from talmudic practice. He does, however, require a further argument in order to justify abolishing a practice recommended by the Talmud as a virtuous act, since R. Judah's will alone does not possess sufficient normative clout for such a step. R. Klatzkin proceeds to limit the scope of the talmudic recommendation to marry one's niece to cases prompted by pure altruism, where there is no ulterior motive such as the youth or physical charms of the niece. He does so by pointing out that the Bible generally forbids relatives from marrying each other.[28] In this respect, an uncle marrying a niece is an exception to the rule. As explained above, the reason for this exception is to ensure that young unmarried female relatives will be supported by older, established family members, and will not be condemned to poverty as a result of the non-availability of grooms outside the family. R. Klatzkin goes on to make the assumption that in order to ensure that marrying a niece would not be tainted by its resemblance to otherwise forbidden alliances, it must have been assumed by the Bible that only those with absolutely pure motives would enter such a marriage. According to R. Klatzkin, such purity of motive is a thing of the past. Today, the majority of uncles who marry their nieces do so on the basis of physical attraction alone. Consequently, R. Klatzkin rules that the better course is to avoid niece-marriages entirely. His ruling is consonant with both the Bible and the Talmud, as well as R. Judah's will. In fact, R. Klatzkin suggests that the purity of motive requirement is the authentic basis of R. Judah the Hasid's rejection of niece-marriages; it is not, as previously thought, a result of the peculiar approach of the *Hasidei Ashkenaz* towards spouse selection in general. Thus, there is no contradiction between the Talmud and R. Judah's ruling. The correct halakhic response to niece-marriage in the present era of

---

[26] See *Encyclopaedia Judaica*, vii. 1382.

[27] See *Resp. Noda Biyehuda*, 2, *Even Haezer*, no. 79; *Resp. Divrei Hayyim, Even Haezer*, no. 8.

[28] See Lev. 18. It is forbidden for a nephew to marry his aunt.

doubtful sincerity is articulated in R. Judah's will, and R. Klatzkin concludes that it is permissible to deviate from the idealized talmudic position and to follow advice based upon genetic knowledge.[29] R. Klatzkin
also refers to various mystical dangers inherent in the union of an uncle
and his niece, which are only avoidable when the motives for the marriage are absolutely pure.[30]

In the light of the above, it is evident that the prevention of hereditary
diseases has a long history in Jewish law. There is no evidence that the fact
that such diseases are the result of natural phenomena means that their
existence must be accepted in a passive fashion.[31] R. Klatzkin's *responsum*
demonstrates that the same approach is to be adopted in the genetic era.
Once recognized as diseases, genetic conditions are no different to non-
genetic maladies for halakhic purposes, and all the measures that should
be adopted with respect to disease prevention in general apply to genetic
defects. Measures to prevent the spread of illness must be undertaken
with respect to all forms of sickness; the fact that a particular malady has
its roots in genetic factors does not detract in any way from the obligation
under Jewish law to attempt to cure it.[32]

3. GENETICS AND ABORTION

One of the first major halakhic problems to arise in the area of genetic
disease prevention in recent times is the abortion of genetically defective
foetuses. As pointed out in Chapter 1,[33] this issue was the subject of a
heated debate between R. Waldenberg and R. Feinstein in the late 1970s
with regard to a foetus suffering from Tay-Sachs disease. Tay-Sachs is a
genetic disease of the immune system affecting Ashkenazi Jews of East
European origin. If two carriers procreate there is a 25 per cent chance that
their offspring will suffer from the disease. The disease results from an
enzyme deficiency caused by a defective gene and sets in by the time a

---

[29] This is the position adopted by modern authorities; see *Resp. Ziz Eliezer*, 15 no. 44.

[30] *Resp. Even Harosha*, no. 31. Also see *Yad Ramah, Sanhedrin*, 76b; *Appei Zutra, Even Haezer*,
2: 6. It is worthwhile mentioning that the purity of motive argument is also used to account
for the preference of *halitzah* over levirate marriage: see M. Elon (ed), *The Principles of Jewish
Law* (Jerusalem, 1974), 406.

[31] Whether or not there is any theological position in Judaism requiring passivity in the
face of disease in general, is a question that will be discussed in Ch. 4. For purposes of the
present chapter, it is assumed that such a position, even if it exists, is not the dominant one.

[32] See Ch. 4 s. 2.

[33] See Ch. 1 s. 5. The supporting arguments and proof-texts for most of the points in the
present section regarding Tay-Sachs and the debate between R. Waldenberg and R. Feinstein
are to be found in Ch. 1, unless indicated to the contrary. The emphasis in the present section
is on the genetic ramifications of the debate, rather than its significance for abortion *halakhah*.

baby afflicted with Tay-Sachs is 1 year old. The baby deteriorates steadily and dies before it reaches the age of 5. There is no cure. Since the early 1970s it has been possible to establish the existence of the disease by examining cells in the amniotic fluid at the fourteenth week of pregnancy; under today's methods, results can be obtained as early as the seventh week. The question as to whether it is halakhically permitted to abort a Tay-Sachs foetus was posed to R. Waldenberg in the late 1970s and was answered in the affirmative. This permission was later extended by R. Waldenberg to foetuses carrying the genetic defect that gives rise to Down Syndrome. It will be recalled that one of the principal precedents relied upon by R. Waldenberg to permit the abortion of the Tay-Sachs foetus was the decision of R. Jacob Emden to allow the abortion of a *mamzer* foetus. The *halakhah* recognizes a wide range of reasons for aborting a foetus, including the mental stress associated with giving birth to a *mamzer*. Such stress is certainly present in the case of a Tay-Sachs child, whose parents have no option but to stand by and watch their child die. Mental stress resulting from the birth of a severely handicapped child is also the basis for R. Waldenberg's permission to abort a Down Syndrome child, although in this case, he confines the permission to parents for whom the idea of bringing such a child into the world is so stressful that it is quite evident that they will be unable to cope with it in terms of both their own health and durability of their marriage.

It will be recalled that R. Feinstein analyses the halakhic sources on foeticide and abortion very differently to R. Waldenberg and reaches the opposite conclusion. According to R. Feinstein, permission to carry out therapeutic abortions in Jewish law is confined to a direct and immediate threat to the mother's life, and the prevention of future parental suffering is not a valid reason for aborting a foetus, even in a case such as Tay-Sachs in which the baby will definitely die before the age of 5. On this view, there would definitely be no justification for aborting a Down Syndrome foetus.

At the end of our lengthy discussion of these two views in the first chapter, it was argued that R. Feinstein's position is based upon the influential moral element in abortion *halakhah*, and that his particularly strong espousal of this element in relation to Tay-Sachs may have been the result, in part, of the fear that a permissive ruling in relation to Tay-Sachs would constitute the beginning of a slippery slope to abortions for non-therapeutic and purely eugenic reasons.[34] This fear would certainly become stronger as our knowledge of the genetic make-up of the human genome becomes more comprehensive, and the line between defective and less-than-perfect children becomes ever more blurred. However, whether the

[34] See Ch. 1 s. 6.

best way of dealing with this slippery slope is to condemn all genetically indicated abortions is questionable. In the long run, a more selective approach would probably be more effective. The line between the therapeutic and the eugenic is not an easy one to draw,[35] and tracing it in any particular case will undoubtedly require complex legal and moral input. The development of a halakhic doctrine in this area is a major challenge for the halakhists of the genetic age.

4. GENETIC TESTING

One of the major practical benefits of modern genetics is the ability to test for certain diseases at the very earliest stages. Once it is established that a particular individual will fall victim to a genetic condition, it is also possible to take action in order to prevent or limit that condition. For example, adult carriers of defective genes may be tested and advised against marrying each other in order to prevent serious diseases such as Tay-Sachs, cystic fibrosis, and neurofibromatosis amongst their offspring. Abortion is an option for foetuses testing positive for genetic conditions of this type. Finally, people are in a position to learn about their genetic dispositions to particular diseases, including a range of cancers and heart conditions, and general physical health. There is, however, a dark side to genetic testing, especially since it is often done on a mass scale and amongst specific populations. There is a risk that mass testing on a specific population will result mainly in stigmatization and discrimination. A classic example is the national screening programme for sickle-cell anaemia set up in the United States in the late 1960s and virtually scrapped a decade or so later.[36] This type of anaemia is a single-gene defect, and it has a high incidence amongst the black population. Mandatory screening programmes were introduced in several states but quickly became the focus of political and racial contention. Since there was no education as to basic issues such as the difference between carriers and those who actually had the disease, both groups were described as suffering from 'bad blood', and the general wisdom was that they were weak and unable to engage in any form of strenuous activity. Carriers of the gene were discriminated against in the job market and were denied insurance on the basis of their defective, though merely recessive gene. There was also basic ignorance with regard to the nature of the disease

---

[35] Sex-selection is an interesting example of what may be eugenic in one culture but therapeutic in another. As far as the present writer is aware, it has not yet appeared as a candidate for justifying abortion in Jewish law.

[36] See *Our Genetic Future*, 191–2; Wilkie, *Perilous Knowledge*, 97–111.

itself. Indeed, in some states laws were passed classifying sickle-cell anaemia as a contagious disease and requiring children suffering from the condition to stay away from school! Cases are on record of physicians assuming that patients were suffering from sickle-cell anaemia rather than acute appendicitis, for example, and their refusal to look beyond their original and mistaken diagnoses sometimes produced results of a fatal nature.

Another issue brought to the fore by the sickle-cell anaemia mass screening project was the gap between knowledge and therapy. Testing produces knowledge, but it does not guarantee a cure. In fact, the anaemia was incurable, and all that the testing did, because of the way it was handled, was to discriminate against both carriers and sufferers. Both were simply branded as invalids. Genetic counselling was not available at the time, and no actual therapeutic benefit accrued to any of the victims of the disease or participants in the screening programme.

On the basis of the sickle-cell experience, it became evident that genetic testing, especially on a mass scale, confronts us with a number of challenges. These include the avoidance of stigmatization and discrimination; the need to close the gap between diagnosis and treatment; the preservation of confidentiality; the importance of education regarding the significance of the results of the screening; and the necessity for counselling and follow-up care. Now, it is true that these challenges are not unique to genetics. However, since the knowledge obtained by means of genetic testing is so wide-ranging and includes actual diseases, predilections to diseases, and general physical and mental competence, the above-mentioned issues are more complex in the genetic context than in that of regular medicine. The time factor is especially significant since much of the testing is aimed at predicting future developments rather than diagnosing current problems. A decision to act now in order to prevent a serious disease in twenty years time raises problems that are not encountered on a day-to-day basis in standard medical practice. These and other features of genetic testing give rise to a number of moral and legal problems that are widely discussed in the general literature in this area.[37]

In the aftermath of the sickle-cell anaemia episode, a President's Commission was set up to investigate the area of mass genetic testing, and in 1983 it issued a report in which it recommended that the elements of confidentiality, counselling, voluntary as opposed to mandatory testing, and public education ought to be incorporated into any future screening programmes in the United States. It also pointed out the need for addressing these issues from a legal perspective and developing adequate models of control for the future.

---

[37] See the sources in nn. 1 and 3.

In contrast to the sickle-cell programme, the Tay-Sachs screening project of the 1980s, which also affected a particular group amongst the population, i.e. Jews of East European Ashkenazi origin, is often cited as an example of successful mass screening. A simple test determines whether or not a particular individual is carrying the defective gene. Mass screening to detect carriers is clearly an important step towards the eradication of the disease, since it will only strike a child whose parents both carry the defective gene. This time, the North American programme, which has since been copied in Israel and in Europe, proved to be extremely effective. Since its introduction the number of babies born with the disease all over the world has decreased quite significantly.

The success of the Tay-Sachs mass screening programme was due to a number of factors, including its voluntary nature, the education of the target population in relation to all aspects of the programme, the great efforts made to ensure confidentiality with respect to results, and the provision of serious guidance and professional counselling services for carriers. Much had been learned in the period between the sickle-cell project and the Tay-Sachs programme.

A special problem arose with regard to the ultra-Orthodox community in North America, the overwhelming majority of which is composed of Jews of East European ancestry. This community, whose co-operation was an important element in ensuring the success of the entire screening programme, is highly sensitive to the preservation of confidentiality in all matters relating to matchmaking and marriage. In order to introduce the programme into this sector of the community, special guidelines aimed at preserving a maximum of confidentiality in relation to the identities of Tay-Sachs carriers were introduced. These guidelines paved the way for the success of the screening programme in this numerically significant sector of the target population.[38]

The major challenge in crafting these guidelines was to strike the right balance between the halakhic prohibition on breaking a confidence and the obligation to inform a prospective bride or groom of the medical disabilities of the intended partner, especially in relation to any serious hereditary diseases which might affect their offspring. The halakhic basis for requiring the preservation of confidentiality is the biblical prohibition on talebearing.[39] This prohibition, which applies to both true and false statements,[40] extends to physicians as well as to the general population,[41]

---

[38] See F. Rosner, 'Tay-Sachs Disease: To Screen or Not to Screen', in F. Rosner and J. D. Bleich (eds.), *Jewish Bioethics* (New York, 1979), 178.   [39] Lev. 19: 16.
[40] *Pesahim*, 113b; Maimonides, *Hilkhot Deot*, 7: 2–3.   [41] *Resp. Ziz Eliezer*, 13 no. 104.

but it is suspended in any case in which the dissemination of information about a person is aimed at preventing serious harm to others. Indeed, any person who becomes aware that another individual is likely to harm someone, including a case in which important information about the health of a proposed spouse is deliberately withheld from the other party,[42] must inform the intended victim as soon as possible. Failure to do so will result in a breach of the biblical commandment 'not to stand idly by your neighbour's blood'.[43] Other sources cited in support of the obligation to break a confidence for the sake of preventing serious harm are the pursuer principle discussed in Chapter 1,[44] and the commandment to restore lost life, mentioned in Chapter 4.[45] In general, Jewish law places the prevention of danger at a significantly higher level than the preservation of confidentiality, and even if the physician promised the patient not to reveal a particular detail, he is justified in so doing if it is evident that withholding this information is likely to put another person in jeopardy.[46]

As already observed, withholding information about the medical condition of a potential spouse from his or her intended, especially when the particular condition has an effect on childbearing and infant health, is defined as serious harm in the context of the *halakhah* governing the breaking of a confidence. Consequently, there is no halakhic bar to running a screening programme for Tay-Sachs carriers and passing on the information to potential marriage partners, although care must be taken to ensure that the information is used solely for the purpose of preventing the marriage of two carriers and for no other end.

It ought to be noted that Jewish law does not recognize a strict duty of confidentiality placed upon a physician by virtue of his profession. Such a duty is found in the common law,[47] and its origins probably lie in ancient Greece during the time when physicians first emerged as a paid group of professionals, and one of the traits that marked them off from the amateur healer was the commitment to confidentiality.[48] The halakhic obligation to preserve confidences is a universal one, transcending all professional boundaries. The same goes for the obligation to break a confidence when the life, health, or general welfare of other people is at stake.[49]

[42] *Pithei Teshuvah, Orah Hayyim*, 156; *Resp. Helkhat Ya'acov*, 3 no. 336; *Resp. Yehave Da'at*, 4 no. 60; *Resp. Ziz Eliezer*, 16 no. 4.   [43] Lev. 19: 16.
[44] Ch. 1 n. 79.   [45] Ch. 4 n. 39.
[46] S. Rafael, 'Medical Confidentiality in a Halakhic Perspective' (Heb.), *Sefer Assia*, 3 (1983), 332–5.   [47] See I. Kennedy and A. Grubb, *Medical Law* (London, 1994), 637–73.
[48] L. Edelstein, *Ancient Medicine* (Baltimore, 1987), 37–8.
[49] For a comparative treatment of medical confidentiality, see D. Mendelson, 'Medical Confidentiality: Australian and Jewish Law', *Jewish Law Annual*, 12 (1997), 217–49.

The application of this complex of halakhic rules and principles to the issue of confidentiality paved the way for the successful implementation of the Tay-Sachs screening programme in the ultra-Orthodox community. Screening was not rejected outright because of the difficulties involved. Instead, the difficulties were addressed and then overcome. This is the type of richly textured casuistic approach that is necessary for dealing with many of the problems facing us in the genetic age.

5. GENE THERAPY

As far as Jewish law is concerned, there is no difference between genetic therapy and any other form of therapy.[50] The curing of disease is an important value in the *halakhah*, and any serious threat to human life over-rides all but the most serious of halakhic prohibitions. It was pointed out earlier that the *halakhah* recognizes the therapeutic validity of taking steps to prevent genetic diseases in the same way that it recognizes the validity of taking preventive steps in relation to non-genetic maladies. The legal core of the halakhic obligation to heal is the mandate to save life.[51] As a result, the wider the gap between a particular medical procedure and the direct saving of life, the less likely it is that the procedure will obtain full halakhic sanction. The major halakhic problem with regard to gene therapy, therefore, is the extent to which it is therapeutic rather than experimental. As long as it remains in the experimental category, its halakhic legitimacy is subject to the fairly restrictive rules governing medical experiments involving human beings in Jewish law. If and when gene therapy becomes standard medical treatment and is proved to be free of risk, it may be assumed that it, too, will receive the same halakhic support as standard medicine.[52]

At the present time, a number of diseases have been targeted by genetic therapy research, including cystic fibrosis, neurofibromatosis, muscular dystrophy, adenosine deaminase deficiency (ADA), cancer, and AIDS. However, the therapeutic value of the treatments administered in all these

[50] A. Rosenfeld, 'Judaism and Gene Design', in Rosner and Bleich (eds.), *Jewish Bioethics*, 401; F. Rosner, 'Genetic Engineering and Judaism', ibid. 417.

[51] See Ch. 4 s. 2 in which it is pointed out, *inter alia*, that if a physician treats a patient but fails to effect a cure, then the standard penalty for inadvertent homicide, i.e. exile, will apply. This is not the case in relation to a teacher who inadvertently kills a student in the course of teaching them Torah or a father who disciplines his son with fatal results. The reason for this discrepancy is the fact that whereas the teaching of Torah and the disciplining of children are independent *mitzvot*, medicine is a halakhically mandated activity only if life is actually saved.

[52] This issue has been addressed by the present writer in 'Medical Experiments on Human Beings in Jewish and Israeli Law', in *Israeli Reports to the 15th International Congress of Comparative Law*, ed. A. Rabello (Jerusalem, 1999), 129–44.

cases is still doubtful, and there are a number of problems that must be overcome before gene therapy becomes standard. One such problem is the use of viral vectors to deliver normal genes into cells that are malfunctioning as a result of damaged genes. These viruses may disrupt the DNA of the cells they infect, with harmful results. Furthermore, weakened viruses can conceivably change inside the body and regain their pathogenic character. A patient may also develop an immune reaction to the virus, resulting in the death of either the virus vector itself or the infected cells before the therapeutic gene has had a chance to help the patient. Non-viral methods for gene therapy are being studied, but they are very much in the experimental stage, and it will probably be decades before they are suitable for use in treating human genetic defects.[53]

The state of gene therapy in strictly therapeutic terms was recently summed up thus: 'Investigators have accomplished the requisite first steps; they have shown that transferred genes can be induced to function in the human body, at times for several years. So far, however, no approach has definitively improved the health of a single one of the more than 2000 patients who have enrolled in gene therapy trials worldwide.'[54] Until this situation changes, gene therapy will remain, at least from a halakhic perspective, more in the nature of experimentation than therapy. Once the situation does change, gene therapy will be no different from any other therapy: as already observed, all healing is endorsed by the *halakhah*.

A particular application of gene therapy that has become the subject of an ethical debate is germ-line therapy, involving the manipulation of the genetic code of future generations. Those opposed to human germ-line therapy base their opposition on three factors: the absence of clear scientific knowledge with regard to its long-term effects, the problems involved in carrying out the necessary research on embryos, and the possibility that other techniques such as pre-implantation are capable of achieving the same therapeutic goal, albeit in a less scientifically dramatic fashion.[55] In this context, it is noteworthy that in its 1995 Report, the Science and Technology Committee of the House of Commons recommended that 'the current prohibition on manipulation of a human germline at any stage without the approval of the Gene Therapy Committee' ought to remain in force.[56]

---

[53] See 'The Genetic Revolution', *Time*, 17 January 1994, 36; P. Felgner, 'Nonviral Strategies for Gene Therapy', *Scientific American*, 276 (1997), 86.

[54] See Felgner, 'Nonviral Strategies', 90.

[55] *Our Genetic Future*, 185. Also see Wilkie, *Perilous Knowledge*, 152–8, for a comment on the darker side of the prospects offered to society by somatic cell gene therapy, i.e. the correction of genetic defects or diseases in the body cells of a patient.

[56] Wilkie, *Perilous Knowledge*, 158–65; *Our Genetic Future*, 185–8.

The basic objection to germ-line therapy is that we are unaware of the full effects of this treatment, and we should therefore desist from passing on our possible mistakes to future generations. However, once the therapeutic benefits of genetic manipulation are proved beyond reasonable doubt, there would not appear to be any genuine distinction between the manipulation of regular cells and those of the germ line. The halakhic approach would probably proceed along lines similar to those suggested in the House of Commons Report, i.e. that nothing should be done with a view to providing genetically improved cells to future generations until it has been proved conclusively that the improvements are entirely risk-free.

The idea that great care should be exercised by those seeking to cure defects in future generations rather than in their own, may underlie a well-known talmudic passage describing how the dedicated and virtuous ruler of Judah, King Hezekiah, is informed that it is not within his authority to determine the fate of future generations and to prevent a son being born to him who is destined to undo all his good work in spreading the word of the Lord in Israel.[57] Now, although the future defect in this case is of a moral, rather than a physical nature, the principle of 'what have you to do with the secrets of the All-Merciful?' articulated in this passage indicates that Hezekiah's obligation to procreate overrides any reservations, even well-based ones, about the nature of his future progeny. Until germ-line therapy becomes well and truly standard, it would be best to follow the talmudic adage regarding the 'secrets of the All-Merciful' and ensure the proper fulfilment of all present responsibilities with regard to the treatment of today's sick. In this respect, the future ought to be left to take care of itself.

6. PATENTING GENETIC MATERIAL AND INFORMATION

The idea of patenting living organisms, especially parts of human bodies, is a legally controversial matter.[58] The debate is particularly heated in relation to human DNA and the genome project. One of the major objections to patent protection of human DNA is that it confers rights of ownership over human body parts, a notion that is repugnant to many commentators on both ethical and legal grounds. In the case of the human genome, it is also necessary to take into account the negative effects of

---

[57] *Berakhot*, 10a.
[58] See the debate surrounding the patenting of the Harvard oncomouse, a genetically modified mouse for use in cancer research: D. Manspeizer, 'Genetically Engineered Wonderland', *Rutgers Law Review*, 43 (1991), 417; R. Dresser, 'Ethical and Legal Issues in Patenting New Animal Life', *Journal of Jurimetrics*, 28 (1998), 399.

patenting upon the sharing of research results in what ought ideally to be an exercise in international co-operation, from both a scientific and a therapeutic perspective. Others, however, argue that patenting is the only realistic way of ensuring that the research will be funded and that the therapeutic promise of the genetic age will be realized.[59]

As far as Jewish law is concerned, the very existence of copyright and patent protection is a matter of debate. Although there is no direct reference to these concepts in classical Jewish law, the repetition of the biblical prohibition on the removal of a boundary marker[60] has been cited as an indication that the protection of exclusive rights to forms of property other than land is recognized by the *halakhah*. Indeed, it was on this basis that printers received protection for their works from the sixteenth century onwards.[61] The major justification for protecting printers from competition for a specified period after the first print run was that if no such protection were offered, printers would not undertake the heavy initial outlay necessary for publishing a work, and Torah study would thereby be neglected due to a dearth of books and the very high prices of existing copies. The novel question that arose in the nineteenth century concerned intellectual property: do authors possess a copyright in the ideas presented in their published works? A positive view on this point was expressed by R. Joseph Saul Nathanson, who based himself both upon the above-mentioned extension of the biblical prohibition on the removal of boundary markers and on 'the law of the land', which provided patents to inventors of various machines and useful artefacts.[62] R. Isaac Schmelkes, on the other hand, maintained that the cause of Torah study would not be furthered by copyrights on intellectual property, and the most he was prepared to concede was a limited restriction in time on the reprinting of the author's work.[63] The majority of views followed R. Schmelkes,[64] indicating that in a conflict between private ownership rights and the welfare of the community in the form of the encouragement of Torah study, the latter prevails. It is likely, therefore, that at the level of policy, sharing genetic information as part of a universal scheme for the betterment of health would also override the principle of patent and copyright. It is noteworthy that both R. Nathanson and R. Schmelkes find strong support for the idea of copyright in non-Jewish, as opposed to Jewish, legal sources.

---

[59] See *Human Genetics*, 64–73; Wilkie, *Perilous Knowledge*, 92–6; *Genetics News*, 13 (Sept/Oct. 1996), 4.   [60] Deut. 19: 14; 27: 17.

[61] See *Resp. Maharshal*, no. 89; I. Herzog, *The Main Institutes of Jewish Law* (London, 1965), i. 127–36; Elon (ed.), *Principles of Jewish Law*, 344–6.

[62] *Resp. Shoel Umeshiv*, 1 no. 44.   [63] *Resp. Beth Yizhak, Yoreh Deah*, 2 no. 75.

[64] See Elon (ed.), *Principles of Jewish Law*, 346.

Assuming that patenting is a halakhically valid enterprise, the next question is whether it is possible to take out a patent for genetic material. The issue that naturally presents itself for discussion in this context is the ownership of a person's body. The majority of authorities maintain that people hold their bodies in trust from God, and hence cannot be said to own them.[65] The Divine ownership principle ought not, however, to preclude the possibility of selling or patenting body parts in the absence of any halakhic provision to the contrary. After all, the same God who 'owns' human bodies is also entitled to allow for their disposal in certain circumstances.[66] Since God's will is expressed in the *halakhah*, the question needs to be answered at the halakhic level,[67] and if there is no specific prohibition on selling one's body, it would appear that it is permitted. Moreover, there is a minority view in the *halakhah* according to which people are the legal owners of their bodies.[68] As far as the sale of organs is concerned, there would seem to be no principled halakhic bar to such sales, especially if the donor is poverty-stricken and requires the fee for his own support or that of his family.[69] Naturally, there is a policy aspect here as well as a purely legal one, and this aspect would undoubtedly play a major role in shaping the *halakhah* in this area. Clearly, no halakhist would be in favour of a system in which the poor are reduced to supplying spare body parts for the wealthy.[70]

In conclusion, although there is probably no legal bar to patenting genetic material or even the human genome itself, the *halakhah* would undoubtedly insist upon rigorous legislative safeguards designed to protect human dignity and freedom before giving a *carte blanche* to patenting and private ownership in the genetic sphere.

7. GENETIC DETERMINISM

The notion that human behaviour is determined by genetics is a popular one, manifesting itself in relation to both criminality and sexual

---

[65] Maimonides, *Hilkhot Rozeah*, 1: 2; *Radbaz, Hilkhot Sanhedrin*, 18: 6; *Resp. Rosh*, no. 68; *Resp. Rivash*, no. 484; *Tur, Hoshen Mishpat*, 384; Zevin, *Leor Hahalakhah*, 318.

[66] Note the argument attributed to Socrates that 'the gods are our guardians, and that we men are part of their property' but if 'God sends some necessity upon him', a person may legally take his own life (*Phaedo*, 6. 62).

[67] See D. Shatz, 'Concepts of Autonomy in Jewish Medical Ethics', *Jewish Law Annual*, 12 (1997), 11.

[68] *Turei Even, Megillah*, 28a; *Minhat Hinukh*, nos. 48, 212; R. Saul Yisraeli, *Amud Hayemini*, no. 16.

[69] *Nishmat Avraham, Hoshen Mishpat*, 420: 1, citing R. Auerbach. Also see S. Rabinowitz, 'Selling Organs' (Heb.), *Assia*, 61–2 (1998), 58–64; H. Tabenkin, 'Issues Relating to the Sale of a Kidney from a Live Donor' (Heb.), *Assia*, 63–4 (1998), 74–93.

[70] See M. Halperin, 'Organ Transplants From Living Donors in Jewish Law', (Heb.), *Assia*, 45–6 (1989), 54–5.

orientation.[71] However, it is abundantly clear that as yet there is little scientific basis for any claimed link between gene variants and abnormal behaviour, and that in any case people are not merely the product of their genes: a genotype is not a phenotype. The role of training and education must not be underestimated, especially in relation to moral behaviour. Genetic determinism is generally rejected in the simplistic form referred to above, a position summed up by this extract from the Report on Human Genetics by the Science and Technology Committee of the House of Commons: 'Our awareness of the power and intellectual excitement of genetic science does not imply a belief that we are merely "programmed by our genes". Human nature is a product of the interaction between genes and environment, which is subject to uncertainty.'[72] Jewish tradition would certainly agree with this position. Maimonides in particular emphasizes the obligation upon every person to work upon themselves and modify their inborn, natural traits.[73] A vivid illustration of this idea is the legend of the portrait of Moses cited by R. Israel Lipschutz in his commentary on the Mishnah.[74] According to this legend, an Arabian king heard about the great exploits of Moses, and sent an artist to paint a portrait of the celebrated Divinely inspired leader of the Israelites. On the artist's return, the portrait was handed over to the king's physiognomists for the preparation of a character analysis of Moses. The results were totally negative and the great leader emerged as a thoroughly evil individual. Dissatisfied with the results, the king decided to visit the Israelite camp in order to check on the accuracy of the portrait. The visit confirmed the artist's claim that his portrait was a faithful reproduction of Moses' face, and the king concluded that the fault lay with his physiognomists. Prior to leaving the camp, however, the king informed Moses of the events that had caused him to make his visit. Moses then assured the king that his physiognomists were as precise as his artist, and that by nature he was even worse than the picture they had painted of him. Without a

---

[71] 'The Genetic Revolution', *Time*, 17 January 1994, 39; 'Search for a Gay Gene', *Time*, 12 June 1995, 52.   [72] See *Human Genetics*, 22.

[73] *Hilkhot Deot*, 1: 5–6; *Eight Chapters*, s. 8. Also see S. Aviner, 'Genetic Engineering, Free Will and Hazardous Experiments on Human Beings' (Heb.), *Assia*, 61–2 (1998), 43.

[74] *Tiferet Yisrael, Kiddushin*, 4: 14. In fact the earliest versions of this story in Jewish sources contain no reference to Moses whatsoever, and the source is probably a passage in Cicero's *Tusculan Disputations* (London, 1927), 4. 80; see S. Leiman, 'R. Israel Lipschutz and the Portrait of Moses Controversy', in I. Twersky (ed.), *Danzig: Between East and West* (Cambridge, Mass., 1985), 49. According to R. Avraham Kook, who criticized R. Lipschutz for incorporating a non-Jewish legend into his commentary, the point, if any, of the story is that notwithstanding Moses' noble birth and excellent inborn personality traits, he still made remarkable progress during his life and reached a stage of perfection achieved by no other individual (*Ein Yaeh, Berakhot*, 1 no. 144).

concerted effort to overcome the evil proclivities to which nature had disposed him, Moses would never have become the servant of God and the greatest prophet in Israel. This legend expresses in dramatic form the Maimonidean doctrine that free will reigns supreme, even in the context of a natural disposition. The establishment of a genetic predisposition is not, therefore, likely to affect the theological doctrine of moral choice, which lies at the very heart of traditional Jewish thought.

8. CLONING

(a) Scientific Background

The word 'clone', derived from the Greek word for twig, or the Latin for colony, was originally used to refer to the asexual production of plants from one original seedling. Any horticulturalist who has successfully planted a clipping has cloning credentials. In very simple terms, a clone is the product of a single parental cell rather than a combination of two parental gametes. Mammals such as cows, sheep, rabbits, and monkeys have been cloned from undifferentiated embryonic cells in recent years, but it was not until July 1996 that a mammalian clone was produced using a differentiated adult somatic cell.[75] This scientific breakthrough was achieved by taking udder cells from a Finn Dorset ewe and starving them of nutrients for five days in order to stop their normal cycle of cell division. This step was necessary in order to ensure that the nuclear DNA of the udder cells would be susceptible to reprogramming after having been inserted into the empty egg cells. In the meantime, an unfertilized egg was taken from a Scottish Blackface ewe and its nucleus removed by suction. The two cells were placed next to each other and electric pulses were applied in order to fuse the nucleus of the udder cell into the egg cell and to jump-start the process of cell division that normally occurs at fertilization. The embryo produced by this process was then placed in the uterus

---

[75] See reports in *Time*, 10 March 1997, 41–55, and *Scientific American*, May 1997, 10–11. Differentiation in relation to cells means that they have undergone the progressive changes that turn them into the two hundred or so different types of tissue cells, e.g. skin, brain, muscles, and hair required for the adult mammalian body. Undifferentiated cells have not undergone this process, and are capable of giving rise to any body cell. In technical terms, differentiation alters the way in which DNA folds up inside the nucleus of the cell. The folding makes vast stretches of DNA inaccessible, thereby ensuring that the cell's genetic programme remains that of a specialized cell, and no irregularities occur. Dolly proved that differentiation is reversible and that under the right conditions, adult somatic cells could be stimulated to unfold and provide the basic genetic code for the development of an entire body.

of another Blackface ewe and the result was Dolly, a Finn Dorset lamb genetically identical to the 6-year-old ewe from whose udder cell she had sprung.

It is, however, important to note that Dolly was preceded by 277 unsuccessful attempts, and she has developed arthritis at a relatively early age for a sheep. There are, therefore, serious and as yet, unanswered questions with regard to both the value of the investment that must be made in order to obtain a cloned mammal, and the clone's state of health. There is also growing evidence of genetic defects amongst cloned animals. Dolly herself manifested signs of premature aging, including the presence of unusually short telomeres in her chromosomes. In February 2003 she was diagnosed with a severe respiratory infection of a fatal nature. She was put out of her misery, and her body is preserved for posterity in Scotland's National Museum. At present, it is not possible to state with any scientific certainty whether her illness and relatively early demise were the result of her being a clone, or pure bad luck.[76]

Not surprisingly, there is widespread opposition to the notion of human cloning in the scientific community, and the only situation in which Ian Wilmot, the leader of the team that produced Dolly, is prepared to condone human cloning is in order to avoid genetic diseases caused by mitochondrial DNA in the cytoplasm of the embryo.[77] This is a far cry from the mass production of genetically selected human beings. Wilmot has also argued in favour of a moratorium on any attempt to produce full human clones.

(b) Comparative Survey

The announcement to the world of the scientific breakthrough in Scotland prompted the President of the United States to turn to the national Bioethics Advisory Committee with a request for a report on cloning to be submitted to him within three months. The report was submitted in June 1997, and found that at the present time the cloning of humans was unacceptable because of both its scientific uncertainty and the profound social unease aroused by the prospect of human cloning. The committee made a number of recommendations, including continuing the ban on federally funded

---

[76] L. Kodner, 'Dolly's Death Raises Doubts with Regard to the Success of Cloning' (Heb.), *Ha'aretz* (17 February, 2003). See also C. Wilgoos, 'FDA Regulation: An Answer to the Questions of Human Cloning and Germline Therapy', *American Journal of Law and Medicine*, 27 (2001), 106.

[77] The mitochondrion is a DNA-bearing structure lying just outside the cell nucleus. Mutations of mitrochondrial DNA can cause serious diseases, including blindness. These diseases could be avoided if the nucleus from an embryo with defective mitochondria is implanted into a donor egg possessing healthy mitochondria. The resulting child will be born free of mitochondrial disease.

Genetics

human cloning research using the 'Dolly method' for a period of three to five years, the encouragement of privately funded institutions to support the ban, and the institution of legislation prohibiting human cloning at both the federal and the state levels.[78] There has been much discussion of cloning in Congress, in particular over the need to distinguish between cloning for reproductive purposes, which is generally condemned, and cloning for research purposes, which is regarded by many people as being essential for scientific process. As a result, no legislation has been passed as yet, and in this respect, the United States is a good example of a country in which the issue of cloning is a highly emotive one, but as yet, the emotionally charged debate has not been translated into law.[79]

In the United Kingdom, assisted reproduction is governed by the Human Fertilization and Embryology Act, 1990. However, this Act applies only to fertilized embryos, i.e. embryos brought into existence by the fusion, at some stage, of an egg and a sperm. Since cloning does not involve such fusion, it is not covered by the Act, and, in theory, the way was open for anyone with appropriate expertise to attempt to clone a human being.[80] The response to this gap in the law was the Human Reproductive Cloning Act, 2001, which provided that placing a human embryo created in a manner other than fertilization into a woman's body constitutes an offence punishable by up to ten years imprisonment or a fine, or both. Clearly, this law does not apply to cloned embryos used for research at the very earliest stages of their development, since they are never put into a woman's body. There would, therefore, appear to be no objection to stem-cell research using cloned human embryos under English law.

The Canadian Royal Commission on New Reproductive Technologies presented its Report in 1993, and recommended the banning of human cloning. Penalties for breaking the law range from five to ten years imprisonment or a heavy fine.[81] The proposal is expected to become law in the near future.[82]

Several European countries prohibit cloning explicitly,[83] and others are drafting bills with a view to regulating it.[84] The German law is particularly

---

[78] *Cloning Human Beings, Report and Recommendations of the National Bioethics Advisory Committee* (9 June 1997).

[79] See E. Shanin, 'International Responses to Human Cloning', *Chicago Journal of International Law*, 3 (2001), 255.

[80] *R (on the application Quintavalle)* v. *Secretary of State for Health* [2001] 4 All ER 1013.

[81] *An Act Respecting Human Reproductive Technologies and Commercial Transactions Relating to Human Reproduction*, 1996.

[82] T. Caulfield, 'Clones, Controversy, and Criminal Law', *Alberta Law Review*, 39 (2001), 341.

[83] Germany (Embryo Protection Act, 1991), Denmark (Act Concerning Biomedical Research Projects, 1992), and Norway (Act Relating to the Application of Biotechnology in Medicine, 1994).

[84] Switzerland (*Loi Fédérale sur la Procréation Médicalement Assistée*, 1995).

detailed, and bans all forms of cloning and genetic mixing. In 1998 the Council of Europe ratified an Additional Protocol to the Convention for the Protection of Human Rights and Dignity of the Human Being with Regard to the Application of Biology and Medicine, banning cloning.

Israel has passed the Prohibition on Genetic Intervention Law, 5759-1999, which places a five-year moratorium on any genetic manipulation aimed at producing a human clone and the performance of germ-line therapy. The Israeli law provides for the appointment of a committee to oversee all human genetic research, and for the Minister of Health to give special permission to carry out genetic research prohibited under the Act, provided that the research does not offend against human dignity.[85]

Both the American and the Israeli provisions incorporate so-called 'sunset clauses', which limit the ban on human cloning to a set number of years. The idea is that the interim period will be used for a full discussion of the issues and the preparation of a sound legal and social infrastructure for what will eventually become a permitted practice. Indeed, there would seem to be a number of infertility cases in which cloning might be a very acceptable solution, from both a legal and a moral perspective. The problem is how to confine human cloning to these cases and to ensure that it is not misused in any way.

In this respect, cloning is not so different from other artificial reproductive techniques that are now widely used, notwithstanding the existence of many legal and moral misgivings when they were first introduced.

One of the major fears expressed in the media at the time of Dolly's cloning was that individuals with an identical genetic make-up would suffer from loss of individuality and personal identity. This fear is clearly fallacious, since nature itself produces such individuals. Identical twins have exactly the same genetic make-up, and there is no denying that they have a capacity for personal growth and individuality. As already stated, genotypes are definitely not phenotypes and the use of vague arguments concerning the destruction of the human capacity for individuality in order to criticize cloning is simply poor logic. This does not mean that great care should not be exercised in relation to the relevant scientific research, but the object of that concern ought to be the people using the technique and not the technique itself.

(c) Jewish Law

As far as Jewish law is concerned, we have already noted that the general rule is that if there is no reason for declaring something forbidden, it is

---

[85] See G. Ben Or, 'Cloning and Artificial Reproduction Techniques' (Heb.), *Assia*, 61–2 (1998), 23–5.

Genetics

permitted without any further justification.[86] There do not appear to be any specific legal grounds for prohibiting cloning, and this probably accounts for the fact that in the first blaze of press responses to human cloning, very few rabbinic authorities joined the fairly raucous caucus of religious voices demanding an absolute ban on the process. Instead these authorities shied away from adopting a blanket prohibitive stance, and tended to leave the matter open for further clarification in the light of ongoing scientific and medical progress.[87] The generally accepted view would appear to be that there are no principled objections, either ideological or halakhic, to cloning humans, but that it ought not to be done until the science has been thoroughly worked out and its therapeutic applications firmly established, and society has been thoroughly prepared, both legally and morally, for its introduction.[88]

The positive side of cloning raises a number of halakhic issues, including the fulfilment of the commandment to procreate and the establishment of legal parenthood. Essentially, many of these issues arose in the context of artificial reproductive techniques and were dealt with in Chapter 2. For example, in relation to AIH, the possibility was raised that even if the use of assisted reproduction would not qualify as fulfilment of the obligation to reproduce at the biblical level, it would certainly do so at the rabbinic one.[89] This is clearly one possible response to the question of the status of the commandment to propagate in the cloning context.

---

[86] See Ch. 2 n. 17.

[87] See *Jerusalem Post*, 28 February 1997, 10; *Pittsburgh Post Gazette*, 1 March 1997, A1; *Jewish Telegraph*, 7 March 1997, 3; *Jewish Tribune*, 2 May 1997.

[88] See A. Steinberg, 'Human Cloning' (Heb.), *Assia*, 61–2 (1998). The argument that a clone resembles a golem, i.e. an 'artificial person' created by mystical means, is clearly inappropriate, since all human clones issue from wombs following a period of pregnancy and are fully human beings as far as the *halakhah* is concerned (*Resp. Haham Zvi*, no. 93; *She'elat Ya'avez* nos. 41, 82; *Resp. Zofnat Paneah*, 2 no. 7; *Pithei Teshuvah, Yoreh Deah*, 62: 2; *Resp. Rivevot Efraim*, 7 no. 385; cf. B. Sherwin, *In Partnership with God* (Syracuse, 1990), 181–208; J.D. Bleich, 'Cloning: Homologous Reproduction and Jewish Law', *Tradition* 32 (1998)). In general, halakhic arguments to the effect that somehow clones are not human would seem to be misguided in that cloning is a natural process, and clones are not substantially different from identical twins. Attempts to raise objections to cloning on the grounds of the prohibition on sorcery also appear to be misguided. Indeed, R. Menahem Hameiri states quite conclusively that 'nothing natural can ever be classified as sorcery, even if people produce beautiful creatures in an asexual fashion... there is no prohibition involved, since sorcery does not apply to that which occurs naturally' (*Sanhedrin*, 67b, s.v. kol). Neither the argument that Judaism insists upon preserving nature as it was at the time of creation, or that the biblical prohibitions on mixing agricultural species or cross-breeding animals require us to desist from crossing 'natural' barriers in relation to reproduction, are particularly convincing. Indeed, the dominant opinion would seem to be that Judaism insists upon changing nature as it was at the time of creation, and that the prohibitions on mixed kinds are inapplicable to human cloning (Steinberg, 'Human Cloning'). See also Aviner, *Genetic Engineering*, 43; J. D. Bleich, 'Cloning', 47.

[89] See Ch. 2 n. 14.

Another fundamental point made in relation to fulfilling the commandment to have children using assisted reproduction is that if the final result is a child, then the method of reproduction ought not to be the decisive issue.[90] Finally, it is arguable that the word 'fruitful' used in the biblical phrase 'be fruitful and multiply' from which the commandment to propagate is derived,[91] may be understood as any means of producing fruit. Fruit-bearing may not be confined to sexual reproduction alone.[92]

Another important halakhic issue is the paternity of cloned offspring. If a somatic nucleus is taken from a woman and induced to develop in embryonic form in her egg, or even in that of a donor, there is absolutely no male biological involvement in the offspring produced as a result of this type of cloning. The closest halakhic analogy to this situation is the child resulting from a union of a Jewish woman and a non-Jewish man. Such a child lacks any halakhically recognized paternity,[93] but may, in certain circumstances, be treated as his maternal grandfather's progeny. For example, the Talmud rules that the son born to the daughter of a levite from a non-Jew is treated as a levite for purposes of exemption from the ritual of the redemption of the firstborn.[94] On the basis of this and other similar rulings, it is arguable that in certain situations, the paternal role may be assumed by the maternal grandfather,[95] although whether this applies to cloning is, of course, a matter of conjecture at the present time.

Another possibility is that a cloned child simply does not have a father. The notion that an artificial method of reproduction results in loss of legally recognized lineage was applied by R. Waldenberg in the context of IVF. Relying upon a phrase in a *responsum* by R. Menahem Azariah of Fano,[96] R. Waldenberg held that a child conceived using IVF lacks any lineage whatsoever because of the artificiality of the process.[97] R. Waldenberg's view was attacked quite heavily in the context of IVF, but may prove to be more palatable in relation to cloning, since in that context, there is simply no candidate for paternal lineage.[98]

Other issues may arise as a result of the use of donor nuclei. What is the halakhic status of a child born to a married woman using a donor male

---

[90] See p. 97.   [91] See the sources cited in Ch. 2 n. 11.
[92] Y. Shilat, 'Genetic Cloning in the Light of the *Halakhah*' (Heb.), *Tehumin*, 18 (1998), 140.
[93] See Ch. 2 n. 41.
[94] *Bekhorot*, 47a. On the redemption of the firstborn, see *Encylopaedia Judaica*, vi. 1308.
[95] *Hiddushe R. Hayyim Halevi, Hilhkot Issurei Biah*, 15.
[96] *Resp. Rima Mifano*, no. 116.   [97] *Resp. Ziz Eliezer*, 15 no. 5.
[98] For a discussion of these and related issues see M. Broyde, 'Cloning People: A Jewish Law Analysis of the Issues', *Connecticut Law Review*, 30 (1998), 503–35. Also see Shilat, 'Genetic Cloning', 140, and Y. Shafran, *'Genetic Cloning in the Light of the Halakhah'* (Heb.), *Tehumin*, 18 (1998), 151.

nucleus? How is the Jewish identity of a child cloned from a non-Jewish somatic nucleus determined? The basis for resolving these questions, should they ever arise in practice, lies in the principles developed in relation to assisted reproduction, and dealt with at length in Chapter 2. There would not appear to be any inherent reason for doubting their applicability to cloning technology.

Above and beyond purely legal issues, it is evident that cloning technology requires us to consider its impact upon parenthood and the family unit. The basis for these very basic relationships has always rested upon sexual reproduction. Cloning is reproduction without any sexual input, and it is not clear how it will impact upon the institution of the family. The process of moving away from the sexual basis of family relationships has, however, already begun. Assisted reproduction provokes profound questions with regard to the definition of parenthood and the family unit; some of these were raised in the fourth section of Chapter 2. The question of the extent to which the law ought to intervene in order to shape these basic relationships in a genetic era is a challenging one, but beyond the scope of the present work. It also requires much more empirical evidence than we have at present for its resolution.

One final comment: the topic of abortion has a long history in both general and Jewish law. The interaction of legal and moral elements, which we traced in the context of the *halakhah* in great detail, is a feature common to both types of law. The use of assisted reproduction technology is a recent phenomenon, and both general and religious systems are still coming to terms with its legal and moral ramifications. In this area, there are as many questions as there are answers, and many of the central legal doctrines and moral positions have yet to be worked out in a definitive fashion. There is, nevertheless, a perceptible trend amongst more contemporary halakhic authorities to accept these techniques, and to eschew the weak form of naturalism relied upon by older rabbinic authorities as a means of condemning them. The application of genetics to the conquest of disease and the improvement of the quality of life is the face of the future. The science is still in its infancy, but the results are expected to be far-reaching in terms of the revolutionary effect of genetic therapy on human life and health. In this area, the legal and, a fortiori, the moral questions far outnumber the answers. The crafting of legal and moral guidelines for the genetic age is one of the major challenges facing both general and Jewish biomedical law in the twenty-first century.

4

The Obligation to Heal and Patient Autonomy

1. INTRODUCTORY REMARKS

The main argument made in the present chapter is that the obligation to heal in Jewish law is not an absolute one: in certain cases, it is possible to follow the wishes of a patient who does not wish to receive medical treatment. A significant part of this argument is based upon the influence of biblical theology according to which human healing is not a religious desideratum. This position influences both the legal approach to the binding status of medical therapy, and the *halakhah* governing the refusal of a terminal patient to receive life-sustaining treatment. We will therefore begin with a discussion of the theological validity of the practice of medicine in the Bible, and the subsequent theological developments in this area. This will be followed by a section on the influence of this theology upon the *halakhah*. The remaining sections deal with the nature of the halakhic obligation to heal, coercive life-saving therapy, the situations in which there is no mandate to compel life-saving medical therapy, and the concept of limited autonomy in Jewish biomedical law. The chapter concludes with two comparative sections. The first compares the position under Jewish law with that under the Common law. The second investigates the influence of the *halakhah* on Israeli law and the attempt by Israeli judges and legislators to combine Judaism and democracy in this area.

2. DIVINE HEALING AND HUMAN MEDICINE IN JEWISH THEOLOGY AND BIBLE COMMENTARY

A good starting point for a discussion of the approach of Jewish theology to the value of human healing is the talmudic interpretation of the biblical passage dealing with physical assault. According to biblical law, the victim of a physical assault is entitled to claim medical expenses from his attacker: 'And [the attacker] shall surely provide for healing'.[1] In drawing a general message about human healing from this verse, the Talmud states

---

[1] Exod. 21: 19.

that 'permission has been given to the physician to heal'.[2] The use of the word 'permission' indicates that the virtue of human healing is not self-evident. If it were, the physician would not require 'permission' to engage in therapeutic activity: he would be commanded or obliged to do so.

In his commentary on the Talmud, Rashi articulates the theological misgivings underlying the use of the word 'permission' in the talmudic interpretation of the biblical passage. According to Rashi, human healers require God's permission because without it, their activities may be construed as an act of rebellion against Him. In Rashi's view, the fundamental biblical position is that both disease and healing are manifestations of Divine providence,[3] and the only method for curing disease is through prayer and the performance of virtuous deeds.[4] Indeed, the Bible singles out Asa, king of Judah, for censure on the grounds that when he became sick, he turned to physicians rather than to God.[5] In terms of its theology, therefore, it would appear that the Bible frowns upon human healing, casting it in a negative light. The Talmud is sensitive to this position, and indicates the theological reservations regarding human healing by using the word 'permission' when interpreting the biblical source for the halakhic legitimacy of medical practice.

This theological ambivalence towards the physician and his activities is reflected elsewhere in the Talmud. Together with numerous positive statements regarding doctors and their profession,[6] the Talmud has on record one of the most strikingly negative remarks ever made about the practice of medicine, i.e. 'the best of physicians are destined for purgatory'.[7] Now, although this statement is understood by many commentators as a homiletical device warning a physician to avoid the pitfalls of overweening pride and excessive self-confidence,[8] it also conveys the existence of reservations within Judaism regarding the desirability of human healing.

The mainstream theological response to the dubious status of human healing is to complement medicine with prayer. This response is found in the Talmud in the passage dealing with the 'permission' to pursue human healing:

Rabbi Aha said: On going in to have one's blood let one should say: 'May it be Your will O Lord, my God, that this operation may be a cure for me, and may You

---

[2] *Berakhot*, 60a; *Bava Kamma*, 85a.   [3] Exod. 15: 26; Deut. 32: 39.
[4] *Bava Kamma*, 85a, *s.v. nitnah reshut.*   [5] 2 Chr. 16: 12.
[6] See *Sanhedrin*, 17b, in which a scholar is warned against living in a city that lacks a physician, and *Bava Mezia*, 85b where the curing of R. Judah the Prince's eye ailment by the Babylonian scholar Samuel is discussed at length. See also *Encyclopaedia Judaica*, xi. 1181–3.
[7] *Kiddushin*, 4: 14.
[8] See S. Kottek, 'The Best of Physicians are Destined for Purgatory' (Heb.), *Sefer Assia*, 2, 21.

heal me for You are a faithful, healing God, and Your healing is sure, since men have no power to heal, but this is a habit with them!'[9]

In R. Aha's view,[10] human medicine is a fundamentally misguided enter-prise; in reality, God is the sole Healer, and turning to the physician demonstrates a lack of faith. However, people have fallen into the bad habit of going to the doctor,[11] and since they are unable to change their ways, the solution is to address a prayer to the real Healer on the way to the surgery. As long as one bears in mind that the true source of healing is God and the physician is merely acting as His instrument, it is legitim-ate to go to the doctor since, apparently, God does not insist that people defy basic conventions in matters of life and death.

This approach was adopted by many authorities throughout the ages,[12] and it has become the standard response in Jewish theology to the issue of human healing. Not only do observant Jews pray as part of the course for dealing with disease, they may also consult with rabbis at the same time as they are seeing the doctor. In the words of R. Abraham Isaiah Karelitz, 'it is necessary to reach a fine balance between reliance upon Divine providence and the pursuit of the appropriate medical cure'.[13]

In the above-mentioned talmudic passage, Abaye takes issue with R. Aha's negative position, arguing against it as follows: 'A man should not speak thus, since it was taught in the school of R. Yishmael: "And [the attacker] shall surely provide for healing". From this we learn that per-mission has been given to the physician to heal.' Abaye understands the 'permission' given to the physician to heal as an unqualified Divine licence to practise medicine. He ignores the theological reservations with regard to human healing discussed above. This view did not gain wide acceptance amongst theologians, although it is reflected in Maimonides' strongly rationalist and extremely positive approach to the practice of medicine, which will be discussed below. It also fails to give expression to the ambivalence of the word 'permission' in the talmudic inference regarding medical practice. If human healing is an unreservedly positive

---

[9] *Berakhot*, 60a.

[10] See *Hagahot R. Zvi Hirsch Hayyes, Berakhot*, 60a, *s.v. R. Abahu*, which casts doubt on the attribution of this statement to R. Aha.

[11] Rashi comments that 'they ought not to have occupied themselves with medicine but rather they should have asked God to show them mercy' (*Berakhot*, 60a, *s.v. she'en darkhan*). See also Rashi's comments on *Berakhot*, 10b, *s.v. sheganaz; Pesahim*, 56a, *s.v. veganaz*. Rashi consistently explains talmudic objections to medicine in terms of a lost opportunity for prayer.

[12] See *Shabbat*, 32a; *Avodah Zarah*, 55a; *Bayit Hadash, Yoreh Deah*, 336; *Resp. Teshuvah Meahavah, Yoreh Deah*, 3 no. 336; *Resp. Hatam Sofer, Orah Hayyim*, no. 177; *Resp. Binyan Zion*, no. 111; *Resp. Divrei Malkiel*, 5 no. 35; *Resp. Ziz Eliezer, Ramat Rahel*, no. 20; *Resp. Yehaveh Da'at*, no. 61.

[13] *Kovez Iggrot Hazon Ish*, no. 136. Also see R. Karelitz's *Inyanei Emunah Uvitachon*, no. 5.

activity, why not give it the status of a Divine commandment (*mitzvah*) or a meritorious deed; why declare it a mere 'permission'?

The tension between human and divine healing also engaged the medieval Bible commentators, for whom the problem was textual as well as theological. They suggested various ways for resolving the contradiction between the text providing for the payment of medical expenses in assault cases, and the text criticizing Asa for going to physicians rather than praying.

Nahmanides is one of the most prominent medieval Bible commentators to discuss this issue. In his view, a distinction must be drawn between the age of prophecy in the biblical period, during which Israel was at a very high spiritual level, and the post-prophetic period, during which the level of spirituality was much lower. In the prophetic period, the sole legitimate means for curing disease was prayer; since Asa lived during that period, he ought to have entrusted his cure to Divine rather than human hands. His reliance upon physicians was tantamount to denying God's providence, and hence, his conduct was censured by Scripture. The situation is different in the post-prophetic era, in which the level of spirituality is much lower. In this period, God has withdrawn from all direct involvement in the therapeutic process, and all healing is mediated by human beings. The biblical verse dealing with medical expenses is directed to the post-prophetic age, in which people are allowed to seek medical help. It is also to this period that Abaye's above-mentioned comment in the Talmud is directed.

This distinction is not a hard and fast one, and Nahmanides himself blurs it in a number of ways. For example, he confines the permissive approach to human healing in the post-prophetic period to physicians, and observes that a sick person who comes to a doctor for a cure is 'not of the congregation of the Lord, whose portion is in this life'. Despite the deficient spiritual status of the patient, 'the physician should, nevertheless, not refrain from healing him'. In this respect, Nahmanides preserves the option of Divine healing even in the post-prophetic era.[14] He also cites a talmudic passage to the effect that virtuous and spiritually inclined

---

[14] *Commentary to the Torah, Leviticus* 26: 11; cf. *Torat Ha'adam, Kol Kitvei Haramban*, ed. C. Chavel (Jerusalem, Mossad Harav Kook, 1962), ii. 42, and see n. 35 below. This distinction between physician and patient is criticized by R. Isaac Arama who claims that 'it would be illogical to permit the physician to heal while at the same time forbidding the patient to seek a cure' (*Akedat Yitzhak, Vayishlah*, Gate 26, 201a). In fact, Nahmanides did not say that it is 'forbidden' for a patient to seek a cure. According to Nahmanides, a patient is not obliged to seek human healing. This does not mean that he is not permitted to do so. Nahmanides' approach is that a person should, in the first place, strive to avoid physicians and throw himself upon God's mercy. Such a step, however, requires great faith, and since most people lack such faith, recourse to physicians is permitted. Nahmanides' distinction is not, therefore, inherently flawed on logical grounds, and R. Arama's critique is capable of being rebutted.

people have no need of physicians, since these qualities protect them from disease.[15]

A different approach to the contradiction between the above-mentioned biblical passages is adopted by Abraham ibn Ezra, who resolves the contradiction by distinguishing between external and internal diseases. Human healing is legitimate in the case of external wounds, such as those sustained in the course of a violent brawl. This is the type of injury that the physician has been permitted to heal. Internal injuries, on the other hand, are solely within God's therapeutic domain. Thus, because Asa was suffering from an internal disease, his recourse to physicians was wrong.[16]

Ibn Ezra's distinction was strongly criticized by R. Moshe Mat, mainly on the grounds of talmudic accounts of famous and respected rabbis who themselves treated internal maladies and achieved successful results.[17] R. Mat concludes that it is inconceivable that great and learned talmudic authorities would have disregarded the law: therefore, ibn Ezra must be wrong. According to R. Mat, the distinction between external and internal injuries carries no normative weight in Jewish law.[18]

R. Mat's objection is not a fatal one. It may be countered with the argument that the point of ibn Ezra's distinction is not whether the problem is on the surface of the body or inside it, but whether the problem is clearly diagnosable. Cast in these terms, it is arguable that any medical problem for which there is a known and well-tried remedy falls within the legitimate purview of the human healer. There is a good deal of wisdom in this approach. Doctors should certainly treat diseases they can easily diagnose and cure with confidence. There are, however, many conditions that do not fall into this category: to leave them in the hands of God, or at least,

---

[15] The Talmud was compiled in the post-prophetic era. The talmudic statement cited by Nahmanides is as follows: 'During all the twenty-two years that Rabbah filled the post of Head of the Academy at Pumpeditha, Rabbi Joseph did not even call a blood-letter to his house' (*Horayat*, 14a; *Berakhot*, 64a). According to Nahmanides, the meaning of this statement is that Rabbi Joseph's great modesty in declining the office of Head of the Academy in favour of Rabbah won him protection from all sickness and disease. This is also the explanation given in *Tosafot Harosh, Horayot*, 14a, s.v. *afilu umna*. Rashi, however, explains that the episode illustrates R. Joseph's great modesty in that he did not even want to summon a blood-letter to his house—which would certainly have been justified in the light of the dignity of his position—but went instead to the blood-letter's surgery for treatment, i.e. he did not stand on his dignity. Nahmanides also quotes a late midrashic aphorism that 'a gate which is not open for the performance of *mitzvot* is open for the physician' (*Shir Hashirim Rabbah*, 6: 17) in support of a viable connection between spirituality and health in post-prophetic times.

[16] *Commentary to the Torah*, Exod. 21: 19. This distinction is also accepted by R. Bahya b. Asher in his commentary on Exod. 21: 19.

[17] R. Mat cites the passage describing how Samuel, a prominent talmudic authority, cured R. Judah the Prince of an eye ailment (see n. 6) to demonstrate that internal medical procedures are legitimate.   [18] *Matteh Moshe, Amud Gemilut Hassidim*, 4.3.

to refrain from adopting a highly interventionist course, might not be
such a bad idea.

3. THEOLOGY AND BIBLE COMMENTARY IN THE
HALAKHIC LITERATURE

An interesting feature of this area of Jewish law is the incorporation of the
views of Nahmanides and ibn Ezra into halakhic texts dealing with the
question of the mandatory nature of medical therapy. In general, views
expressed in Bible commentaries do not carry normative weight,[19] but
this is not the case in this context. The views of Nahmanides and ibn Ezra
are cited with approval by halakhic writers. The reason for this exception
is that the theories developed by these commentators in order to solve
their textual problems readily lend themselves to application in a legal
context, thereby allowing halakhists to resolve the deep tension between
Divine and human therapy in this area.

As pointed out above, Nahmanides' distinction between the prophetic
and the post-prophetic periods is not a hard and fast one. He indicates
quite clearly that reliance upon Divine healing is also a viable option in the
latter period. This position is cited in a halakhic context by R. Ze'ev Nahum
of Biala, in nineteenth century Poland. According to R. Ze'ev Nahum,

---

[19] This is certainly the case in relation to ibn Ezra (see *Tashbetz*, 1 no. 5; *Resp. Yehave Da'at*,
no. 61) but is less true as far as Nahmanides is concerned. Unlike ibn Ezra, Nahmanides is a
prominent halakhic authority, and views expressed in his *Commentary on the Torah* are often
given full normative weight by later scholars. Nevertheless, the option to disagree with
them on the basis of their origin in a biblical commentary is left open. One example of this
phenomenon is Nahmanides' statement in his *Commentary* that the scales that constitute a
sign of the dietary fitness (*kashrut*) of fish under biblical law must be capable of being
removed by hand. If they are fixed too strongly to the body of the fish, then they do not qualify as a sign that the fish is fit for consumption (Lev., 11: 9). The need for manually removable scales is cited with approval by halakhic codifiers (*Maggid Mishneh, Hilkhot Ma'akhalot
Asurot*, 1: 24; Rema, *Yoreh Deah*, 83: 1). The question of the *kashrut* of the sterlet (a fish), the
scales of which could only be removed by soaking it in a caustic solution, arose in Bohemia
in the 18th cent., and R. Ezekiel Landau of Prague ruled that the sterlet was *kosher*. In the
course of his argument he emphasized that 'the stricture imposed by Nahmanides in relation to removal by hand' is in 'his *Commentary on the Torah*', and need not, therefore, be
applied in a rigorous fashion. Hence, any method of removing the scales is acceptable (*Resp.
Noda Biyehudah*, 2, *Yoreh Deah*, no. 28; *Arukh Hashulhan, Yoreh Deah*, 82: 13). Another example
is Nahmanides' tentative assertion in his *Commentary* (Lev., 18: 20) to the effect that the biblical prohibition on adultery may also extend to any act which confuses the lineage of a child
by obscuring his or her paternity. This statement became a major issue in the debate between
R. Feinstein and R. Teitelbaum concerning the halakhic acceptability of AID (see Ch. 2 s. 2 n.
54) and in that context too, R. Feinstein, who does not accept Nahmanides' position,
attempts to weaken it by implying that it was added by an errant disciple, and is not the
work of Nahmanides himself. It is unlikely that the same charge would be made as readily
against a statement expressed in Nahmanides' strictly halakhic works.

a person is permitted to refuse life-saving medical therapy if it involves the consumption of ritually-forbidden foods. This decision is at odds with mainstream *halakhah* which, as will be explained below, requires people to ignore halakhic prohibitions in order to save their lives.[20] His main precedent is Nahmanides' theory of spiritual healing for the virtuous and spiritually inclined, on the basis of which he argues that the very fact that a person refuses life-saving therapy on the grounds that it involves breach of halakhic considerations, automatically endows him with the status of a virtuous and spiritual individual. According to Nahmanides, this status carries with it the privilege of Divine healing, and obviates the need to visit the doctor.[21] Hence, R. Ze'ev Nahum's ruling that it is not mandatory to follow a medical regimen which involves a breach of the dietary laws.

This ruling is certainly a minority view, and it may be explained against the background of nineteenth century Polish medicine, the standard of which was such that reliance upon Divine healing rather than human therapy may well have been eminently justifiable on empirical as well as spiritual grounds! Nevertheless, R. Ze'ev Nahum's view received some support in other halakhic sources,[22] and it is cited in support of the proposition that the obligation to heal becomes less binding in circumstances in which there is little likelihood of a full recovery.

Another application of Nahmanides' approach is found in relation to the non-enforcement of life-saving therapy in the case of terminally ill patients who wish to place their fate in the hands of God, rather than in those of human healers.[23] There is, of course, a world of difference between the track record of modern medicine and that of medical practice in nineteenth-century Poland; therefore, it is not as a primary source—as in the *responsum* of R. Ze'ev Nahum—but as a secondary one, that Nahmanides' position is cited in relation to today's highly advanced medical context. Also, the focus is on the terminal condition only. Nahmanides' approach is, as stated, an important secondary support for the claim made in section 5, that a competent, terminal patient seeking to exercise an autonomous choice to refuse life-support may do so under the *halakhah*. It must be emphasized that Nahmanides' position does not supplant the basic *halakhah* governing this area, but it does supplement it, providing an extra argument for the exercise of patient choice in difficult issues of life and death. It also seems to be rather wise in that it allows

---

[20] See nn. 62–3.   [21] *Resp. Avnei Nezer, Hoshen Mishpat*, no. 193.

[22] Also see *Resp. Haelef Lekha Shlomo*, no. 351, for a similar position.

[23] See S. Rafael, 'Forcing Medical Therapy on a Patient' (Heb.), *Torah Shebal Peh*, 33 (1992), 74; M. Raziel, 'Forcing a Patient to Receive Medical Treatment' (Heb.), *Tehumin*, 2 (1981), 325.

terminal patients to rely on their own spiritual resources during their last days or months, and grants them the freedom to make that choice.

Ibn Ezra's distinction between external and internal maladies is also found in halakhic writings in terms of a distinction between easily diagnosable conditions and those in relation to which there is no such medical certainty and the physician is basically working in the dark. Treatments prescribed by the physician for the former type of condition are mandatory; those prescribed for the latter are not. According to R. Emden, medical therapy is only halakhically mandatory if it is a well-tried cure in which people have full confidence. He provides various examples of such types of cures: trimming wounded flesh, manipulating an abscess, binding a fractured limb, or performing an amputation. These are all examples of 'external maladies'. 'Internal cures', to which a person may not be forced to submit, are defined by Rabbi Emden thus:

drugs which the patient must ingest in order to cure a disease hidden in the inner parts of the body and concealed from the human eye. In such cases, the physician himself is unsure as to the outcome of the treatment, and his role is nothing more than that of an experimenter applying his own personal estimation of the therapy to be applied.[24]

R. Emden focuses the distinction between internal and external diseases on the medical certainty of the treatment and, in the context of coercive medical treatment, his approach to the distinction is a highly influential one. R. Emden's position is followed by many halakhists, and in this respect ibn Ezra's exegetical analysis has gained halakhic force.

It is noteworthy that ibn Ezra's view is also cited, along with that of Nahmanides, in the *responsum* of R. Ze'ev Nahum on the right to refuse mainstream medical treatment and to opt instead for Divine healing, as discussed above.

No discussion of the theology of medicine in Judaism would be complete without reference to the minority view of Maimonides who, in conformity with his rationalist bent, had no reservations whatsoever with regard to the legitimacy of human healing. His fundamental position is elucidated in a comment on the talmudic statement that King Hezekiah 'concealed the *Book of Cures* and the sages concurred with him'.[25] The talmudic context of this statement is Hezekiah's prayer to God for relief from his sickness.[26] On this basis, Rashi and other commentators explain that Hezekiah's concealment of the *Book of Cures* was 'so that people should entreat God and not simply rely upon the cures contained in the book'.[27] Maimonides takes strong exception to this explanation: 'It is vain

---

[24] *Mor Ukeziah*, no. 328.   [25] *Berakhot*, 10b; *Pesahim*, 56a.   [26] *Berakhot*, 10b.
[27] Ibid. *s.v. sheganaz*, and see n. 11.

and bizarre, and attributes to Hezekiah such folly as is attributable only to the most vulgar elements of society.'[28] According to Maimonides, the reason for the concealment of the *Book of Cures* was that the 'cures' contained in it were irrational; only therapies based upon rational proof and empirical evidence are permitted. Not only does Maimonides dismiss out of hand the idea that prayer is preferable to medicine; he also takes the opportunity presented by the account of Hezekiah's deed to find talmudic support for rational medicine. It is noteworthy that Maimonides emphasizes the need for a 'rational and empirical' approach to medicine throughout his writings,[29] and he was prepared to strike out on an independent course with regard to issues of talmudic law and lore on the basis of the best medical science of his time.[30] In expanding his argument, Maimonides draws an analogy between food and therapy, arguing that just as no one would accuse a hungry person who eats bread of not trusting in the Lord, so too a sick person who takes medicine is not to be regarded as lacking in faith.[31]

It is important not to overstate Maimonides' argument. As a devoted physician he would, undoubtedly be prepared to admit that there are situations in which refraining from attending the physician may very well be the wiser course. His major concern is that prayer not be substituted for mainstream, rational medicine in cases where the health of the patient is at stake; things may very well be different in the terminal condition. It is, after all, Maimonides who uses the biblical law of returning lost property as the basis for the obligation to practise medicine in order to save

---

[28] *Commentary to the Mishnah, Pesahim*, 4: 10.

[29] See *Eight Chapters*, ch. 5; *Guide for the Perplexed*, bk. 3: 33; *Iggerot Harambam*, ed. Y. Kafah (Jerusalem, 1972), 26–8; *Hilkhot Deot*, 1: 4; *Commentary to the Mishnah, Yoma*, 8: 4; I. Twersky, 'Halakhah and Science: Perspectives on the Epistemology of Maimonides' (Heb.), *Shenaton Hamishpat Haivri*, 14–15 (1988–9), 135–40: D. Sinclair, 'Torah and Scientific Methodology in Rambam's Halakhic Writings', *Le'ela* (April 1995), 30–3.

[30] See *Hilkhot Avel*, 14: 5; *Commentary to the Mishnah, Yoma* 8: 2. In his commentary to *Kelim*, 1: 5, Maimonides observes that 'the *halakhah* is not in accordance with the view of R. Judah but we inspect each organ individually in accordance with standard medical practice'. See also his *Sefer Harefuot*, ch. 30. In this context, Maimonides' strong opposition to astrological medicine is worthy of mention (see *Hilkot Avodah Zarah*, 11: 12; *Resp. Harambam*, no. 218; *Hilkot Mezuzah*, 5: 4), as is the strong contrast between his view and that of Nahmanides. According to Rashba, a student of Nahmanides, the latter used talismans such as the image of a gold, tongueless lion in order to cure patients suffering from kidney disease (*Resp. Rashba*, nos. 167, 413, and 652). Nahmanides advocates a qualified acceptance of astrology and his position is probably closer to the codified *halakhah* than that of Maimonides (see *Resp. Ramban*, no. 282; *Beth Yosef, Yoreh Deah*, 179; *Shulhan Arukh, Yoreh Deah*, 179: 1; *Rema* and *Hagahot Hagra, Yoreh Deah*, 179: 2). Maimonides provides two very interesting examples of the use of medical science in order to shape *halakhah* in the laws relating to both human and animal *terefot* (see Ch. 6, nn. 39–46). Also see D. Sinclair, 'The Relationship Between the Process of Reasoning and the Legitimacy of Medical Therapy in Medieval Spanish *Halakhah*', in S. Kottek and L. Garcia-Ballester, (eds.), *Medicine and Medical Ethics in Medieval and Early Modern Spain* (Jerusalem, 1996), 173, for the relationship between science and *halakhah*.

[31] There is a midrashic source for this idea; see *Midrash Temurah*, 2, *Ozar Midrashim*, ed. J. Eisenstein (New York, 1915), 580–1.

life. If there is no health to restore, then presumably, the obligation to treat lapses.[32]

Maimonides' strongly rationalist position is often cited by modern halakhists in order to oppose alternative medicine. His emphasis on 'rational and empirical' evidence implies that only rationally compelling treatments are valid, and that non-rational treatment ought to be eschewed. It is noteworthy that Maimonides is cited as a primary source by those opposed to homeopathic and other forms of so-called alternative medicine in the contemporary debate.[33]

Maimonides' strongly rationalist approach to medicine is certainly more in vogue today than in the past. This may be the result of the fact that human healing is not as hazardous to life and health as it was in previous generations. R. Ze'ev Nahum's view is definitely not part of contemporary *halakhah*, and Nahmanides and ibn Ezra are of significance only in cases involving complex choices with regard to patient welfare, and the terminal situation. Nevertheless, the belief in God's input into human healing is still a powerful component of the Jewish approach to healing. The modern period has seen greater confidence in human therapy,[34] but the belief that God plays a vital role in the cure is as powerful as ever. Faith has merely been complemented by a halakhic requirement to obtain all necessary medical treatment without delay. In this sense, both R. Aha and Abaye coexist within the framework of modern Jewish medical theology.

4. NAHMANIDES AND MAIMONIDES ON THE LEGAL STATUS OF MEDICAL PRACTICE IN JEWISH LAW

There is no simple answer to the question of whether medical practice has the formal status of a legal obligation (*mitzvah*) under Jewish law. In this section it will be argued that theology and law are particularly closely intertwined in this context, and any conclusion as to the status of medical practice as a *mitzvah* turns, to a great extent, on a person's understanding of the religious role of human healing. The major debate on this issue is between Nahmanides and Maimonides, which we will explain in terms of Nahmanides' theological reservations regarding human healing on the one hand, and Maimonides' strong approval of 'rational and empirical' medicine on the other.

---

[32] This matter is discussed at length in the following section on the halakhic status of medical practice.

[33] In this context, see the discussion of homeopathy in halakhic sources in G. Rabinowitz, 'A *Responsum* Regarding Homeopathy' (Heb.), *Halakhah Urefuah*, 3 (1983), 249; H. Regensberg, ibid. 244; *Resp. Aseh Lekha Rav*, 5 no. 13.

[34] See the sources cited in n. 12.

In his halakhic monograph on sickness and death,[35] Nahmanides begins his discussion of the legal status of medical practice by citing both the biblical law regarding compensation for medical expenses and the talmudic statement that 'permission has been given to the physician to heal'.[36] He proceeds to explain that the 'permission' mentioned in the Talmud 'is the permission of a *mitzvah*'. The phrase 'permission of a *mitzvah*', as opposed to simply 'a *mitzvah*', would seem to indicate that Nahmanides, who was a physician by profession, is obviously not entirely happy with the idea that medicine is merely a permitted activity in Jewish law, devoid of any formal *mitzvah* content. He therefore adds the phrase, 'of a *mitzvah*', to the term 'permission', thereby removing medicine from the category of the purely optional, but not giving it full *mitzvah* status. According to Nahmanides, the *mitzvah* quality of the physician's craft is based upon the idea that any act that brings about the saving of human life constitutes fulfilment of a number of important *mitzvot*. These include the biblical commandments to love one's neighbour as oneself;[37] not to stand idly by the blood of one's neighbour,[38] and to restore lost property,[39] which is extended by the Talmud to the restoration of an individual's health and life.[40] The addition of the phrase 'of a *mitzvah*' to the word 'permission' indicates that healing is consistent with this cluster of legal obligations and prohibitions. In this fashion, Nahmanides preserves the normative ambivalence of the talmudic source, i.e. medicine as a 'permission', while making the obligation to heal as strong as possible without actually categorizing it as an independent '*mitzvah*'.

It ought to be pointed out that Nahmanides' formulation also has practical ramifications. Implied in his formulation is the proposition that medical treatment assumes a *mitzvah* quality only if life is actually saved. If the patient dies, it will be clear—albeit retroactively—that the physician was not, in fact, engaged in a *mitzvah* and consequently, he will not be entitled to the protection normally given to those causing death in the course of performing a *mitzvah*. This aspect of Jewish criminal law and its significance for Nahmanides' approach to the halakhic status of medical practice is discussed in detail below. Finally, throughout *Torat Ha'adam* there is great emphasis on the necessity for the physician to be a genuine expert in his craft. The *mitzvah* is to save life, not to practise medicine per se; hence the doctor must be an expert, since the saving of life is only likely if he really knows what he is doing.[41]

---

[35] *Torat Ha'adam, Kol Kitvei Haramban*, 2, ed. C. Chavel (Jerusalem, 1964), 41–5. For a recent comment on this work, see S. Kottek, 'Medical Practice and Jewish Law: Nahmanides' *Sefer Torat Ha'adam*', in Kottek and Garcia-Ballester, *Medicine and Medical Ethics*, 163–72.
[36] See nn. 1–2 above.   [37] Lev. 19: 18.   [38] Lev. 19: 16.   [39] Deut. 22: 2.
[40] *Sanhedrin*, 73a; *Bava Kamma*, 81b.   [41] *Torat Ha'adam*, ed. Chavel, 42–4.

Nahmanides' ambivalent approach to the legal status of medical practice is analysed by a number of halakhic authorities. R. Joshua Falk, in his commentary on the *Tur* code, describes it as a 'two-tier' model.[42] The first tier is the optional talmudic baseline. There is no obligation and no *mitzvah* quality at this level. However, should an individual study medicine and practise it, the second tier becomes operative, and what that person is doing gains *mitzvah* quality, but only in so far as it constitutes fulfilment of one of the general commandments to save and preserve human life in Jewish law.

It is reasonable to suppose that Nahmanides' insistence upon preserving the normative ambivalence of the physician's role in his *Torat Ha'adam* stems in no small measure from his theological position in his commentary on the Bible. It will be recalled that in that commentary, Nahmanides indicated that highly spiritual individuals would do best by eschewing human healing, even in the post-prophetic period. Clearly, medicine cannot be a fully fledged *mitzvah* if it is subject to this type of reservation. In his *Torat Ha'adam*, Nahmanides also takes care to preserve the distinction, made in his *Commentary on the Torah*, between the physician and the patient, i.e. any obligation to heal devolves solely upon the physician and not upon the patient. A person is under no obligation to seek medical advice, but if he chooses to go to a doctor, the doctor has a duty to treat him.

As explained above, Maimonides had absolutely no theological reservations about the validity of empirical and rational medicine.[43] Indeed, if there are any theological errors to be made in this context, they are the lot of those who deny the validity of human healing and rely instead upon miracles. In his codification of the *halakhah*, therefore, Maimonides states quite simply that medical therapy is a *mitzvah*. The context of this statement is the laws of oaths, and Maimonides deals with the question of whether a person's oath to refrain from giving benefit to another individual because of a serious rift between them, does, in fact, prevent the former from administering medical treatment to the latter. Maimonides articulates the mishnaic ruling permitting medical assistance in these circumstances as follows:

There is no prohibition on curing a sick person [whom one vowed not to benefit], since it is a *mitzvah* to do so, and the physician is required by the law to heal the sick of Israel. The source for this obligation is the verse, 'And you shall restore it to him'.[44] This commandment extends to a person's body. If a person sees another individual perishing, and there is a possibility of saving him, that person is obliged to use his body, his property or his knowledge, in order to effect a rescue or cure.[45]

---

[42] *Perishah, Yoreh Deah*, 336: 4.　　　[43] See nn. 25–32.　　　[44] Deut. 22: 2.
[45] *Commentary to the Mishnah, Nedarim*, 4: 4; *Hilkot Nedarim*, 6: 8.

According to Maimonides, there is a specific *mitzvah* to practise medicine, and its biblical source is not the classical verse dealing with medical expenses, but the verse regarding the restoration of lost health. It ought to be noted in passing that both verses are mediated by rabbinic exegesis. Maimonides' choice of the verse concerning the restoration of health, rather than the more widely used one regarding medical expenses,[46] may have been motivated by a desire to avoid the ambivalence in the talmudic interpretation of the medical expenses verse, which is cast in terms of a permission to heal, not an obligation to do so.[47]

In general, Nahmanides and Maimonides differ consistently in their halakhic solutions to biomedical issues. These differences may all be explained in the light of their diametrically opposed views on the theological significance of human healing.[48] The link between the theological positions of these scholars and their halakhic rulings is a good example of the relationship between theology and law in medical *halakhah*.

In terms of the later halakhic development with regard to the legal status of medicine, it would appear that Nahmanides' view prevailed.[49] The basis for this conclusion is the law governing the negligent killing of a patient by a physician. Under Jewish law, inadvertent homicide carries the penalty of exile.[50] An exception is made in cases in which the inadvertent homicide occurred during the course of the fulfilment of a *mitzvah*, as when a child dies as a result of being chastised by his father, or a teacher's disciplining of his student brings about the student's death.[51] In both these

---

[46] Maimonides often uses different proof-texts from those found in the Talmud; see B. Z. Benedict, 'On Maimonides' Methodology' (Hch.), *Sefer Hayovel Lerabbi Hanokh Albeck* (Jerusalem, 1963), 52.

[47] See *Torah Temimah, Deuteronomy*, 22: 2 no. 18. An interesting result of Maimonides' choice of this source is that it provides the basis for arguing that there is no obligation to heal unless the patient can be restored to full health, since the commandment to restore lost property only applies so long as that particular piece of property is fully restorable to its owner. Once this is no longer the case, then the obligation lapses. It may, therefore, be inferred that if a person's health is no longer restorable, i.e. their lives may be saved but they will not be 'restored' to the state of health that they previously enjoyed, then the obligation to heal also lapses; see I. Jakobovits, 'The Law Relating to the Precipitation of Death of a Terminally Ill and Suffering Patient' (Heb.), *Hapardes*, 31 (1957), 18.

[48] See A. Steinberg, *Encyclopaedia of Jewish Medical Ethics* (Jerusalem, 1988–98), vi. 186–94.

[49] In this context, it is noteworthy that Nahmanides' view also prevailed in the debate over the status of laws derived by the rabbis on the basis of the application of hermeneutical principles. Maimonides maintains that such laws are rabbinic in status, whereas Nahmanides upgrades them to biblical status. The majority of halakhic authorities accept Nahmanides' view that all laws deduced by means of the hermeneutical principles used by the rabbis are biblical, unless the Talmud specifically relegates them to the rabbinic category; see M. Elon, *Jewish Law* (Philadelphia, 1994), 209–10. The basis for the consensus in favour of Nahmanides would appear to be a theological one, i.e. it would be theologically risky to relegate the vast majority of the *halakhah* to rabbinic status; see: D. Sinclair, 'Legal Reasoning in the Writings of Maimonides and Nahmanides' (Heb.), *Minhah Leish* (Jerusalem, 1991), 354.

[50] See M. Elon (ed.), *The Principles of Jewish Law* (Jerusalem, 1974), 530–2.

[51] *Makkot*, 8a; Maimonides, *Hilkhot Rozeah*, 5: 6.

cases the fact that the fatality occurred during the performance of a *mitzvah* means that there is no exile. On the other hand, a physician who negligently kills a patient is not exempt from exile. This rule is attributed to the *Tosefta*, which states quite simply that 'a physician who causes death is liable to exile'.[52] It is also codified in the *Tur*[53] and the *Shulhan Arukh*,[54] with the qualification that only a physician who realizes that his negligence has caused the death of the patient is exiled.[55] Nevertheless, the fundamental implication of this provision is that medical treatment is not a fully fledged *mitzvah* with respect to the imposition of exile; if it were, the physician— like the father and the teacher—would be exempt from this penalty. Various suggestions have been made with a view to explaining this law, and it is generally agreed that an important factor in the imposition of exile upon a physician who inadvertently kills a patient is that it is less of a *mitzvah* to practise medicine than it is to teach Torah or to educate children.[56]

Amongst these suggestions is that of Rabbi Abraham Maskil-Le'eitan, a commentator on the *Shulhan Arukh*, who makes the following distinction between chastisement and medical therapy: 'No *mitzvah* has been performed if the patient dies, unlike the cases of the father and teacher, in which the *mitzvah*-quality of the acts of instruction and teaching are independent of the inadvertently fatal result of the chastisement.'[57] Accordingly, medical treatment is not a *mitzvah* per se. If the patient is cured, the physician has fulfilled the *mitzvah* of saving a human life. If he fails, however, no *mitzvah* has been fulfilled, and the physician must go into exile. By contrast, in the case of chastisement by a father or teacher, the very act of chastisement is an integral part of the performance of the *mitzvah* of education. Consequently, even if the child or pupil dies as a result, a *mitzvah* has been performed, and neither the father nor the teacher are required to go into exile for their inadvertent homicide.

A more radical approach in terms of the link between the theology of medicine and the *halakhah* is that of Rabbi Joseph Engel, who specifically bases himself upon Nahmanides' approach to the theological status of medicine as explicated above. Under that approach, human healing is a

---

[52] *Tosefta, Makkot*, 2: 5; *Tosefta Bava Kamma*, 9: 3; *Tashbez*, 3 no. 82; *Biur Hagra, Yoreh Deah*, 336: 6. This ruling is also cited by Nahmanides in *Torat Ha'adam*, ed. Chavel, 42–3.

[53] *Yoreh Deah*, 336.

[54] *Yoreh Deah*, 336: 1. See *Arukh Hashulhan, Yoreh Deah*, 336: 2, where the point is made that in the absence of negligence, there is no exile for a physician who inadvertently kills a patient.

[55] See *Bayit Hadash, Yoreh Deah*, 336, for the significance of the expression 'becomes aware' in the formulations of both the *Tosefta* (see n. 52) and the *Shulhan Arukh* (see n. 54), and the required causal nexus between treatment and death.

[56] Some authorities simply pointed out the apparent discrepancy, e.g. *Tashbez*, 3 no. 82, in which R. Duran observes that 'there is a distinction between the cases', but makes no attempt to spell the distinction out.   [57] *Yad Avraham, Yoreh Deah*, 336: 1.

fundamentally negative activity: the person of faith ought to place his trust squarely in Divine hands. In the light of this negative attitude towards medicine, Rabbi Engel reasons that 'it is not considered a *mitzvah* to the extent of exempting a doctor who is guilty of inadvertent homicide from exile'.[58]

It may, therefore, be concluded that the practice of medicine does not have the same obligatory force in Jewish law as other *mitzvot*. It is both dependent upon the saving of life for its justification—Nahmanides' two-tier approach—and circumscribed by ideological reservations. On the point of the legal status of medical practice, therefore, Nahmanides would seem to have won out over Maimonides.

It is, however, important to limit the debate between Maimonides and Nahmanides to the issue of the legal status of medicine in theory, rather than in practice. On the theoretical level, medicine per se may not have full *mitzvah* status, but there is no question that the *mitzvot* upon which it is based, i.e. the obligations to both save life and to have one's life saved, are binding, thus imbuing any potentially life-saving treatment with *mitzvah*-quality. This is certainly the view of Nahmanides himself, who, as pointed out above, always takes care to list the *mitzvot* requiring the saving of life as the basis for the 'permission' granted to the physician to heal, whenever he deals with the obligation to practise medicine.

In theory, life-saving therapy may be forced upon a patient. The basis for coercive life-saving therapy and the situations in which it is applicable are discussed in the following section, together with the exceptions to the coercion rule, and the notion of a doctrine of limited patient autonomy in this area. We will also explore the scope, if any, for the influence of Nahmanides' approach to the theological standing of human healing and the legal status of medical practice, on the limited autonomy concept in Jewish biomedical law.

5. COERCIVE LIFE-SAVING MEDICAL THERAPY AND LIMITED PATIENT AUTONOMY

The obligation to save human life is grounded in a number of biblical texts,[59] and it is settled law that this obligation overrides all but three prohibitions: murder, idolatry, and unlawful sexual relations.[60] In all other

---

[58] *Gilyonei Hashas, Berakhot,* 60a.   [59] See nn. 37–40.

[60] Lev., 18: 5, *Yoma* 85a. Martyrdom is also required in a situation in which a Jew is faced with a choice between death and the violation of any religious norm, which, in the light of the objective circumstances, may be understood by others as a public renunciation of his faith (*Sanhedrin,* 74a–b; *Shulhan Arukh, Yoreh Deah,* 157).

cases, the saving of life is paramount, and even the Sabbath and the Day of Atonement are overridden by the obligation to save life.[61] The Jerusalem Talmud goes as far as to brand a rabbi who has failed to teach this rule to his flock and, as a result, is asked a question concerning the permissibility of breaking the Sabbath in order to save a life, a 'despicable individual'.[62] This is because the first thing that the rabbi ought to have done was to teach this rule, so that if a life-threatening situation arose on the Sabbath, there would be no need to waste time in asking a question.

The obligation to break the Sabbath in order to save human life often arises in relation to medical treatment. If a patient is diagnosed as being in danger of losing his or her life unless they receive immediate medical attention, the *halakhah* requires that they receive that attention even at the cost of breaking the Sabbath. Indeed, many authorities maintain that any religious obligation that is fulfilled in defiance of life-saving medical advice is halakhically invalid.[63] In the nature of things, it is physicians who determine that the life of any particular person is in danger, and it is on the basis of their considered diagnoses and recommended treatments that the *halakhah* permits the sanctity of the Holy Days to be overridden by the need to save life.[64]

Now, since it is not medical treatment per se that is obligatory, but the saving of life, the question that must be asked before breaking the Sabbath is whether the recommended procedure is actually going to save human life. This was certainly a wise course in the past when medicine was far less effective in the saving of life than it is today. Only a procedure characterized by a high level of medical effectiveness overrides the dietary laws or the Sabbath. In a case involving the use of ritually forbidden substances for life-saving purposes, R. Moses Isserles ruled that a sick person may ingest such substances only 'if the cure is well-known or it is recommended by an expert'.[65] The same requirement is applied to a cure for epilepsy containing insects prohibited for consumption under Jewish law. Notwithstanding the fact that in halakhic terms, epilepsy is treated as a life-threatening disease, owing to the possibility that the epileptic might fall into a fire or a river during a fit, the potion is only permitted if it is a 'known cure'.[66] The halakhic position on this point is summed up by R. Abraham Gombiner, who rules that only 'known cures or therapies

[61] *Shulhan Arukh, Orah Hayyim*, 328, 618.
[62] *Yoma*, 8: 5. In the same *dictum*, the *Jerusalem Talmud* states that one who asks whether or not it is permissible to break the Sabbath in order to save life is considered 'a shedder of blood' since during the time it takes to pose the question, the individual concerned could have had his or her life saved.
[63] See *Resp. Mahari Asad, Orah Hayyim*, no. 160; *Resp. Maharam Shick, Orah Hayyim*, no. 260; *Resp. Minhat Yizhak*, 4 no. 102.   [64] See *Shulhan Arukh, Orah Hayyim*, 328, 618.
[65] *Yoreh Deah*, 155: 3.   [66] See *Hagahot Maimoniot, Hilkhot Ma'akhalot Asurot*, 14: 2.

recommended by an expert' override the prohibitions of the Sabbath day.[67] Only after the recommended procedure satisfies the practical test of medical effectiveness does it qualify as a life-saving therapy for the purpose of overriding the dietary laws or the sanctity of the Sabbath and the other Holy Days.

What is the position with regard to a person who is diagnosed by doctors as being in immediate need of life-saving treatment by means of a medically proven procedure, but who insists upon remaining untreated for the duration of the Holy Day since he does not wish to violate the holiness of the Sabbath or the Day of Atonement? The standard reply to this question is that individuals who do not wish to be treated are to be forced to follow medical advice in order to save their lives. Saving one's life overrides all but the three prohibitions referred to above, and not breaching the sanctity of the Holy Days is not included in that list. The recalcitrant individual is compelled to follow the halakhic mandate regarding coercive medical therapy for the sake of saving human life, and physical force may be used in order to ensure that the therapy is administered to the patient.[68]

A person who refuses life-saving therapy on a weekday is subject to coercion, on the basis of an a fortiori argument from the Sabbath and the Holy Days. If an individual is to be coerced into breaking the Sabbath for the sake of saving his life, then a fortiori he is to be compelled to have his life saved on a weekday. Indeed, the title of the section of R. Emden's halakhic work dealing with this issue is: 'The Law Regarding Someone Who Refuses Life-Saving Treatment on the Sabbath and on Weekdays'.[69] It will be recalled that R. Emden opines that only easily diagnosable diseases with certain cures fall within the domain of the human healer. Consistent with this position is his ruling that it is only to such diseases that the coercion rule applies. In the same way that only medically certain life-saving therapy is mandatory on the Sabbath, it is only to be forced on an individual during the week if it passes the certainty test.

R. Emden's list of examples of halakhically coercible medical treatments includes amputations, and in this context, it is noteworthy that the *Tosefta*, a parallel work to the Mishnah, uses the example of life-saving coercive amputations in order to justify the principle that people may be forced to do things for their own benefit, even if they object at the time. According to the *Tosefta*, the property of Israelites who have not paid their annual contributions to the Temple fund by a certain date is to be confiscated until the payment is made. In order to explain this step, the *Tosefta*

---

[67] *Magen Avraham, Orah Hayyim*, 339: 1. See also *Nishmat Avraham, Yoreh Deah*, 155: 1.

[68] *Resp. Radbaz*, 4 no. 1139; *Mor Ukeziah*, no. 328; *Magen Avraham, Orah Hayyim* 328: 6. See also *Shulhan Arukh Harav, Orah Hayyim*, 328: 11.   [69] *Mor Ukeziah*, no. 328.

makes a medical analogy, comparing the action of the court in forcefully appropriating private property to that of a physician who 'compels a person with a diseased leg to undergo an amputation; he does so for the sake of obtaining a cure'.[70] At the end of the day, the patient will be grateful to the doctor for saving his life. In a similar fashion, the person whose property has been appropriated in order to force him to pay his contribution to the Temple will gratefully acknowledge the fact that force was applied, since the benefit of paying far outweighs the unpleasantness of the appropriation.

The high value attached to the preservation of human life in Jewish law is also expressed in other ways, such as the prohibitions on suicide[71] and self-endangerment.[72] According to Maimonides and other halakhists, the theological principle underlying these and other laws aimed at the preservation of human life is that 'a person's life is not his property; it is the property of the Holy One blessed be He'.[73] This theory of the Divine

---

[70] *Tosefta, Shekalim,* 1: 6. A number of commentators on the *Tosefta* observe that since sacrifices purchased with money not freely given are invalid, there must be some form of retroactive consent in this case. The dominant view amongst the commentators is that once the Israelites whose property has been seized realize the spiritual benefits accruing to them by virtue of the observance of the sacrificial services, they would be happy to ratify their contributions retroactively (see *Tosefta, Kifeshuta Shekalim,* 1: 6, *s.v. vekhavanat habrayta*). There is thus a notion of retroactive consent underlying the coercive principle in relation to sacrifices, which ought also to extend to medical therapy. This point is of interest in terms of comparative jurisprudence, since the common law also uses the notion of retroactive consent in order to justify non-consensual treatment in cases in which such consent will most likely be forthcoming (see P. Skegg, *Law, Ethics and Medicine* (Oxford, 1984), 115). Reasonably foreseeable retroactive consent is one of the conditions required by section 15 of the Israeli Patient's Rights Law, 5756-1996, for the administration of coercive medical treatment (p. 176 below).

[71] Elon (ed.), *The Principles of Jewish Law,* 477.

[72] Deut. 4: 9. In *Hilkhot Rozeah,* 1: 4, Maimonides states that 'whoever transgresses the decrees of the Rabbis concerning self-endangerment, and says that as long as he is prepared to take the risk, his actions should be of no concern to others, is to be beaten for his rebelliousness'. On the prohibition on self-injury in the context of live organ donation, see Ch. 6 s. 3.

[73] Maimonides, *Hilkhot Rozeah,* 1: 4, in relation to the law that a ransom may not be accepted for the life of a murderer. Radbaz, *Hilkhot Sanhedrin,* 18: 6, uses this idea to explain the inadmissibility of confessions in capital cases under Jewish law. See also F. Rosner and J. D. Bleich (eds.), *Jewish Bioethics* (New York, 1979), 18–9. The idea that life is Divine property and may not be damaged by its human stewards is also found in the Greek tradition. Plato's *Phaedo* contains this exchange between Socrates and Cebes: 'But I do think, Cebes, that it is true that the gods are our guardians and that we men are part of their property. Do you not think so? I do, said Cebes. Well then, said he, if one of your possessions were to kill itself, though you had not signified that you wished it to die, should you not be angry with it? Should you not punish it, if punishment were possible? Certainly, he replied.' Socrates uses this argument to refute the legitimacy of suicide in circumstances other than those mandated by the gods (*The Trial and Death of Socrates,* trans. F. Church (London, 1910), 113). The idea that self-destruction is an offence against the gods was part of the teachings of the Pythagorean and Hippocratic Schools, as a result of which it became part of Western medical ethics; see L. Edelstein, 'The Hippocratic Oath', in C. Burns (ed.), *Legacies in Ethics and Medicine* (New York, 1977), 26.

ownership of the body is cited by many halakhic authorities as the ideological springboard for their endorsement of coercive life-saving treatment in Jewish law.[74]

It would be wrong to assume that Jewish law has no room at all for
patient autonomy in relation to questions of life and death.[75] Both the
coercion rule and the Divine ownership principle reflect the starting point
of the halakhic approach, which is the supreme value of human life and
the absence of personal choice as to whether to dispose of it. However, in
complex cases involving clashes between competing halakhically and
morally valid options, patient choice may well be the halakhic answer. An
example of such a case, and its resolution using patient autonomy, is
R. Feinstein's *responsum* concerning a person's decision to undergo a very
risky operation in order to achieve a life expectancy of five to ten years,
even though it is possible to survive for a short period of time without it.
In halakhic terms, the obligation to preserve life applies equally well to
the short as to the long term.[76] Hence, it might have been assumed that an
individual faced with a hazardous procedure ought to forgo the risky
treatment in the light of the serious threat to their life expectancy, short
though it may be. After all, in matters of life and death, the preferable
course is 'to sit and do nothing' rather than transgress the prohibition
against shortening life.[77] Nevertheless, R. Feinstein argues that in this
type of situation, the individual concerned is permitted to choose the
operation, and need not remain passive. It is significant that R. Feinstein
recognizes the desire to achieve a normal lifespan as a legitimate one in
terms of the *halakhah*, and takes it into account in his ruling in favour of
patient choice in this case. The chance, however slim, of a successful result
to the operation overrides the prohibition on shortening life. R. Feinstein
argues that in situations like these, 'people own their own bodies with
respect to improving the quality of their lives'. Notwithstanding the concept that the ownership of human bodies is vested in God, and the notion
flowing from this concept that people are no more than stewards of their
own bodies, R. Feinstein places the solution in this case in the hands of the
individual concerned, and uses the rather dramatic image of the ownership of the body being transferred by God to that person, in order to provide some theological justification for his ruling.[78]

In his ruling, R. Feinstein states quite explicitly that the motivation for
undergoing the life-risking operation is the patient's desire to improve his

---

[74] See *Nishmat Avraham, Yoreh Deah*, no. 155.
[75] See D. Shatz, 'Concepts of Autonomy in Jewish Medical Ethics', *Jewish Law Annual*,
12 (1997), 3–43, for an illuminating and sustained analysis of the concept of autonomy in the
halakhah in this area.   [76] *Yoma*, 85a.
[77] *Resp. Noda Biyehuda*, pt. 2, *Yoreh Deah*, no. 59.
[78] *Resp. Iggrot Moshe, Yoreh Deah*, 3 no. 36.

quality of life. He also points out that many people in this position would opt for the operation. According to R. Feinstein the quest for quality of life is acceptable as a counterweight to the halakhic principle of avoiding risk to even short-term life, especially if the quality concerned is not unreasonable in terms of the average person's expectations. The implication here is that the *halakhah*, therefore, justifies the placing of the final decision in the hands of the patient, even when the choice is between a rational principle such as the quality of life, and a well-established legal one—in our case, that of the preservation of short-term existence.

Another illustration of the application of individual autonomy in order to resolve hard cases in the area of life and death is the rule that people may risk their lives for purposes of earning a living, notwithstanding the above-mentioned prohibition on self-endangerment. Clearly, the extent to which life and limb are going to be put at risk is highly relevant in this context. However, it is established *halakhah* that a person may undertake a profession or calling that regularly poses some risk to life and limb, as long as there are others who also follow this particular lifestyle, and the sole purpose is to earn a living for the person concerned and his family. Here too, the existence of a morally justifiable activity, i.e. choice of a livelihood, is sufficient to counterbalance the clear-cut halakhic prohibition on self-endangerment.[79]

The type of autonomy that emerges from these examples is limited, in the sense that the maximization of personal autonomy is not an ideal to which the halakhic system aspires. On the contrary: in general the *halakhah* seeks primarily to define and enforce obligations. In these two examples, however, individual autonomy is used as a tool for resolving hard cases. The difficulty involved is the result of a clash between a rational principle and a well-established halakhic norm. In both cases, the halakhic response is to pass the decision over to the individual concerned, and that decision constitutes the appropriate halakhic solution to the problem. In addition to being sound in rational terms, it is evident that striving to achieve goals such as an improved quality of life, and a decent livelihood are also valid moral aspirations. It may, therefore, be concluded that Jewish law is prepared to grant a measure of personal autonomy to individuals struggling to find the right balance between their rational and moral aspirations, and halakhic norms.

Since it does not recognize a strong form of autonomy, Jewish law would support coercion both in order to maintain short-term life and to prevent the pursuit of a dangerous occupation, if the risk was morally and rationally unjustifiable. This would be the case even if the individual concerned really

---

[79] *Resp. Noda Biyehuda*, pt. 2, *Yoreh Deah*, no. 10; *Resp. Iggrot Moshe, Hoshen Mishpat*, 1, no. 104.

wanted to risk his life, and even if no harm to others was involved. It is only in cases of genuine clashes between morality and law that the limited autonomy principle comes into play. The issue of autonomy will be discussed further in the next section, which compares the limited form outlined here with the stronger form adopted by common law in modern times.

It is important to emphasize that the above examples of limited autonomy in Jewish law are confined to cases in which individuals choose a morally justified, life-enhancing course of action—a greatly improved quality of life or a decent livelihood—at the expense of a competing halakhic norm. We have yet to discuss a patient's right to refuse medically certain life-saving treatment when the result will be his death. Before embarking upon a discussion of the possibility of justifying the refusal of life-saving therapy in such a situation, it is necessary to examine two related ideas: patient input into the definition of medical certainty, and the negative effects of coercive medical treatment upon a terminal patient.

It would appear that for purposes of justifying coercive life-saving therapy, the definition of medical certainty consists of both a subjective and an objective element. Both elements are mentioned by R. Emden in his seminal ruling in this area.[80] According to R. Emden, a person is to be compelled to submit to medical treatment only if the recommended cure is a well-tried one and 'the patient has full confidence in it'. R. Emden was writing in the eighteenth century, and the idea that the patient must have full confidence in the therapy is probably reflective of the generally uncertain outcome of all but the most straightforward of medical procedures in this period. R. Emden's ruling is widely cited in halakhic literature, and patient confidence is a recognized element in the establishment of medical certainty for halakhic purposes.[81] In the absence of patient confidence in the proposed therapy, the obligation to coerce would not apply, despite the objective medical evidence in its favour.

A person's subjective assessment of his condition also plays an important role in determining whether the Sabbath or the Day of Atonement should be broken on his behalf. For example, if the objective, medical evidence does not indicate that forbidden activities should be permitted, but the person insists that without a breach of the law, his life will be in danger, his subjective assessment of the situation overrides the medical evidence.[82] Scriptural proof is adduced for this position from the verse in Proverbs: 'The heart knows its own bitterness'.[83] Once again, although this position may reflect the state of medicine in the past, it has been

---

[80] *Mor Ukeziah*, no. 328.

[81] R. Emden's ruling is widely cited, see *Mishneh Berurah, Orah Hayyim*, 328: 5; *Resp. Ziz Eliezer*, 15 no. 40; *Resp. Iggrot Moshe, Hoshen Mishpat*, 2 nos. 73–4; *Aseh Lekha Rav*, 4: 64.

[82] *Yoma*, 82a; *Shulhan Arukh, Orah Hayyim*, 328: 5, 619: 1; *Shulhan Arukh Harav, Orah Hayyim*, 328: 12. [83] Prov. 14: 10.

incorporated into halakhic doctrine, and must be taken into account when making decisions with regard to coercive life-saving medical therapy in Jewish law.

The importance of the patient's own assessment of his medical needs also finds expression in the following *responsum*, which deals with homeopathic remedies in a life-threatening situation. R. Hayyim David Halevy discusses a case involving a young man who refused to undergo chemotherapy for his cancer, and opted instead for homeopathic medicine. In his discussion of the issue of compulsion in these circumstances, R. Halevy points out that in this case, since the physicians advocating the chemotherapy could not claim absolute medical certainty regarding a cure, the cancer was an 'internal disease' according to R. Emden's definition, and as such, the coercion rule does not apply. Moreover, the patient was utterly convinced that the chemotherapy would not be effective. On the basis of this reasoning, R. Halevy concluded that there was no halakhic justification for forcing the young man to receive chemotherapy, as opposed to homeopathic treatment in this case.[84]

Does the patient's subjective assessment of his situation ever justify refusal of all medical assistance, be it mainstream or alternative? A precedent that deals directly with this question is the account of the death of R. Isaac b. Asher, a medieval Tosafist known by the acronym Riba.[85] Riba refused to eat on the Day of Atonement, despite his physician's warning that unless he broke his fast, he would surely die. In the physician's view, there was a chance that if he ate he would survive, but he could not guarantee that Riba would live, even if he broke his fast. Riba was sure that he would die in any event, and is reported to have stated, using standard halakhic terminology,[86] that his certainty with regard to his own death was superior to the doubtful possibility offered to him by his doctor that if he ate, he might survive. He chose, therefore, to fast and did, indeed, die.[87] In reconciling Riba's conduct with the obligation to place human life over and above the preservation of the sanctity of the Day of Atonement, R. David b. Zimra (Radbaz) applies the above-mentioned verse in

---

[84] 'Non-Consensual Medical Treatment' (Heb.), *Hazofeh*, 18 July 1991. An opposing view was expressed by Y. Metzger, 'Is There an Obligation to Force a Patient to Receive Medical Treatment in Jewish Law?' (Heb.), *Hazofeh*, 5 July 1991, mainly on the grounds that homeopathy is not a valid form of therapy under Jewish law. R. Halevy is perfectly prepared to accept homeopathy as a legitimate form of medicine. This disagreement seems to reflect the classical dispute between Maimonides and Nahmanides referred to above.

[85] See E. Urbach, *Baalei Hatosafot* (Tel-Aviv, 1980), 165–73.

[86] See *Encyclopaedia Talmudit*, iv. 199.

[87] *Piskei Recanati*, no. 166; see also E. Ben Shlomo, 'Rejecting Medical Therapy on Grounds of Piety' (Heb.), *Assia*, 49–50 (1990), 173, in which an attempt is made to explain Riba's conduct as part of a typically Ashkenazic approach to the relationship between medicine and *halakhah*, and to contrast it with an opposing Sephardic model of behaviour in similar circumstances.

Proverbs, and concludes that a patient's certainty regarding his or her demise may, in certain cases, outweigh the uncertainty of the doctors with regard to the chances of recovery, and may justify the refusal of any form of medical treatment.[88] It may be assumed that Radbaz's motivation for this analysis is to clear Riba of any suspicion of having broken the law; after all, eminent Tosafists are not supposed to ignore basic *halakhah*. Radbaz also makes it very clear that his explanation of Riba's conduct is not meant to be taken as a precedent for the general public, but is confined to rare cases involving individuals of significant spiritual stature. It has, nevertheless, become part of the *halakhah* in this area and, as we will shortly point out, it surfaces in a modified form in modern *responsa* regarding the treatment of the terminally ill.

The stage is now set for a general exploration of the views of modern authorities on the question of refusing life-saving treatment in contemporary *halakhah*. The first two matters to be discussed are high risk and medical uncertainty as to therapeutic outcome. This will be followed by a discussion of the weight to be attached to a patient's subjective opinion as to the risk involved in any particular procedure, and the need to avoid the potentially traumatic effects of coercive medical treatment in the case of a competent terminal patient.

The general trend amongst modern authorities is to allow patients to refuse any treatment that poses a risk to life, even if their prospects for long-term survival without the procedure are poor. The scope for exercising such decisions has expanded rapidly with the rise of geriatric medicine and in the light of the phenomenon of increasingly high numbers of chronically ill patients being treated for longer periods of time. Many standard medical procedures for the young and middle-aged are much riskier for the elderly and the chronically sick. Since a large portion of modern medical therapy is administered to the latter category of patient, the possibility of choice is much more widespread today than in the past. As already observed, R. Feinstein ruled that a person is allowed to choose to undergo a risky procedure, notwithstanding the risk to his short-term lifespan.[89] However, the choice belongs to the person concerned, and he may also exercise it in favour of declining the risky operation.[90] This point is made by R. Aryeh Grossnass, who emphasizes the fact that the permission given to a sick individual to decide whether to undergo a risky treatment, with the object of significantly improving his quality of life, may also be used in order to decide against the procedure.[91] The risk factor is also an element in R. Shlomo Zalman Auerbach's well-known decision that a 50-year old man suffering from chronic diabetes, blindness, blocked

---

[88] *Resp. Radbaz*, 3 no. 485.   [89] *Resp. Iggrot Moshe, Yoreh Deah*, 3 no. 36.
[90] *Sefer Hahayyim, Orah Hayyim*, no. 328.   [91] *Resp. Lev Aryeh*, 2 no. 35.

arteries, and various infections, is not required to undergo the amputation of his gangrenous leg. Any operation of this type is dangerous; in this case, however, the patient's condition greatly magnified the risk involved. The outcome of the operation would not be the restoration of the patient to full health: it would merely stave off his death from other causes for a few months. As such, the procedure was also medically uncertain in terms of obtaining a life-saving cure, and, as such, not amenable to the coercion principle.[92]

The element of medical uncertainty is a major aspect in the approach of modern *halakhah* to the issue of coercive life-saving therapy. According to R. Immanuel Jakobovits, uncertainty is an integral feature of modern geriatrics, particularly in relation to the care and treatment of the terminally ill. The choice of treatment is much broader today than it was in the past, and the range of factors that must be taken into account in deciding on what is best for a patient is also much more extensive than it was a few years ago. At the same time, physicians are being trained to present the various treatment options to the patient, as opposed to determining the proper course of action in an authoritarian manner. This training means that it will become progressively more difficult to establish objective medical certainty in complex terminal cases. The scope for coercion is, therefore, becoming increasingly limited, and in practice, patient consent is likely to become much more the norm in Jewish biomedical law than it was in the past.[93]

R. Saul Yisraeli takes up the question of an equivocal medical opinion and argues that in this type of situation it is up to the patient to decide whether to undergo a particular treatment. The majority of authorities are of the opinion that people hold their bodies in trust from God.[94] R. Yisraeli belongs to the minority who recognize a person's right of ownership to his or her body.[95] On the basis of right, R. Yisraeli rules that patient choice is the solution in situations in which there is no decisive medical view as to the best treatment for the individual in question.[96]

R. Auerbach's decision, referred to above in relation to the question of high-risk treatment,[97] turns mainly on the issue of medical uncertainty. Since the patient in that case had only a very slim chance of survival, the therapeutic outcome of the amputation, even for the short term, must

[92] See *Nishmat Avraham, Yoreh Deah*, 155: 2.

[93] 'Some Modern *Responsa* on Medico-Legal Problems', *Jewish Medical Ethics*, 1 (1988), 6.

[94] *Resp. Rosh*, no. 68: 10; *Resp. Rivash*, no. 484; *Tosefta, Hoshen Mishpat*, no. 384; *Shulhan Arukh, Hoshen Mishpat*, 97: 15; R. Shlomo Zevin, *Leor Hahalakhah*, 318.

[95] 'The Kibiyeh Incident in the Light of the *Halakhah*' (Heb.), *Hatorah Vehamedinah*, 4–6 (1953–4), 109.

[96] See *Biomedical Legal Decisions* (Heb.) (Israel Medical Association, Tel Aviv, 1989), 194.

[97] See *Nishmat Avraham, Yoreh Deah*, 155: 2.

have been in doubt, and coercion was therefore out of the question. It is noteworthy that in that case, R. Auerbach ruled that not only was the patient not to be coerced to lose his remaining leg; he was not even to be persuaded verbally to consent to the operation.

There is an important connection between the limitation of coercive treatment to situations in which it is medically certain, and the law of the *terefah*. This law, which is dealt with at length in Chapter 5 section 5, provides that if a person is suffering from a condition which, according to well-founded medical opinion, will definitely cause death within a twelve-month period, it is no longer necessary to make the same efforts to keep him alive as would be done in the case of a non-*terefah*. Since many of the difficult cases in modern bioethics involve terminally ill patients, the law of the *terefah* would appear to militate in favour of expanding patient choice rather than increasing the scope of coercive treatment.

R. Feinstein discusses the question of the weight to be attached to a patient's belief that the life-saving medical procedure that is being proposed is extremely risky, even if this belief has no sound medical basis.[98] In his view, if a patient refuses the treatment on the grounds that it is risky, even if that belief is medically unjustified, the choice is to be respected. It should also be noted that in Rabbi Feinstein's view, a patient's choice to refuse risky treatment on subjective grounds is justified, not only in cases of a perceived threat to short-term life, but even in the case of a less than fatal risk.[99]

R. Feinstein's major contribution to this area is his argument that if the proposed coercive treatment will traumatize a terminal patient, it ought not to be carried out. In the course of two consolidating *responsa* on medical *halakhah*, R. Feinstein rules that physical force may not be applied to a competent, terminal adult patient in order to make him or her submit to a particular life-saving treatment, if the outcome of the coercion is likely to be the traumatization of the patient as a result of having his personal wishes overridden by force, or even knowing that such a course of action will take place. This type of trauma may very well lead to injury or even death, both of which must be avoided at all costs.

In the first of these *responsa*, R. Feinstein addresses the question of giving medication to a terminally ill person against his or her wishes:

If all doctors in the hospital agree that a particular therapy is necessary, the patient may be forced to undergo the treatment, provided that he will not be traumatised by it. If, however, the patient will be traumatised, then even if his grounds for refusing the treatment are entirely irrational, no steps may be taken to force the

[98] *Resp. Iggrot Moshe, Hoshen Mishpat*, 2 no. 73.

[99] See M. Feinstein, 'Endangering Transient Life for the Sake of a Doubtful Recovery' (Heb.), *Halakhah Urefuah*, 1 (1980), 131.

therapy upon him, since such steps may lead to injury, and possibly death, as a direct result of the force applied to him...and the doctors must consider the situation very carefully before embarking upon the non-consensual treatment of an adult patient, since coercive measures in such a case are likely to be of no avail. In general, all their actions must be for the sake of Heaven.[100]

R. Feinstein takes pains to emphasize that even if the grounds for refusing treatment are of an irrational nature, the chance of traumatization is real and must be avoided, even at the cost of withholding life-sustaining therapy.

In his second *responsum*, R. Feinstein deals with the forced intravenous feeding of a suffering, terminal patient:

One may not apply physical force to an adult in order to make him eat, especially if he believes that such a step will cause him harm. This is the case even if his doctor insists that he eat and that eating is beneficial for him...The reason for this is that in light of the patient's belief that eating is harmful to his welfare, force-feeding is likely to endanger his life (i.e. the trauma of being forced to eat in such a situation will threaten the patient's physical and mental health)...One is only permitted to try and persuade such a patient to follow medical advice. If persuasion does not work, nothing may be done. Feeding the patient without his knowledge is also possible, provided that it is unanimously agreed that eating will not cause the patient any danger whatsoever.[101]

This *responsum* is of particular significance since, as will be pointed out in Chapter 5 section 2, R. Feinstein maintains that under normal circumstances, neither artificial nutrition nor hydration—as opposed to therapeutic procedures such as amputations and the administration of antibiotics—may be removed until the establishment of death.[102] In the case of force-feeding, it is the need to avoid traumatizing the patient that militates against compelling artificial nutrition, and in this respect, R. Feinstein's *responsum* constitutes a new and powerful precedent for respecting patient choice in this type of situation. Under the *halakhah*, the refusal of any life-support, such as a naso-gastric tube, by a competent terminally ill patient must be taken seriously and if necessary, complied with.

In constructing his argument, R. Feinstein cites the talmudic law concerning dying individuals who wish to dispose of their property, even though the formal means for so doing, e.g. witnesses and documentation, are unavailable to them. Under talmudic law, the wishes of such a person are to be respected, and the property is transferred, irrespective of the lack of formality at the time of the deathbed disposition. The reason for this leniency is the fear that a refusal to implement the wishes of the dying will

---

[100] *Resp. Iggrot Moshe, Hoshen Mishpat*, 2 no. 73.   [101] Ibid. no. 74.

[102] Ibid. no 73. A full discussion of the objective halakhic criteria relating to the treatment of the dying and the terminally ill will be found in Ch. 5. The focus of the present discussion is confined to the issue of patient autonomy. A combined model comprising both objective and subjective criteria for dealing with end-of-life decisions is presented in Ch. 5 s. 8.

cause them mental distress, which may, in turn, result in a worsening of their condition to the extent of precipitating their death.[103] R. Feinstein argues that the medical welfare of the dying is surely worthy of even more serious consideration, as far as trauma-avoidance is concerned, than the disposition of their property.

It is noteworthy that the justification for leniency in relation to the formalities of a deathbed disposition would appear to be understood by some commentators on the Talmud in terms of mental suffering alone.[104] Others seem to indicate that the real fear is that of injury or sudden death caused by the mental stress of being unable to give effect to one's dying wishes.[105] The latter approach is broader than the former in that it justifies modifying the *halakhah* governing the transfer of property on the basis of a concern for the purely mental comfort of the dying individual. The application of such an approach in the context of the rejection of medical treatment by a terminal patient at the end of life would present us with a number of challenging issues, including the role of purely mental suffering as a factor in halakhic decisions with regard to the treatment of the terminally ill. However, R. Feinstein clearly adopts the former approach, and one is left to speculate as to the significance of the latter one for the care of the dying under Jewish law.

The modern *responsa* expand and deepen the concept of limited autonomy referred to earlier in this section. Patient choice is now clearly recognized as a factor in halakhic decisions regarding the medical treatment of the terminally ill, even if the result of that choice is a speedier death. R. Feinstein's *responsa* in particular, add an important dimension to this trend. They emphasize the subjective element in patient choice, and the psychological, as well as the physical needs of the terminal patient. Although there is still a significant gap between the autonomy-driven ethos of modern, liberal legal systems and the limited autonomy principle in Jewish law, it has become somewhat narrower than in the past. The rise of patient autonomy in Jewish biomedical law also imposes an obligation upon rabbis specializing in this area to recognize this autonomy and to factor it into their decisions in the field.

6. PATIENT AUTONOMY IN JEWISH AND COMMON LAW

It is interesting to compare the position under Jewish law with that of the common law. The common law has a well-established doctrine of patient autonomy, and the right of a competent adult to refuse medical treatment

---

[103] See *Bava Bathra*, 147b, 156b, and *Ketubot*, 70a.
[104] Rashbam, *Bava Bathra*, 17b, *s.v. matnat.*
[105] R. Gershom, *Bava Bathra*, 147b, *s.v. ika deamri.*

is well entrenched in both criminal and tort law.[106] This right was recently emphasized by the House of Lords in *Airedale NHS Trust* v. *Bland*,[107] in which Lord Goff said that doctors must give effect to the wishes of 'an adult patient of sound mind [who] refuses, however unreasonably, to consent to [life-sustaining] treatment'. Under the common law, legal doctrines such as necessity[108] and the best interests of the patient may not be used in order to justify the coercive medical treatment of competent adults. Doctors who wish to override an adult patient's wishes in order to save his life must be prepared to argue either patient non-competence,[109] or that the patient's refusal is based upon religious grounds, in which case, the court will usually find a way to override that refusal.[110]

It is worth mentioning that the principle of patient autonomy is much weaker in relation to minors, especially when their parents reject medical advice on religious grounds. Notwithstanding the principle laid down in the late nineteenth century that 'in exercising the jurisdiction to control or ignore the parental right, the court must act cautiously... and only when judicially satisfied that the welfare of the child requires that the parental right should be suspended or superseded',[111] English courts have consistently tended to prefer doctors to parents,[112] especially in situations in which refusal of life-saving treatment is based upon religious beliefs. In a case involving the religious beliefs of Orthodox Jewish parents, the court held that 'to follow the wishes of the parents would be tantamount to

---

[106] See *Schloendorff* v. *Society of New York Hospital*, 211 NY 125, 105 NE 92, 93 (1914); Skegg, *Law, Ethics, and Medicine*, Ch. 2.   [107] (1993) AC 789, 864.

[108] The defence of necessity was used by the Court of Appeal to justify separating very young Siamese twins sharing one heart, and effectively killing the weaker one, who could not survive, in order to give the stronger one a chance to live (*Re A (Children)* (2001) 2 WLR 480). This case involved a conflict between the religious belief of the parents of the twins that preferring one over the other was wrong and the correct course was to remain passive, and their physicians' belief that the only way the stronger twin could survive was to kill the weaker one, since without the separation, both twins would die. The significance of this case for the issues of the treatment of minors against the wishes of their parents and the correct balance between medical opinion and religious belief is discussed below (nn. 111–13). The case also raises the question of the defence of necessity in circumstances in which one innocent life is sacrificed in order to save another innocent life. This aspect of the case is discussed at length in Ch. 5 s. 6. It is particularly interesting that in its discussion of the necessity defence in a criminal law context, the Court of Appeal had recourse to Jewish law, and cited a halakhic decision by R. Feinstein on the question of separating Siamese twins in the course of its judgment.

[109] See L. Skene, 'When Can Doctors Treat Patients Who Cannot or Will Not Consent?', *Monash University Law Review*, 23 (1997), 84–91.

[110] This trend is particularly pronounced in relation to faiths that are opposed to blood transfusions, see *Re T* [1992] 4 All ER 649 and Skene, 'When can Doctors Treat Patients?', 88–9.

[111] *R v. Gyngall* [1893] 2 QB 232.

[112] See *Re J 2 (A Minor)* (1992) 2 FLR 165, 172. In this case, Lord Donaldson gave expression to the view that he could not conceive of any situation in which it would be appropriate to order a doctor 'to treat a child in a manner contrary to his or her clinical judgment'.

requiring the doctors to undertake a course of treatment which they are unwilling to do. The court could not consider making an order which would require them to do so.'[113] This particular decision was criticized by two learned authors as 'being at best paternalistic, and at worst, a case of cultural imperialism'.[114] The recent case involving the separation of Siamese twins, which will be discussed in Chapter 5, is yet another illustration of this trend in English law.[115]

In the United States, the right of competent adults to refuse medical treatment is protected under both the common law and the constitutional right of privacy.[116] The right to refuse treatment extends to life-threatening conditions, and in *Bouvia* v. *Superior Court*,[117] the Court issued a writ requiring a public hospital to remove a naso-gastric tube inserted into a quadriplegic patient without her consent, even though it might save or prolong her life. The Court also held that the constitutional right to refuse treatment is not limited to an adult human being of sound mind, but may also be exercised on behalf of an incompetent patient.[118] The constitutional right of a competent patient to refuse treatment was affirmed by the Supreme Court of the United States in the 1990 case of *Cruzan* v. *Director of the Missouri Department of Health*. In *Cruzan*, the Court assumed that 'the United States Constitution would grant a competent person a constitutionally-protected right to refuse life-saving hydration and nutrition'.[119] In the nature of constitutional rights law, cases will occur in which the state's interests outweigh a competent adult's right to refuse treatment. In these cases, the reasons for preferring the interest of the state in preserving life over that of the patient to end it include the value of preserving life, the prevention of suicide, the maintenance of the ethical integrity of the medical profession, and the protection of innocent third parties such as potential orphans.[120] However, any attempt to compel a competent adult to undergo medical treatment will be successful only if it is grounded in legal doctrine and authorized by a court order, declaratory judgment, or guardianship board. Coercive medical treatment of a competent adult is, therefore, a rare phenomenon.[121]

---

[113] *Re C (A Minor)* (1997) 40 BMLJ 31, 37.
[114] J. Mason and R. McCall Smith, *Law and Medical Ethics* (London, 1999), 251.
[115] See n. 108.
[116] *In Re Quinlan*, 70 NJ 10. 355 A. 2d 647 (1976); N. Cantor, *Legal Frontiers of Death and Dying* (Indiana, 1987). For the common law right, see *Schloendorff* v. *Society of New York Hospital*, 211 NY 125, 105 NE 92, 93 (1914).
[117] 179 Cal. App. 3d 1127, 225 Cal. Rptr. 297 (1986).
[118] See *In re Quinlan*, 70 NJ 10. 355A. 2d 647 (1976).   [119] 110 S. Ct. 2841 (1990).
[120] See N. Cantor, 'A Patient's Decision to Decline Life-Saving Medical Treatment', *Rutgers Law Review*, 26 (1973), 228, and R. Scott, 'Autonomy and Connectedness: A Re-Evaluation of *Georgetown* and its Progeny', *The Journal of Law, Medicine and Ethics*, 28 (2000), 56.
[121] See Skene, 'When can Doctors Treat Patients?', 90–1.

In modern common-law systems, the concept of autonomy is at the centre of the physician–patient relationship, and constitutes a value to which the courts attempt to give as full expression as possible.[122] In contrast, Jewish law is often characterized as a system totally lacking any concept of patient autonomy. As we have already demonstrated, this characterization is too strong, and a limited form of patient autonomy exists in Jewish law in the sense that there are complex situations in which the *halakhah* mandates patient choice as the operative solution. The grant of patient autonomy in such cases is not because autonomy is an ideal in Jewish law, but because the complexity of a particular situation, and the competing values involved in it, make patient choice the best halakhic course. The major champion of this form of autonomy is R. Feinstein; attention has already been drawn to his statement that in this type of complex case, the 'ownership' of the body passes from God to the individual.[123]

Now, it is important to point out that both Jewish and common law, in effect, ameliorate their starting positions in difficult and complex cases. This process in Jewish law has been discussed in detail throughout this chapter. Under the common law, the list of exceptions to the strong autonomy principle grows as the features of the case become morally complex. A simple example is the incompetent patient. Clearly, the determination of incompetence is an open-ended exercise that is affected, both legally and medically, by the circumstances of the case.[124] More difficult examples are the cases involving adults who refuse life-saving blood transfusions on religious grounds,[125] and those in which pregnant women refuse medically indicated Caesarean sections.[126] In both types of case, the court finds itself in a conflict situation and struggles to balance opposing moral principles as well as conflicting legal doctrines. In some case, it achieves this balance more successfully than others. In the common law too, therefore, the starting position is modified in complex cases.

As far as their respective starting points are concerned, there is a clear difference between the two systems. In practice, however, they are not so different from each other. There are also important lessons that Jewish law

---

[122] Israeli law goes to an extreme in this area and awards damages in tort for injury to a patient's autonomy (*Ali Da'aka v. Carmel Hospital* CA 2781/93, PD 56 (3) 727).

[123] *Resp. Iggrot Moshe, Yoreh Deah*, 3 no. 36.   [124] See n. 109.

[125] In *Re T* [1992] 4 All ER 649, the court justified ignoring the wishes of an adult who refused a blood transfusion on religious grounds. It did so on the basis of a conversation between the patient and her mother prior to the refusal which it categorized as undue influence upon the former in relation to the refusal of treatment. The court also found that the patient herself was not really so committed to the faith as to justify her refusal of treatment!

[126] In *In Re T* [1992] 4 All ER 649, 652–3, Lord Donaldson stated the principle of autonomy in no uncertain terms but added that 'the only possible qualification is a case in which the choice may lead to the death of a viable fetus'. See also Mason and McCall Smith, *Law and Medical Ethics*, 265–9.

can learn from the common-law position and *vice versa*. For example, Jewish law would do well to expand its use of the concept of limited patient autonomy, and prepare both rabbis and patients to use it wherever the opportunity arises; the common law might benefit society by articulating the notion that life is not entirely a matter of choice, but also carries with it an obligation. More will be said on this matter in the section on Israeli law, in which an attempt is made to combine the autonomy principle of the common law with the obligation approach of Jewish law.

7. *HALAKHAH* AND DEMOCRACY: COERCIVE LIFE-SAVING MEDICAL THERAPY IN ISRAELI LAW

An interesting illustration of the application of the halakhic principle of coercive medical treatment to Israeli law is the case of *Kurtam* v. *State of Israel*,[127] in which the appellant, a suspected drug dealer, was operated on by a police surgeon against his express wishes, and two packages of heroin removed from his stomach without his consent. The operation was carried out under the authority of a court order, and the justification given by the judge for the order authorizing the invasive, non-consensual stomach surgery was that without it the suspect would have died. Upon his recovery, the appellant was charged with using heroin, and the packages of drugs obtained from his stomach were used in evidence against him. Kurtam sought to have this evidence rejected on the grounds that he had refused consent to the procedure, and it had, therefore, been obtained by illegal means. Non-consensual medical procedures offended against both Israel's law governing privacy and the principles of democracy.

The Supreme Court ruled that the evidence was admissible, and one of the justices cited Jewish law in support of this ruling. According to Beiski J., the *halakhah* mandates coercive life-saving therapy. Indeed, under Jewish law, 'the patient's wishes are of no account...and his lack of consent is irrelevant'.[128] Beiski J. pointed out that the Judaic principle of the sanctity of human life had been incorporated into Israeli law by the Supreme Court in a precedent involving the issue of the freedom of contract in the 1962 case of *Zim* v. *Maziar*.[129] In that case, the Court held that there was no freedom to make a contract in defiance of the Jewish law principle of the

---

[127] Cr. A. 480/85, 527/85, 40 (31 PD 673). Also see D. Sinclair, 'Jewish Law in the State of Israel', *Jewish Law Annual*, 11 (1994), 237.　　　[128] Ibid. 697.

[129] Cr. A. 480/85, PD 40 (3) 637. In this case, which involved a serious case of food poisoning on the petitioner's passenger ship, the Court referred to the Jewish sanctity of life principle in relation to the need to limit the principle of freedom of contract and to prevent its application to an agreement that carried an exemption clause effectively allowing one of the parties to engage in life-threatening conduct.

sanctity of human life. In the present case, therefore, it was perfectly legal to carry out the invasive life-saving therapy against Kurtam's express wishes. The heroin obtained as a result of that operation was not tainted by illegality, and could be used in evidence against him.

Bach J. approached the issue both from the perspective of the Israeli Protection of Privacy Law, 1981, and the common-law exceptions to the principle of patient autonomy. He found that there was a general principle of judicial discretion in this area and that the present case fell well within this discretionary area. However, in the course of his judgment, he also referred to the Jewish tradition incorporated by Israeli courts in relation to the need to preserve the sanctity of human life.[130]

Even though the *halakhah* would have reached the same result as the Supreme Court in this case, provided that the operation was medically certain and of low risk, and if its coercive nature was unlikely to traumatize the appellant to the extent of threatening his health, the Court missed an opportunity to direct attention to the doctrines of patient autonomy and the theological ambivalence regarding human healing which are part of the halakhic position on this matter. It is certainly not the case that according to the *halakhah*, the patient's wishes are of 'no account' and consent is 'irrelevant'.[131] On the contrary, as shown above, there is room for the patient to choose to reject life-saving treatment, depending upon the circumstances of the case. This omission was, however, rectified in the *Sheffer* case, which will be discussed shortly.

It is noteworthy that coercive life-saving therapy is now a statutory option in Israeli medical law. It is codified in section 15 (2) of the 1996 Patient's Rights Law. According to this section, the Ethics Committee of a hospital is qualified to approve coercive life-saving therapy if the patient is fully informed of the decision to coerce, if it is agreed by all the physicians involved in the case that the procedure in question is the only way to save the patient's life, and 'if there is a reasonable possibility that the patient will consent retroactively'. Clearly, the last requirement is an attempt to combine patient autonomy with halakhic obligation, representing the democratic element in this synthesis. In the light of *Kurtam* and section 15 of the Patient's Rights Law, therefore, it is evident that Israeli law is not going down the path of strong patient autonomy associated with American law.[132] The traditional Jewish approach to the value of human life is still an influential one in Israeli law.

---

[130] In addition to the *Maziar* case, he also cited *Garti v. State of Israel*, CA 322/63, PD 18 (2) 449.
[131] See S. Shilo, 'Comments and Some New Light on the Foundations of Law Act' (Heb.), *Shenaton Hamishpat Haivri*, 13 (1987), 351. See also A. Shapira, 'Informed Consent to Medical Procedures' (Heb.), *Iyyunei Mishpat*, 14 (1989), 225.   [132] See n. 106.

The issue of the balance between obligation and autonomy in Jewish law and the difference between the Jewish approach and that of the common law was addressed by Elon J. in the Israeli Supreme Court decision in *Yael Sheffer* v. *State of Israel*.[133] The appellant in this case was born in 1986 with Tay-Sachs disease. Her mother had applied to the District Court, in her capacity as Yael's natural guardian, for an order sanctioning the withholding of artificial respiration and intravenous medicine in the event that her daughter developed a lung infection or any other disease normally treated by these methods. The administration of analgesics was specifically excluded from the request. The District Court rejected Mrs Sheffer's petition on the grounds that her husband, Yael's father, was not a party to it. It was Mr Sheffer's practice to spend some time at his sick daughter's bedside every evening after work, whereas Mrs Sheffer spent most of her time with the couple's other, healthy daughter. Although Mr Sheffer did not actively oppose the petition, his non-participation in it was regarded as a significant matter by the Court. In the final analysis, the Court held that the relief requested was of too grave a nature to be granted at the request of one parent alone. This decision was upheld by the Supreme Court, in a decision written after Yael's death in 1988.

Although much of Elon J.'s lengthy judgment deals with the objective criteria governing the question of the withdrawal of life-support, his major point is that a balance needs to be struck between the principle of the sanctity of human life and respect for the dignity of the terminally ill and their families. He approved of the general approach adopted by Beiski J. in the *Kurtam* case, and criticized Israeli supporters of the strong doctrine of patient autonomy. Elon J. did, however, observe that although in principle, both physician and patient are under an obligation to engage in life-saving medical therapy, various exceptions to this principle, e.g. risky and uncertain therapies, have been developed by halakhic authorities over the ages.[134] In this respect, Elon J. presents a more complete picture of the halakhic approach to the issue of coercive treatment than did Beiski J. in the *Kurtam* case.

A lengthy section of Elon J.'s opinion is devoted to the legal position regarding the terminally ill in the United States and the Netherlands. A wide-ranging survey of United States law on the issues of patients' rights under the Constitution, the balance between these rights and the interest of states in the preservation of life, together with the therapeutic

---

[133] CA 560/88, 48 (1) *PD* 87. This case is referred to in Ch. 5 n. 66, and in the Appendix, n. 2.

[134] In addition to the material already discussed in this chapter, see D. Sinclair, 'Non-Consensual Medical Treatment of Competent Individuals in Jewish Law with Some Comparative Reference to Anglo-American Law', *Tel-Aviv University Studies in Law*, 11 (1992), 227.

ethos of the medical profession, the standard of evidence required in exercising substituted judgement on behalf of an incompetent patient, and the issue of advance medical directives, concludes with a recommendation that the Israeli legislature pay careful attention to the widely used system of ethics committees in United States hospitals. Such committees have many advantages and would help, in Elon's view, to strike the right balance between Jewish values and democratic rights in individual cases.[135]

Elon J. expressed strong reservations regarding the Dutch approach, according to which physicians who practise mercy-killing are exempt from criminal liability provided that their actions follow set guidelines aimed at ensuring that the patient requested euthanasia voluntarily and there was no medical possibility of the relief of his or her suffering.[136] In Elon J.'s view, such an approach constitutes the beginning of a slippery slope to the type of involuntary euthanasia programmes associated with the Nazi regime.

Elon J. pointed out that Israeli law currently rejects the Dutch model of active euthanasia, but does respect the wishes of the terminally ill with regard to the withholding of life-saving therapy. Whereas the starting point in Israeli law remains that of the notion of the sanctity of human life, a number of cases have established the principle that competent adults in a terminal condition may refuse life-sustaining procedures. In *Eyal v. Wilenski*,[137] the Tel Aviv District Court held that no criminal charge or civil suit would lie against a physician who, in accordance with the wishes of the patient, failed to insert a tracheal tube into the throat of a competent adult suffering from amyotrophic lateral sclerosis. The Court required that the patient be conscious at the time the fateful decision is made and that the dying process must already have commenced.

In *Zadok v. Beth Haelah*,[138] the District Court was prepared to accept advance directives regarding the termination of life-support in the form of both a written memorandum and a tape-recorded message made by Mrs Zadok, an Alzheimer's victim, who was clearly suffering from senile

---

[135] The combination of 'Judaism and democracy' is referred to in section 1 of Israel's Human Dignity and Freedom Law, 5752-1992, as the basis for resolving conflicts between state laws and democratic rights. Elon J. held that the Foundations of Law Act, 5740-1980, provides the framework for achieving a synthesis of these two values.

[136] On the medical and legal position in the Netherlands, see M. Otlowski, *Voluntary Euthanasia and the Common Law* (Oxford, 1997), 391–455. In the past, physicians who practised mercy-killing were able to invoke the defence of necessity under Dutch criminal law in accordance with a number of guidelines laid down by the Dutch courts. Now, the situation regarding active euthanasia is governed by statute (*Time*, 23 April 2001).

[137] PM 1141/90, PM 51 (3) 187.

[138] PM 759/92, PM 52 (2) 485. There are a number of recent, unpublished District Court decisions in this area, all of which tend to favour the principle of patient autonomy without directly breaching the parameters outlined in the *Sheffer* case (CA 560/88, 48 (1) PD 87) See also Appendix, n. 2.

dementia at the time that the memorandum and the recording were deposited with her lawyer. On the basis of these directives, the family of the sick woman ordered the physicians in the medical facility in which Mrs Zadok was hospitalized to terminate her artificial respiration. This step was opposed by her physicians on ethical grounds; they were not prepared to stand by after the disconnecting of the respirator and watch their patient suffocate to death. Talgam J. accepted the legal validity of the advance directives but did not rule in favour of the family. In his view, it is always necessary in this type of case to distinguish between the withdrawal of short-term life-sustaining measures, and the removal of long-term procedures. In the final analysis, it is all a matter of timing. In the early stages of the treatment of this type of patient, the ethos of the medical profession is the dominant value and it is necessary to provide full life-support. However, as time goes by and the prospects for improvement become dim, the value of patient autonomy gains the upper hand, and if it becomes evident that the best interests of the patient will be served by disconnection from life-support, then that is the appropriate course of action. Talgam J. limited his decision to the short term, and ruled in favour of the physicians.

It is noteworthy that in both *Eyal* and *Zadok*, reference was made to the principles of Jewish law governing the treatment of the terminally ill. These principles will be discussed in the next chapter.

Elon J. concluded his survey of Jewish, United States, Dutch, and Israeli law on the treatment of the terminal patient with a plea for the synthesis of Judaism and democracy as the model for Israeli jurisprudence in this area of the law.

In relation to the specific circumstances of Yael Sheffer, Elon J. found that it had not been demonstrated that she was undergoing undue suffering, nor was it proved that she was no longer in touch with her environment. She cried like all children when she was hungry or needed routine attention. In these circumstances, the balance between the Jewish value of the sanctity of life and the democratic value of patient autonomy ought to be struck in favour of the former. This conclusion was justified by the fact that her father was not a party to the petition, and there was no basis for presuming tacit consent on his behalf to the petition presented by his wife. In terms of the law regarding minors, there is a particularly strong obligation to act in their best interests,[139] and in the present case it had not been proved that withholding artificial respiration and intravenous medicine was clearly and convincingly in Yael Sheffer's best interests.

---

[139] See *Attorney General* v. *A.*, CA 698/86, PD 42 (2) 661; D. Sinclair, 'Kidney Donations from the Legally Incompetent in Jewish and Comparative Law', *Israel Law Review*, 27 (1993), 587.

It is interesting to note that in the course of his judgment in the *Zadok* case, Talgam J. referred to the talmudic law requiring the declared wishes of a dying person with regard to the disposition of his property to be honoured, even if the formal means for validating such a disposition are unavailable at the time of the declaration.[140] The effect of this reference was to strengthen the case for accepting advance directives in Israeli law: in *Zadok*, these consisted of a written memorandum and a tape-recorded message. This very aspect of talmudic law was cited by R. Feinstein in his *responsum* regarding the need to avoid traumatizing a terminal patient by providing him with artificial nutrition against his express wishes.[141] In that context, however, the dying person was still competent, and the justification for not insisting upon all the formalities of the laws of gifts for the purposes of a deathbed property disposition was to avoid traumatizing the dying person. In general, there is no evidence that *halakhah* would recognize an advance directive made in anticipation of incompetence as a binding instrument. All that may be said is that a combination of the talmudic principle of the deathbed will, the halakhic doctrine of limited autonomy, and the theological approach that eschews human healing in favour of Divine succour, would possibly be sufficient to ground a concept of advance directives in Jewish law.[142] There is, however, no clear evidence either way, and the question remains open.

The tension between the obligation to heal and the patient's own wishes—including the rejection of medical therapy—is at the very core of Jewish medical law and ethics in the modern era of patient autonomy and rights-driven jurisprudence. In the course of this chapter it has been argued, in terms of both *halakhah* and theology, that the scale tips in favour of a limited concept of patient autonomy in terminal cases. It remains to be seen how halakhic authorities develop and apply this concept in the twenty-first century.

---

[140] R. Gershom, *Bava Bathra*, 147b, *s.v. ika deamri*.

[141] Rashbam, *Bava Bathra*, 17b, *s.v. matnat*.

[142] See D. Sinclair, 'Patient Self-Determination and Advance Directives', *Jewish Law Association Studies*, 8 (1996), 173.

5

The Terminally Ill Patient

1. INTRODUCTION TO THE LAW OF THE DYING PERSON (*GOSES*) IN HALAKHIC SOURCES

The talmudic word for a person whose death is imminent is *goses*. The features traditionally associated with the dying process (*gesisah*) are the emission of a death rattle and the inability to swallow.[1] In legal terms, the *goses* is considered a 'living person in all respects',[2] and his murderer is subject to the same penalty as the murderer of a 'regular' person, i.e. capital punishment.[3] The Talmud compares the *goses* to a flickering lamp which, when touched, is immediately extinguished,[4] and it is generally forbidden to come into physical contact with a *goses* for fear of precipitating his death.[5]

The Talmud itself does not specify the period of *gesisah*, although according to R. Joshua Falk (sixteenth century), a *goses* is not capable of surviving for more than three days.[6] R. Falk's three-day limit does not apply nowadays, since 'it was propounded by the early authorities on the basis of the medical science of their time'.[7] Most contemporary authorities treat *gesisah* as a physical condition in which death is likely to occur in the not too distant future.[8]

---

[1] Maimonides, *Commentary to the Mishnah, Arakhin*, 1: 3; *Tiferet Yisrael, Arakhin*, 1: 3; *Arukh Hashalem s.v. gasas*. The plural form of *goses* is *gosesim*. The definition of death is discussed at length in Ch. 6 ss. 1 and 2, which deal mainly with the permissibility of heart transplants in Jewish law. There are, in fact, two principal schools of thought amongst modern halakhists with regard to the definition of death. According to one school, death is defined by the cessation of both independent breathing and heartbeat. The other school is prepared to accept irreversible cessation of all brain-stem activity, sometimes referred to as 'whole brain death', as a definitive indication of death under Jewish law. Since, the definition of death is the major halakhic issue in that discussion, its detailed analysis is reserved for Ch. 6. This chapter is devoted to the treatment of the terminally ill patient who is still in the final phase of his or her life, and in this context, the definition of death is not of such great relevance.

[2] *Semahot*, 1: 1, *Encyclopaedia Talmudit*, v. 393.

[3] *Sanhedrin*, 78a; Maimonides, *Hilkhot Rozeah*, 2: 7.   [4] *Semahot*, 1: 4; *Shabbat*, 151b.

[5] *Semahot*, 1: 4; Maimonides, *Hilkhot Avelut*, 4: 5, *Siftei Cohen, Yoreh Deah*, 393: 5; *Resp. Iggrot Moshe, Hoshen Mishpat*, 2 no. 73. In modern times, this prohibition retreats in the face of medical treatment and care (*Resp. Ziz Eliezer*, 8 no. 15). Also, an impediment to death may be removed even if slight physical contact with the *goses*'s body is involved (n. 22).

[6] *Perishah, Yoreh Deah*, 339: 5.

[7] G. Rabinowitz, 'The Dangerously Ill, the *Goses* and the Definition of the Time of Death' (Heb.), *Halakhah Urefuah*, 3 (1983), 114. In the context of modern life-prolonging technology, *gesisah* may certainly last for a much longer period of time than the traditional three days.

[8] *Resp. Iggrot Moshe, Hoshen Mishpat*, 2 no. 73; J. D. Bleich, 'The Quinlan Case: A Jewish Perspective', in F. Rosner and J. D. Bleich (eds.), *Jewish Bioethics* (New York, 1979), 275 n. 2.

The most important aspect of the law of the *goses* is the distinction between accelerating the death of a *goses*, which is prohibited, and merely removing an impediment to the dying process, which is permitted. The major source for this distinction is the discussion in the *Sefer Hasidim*[9] regarding the spiritual and mystical evils involved in preventing the soul leaving the body at the appointed time. The *Sefer Hasidim* interprets the biblical verse, 'there is a time to die',[10] as a warning against doing anything that will prevent the soul emerging from the body at the predetermined moment of death. It is, therefore, forbidden for another person to cry out at the time the soul of the *goses* leaves his body, since the cry will either prevent the emergence of the soul or force it to return after it has emerged. In both cases, great spiritual suffering is caused to the *goses* as a result of this death-impeding act.[11]

The timely release of the soul is not, however, an operative halakhic principle.[12] Halakhic prohibitions regarding the treatment of the *goses* override any spiritual and mystical concerns regarding the suffering caused by untimely death. For example, if the *goses* claims that his soul can depart only if he is moved to a particular place, his wish may not be acted upon, since the Talmud prohibits the touching of a *goses* for fear that his death will be precipitated as a result of the physical contact. In order to avoid coming into conflict with binding *halakhah*, the *Sefer Hasidim* distinguishes between acts aimed solely at preventing the *goses* from suffering the pangs caused by preventing the soul from departing, and acts that also involve the precipitation of death and are forbidden because they are in breach of talmudic law:

Death is not to be delayed. For example, if there is a woodchopper in the vicinity of the *goses*, and the soul is thereby prevented from emerging, the woodchopper may be removed. Salt is not to be put on the tongue of the *goses* in order to keep him alive.[13] If, however, the *goses* claims that he cannot die unless he is moved to another place, he is not to be moved.[14]

According to the *Sefer Hasidim*, the noise of the woodchopper falls into the same category as the cry of another person at the moment of the departure of the soul of the *goses*: they are both pure impediments to death in

---

Also see s. 2 (a) below for a more detailed discussion of the definition of the *goses* in contemporary times.

[9] This work was produced by the 13-cent. Ashkenazi pietist group known as the *Hasidei Ashkenaz*, which exercised a not inconsiderable influence on mainstream *halakhah* (see Ch. 3 n. 24). Also see I. Baer, 'The Religious-Social Tendency of *Sefer Hasidim*' (Heb.), *Zion*, 1 (1948), 3; H. Soloveitchik, 'Three Themes in Sefer Hasidim', *Association of Jewish Studies Review*, 1 (1976), 311.   [10] Eccles. 3: 2.

[11] *Sefer Hasidim*, no. 234.

[12] See *Resp. Hatam Sofer, Yoreh Deah*, no. 339 in which it is pointed out that we are no longer able to determine the time for the soul's departure.

[13] See J. Trachtenberg, *Jewish Magic and Superstition* (London, 1939), 160. Salt, in particular, was believed to possess supernatural qualities for warding off demons and evil spirits.

[14] *Sefer Hasidim*, no. 722.

that neither involves any physical contact with the *goses*. As such, they ought to be removed, even though maintaining them might extend the duration of life. Moving the *goses* from one place to another, however, does involve physical contact and falls under the talmudic definition of a death-precipitating deed. It is in breach of the talmudic warning against extinguishing the 'flickering lamp' and consequently, it is prohibited. The non-placement of salt on the tongue, on the other hand, does not implicate any talmudic ruling since it is an omission, and the talmudic prohibition on touching a *goses* applies only to acts. The *Sefer Hasidim* is, therefore, on safe ground in relation to acts that do not involve physical contact with the *goses* and omissions. In both cases, no talmudic prohibition is implicated, and the way is clear for the *Sefer Hasidim* to teach that the spiritual value of a timely death overrides the natural desire to keep people alive for as long as possible.

The distinction in the *Sefer Hasidim* between permitted and prohibited acts in relation to a *goses* is the major source for the *halakhah* governing the treatment of the dying in Jewish law. Before proceeding to an account of the way in which this area of the law developed, it is worthwhile commenting upon the actual practices for keeping people alive recorded in the above passages from the *Sefer Hasidim*. These practices were the subject of much rabbinic criticism but managed, nevertheless, to survive and flourish because of their popular appeal. The tension between the *halakhah* and these popular practices is reflected in many halakhic sources in this area. In addition to woodchoppers and grains of salt, there were many other ways of preventing the dying from quitting their mortal lives. One particularly controversial method, common to Jews and non-Jews alike, was the removal of pillows made from birds' feathers from beneath the head of a dying person. This practice was based upon the belief that the feathers in the pillow prevented the soul from leaving the body.[15] In the light of the talmudic rule forbidding physical contact with the body of the *goses*, and the above-mentioned distinction in the *Sefer Hasidim*, this practice ought to have been strongly condemned by the halakhic authorities of the time, since it involves moving the head of the *goses* in order to remove the pillows. Indeed, this was the position adopted by R. Joshua Boaz,

---

[15] According to Trachtenberg, *Jewish Magic*, the removal of such pillows was an anti-demonic practice prevalent in the Middle Ages. The widespread nature of this practice is attested to in a Christian work devoted entirely to its evil nature. In the preface to *De Pulvineri Morientibus Non Subtrahendo* (Jena, 1678), 1. 7, Caspar Questelius, a cleric, strongly protests against this 'particularly detestable' practice, which 'although frequently practised is quite obnoxious and inexcusable'. In the body of his text, Questelius further emphasizes the entrenched nature of the practice. 'Even if such a custom had existed for a thousand years, its origin is uncertain, and now that we have grasped its inherent wickedness, it is a proper time to correct it, and there is a necessity to correct it.'

a sixteenth-century Italian scholar, who wrote that he 'strenuously opposed the practice', and found support for his position in the *Sefer Hasidim*.[16] However, R. Boaz also mentions that his 'own teachers ruled to the contrary, and [that] R. Nathan of Igra, a prominent scholar, permitted the practice'.[17] It is evident from his comments that R. Boaz faced an uphill struggle to uproot the practice of pillow-removal from the heads of the dying in his community, and that in the end, his efforts were not crowned with success. In his codificatory glosses on the *Tur*, R. Joshua Falk analyses R. Boaz's comments and comes to the startling conclusion that in the final analysis, R. Boaz did permit pillow-removal, albeit grudgingly.[18] R. Falk's basis for this contention involves some highly creative syntactical suggestions that probably reflect a desire to bring *halakhah* into line with prevalent practice rather than an attempt to achieve an authentic understanding of R. Boaz's text.[19] R. Falk does, however, insist that the pillow be removed in a gentle fashion without any jostling of the *goses*. In the following century a Turkish authority, R. Hayyim Benveniste, struggled with the same issue. R. Benveniste also mentions the tension between popular practice and the *halakhah* in this area, and makes it fairly clear that he consciously chose to bend *halakhah* to popular will. In his view, the fact that pillow-removal was permitted by some scholars in the past provides important support for permitting it to continue, despite its lack of halakhic credibility.[20]

To return to the main theme, the distinction in the *Sefer Hasidim* between removing an impediment and precipitation of death was incorporated by

---

[16] *Shiltei Hagiborim, Moed Katan*, 3 (16b no. 4).

[17] R. Nathan of Igra was a German scholar who travelled to Italy, and served in various Italian communities in the second half of the 15th cent. R. Boaz was one of his disciples, and he is cited elsewhere in *Shiltei Hagiborim*, see N. Hacohen, *Otsar Hagedolim* (Bnei Berak), 7 (151 no. 119). He is to be distinguished from the R. Nathan of Igra of the same period who was widely accepted as the outstanding Ashkenazic authority and teacher of his age (Hacohen, ibid. 149 no. 118). In the light of the strong influence of the Hasidei Ashkenaz on German Jewry, it is not surprising that R. Nathan issued a ruling of this nature. Note that both R. Boaz and R. Hayyim Benveniste, a Turkish scholar whose views are cited below, are not particularly happy with the *Sefer Hasidim*'s finessing of the strict talmudic prohibition on interfering with a *goses*. Clearly, Ashkenazic scholars of the earlier period did not share this attitude.   [18] *Derishah, Yoreh Deah*, 339.

[19] '[E]ven though he [R. Boaz] begins with the statement that the practice of removing a pillow made of birds' feathers would appear to be in breach of a prohibition, nevertheless, his conclusion, in which he reconciles the various acts mentioned in the *Sefer Hasidim* on the basis of the distinction between impediment removal and death-precipitation, implies that . . . removing a pillow gently in order to get rid of the feathers which act as an impediment is permitted. In this light, we may now understand correctly the opening statement that the practice of removing pillows would appear to be in breach of a prohibition i.e. this was how the matter appeared originally; in the final analysis, and in the light of this resolution of the passage of the *Sefer Hasidim*, however, it is evident that this is not the case (i.e. pillow removal is permitted).' This reading of R. Boaz's words is more ingenious than it is convincing!

[20] *Sheirei Knesset Hagedolah, Yoreh Deah, Hilkhot Bikkur Holim*, 339: 4.

R. Moses Isserles, the great sixteenth-century Polish codifier of Jewish law, into his glosses on the *Shulhan Arukh*. R. Isserles combines both the ruling in the *Sefer Hasidim* and R. Boaz's ruling on pillow-removal in his formulation of the *halakhah*:

It is forbidden to hasten death, for example if a person is undergoing prolonged death throes and his soul cannot depart, it is forbidden to remove his pillow... notwithstanding the popular belief that the feathers of certain birds contained in the pillow... prevent the soul from departing. The *goses* may not be moved... in order to facilitate the departure of his soul. If, however, there is something hindering its departure, for example the presence near the house of a knocking sound such as the chopping of wood, or salt on the tongue, it may be removed. No act is involved in such a case: it is merely the removal of an impediment.[21]

R. Isserles interprets the *Sefer Hasidim* in the same way as R. Boaz: pillow-removal is forbidden because of physical contact with the *goses*. Nevertheless, he permits some contact with the *goses* since he allows salt to be removed from his tongue. It is noteworthy that the *Sefer Hasidim* itself did not mention the removal of salt; it only deals with the issue of not placing it on the tongue in the first instance. Presumably, R. Isserles is of the opinion that some physical contact with the *goses* is permitted in the course of removing an impediment to death, provided that it does not constitute serious jostling. This point is brought out by casting the salt example in terms of its removal; it would not have emerged from the original example in the *Sefer Hasidim* which relates only to omissions.[22] Another explanation for R. Isserles's permission to remove salt is based upon the fact that it ought not to have been placed on the tongue in the first place; since it was put there in contravention of the *Sefer Hasidim*'s ruling, its removal qualifies as a *mitzvah* and is required by the law.[23] In any case, the significant point that emerges from R. Isserles's ruling on removing salt is that physical contact with the *goses* does not act as an absolute bar to impediment-removal.

The transition from concern with avoiding any physical contact with the *goses* to a more general conception of the distinction between precipitating death and removing an impediment begins to take place in the writings of halakhic authorities after R. Isserles. In dealing with the question posed by the permission to remove salt, R. Mordekhai Jaffe, a disciple of R. Isserles, emphasizes that the issue is not physical contact but the effect of removing the alleged impediment. If it is established that the removal of a particular substance will definitely accelerate death, then that substance does not qualify as an impediment even if its removal does not involve any physical contact with the *goses*. Salt is not an established

[21] *Yoreh Deah*, 229: 1.
[22] *Siftei Cohen*, *Yoreh Deah*, 339: 7; see *Resp. Ziz Eliezer*, 13 no. 89; *Resp. Ziz Eliezer*, 14 no. 80.
[23] *Beth Lehem Yehudah*, *Yoreh Deah*, 339: 1.

death-precipitator, hence its removal is permitted even though some physical contact is involved. The death-precipitating nature of pillow-removal, on the other hand, is well established and therefore prohibited.[24]

As the world of salt and woodchoppers was gradually replaced by the new reality of empirical medical science, the definition of impediments and precipitators also became more scientifically sophisticated. Medical science, rather than tradition or folk practice, would now dictate what was to be classified as an impediment to death and what constituted an acceleration of the *goses*'s demise. Writing in Eastern Europe in the late nineteenth century, R. Yehiel Epstein rules that anything may be removed from the *goses* or his vicinity which 'is not because of his body'.[25] This somewhat obscure phrase probably means that only those procedures that, from the point of view of rational medical practice, are supporting the *goses*'s physical functioning, are to be maintained in the final phase of life. All other procedures may be discontinued even if they are tradition-ally regarded as effective impediments to death.[26]

This brief survey of the pre-modern law of the *goses* sets the scene for a detailed discussion of the attempts by modern halakhic authorities to deal with the complex and morally challenging debate surrounding the with-drawal of sophisticated life-support technology from terminally ill patients. The gap between the natural death context of the old sources and the hospitalized terminal patient of contemporary times is a dramatic one, giving rise to a host of legal and moral issues. In addition, there is the very basic question of how to read halakhic sources set in an ancient medical setting in a way that will endow them with significance for contemporary times. The transition from woodchoppers to respirators is hardly a simple one,[27] and it is to a description and analysis of this transition that the following section is devoted.

2. APPLYING THE LAW OF THE *GOSES* TO THE TERMINALLY ILL PATIENT IN MODERN MEDICINE

(a) Defining the *Goses*

The very word *goses*, with its etymological association with death rattles and the like, takes us back to an era of natural death in which people took

---

[24] *Levush Mordekhai, Yoreh Deah*, 339: 1. A similar approach is adopted by R. Benveniste, *Sheirei Knesset Hagedolah, Yoreh Deah, Hilkhot Bikkur Holim*, 339: 4. See also *Resp. Ziz Eliezer*, 13 no. 89.   [25] *Arukh Hashulhan, Yoreh Deah*, 339: 4.
[26] This interpretation of R. Epstein's phrase is offered by a number of more recent author-ities, see *Resp. Ziz Eliezer*, 13 no. 89, and *Resp. Lev Aryeh*, 2 no. 37.
[27] See L. Newman, 'Woodchoppers and Respirators: The Problem of Interpretation in Contemporary Jewish Ethics', in E. Dorff and L. Newman (eds.), *Contemporary Jewish Ethics*

to their beds, surrounded themselves with family and friends, and played out their role in one final ritual. The great change that has come in relation to how we die is eloquently expressed by P. Aries in his wide-ranging study of Western attitudes towards death:

Death in the hospital is no longer the occasion of a ritual ceremony, over which the dying person presides amidst his assembled relatives and friends. Death is a technical phenomenon obtained by a cessation of care...Indeed in the majority of cases the dying person has already lost consciousness. Death has been dissected, cut to bits by a series of little steps, which finally makes it impossible to know which step was the real death, the one in which consciousness was lost or the one in which breathing stopped. All these little silent deaths have replaced and erased the great dramatic act of death, and no one any longer has the strength or patience to wait over a period of weeks for a moment which has lost part of its meaning.[28]

A similar development has taken place in modern Jewish society. Most people no longer die at home, and death rattles and the accumulation of saliva at the back of the throat[29] are no longer a part of domestic Jewish lore. Contemporary halakhists have relegated the traditional symptoms of *gesisah* to obsolescence, and rely instead upon criteria of a purely medical nature.[30] R. Moshe Hirshler points out quite simply that since 'it is now possible to clear out the respiratory tract and thereby ensure the patient's continued existence', the emission of a death rattle is no longer to be considered as a sign of dying. He also makes a general statement to the effect that the traditional symptoms associated with *gesisah* are no longer definitive.[31] This is certainly the approach that emerges from the decisions of the majority of modern authorities, whether they admit to it or not. The traditional symptoms of *gesisah* have been relegated to history, and their place has been taken by the concept of the terminal patient, i.e. a person who is beyond medical assistance, and whose death is inevitable within a short period of time.[32]

R. Eliezer Waldenberg argues that there is even halakhic support for ignoring the traditional signs of *gesisah*. He points out that nowhere does the Talmud itself actually offer a physical definition of the *goses*. The Talmud simply uses it as a legal category for dealing with people in

and Morality (Oxford, 1995), 140. Note that almost all the rabbinic authorities cited in the rest of this chapter are modern and many of them are contemporary.

[28] *Western Attitudes Towards Death from the Middle Ages to the Present* (Baltimore, 1974), 88. See also R. Veatch, *Death, Dying and the Biological Revolution* (Yale, 1976), 21–45.

[29] See n. 1.   [30] See n. 8.

[31] 'The Obligation to Save the Lives of Sick and Dangerously Ill Individuals' (Heb.), *Halakhah Urefuah*, 2 (1981), 35.

[32] See A. Steinberg, *Encyclopaedia of Jewish Medical Ethics* (Heb.) (Jerusalem, 1988–98), iv. 370–2.

the final stages of their lives.[33] Thus, whilst the traditional symptoms are reflected in the etymology of the word *goses*, they are not halakhically binding.

(b) Applying the Distinction Between Impediment Removal and Death Precipitation to Modern Life Support

The aspect of the law of the *goses* with which modern authorities are concerned is the application of the distinction between impediment removal and death precipitation to modern life-support, i.e. artificial respiration, nutrition, and hydration. The removal of artificial nutrition or hydration from a patient who cannot eat or drink independently inevitably leads to death. A similar situation, depending upon the patient's physical condition, may arise in relation to artificial respiration. The indirect killing of a person, e.g. by depriving them of air or food,[34] is considered murder under Jewish law.[35] None of the traditional halakhic sources dealing with the distinction between impediment-removal and death-precipitation address questions of nutrition or respiration. They are all concerned with practices such as the maintenance of woodchoppers in the vicinity of the *goses*, salt on his tongue, certain types of pillows under his head, or synagogue keys beneath his pillow. None of these practices possess the physiological significance of nutrition, hydration, or respiration. Indeed, it is likely that one of the reasons behind the toleration of these practices by rabbinic authorities was their awareness that they really had no effect upon the physical state of the *goses*, and they were therefore permitted as long as they did not entail any breach of Jewish law in the form of palpable physical contact with the *goses*. It is also clear that in terms of the principles governing causation in Jewish criminal law, the removal of woodchoppers, salt, and the other items referred to above is not an act of murder. In direct contrast to this situation, today's *gosesim* are inevitably in hospital, having their respiration, nutrition, and hydration supported by artificial means. This type of life-support would not appear to lend itself easily to classification as a removable impediment to death. Accordingly, one would expect that a major question for modern authorities would be whether the traditional *halakhah* in this area has been rendered obsolete by the sophistication of modern life-support technology.

---

[33] *Resp. Ziz Eliezer*, 13 no. 89.

[34] The indirect nature of the act, e.g. locking a person in a sealed room so that he or she either suffocates or starves to death, results in it carrying a Divine rather than a human sanction, see *Sanhedrin*, 77a.

[35] The killer in such circumstances is a murderer who will surely be punished by God, who seeks restitution for spilt blood (Maimonides, *Hilkhot Rozeah*, 3: 10). For a detailed analysis of the significance of the exemption from capital punishment in Jewish criminal law, see s. 5. See also the discussion in Ch. 1 s. 3.

Surprisingly, there is one such authority who has no particular problem with making a simple transition from grains of salt to respirators. According to R. Hayyim David Halevy, all artificial forms of life-support are considered impediments and may be removed in the final phase of life. R. Halevy argues that any interference with the natural status quo constitutes an impediment to death, and may be removed once it is medically proven that the patient cannot function in an independent manner.[36] Although he does not define independent function, R. Halevy finds no difficulty in making a simple and direct analogy between the grain of salt discussed by the earlier authorities and the artificial respirator of contemporary times:

The law regarding the salt is a perfect precedent for the disconnection of an artificial respirator... A dangerously ill patient is brought into the hospital and is kept alive artificially by a respirator in order to give the physicians a chance to effect a cure. Once it becomes evident that no cure is possible, it is clearly permissible to disconnect the patient from the respirator.

R. Halevy also cites the theory that R. Moses Isserles' permission to remove the salt from the tongue of the *goses* is based upon the fact that it ought never to have been put there in the first place.[37] From this explanation of R. Isserles' position, he deduces that any form of life-support that was introduced before the patient's condition was clearly established must be removed once it becomes evident that recovery is no longer possible. Utilizing it in the first place was wrong. This original wrong ought not to be compounded by a further one; the impediment must be removed. Finally, R. Halevy marshals further support from the idea of the time of the departure of the soul referred to in *Sefer Hasidim*.[38] In his view, artificial barriers should not be erected in order to detain the soul within the body beyond this time.

R. Halevy's simple comparison between salt and respirators is somewhat problematic. As already observed, a large part of the reason for the rabbinic leniency with respect to the removal of salt and woodchoppers is precisely the fact that their life-preserving qualities are not empirically proven. If they were, there would be no difference between removing a grain of salt and moving the *goses*: both would be considered acts intended to hasten death. If anything, removal of respirators and artificial nutrition and hydration are to be compared to moving the *goses*, both in terms of their empirically proven fatal effects, and the physical contact with the *goses* that is involved. Moreover, implicit in R. Halevy's approach is the argument that it is never wrong to restore an individual to his

---

[36] 'Removing a Patient with No Chance of Recovery from an Artificial Respirator' (Heb.), *Tehumin*, 2 (1981), 304–5. See also *Resp. Lev Aryeh*, 2 no. 37, for a similar argument.

[37] *Beth Lehem Yehudah, Yoreh Deah*, 339: 1.   [38] See n. 10–11.

'natural' status quo by the removal of any medical device or procedure. Presumably, a treatment such as insulin for a diabetic would also fall into the category of an impediment under this view. This is a very strong form of naturalism indeed, and it highly unlikely that even R. Halevy himself would wish to subscribe to such an extreme naturalist position *vis-à-vis* the status of medical therapy.[39]

A similar critique may be levelled at R. Halevy's argument that impediments are by definition wrongfully put into place and ought to be removed. The impediments in question are not empirically proven, hence their removal is not really problematic. As far as the argument from the time of death is concerned, it is generally agreed that in Jewish law there is no practical method of defining the time to die, and the concept of 'a time to die' is entirely lacking in practical, normative significance.[40]

Finally, R. Halevy's argument that life-support that does not effect a cure may be removed, even if the result is certain death for the patient, raises the serious issue of defining the difference between ceasing futile therapy and killing a person, including a *goses*, by depriving him of his basic physiological needs. As already observed, there is a difference between these two types of activity, and R. Halevy's formulation does not do justice to the seriousness of this problem. His position remains a minority one, even though it follows the classical halakhic sources on the *goses* more literally than any of the approaches offered by other modern halakhic authorities.

R. Eliezer Waldenberg's approach is less simplistic, taking account of the need to define carefully the stage at which removing life-support from a *goses* no longer constitutes a criminal offence.[41] He begins by stating that a 'new type of *goses*' has arisen as a result of modern medical science.

---

[39] Of course, there is a notion in Jewish sources that medicine is indeed 'artificial', since people really ought to rely on God for their physical well-being and not seek human healing: see Ch. 4 s. 2. This notion, however, is not normative, and it is highly unlikely that R. Halevy would subscribe to it: see N. Zohar, *Alternatives in Jewish Bioethics* (New York, 1997), 47–8.

[40] R. Moses Sofer lays down the principle that there is no precise definition of the time of the emergence of the soul in the *halakhah* (*Resp. Hatam Sofer, Orah Hayyim*, no. 199). R. Waldenberg, however, takes issue with this finding and maintains that it may be established by both tradition and medicine (*Resp. Ziz Eliezer*, 14 no. 81). It is evident, however, that R. Waldenberg himself does not intend to offer any precise definition of this 'time', and is merely using it as a conceptual aid to his theory of *gesisah* and his approach to the application of the impediment-removal principle to modern life-support. The majority of halakhic commentators agree that the concept of the time of the soul's departure is a spiritual one, and as such, does not play any direct role in halakhic decisions relating to the treatment of the dying. A similar point is made by R. Moses Feinstein in reference to the nature of the suffering caused by delaying the departure of the soul. According to R. Feinstein, this suffering is entirely spiritual in nature and nothing can be learned from it with respect to the halakhic question of a dying individual who is experiencing severe physical suffering (*Resp. Iggrot Moshe, Yoreh Deah*, 2 no. 174).   [41] *Resp. Ziz Eliezer*, 13 no. 89.

Neither the traditional symptoms of *gesisah*, nor the impediments listed in the halakhic sources, are of relevance to this type of *goses*. In order to apply the law of the *goses* to the terminal hospitalized patient of contemporary times, it is necessary to focus on the physical state of the individual concerned.[42] R. Waldenberg takes his cue from the above-mentioned formulation of R. Epstein, i.e. anything 'which is not because of the body of the *goses*' may be removed.[43] This expression is understood by R. Waldenberg to mean that in 'the absence of any medically proven capacity for independent life', all life-support may be terminated. R. Waldenberg's shift of focus to the medically defined terminal nature of the patient's condition as the key to any decision to discontinue life-support is certainly more in accord with modern realities than R. Halevy's general reference to independent existence and his simple analogy between woodchoppers and respirators.

In order to remove any doubts, from the point of view of the criminal law, regarding the halakhic legitimacy of disconnecting a patient who has lost all capacity for independent life from a respirator, R. Waldenberg recommends that the actual disconnecting be done in an indirect manner, such as by connecting the respirator to a time-clock which will shut it down without any particular individual actually being required to 'pull the plug'. It must be emphasized that this appeal to the principle of indirectness is peripheral to R. Waldenberg's main argument, which relates to the medical condition of the patient and not to the nature of the disconnecting act.

It is noteworthy that R. Waldenberg's idea that life-support be connected to a time-clock so that its termination does not constitute a direct act is, in fact, recommended as a possible secondary justification for permitting the withdrawal of such support in the final phase of life in the recent report of the Israeli committee investigating the treatment of the terminally ill patient. This report, together with the draft bill on the terminal ill patient drawn up by the committee, is outlined in the Appendix.

R. Waldenberg also mentions the concept of timely death. However, he does not attach any halakhic weight to it, but uses it in a general way to explain the need to clarify the law in this area. It is not correct to adopt the approach that everything should be done in every case to continue life. There is 'a time to die', and an effort should be made to investigate the conditions under which the *halakhah* permits the discontinuation of artificial life-support. Unlike R. Halevy, R. Waldenberg does not contend that the value of dying on time is sufficiently strong to overcome the

---

[42] A similar idea may be found in R. Hayyim Benveniste's *responsum* from the 16th cent. *Sheirei Knesset Hagedolah, Yoreh Deah, Hilkhot Bikkur Holim*, 339: 4.

[43] *Arukh Hashulhahn, Yoreh Deah*, 339: 4.

prohibition on indirect homicide involved in bringing about a person's death by terminating his life-support.

R. Waldenberg's most significant contribution to the application of the law of *goses* to modern medical realities is the fact that his analysis centres on the physical circumstances under which the permission to remove an impediment applies, although his definition of these circumstances is not problem free. According to R. Waldenberg, artificial life-support is to be removed once the *goses* no longer possesses the 'capacity for independent life', i.e. he manifests no signs of life in either the brain (including the brain-stem) or the heart. Clearly, such a patient would be dead under any contemporary medical definition of death: once there is no sign of life in both heart and brain, we are surely dealing with a corpse! Indeed, the lack of any ability to breathe independently, together with the absence of a heartbeat, constitute, as we explain in detail in Chapter 6, a valid halakhic definition of death under the most stringent of modern schools of thought on this issue. On being pressed on this point, R. Waldenberg responded that it might have been thought that even in such a case, the *halakhah* requires the continuation of life-support, since there might still be some 'as yet undetected life in the body of the *goses*', and that because of this possibility, life-support should be continued until artificial respiration is no longer capable of maintaining vital functions. R. Waldenberg makes it quite clear that there is no need for such a concern, and that once medical science has established that there is no longer any life in the brain and the heart, all life-support is to be discontinued.[44] This very narrowly drawn definition of lack of independent function means that, in effect, the concept of impediment-removal is rendered practically irrelevant.

This criticism notwithstanding, sight should not be lost of R. Waldenberg's important contribution to the development of the doctrine of the *goses* in modern *halakhah*. He grapples with the issue of defining the *goses* in a modern clinical context, and introduces the 'indirectness' principle as a useful secondary argument in dealing with the issue of the cessation of life-support in terminal situations.

The majority of modern halakhists have chosen to replace the traditional distinction between precipitating death and removing an impediment, with a distinction between medical therapy which is effective only in the short term, and the maintenance of basic physical functions. Any medical therapy that cures a particular aspect of the patient's condition, but fails to provide him with any extra life expectancy, is considered as an impediment to death and may be removed. A typical example is that of a person suffering from terminal cancer who develops gangrene in his leg. Amputation of the leg effectively ensures that the cancer will take its

---

[44] *Resp. Ziz Eliezer*, 14 no. 81.

course and nothing else of any therapeutic value. It will not restore the patient to health or add any years to his lifespan.[45] Air, food, and liquids, on the other hand, are basic physical necessities: their removal constitutes indirect homicide and is forbidden until the establishment of death.

This view avoids R. Halevy's simplistic view of modern life-support without tying impediment-removal to a tightly drawn definition of the final phase of life, as does R. Waldenberg. It does not insist that a patient be effectively medically dead before an impediment may be removed. It does, however, insist that basic life-support be continued until the establishment of death. In general, this approach fits in with many of the medical realities of contemporary dying, as well as being in line with much contemporary theological and legal thinking in this area. Still, a number of questions arise: Is the line between therapy and the maintenance of basic physical functions a clear one? Does it make sense to insist upon the support of basic functions, even though they are being supplied in an artificial manner? These questions have generated a not insignificant debate amongst modern halakhists.

The distinction between short-term medical therapy and the maintenance of basic physical functioning as the fundamental distinction in the law of the *goses* first appeared in a halakhic journal in the early part of the twentieth century.[46] It has since been most clearly articulated by R. Immanuel Jakobovits, in an article published in 1957.[47] R. Jakobovits begins by tackling the issue of the obligation to heal in Jewish law, which he limits to cases in which the patient may be restored to full health. A major source in support of this position is Maimonides' scriptural proof-text establishing the obligation to engage in the practice of medicine. Maimonides derives the obligation from the biblical law requiring the finders of lost property to restore their findings to their true owners, which the Talmud extends to the restoration of lost health.[48] According to R. Jakobovits, the use of this verse, rather than the more familiar biblical passage dealing with the medical expenses of an assault victim, indicates that Maimonides limits the obligation to practise medicine to those cases in which a cure is likely to be achieved. If a cure is not achievable, there is no obligation to administer therapy, just as the commandment to return

---

[45] The case of the man with the gangrenous leg also suffering from a host of other complications, was mentioned in Ch. 4 n. 92. In addition to the risk involved in the amputation of the leg as a result of his generally poor condition, the distinction between therapy and the maintenance of basic functions played an important role in the decision not to amputate.

[46] See R. David Katzberg's editorial comment in *Tel Talpiot*, 30 (1923), 66 no. 42. This source is cited by R. Jakobovits, *Jewish Medical Ethics* (New York, 1975), 350 n. 46.

[47] 'The Law Relating to the Precipitation of the Death of a Hopeless Patient Who is Undergoing Great Suffering' (Heb.), *Hapardes*, 31 (1957), pt. 1, 28–31; pt. 3, 16–19.

[48] Deut. 22: 2; *Sanhedrin*, 73a; *Bava Kamma*, 81b; Maimonides, *Commentary on the Mishnah*, *Nedarim*, 4: 4.

lost property ceases to apply in the absence of an object worthy of restoration to the owner.[49] R. Jakobovits infers from Maimonides that there is no obligation to continue with any therapy at all if the patient's death is inevitable. From this it follows that no criminal liability will devolve upon a doctor who either withholds or withdraws therapy of a short-term nature from a dying patient. Since proximity to death is part of the definition of a *goses*, R. Jakobovits concludes the first part of his argument with the contention that all short-term medical therapy may, in principle, be withdrawn from a terminal patient.

The second stage in the argument is to link the withdrawal of medical treatment to the rationale underlying impediment removal. R. Jakobovits is of the view that impediments to death may be removed in order to prevent suffering to the *goses*. Similarly, the extension of a miserable and painful existence for a short time by means of medical therapy offends against the principle of preventing suffering; consequently, it is not halakhically mandatory. The concept of timely death is also introduced by R. Jakobovits at this stage of his argument in order to support his point that once a particular treatment is not halakhically mandated, its continuation in the case of a terminal individual also offends against the spiritual and mystical idea that death should not be impeded.

The removal of air, food, and drink is an entirely different matter. Their removal is absolutely forbidden until the establishment of death. R. Jakobovits emphasizes the prohibition on indirect homicide in Jewish law,[50] and has no hesitation in declaring that the withdrawal of the artificial support of basic functions such as respiration and nutrition constitutes an act of homicide.

R. Jakobovits' conceptually refined formulation of the traditional distinction provides the basis for almost all the modern halakhic discussion of the treatment of the terminally ill and the contemporary application of the laws of the *goses*.

Incidentally, R. Jakobovits' approach is also reflective of Catholic teachings in relation to the treatment of the dying, which he refers to in his English bioethical writings.[51] In 1957, Pope Pius XII issued a directive requiring that only 'ordinary' means need be used in order to preserve the life of a terminally ill patient.[52] The distinction between 'ordinary' and 'extraordinary' means is a basic element in Catholic teaching in this area,[53]

---

[49] See *Torah Temimah, Deuteronomy*, 22: 2 no.18, and Ch. 4 n. 47.   [50] See nn. 34–5.

[51] Jakobovits, *Jewish Medical Ethics*, 124.

[52] 'The Prolongation of Life', *Acta Apostolicae Sedis*, 49 (November 24, 1957), 1027–33.

[53] Congregation for the Doctrine of the Faith, 1980, 'Declaration on Euthanasia', *Origins*, 10 (1980), 154–7. This approach is also adopted by the Anglican Church, see: Rev. D. Coggan, 'On Dying and Dying Well', *Proceedings of the Royal Society of Medicine*, 70 (1977), 75. See also J. K. Mason and R. McCall Smith, *Law and Medical Ethics* (London, 1994), 324.

and is most commonly understood in terms of the efficacy of the treatment in question. In other words, effective treatment is considered ordinary and must be continued; medically futile treatment, on the other hand, is extraordinary, and may be discontinued. This only applies to therapy; it does not apply to bringing about a person's death by depriving him of air, food, and water, which is always prohibited.[54]

The first problem to emerge in relation to this approach is the dividing line between therapy and basic maintenance. In his article, R. Jakobovits uses the case of a terminal cancer patient suffering from diabetes in order to illustrate the difference between therapy and basic maintenance. In his view, insulin need not be administered to such a patient, even though withholding it will precipitate his death. Since the terminal patient will gain nothing by the administration of the insulin other than a longer period in which to die of a painful cancer, the insulin is to be regarded as a short-term medical therapy that falls into the category of an impediment to death, and may be withheld or discontinued. Whereas the basic distinction between futile therapy and maintenance is a widely accepted one, this particular illustration has come under attack, thereby revealing a basic weakness in the approach. According to R. Shlomo Zalman Auerbach, insulin for a diabetic is exactly the same as food and drink for a regular person. It is therefore forbidden to withdraw insulin, just as it is forbidden to starve a *goses* to death.[55] Clearly, the line between medical therapy and basic biological functions is not easy to draw, especially in an era in which so many of our physical activities may, if necessary, be supported in an artificial fashion. As far as insulin is concerned, it is noteworthy that there is a suggestion that if the insulin is reduced in a gradual manner, it might eventually be terminable, even according to the view that it is food rather than medical therapy.[56]

In addition to the problem of line-drawing, another contested point in relation to this position, from the perspective of contemporary medical practice, is the conclusion that respiration, alimentation, and hydration must be maintained until the establishment of death, even if they are being administered in an artificial fashion. The lack of any distinction between natural and artificial life-support was not particularly significant in 1957 when R. Jakobovits wrote his seminal article; it is much more significant today, when an increasingly large number of terminally ill

---

[54] See Congregation for the Doctrine of the Faith, 'Declaration on Euthanasia', 155–6; G. Grisez, 'Should Nutrition and Hydration be Provided to Permanently Comatose and Other Mentally Disabled Patients?', *Linacre Quarterly*, 57 (1990), 31. See also A. Fisher, 'Theological Aspects of Euthanasia', in J. Keown (ed.), *Euthanasia Examined* (Cambridge, 1995), 330–2.

[55] *Nishmat Avraham, Yoreh Deah*, no. 339.

[56] *Encyclopaedia of Jewish Medical Ethics*, iv. 410 n. 381a. This view is, in fact, attributed to R. Shlomo Zalman Auerbach.

patients are receiving highly sophisticated artificial life support. Both the
House of Lords[57] and the American Supreme Court [58] have ruled that artificial life-support is a therapeutic procedure falling squarely within the
rubric of medical treatment and subject to standard medical law. The
House of Lords held that artificial life-support could be withdrawn by a
medical team on the basis of the criterion of good medical practice, and
the United States Supreme Court permitted the removal of artificial life-
support on the basis of patient autonomy. In both systems, a physician
who stops the supply of artificial respiration or nutrition on the basis of
the criteria laid down for so doing is not regarded as being in the same
moral or legal category as a person who refuses to feed someone they are
meant to be looking after, or a person who wilfully deprives another individual of the air he needs in order to breathe. Artificial life support
involves medical expertise for its installation, as well as constant medical
supervision and treatment for infections resulting from intubation; it is a
fully fledged medical procedure, subject to the legal ramifications of such
procedures.

By contrast, the position under contemporary Jewish law is that artificial life-support must be maintained until the establishment of death, and
it is not subject to the principles governing the withdrawal of short-term,
life-saving therapy in the case of a terminal patient.[59] At the same time, it
ought to be noted that switching from intravenous feeding to oral feeding, or substituting a mixture of water and glucose for a full intravenous
feed in the case of a suffering terminal patient, is permitted.[60]

A medically refined application of the distinction between life-support
and short-term therapy is an important element in the recent Israeli draft bill
on the terminal patient, an outline of which is presented in the Appendix.

This position may change as Jewish law encounters secular practice in
relation to the treatment of the terminally ill. The argument that artificial
nutrition is a form of medical therapy, and as such may be refused by a
terminal patient, was used in a halakhic decision regarding the binding
nature of a legally valid advance directive (living will) upon a Jewish
nursing facility in New York.[61] The facts of the case are as follows: an
Orthodox nursing home in New York refused to follow an advance directive requiring the withdrawal of artificial nutrition and hydration from

---

[57] *Airedale NHS Trust v. Bland* [1993] I All ER 821.

[58] *Cruzan v. Missouri Department of Health* 58 USLW 4916 (1990).

[59] *Resp. Ziz Eliezer*, 13 no. 89; *Resp. Mishnah Halakhot*, 7 no. 287; *Encyclopaedia of Jewish Medical Ethics*, iv. 405–6.

[60] *Encyclopaedia of Jewish Medical Ethics*, iv. 405 n. 361a. This view is attributed to R. Shlomo Zalman Auerbach.

[61] Z. Schostak, 'Ethical Guidelines for the Treatment of the Dying Elderly', *Journal of Halakhah and Contemporary Society*, 20 (1991), 62.

a patient once he became incompetent. The refusal was based on the assumption that *halakhah* forbids withdrawal in these circumstances. The directive was valid under New York law and the patient was clearly incompetent. Under New York law, there was no basis for preferring the religious scruples of the nursing home over the legally valid advance directive. The only way in which the nursing home could have avoided fulfilling the directive would have been to turn the patient away after referring him to a different facility.[62] Not having done so, it was required to act in accordance with the directive. The nursing home management sought halakhic advice, and was informed that artificial nutrition and hydration fall into the category of medical procedures that may be withheld at the direction of the patient. This is clearly not in keeping with R. Jakobovits' position as outlined above. Also, it was pointed out that under Jewish law, there is an established talmudic principle that 'the law of the land is the law', and in a case of conflict such as the present one, halakhic scruples must retreat in the face of New York law.[63] Undoubtedly, the fact that resistance to local law would probably have led to the financial ruin of the home and its staff, and to possible criminal and professional sanctions against them influenced this decision. Nevertheless, the decision does indicate that in particularly difficult circumstances, the *halakhah* in this area is prepared to transfer artificial nutrition from the category of basic maintenance to that of medical therapy.

It should also be pointed out that although under normal circumstances, halakhic authorities are opposed to the removal of artificial respiration until death has been established, there is a view that the oxygen content in a terminal situation may be reduced to 21 per cent, which is the percentage of oxygen in regular air.[64] The obligation to preserve the basic function of breathing becomes weaker as the artificial nature of that function becomes more pronounced, and practical steps may be taken in the light of that weakness. It would appear that the *halakhah* does, in fact, take into account the highly artificial nature of procedures such as artificial respiration, and is prepared to countenance their gradual withdrawal if the patient's condition is hopeless. Any more significant step in this direction would require a distinction to be made between 'natural' and

---

[62] See *Elbaum v. Grace Plaza*, 148 AD 2d 244, 544, NYS, 2d 840 (1989).

[63] It is noteworthy that the halakhic principle of 'the law of the land is the law' was also used in this case to provide a basis for accepting the advance directive and withdrawing the artificial nutrition and hydration. However, this approach is hardly a tenable one, since the principle of the 'law of the land' is normally confined to civil law cases and is not applicable to matters of such profound moral and religious significance as the withdrawal of life-support from a terminal patient: see M. Elon (ed.), *The Principles of Jewish Law* (Jerusalem, 1974), 710.

[64] See *Encyclopaedia of Jewish Medical Ethics*, iv. 408. This view is also attributed to R. Shlomo Zalman Auerbach.

'artificial' maintenance, and guidelines would need to be laid down for so doing. In other words, the halakhic distinction between impediment removal and death precipitation would need to be adjusted once again to accommodate the realities of medical science. Such an accommodation is not a new phenomenon since, as outlined above, the distinction between impediment-removal and precipitating death underwent several metamorphoses in conformity with changing ideas and concepts. In principle, an accommodation that is capable of integration into the basic framework of the distinction between impediment removal and death precipitation ought to be perfectly acceptable, especially if it is designed to reflect well-founded changes in medical science. After all, this type of accommodation has always been a feature of the *halakhah* in this area.

Thus far, the major focus of our discussion has been the termination of life-support. This is a result of the controversial nature of this issue in both older and contemporary halakhic sources. Non-treatment is, however, much less controversial and, as observed in relation to the removal of salt from the mouth of the *goses* discussed in section 1, omissions are much more easily justifiable than commissions in this area of Jewish law. The distinction between withdrawing and withholding life-maintaining procedures is, nevertheless, an important one in modern biomedical *halakhah*, and it deserves a mention, albeit brief, especially since it constitutes a significant element in the recent Israeli draft bill on the terminal patient outlined in the Appendix.

In the light of our analysis, it is evident that Jewish law has always recognized that neither the prohibition on homicide, nor the principle that the preservation of human life is of paramount value, apply with their full rigour to the terminal situation. This recognition of the value of a humane death finds its expression in the *halakhah* in the distinction between impediment removal and death precipitation, and in the halakhic development of this distinction through the ages.[65]

Before concluding this section, mention ought to be made of the *Sheffer* case, discussed at the end of Chapter 4.[66] In the course of his

---

[65] The general concept of distinguishing between direct and indirect acts in this context has come under heavy attack, principally on the part of philosophers but also by some jurists and judges, on the grounds that it is both logically confused and morally mistaken. At the same time, however, it has enjoyed a long tradition in law, medicine, and many different moral theories. Indeed, it has been observed by more than one commentator that there is a certain value in maintaining a distinction that has survived the test of practical application over a long period of time. Such distinctions become part of our moral intuition and should not easily be set aside because of purely intellectual criticism: 'Our gut intuition tells us that there is a difference between active and passive euthanasia and we are not going to be browbeaten into changing our minds by mere logic' (*Lancet*, 1 (1986), 1085). There are also many logical and philosophical defences of the distinction between direct and indirect acts leading to the death of a terminal patient in modern bioethical literature: see D. Sulmasy, 'Killing and Allowing to Die: Another Look', *Journal of Law, Medicine and Ethics*, 26 (1998), 55.

[66] See Ch. 4 n. 133.

wide-ranging judgment, Elon J. applied the traditional distinction between death-precipitating and impediment-removal acts, and implied that it corresponded to the one made by R. Jacobovits between basic survival and treatments aimed at short-term improvements only. He did, however, emphasize the need for both medical knowledge and human sensitivity in applying this distinction. Elon J.'s recommendation was followed in the recent Israeli draft law on the treatment of the terminally ill, which seeks to apply the halakhic distinction between procedures necessary for the maintenance of basic survival and those aimed at short-term therapy, in as medically sound and humane a way as possible.

3. PREVENTION OF SUFFERING IN THE DYING PROCESS

Running like a golden thread throughout the halakhic literature on the law of the *goses* is the principle that the dying should be spared as much physical and mental suffering as possible.[67] This principle is cited by all the modern authorities who deal with this area, and may be traced back to the biblical verse cited by the *Sefer Hasidim*, 'there is a time to die'.[68] The meaning of this verse is that there are times in which death is a positive thing, and it ought to be regarded as such. In classical halakhic thought, the verse teaches the value of death within the framework of the *halakhah*, i.e. the distinction between removing an impediment to death and precipitating it. The scope for applying this distinction is particularly strong when the alternative is suffering for the *goses*. A striking talmudic passage, albeit of an aggadic rather than a halakhic nature, in which the link between the prevention of suffering and the permission to remove an impediment is expressed, is that which recounts the martyrdom of R. Hanina b. Teradyon.[69] The Romans wrapped R. Hanina in a Torah scroll and lit a fire underneath him. They also placed wet tufts of wool next to his skin in order to prolong his agony. When his student suggested that he open his mouth so that 'the fire would enter and he would die more quickly', he refused on the grounds that he would not take his own life. When his Roman executioner offered to remove the wet tufts and increase the fire in return for a share in the world to come, R. Hanina accepted the offer, and backed up his assurance to the executioner of his place in the Hereafter with a solemn oath. As soon as the tufts were removed and the fire increased, R. Hanina died. The executioner then jumped into the fire, and a heavenly voice was heard proclaiming: 'R. Hanina and his executioner are to be received into the life of the World-to-Come.' Rabbinic

---

[67] See *Encyclopaedia of Jewish Medical Ethics*, iv. 394–6.   [68] See nn. 10–11.
[69] *Avodah Zarah*, 18a.

commentators point out that the passage is not a strictly normative one,[70] but they still use it as a dramatic illustration of the nexus between the prevention of suffering and impediment-removal in the Talmud.

Another area in which the principle of preventing suffering to the dying finds expression in Jewish law is the issue of praying for the death of a suffering person. The Talmud[71] recounts that when R. Judah the Prince became seriously ill, the rabbis prayed for his life to be preserved. His handmaid prayed in a similar vein. Upon observing the amount of severe physical and mental suffering he was undergoing, however, she changed her prayer and asked that he be allowed to die. She also caused a disturbance, with the result that the rabbis momentarily ceased their prayers, and at that instant, R. Judah's soul departed to its eternal rest. The handmaid's conduct seems to be perfectly in order as far as the Talmud is concerned, and it is tempting to observe that it took the wisdom of a handmaid to realize that any spiritual benefits accruing from the continued existence of R. Judah were far outweighed by the physical and mental suffering he was undergoing as a result of the prolongation of his life. This talmudic passage serves as the major source for the halakhic permission to pray for the death of a person who is clearly experiencing great suffering and for whom death would come as welcome release. Praying for the death of a suffering person is permitted under Jewish law,[72] although care should be taken to ensure that only those with the purest of motives do the actual praying.[73]

The idea that there may be an analogy between praying for the death of a suffering person and taking active steps to hasten his end is canvassed by some modern commentators.[74] However, it has been rejected by halakhic authorities on the grounds that praying for a person's death still leaves the mechanics of bringing about the death to God, whereas taking active steps to bring about the demise of a terminal patient involves the people concerned in the crime of homicide.[75] Praying for death and taking active steps to end life are two very different things, and no analogy may be drawn between them. In the *halakhah*, the desire to prevent suffering finds expression within the framework of the law, not in defiance of it.

---

[70] *Resp. Beth Avi*, 2 no. 153; Hirshler, 'Obligation to Save Lives', 35; *Resp. Iggrot Moshe, Hoshen Mishpat*, 2 no. 73. Earlier authorities were, however, prepared to draw fully fledged legal conclusions from the story of R. Hanina, see M. Wolner, 'The Physician's Rights and Jurisdiction' (Heb.), *Hatorah Vehamedinah*, 7–8 (1956–7), 318; S. Werner, 'Mercy Killing in the Light of Jewish Law' (Heb.), *Torah Shebal Peh*, 18 (1976), 39.   [71] *Ketubot*, 104a.
[72] *Ran, Nedarim*, 40a, *s.v. en mevakesh*.   [73] *Resp. Hikekei Lev, Yoreh Deah*, no. 50.
[74] See S. Freehof, *Reform Responsa* (New York, 1973), 119; B. Sherwin, *In Partnership With God* (Syracuse, 1990), 97.
[75] *Resp. Iggrot Moshe, Hoshen Mishpat*, 2, no. 73; *Resp. Ziz Eliezer*, 13 no. 89; J. Gershuni, *Kol Zafayikh*, 335. There is also support for this approach amongst Conservative rabbis, see A. Reisner, 'A Halakhic Ethic of Care for the Terminally Ill', *Conservative Judaism*, 43 (1991), 56.

R. Yehiel Epstein expresses this point as follows: 'Even if the *goses* is suffering greatly and one might have thought that it would be a *mitzvah* to precipitate death, it is nevertheless forbidden to carry out any such direct act.'[76] Even though the prevention of suffering is a recognized value in Judaism, it is prohibited to take any practical step that might precipitate the death of the *goses*. Only in the context of impediment-removal does the prevention of suffering become an operative principle in the law of the *goses*.[77]

There is one exception to this prohibition. Several modern authorities have addressed the issue of administering analgesics to a *goses*, all of whom have been prepared, in principle, to sanction the administration of analgesics, even if they result in the shortening of life.[78] According to R. Shlomo Zalman Auerbach, the reason for permitting such a course of action is that no one single dose is sufficient to cause death. Under Jewish criminal law, there is no legal culpability in such a case.[79] Here too, it is the *halakhah* that provides a legal framework for the principle of preventing the *goses* from undergoing great suffering.

4. THE PERSISTENT VEGETATIVE STATE (PVS)

The halakhic model for the treatment of the terminally ill outlined above comprises three major elements: an updated definition of *goses*, a distinction between futile or purely short-term therapy and the maintenance of basic physical functions, and the principle that the dying person should be exposed to as little suffering as possible. The difficult case that exercised both Jewish and general law in this area for much of the second half of the twentieth century was that of the patient in a persistent vegetative state (PVS), and it may be interesting to test out this halakhic model on the case of a PVS patient. PVS must be distinguished from whole brain death, which is properly defined as the irreversible dysfunction of the brain-stem. The brain-stem is that part of the brain that controls 'vegetative' activities: breathing, digestion, the sleep/wake cycle, and other involuntary processes. The PVS patient's brain-stem remains largely intact; therefore, he is still alive.[80] Indeed, there are a few documented cases of patients who were properly diagnosed as being in the relatively early stages of PVS, and who subsequently achieved full or partial

---

[76] *Arukh Hashulhan, Yoreh Deah*, 339: 4.   [77] *Resp. Ziz Eliezer*, 5, *Ramat Rahel*, no. 5.

[78] See Wolner, 'Physician's Rights', 293; *Resp. Ziz Eliezer*, 13 no. 87.

[79] *Nishmat Avraham, Yoreh Deah*, no. 339.

[80] President's Commission for the Study of Ethical Problems in Medicine and Biomedical and Behavioural Research, *Deciding to Forgo Life-Sustaining Treatments* (Washington, DC, 1983), 173.

recovery.[81] Medical opinion generally regards PVS patients as 'severely impaired' rather than dead.[82] The question that arises is the possibility of withdrawing a PVS patient's life-support in especially serious cases of grave and irreversible damage to the rest of the brain.

Leading decisions in the English House of Lords[83] and the American Supreme Court[84] have permitted the removal of artificial life-support in the form of nutrition and hydration from severe PVS patients. As observed in the previous section, both Courts ruled that artificial nutrition and hydration fall into the category of medical therapy, the termination of which is subject to medical discretion rather than the standard doctrines of the law of homicide. The House of Lords used the criterion of 'good medical practice' as the main grounds for justifying the withdrawal of artificial nutrition from a severe PVS patient, whereas the American Supreme Court concentrated on the need to obtain 'clear and convincing evidence' of the patient's wishes prior to his becoming incompetent, in order to decide on the termination of life-support.

In terms of the three-part halakhic model, the first issue is the definition of *gesisah* in relation to a PVS patient. Although the definition of *goses* has been updated, and the three-day limit is no longer a definitive one, the potential of some PVS patients to live for many years poses something of a problem with regard to including PVS under the rubric of *gesisah*.[85] On the other hand, the modern trend to focus on the nature of the patient's condition, rather than its duration, might make it easier to apply the *goses* law to a PVS patient today than in the past. Still, the issue of the lengthy duration of the persistent vegetative state requires careful consideration.

The second element in the model is the distinction between futile or short-term therapy and basic maintenance. Short-term procedures may be withheld or withdrawn, whereas basic maintenance must be continued until the establishment of death in accordance with the criteria discussed in Chapter 6. Since the issue with regard to PVS patients is the termination of maintenance and not therapy, it would appear at first glance that there is no basis for applying the *goses* category to the PVS state. It was pointed out above, however, that in one case at least, artificial nutrition and hydration were classified as therapy rather than basic maintenance,[86] and due to the growing general trend to adopt this classification, the halakhic position on this issue may, indeed, change. In the light of this

---

[81] See President's Commission (n. 80), 120; B. Steinbock, 'Recovery from Persistent Vegetative State?: The Case of Carrie Coons', *Hastings Centre Report*, 19 (1989), 14; 'The Case of Rev. Harry and Mrs Cole', *Time*, 19 March 1990, 62.

[82] See J. Younger and E. Bartlett, 'Human Dignity and High Technology', *Annals of Internal Medicine*, 99 (1982), 252.   [83] *Airedale NHS Trust v. Bland* (1993) I All ER 821.

[84] *Cruzan v. Missouri Department of Health* 58 USLW 4916 (1990).

[85] See Bleich, 'Quinlan Case', 275 n. 2.   [86] See Schostak, 'Ethical Guidelines', 62.

possibility, the applicability of the *goses* category to the PVS patient is not as inconceivable as it may have been in the past.

The third element in the model is the principle of preventing suffering. The extent to which a PVS patient is physically capable of feeling pain is still unclear, and it is precisely this inability to make a strong claim that a PVS patient is undergoing great suffering that makes the issue of withdrawing his life-support so difficult.[87] In the absence of clear evidence of such suffering, there is little basis for applying the rule permitting impediment removal; indeed, there would seem to be a good reason for not doing so.[88] The most that contemporary halakhic authorities are prepared to concede in relation to PVS is that if it can be proved that a patient is suffering, no life-prolonging measures need be taken in the first instance.[89] As far as removing life-support is concerned, it is generally agreed that it may not be withdrawn.[90]

One possible avenue for future exploration is the relevance, if any, of the suffering of others for the question of withdrawing life-support from a PVS patient. Clearly, opening up the principle of the prevention of suffering to persons other than the *goses* him- or herself is a risky step, since it involves complex and difficult decisions regarding the balance of suffering and peoples' inner intentions. Still, the prevention of suffering is such a powerful principle that in those cases in which the suffering of others is extremely great, there is a possibility that it may be taken into account in order to produce a decision in favour of termination of life-support. Such a decision would, presumably, be rendered on an individual basis only, and every attempt would be made to keep it confidential. This is the traditional path of Jewish law in hard cases of this type.

5. CRIMINAL LIABILITY FOR THE KILLING OF A FATALLY ILL PERSON (*TEREFAH*) IN JEWISH LAW

The law of the *goses* is the standard legal framework for the treatment of the terminally ill and the dying. It arose in the context of domestic death, and was developed by modern authorities in order to provide guidelines for patients, families, physicians, and rabbis dealing with

---

[87] See n. 187.

[88] Some Conservative authorities are also reluctant to permit the removal of life-support from a PVS patient, arguing that since the matter is halakhically doubtful, any error should be made in favour of preserving life, however limited that life may be (see n. 75). The debate between Conservative scholars on this issue is referred to below in relation to the *terefah* issue.

[89] *Resp. Iggrot Moshe, Hoshen Mishpat*, 2 no. 75; *Encyclopaedia of Jewish Medical Ethics*, iv. 414. [90] *Encyclopaedia of Jewish Medical Ethics*, iv. 413.

death in a highly sophisticated medical context. The law of the *terefah*, on the other hand, originates in the criminal law and is applied to 'tragic choice situations', such as the sacrificing of one individual for the sake of saving a whole group of people. There is, however, certain scope for the application of the law of the *terefah* to some of the pressing problems regarding the treatment of the terminally ill in the *halakhah*, and it is to an exploration of this issue that the present section is devoted.

(a) Defining the *Terefah*

A *terefah*[91] is an individual who is suffering from a fatal illness that will result in death within a period of about twelve months. The term *terefah* is commonly used in the Jewish dietary laws, and the distinction between the animal *terefah* and the human one is a useful starting point for a discussion of the human *terefah* in the law of homicide.

In the context of the dietary laws, the term *terefah* refers to any animal afflicted with a fatal organic defect, such as a pierced windpipe or gullet, that renders the animal unfit for consumption.[92] The Talmud provides a list of those defects that constitute *tarfut*.[93] It also specifies that a *terefah* animal is, by definition, incapable of surviving for longer than twelve months.[94] The halakhic position is that this list is a closed one and remains unaffected by new developments in veterinary science.[95] A human *terefah*, on the other hand, is defined in purely medical terms, i.e. a person suffering from a fatal condition for which there is no cure known to medical science.[96] Moreover, human *tarfut* is not limited to organic defects, as in the case of the animal *terefah*. On the basis of a *responsum* written by R. Hayyim Ozer Grodzinski, it would appear that any fatal condition qualifies an individual to become a *terefah*, even if it is not included in the list of animal *terefot*, and even if it is a disease rather than an organic defect.[97] It is also important to note that the twelve-month limit relating

---

[91] The root of the word is *taraf*, meaning 'to tear' and is used specifically in the context of an attack by wild beasts, see e.g. the biblical passage in which Jacob points out that as a shepherd working for his father-in-law Laban, he personally bore the loss of every *terefah* (Gen. 31:39), i.e. a sheep 'torn and killed by a lion or a wolf'. Also see Gen. 37:33. The plural form is *terefot* and the state of being a *terefah* is referred to as *tarfut*.

[92] *Hullin*, 42a: Maimonides, *Hilkhot Shehitah*, 9:1; S. Levin and E. Boyden, *The Kosher Code* (New York, 1969).   [93] *Hullin*, 54a; Maimonides, *Hilkhot Shehitah*, 10:12–13.

[94] *Hullin*, 58a; *Shulhan Arukh*, *Yoreh Deah*, 57:18.

[95] Maimonides, *Hilkhot Shehitah*, 10:13. *Tur*, *Yoreh Deah*, 57. For a general discussion of the relationship between science and *halakhah*, see D. Sinclair, 'Torah and Scientific Methodology in Rambam's Halakhic Writings', *Le'ela*, 39 (5755), 31–2.

[96] Maimonides, *Hilkhot Rozeah*, 2:8.

[97] *Resp. Ahiezer*, *Yoreh Deah*, no. 16. The case involved a patient who wished to undergo a highly dangerous operation which, if successful, would keep him alive for a number

to the animal *terefah* is applied in a much less rigid manner with regard to the human *terefah*.[98]

The physical difference between the *terefah* and the *goses* turns, therefore, on the issue of the certainty of death. Whereas there is a chance, albeit very small, of a person remaining alive for many years even after manifesting the symptoms of *gesisah*, the death of a *terefah* within a year or so is a medical certainty. This distinction is clearly reflected in the *halakhah* according to which the wife of a man who manifested the signs of *gesisah* is not permitted to remarry until her husband's death is independently established. The rationale behind this rule is that the husband may belong to the small minority of those who manifest the signs of *gesisah* but do, in fact, recover.[99] On the other hand, the deserted wife of a *terefah* is permitted to remarry solely on the strength of her husband's *tarfut*. The inevitability of the *terefah*'s death is tantamount to its establishment,[100] and the only question is whether the twelve months are counted from the time of the *tarfut*, or from the date on which the information regarding his condition was brought to the wife's attention.[101] The halakhic literature also contains discussions on issues such as whether *terefah* offspring render their widowed mother liable to the levirate marriage,[102] and whether the biblical prohibition on marrying the sister of a living wife applies if the wife is a *terefah*.[103] Medically established certainty of death is the fundamental physical distinction between the *goses* and the *terefah*.

---

of years. The alternative was death within a few months. The legal issue was whether or not guaranteed short-term life could be risked to a great extent in the hope of gaining a significant number of years. The advantage of being classified as a *terefah* in this context will become clear shortly but the relevant point here is that R. Grodzinski was prepared to define a person whose condition did not fit into any of the categories of animal *terefot* as a human *terefah* for the purposes of Jewish criminal law. Also see *Encyclopaedia Talmudit*, xxi. 4–7.

[98] *Tosafot, Gittin*, 57b, s.v. *venikar bemoho; Tosafot, Eruvin*, 7a, s.v. *kegon shidra; Tosafot Yom Tov, Yevamot*, 16: 4.

[99] *Tosafot, Yevamot*, 120b, s.v. *lemimra; Tosafot Yevamot*, 36b, s.v. *ha; Tosafot, Bekhorot*, 20b, s.v. *helev; Rosh Bekhorot*, 3: 2; *Pithei Teshuva, Even Haezer*, 17: 131, and *Yoreh Deah*, 339: 3; *Resp. Noda Biyehuda*, 1 no. 59; cf. *Beth Shmuel, Even Haezer*, 17: 94.

[100] *Yevamot*, 120b–121a; Maimonides, *Hilkhot Gerushin*, 13: 16–18; *Tur, Even Haezer* 17; *Shulhan Arukh, Even Haezer*, 17: 30–2.

[101] Nahmanides, *Yevamot*, 120b, s.v. *umi mazit*; Rash, *Yevamot*, 120b, s.v. *umi mazit; Maggid Mishneh, Hilkhot Gerushin*, 13: 16; *Kesef Mishneh, Hilkhot Gerushin*, 13: 16; *Tur, Even Haezer*, 17 *Shulhan Arukh, Even Haezer*, 17: 30–2. See also *Resp. Mishpetei Uziel, Even Haezer*, no. 79, and *Resp. Ziz Eliezer*, 1 no. 23.

[102] *Resp. Ginat Varadim*, 2, *Even Haezer*, no. 2.

[103] *Resp. Maggid Mereshit*, no. 2. Cf. *Resp. Hikrei Lev Even Haezer*, no. 11; *Petah Hadevir*, 2; *Orah Hayyim*, 199; 4: 229; *Resp. Mishpetei Uziel, Even Haezer*, no. 79; *Resp. Yabia Omer*, 4, *Even Haezer*, no. 1.

(b) The Legal and Moral Consequences of Killing a *Terefah*

Maimonides states the law governing the killing of a human *terefah* thus:

If one kills another who suffers from a fatal organic disease, he is exempt from human law even though the victim ate and drank and walked out on the streets. But every human being is presumed to be healthy, and his murderer must be put to death, unless it is known for certain that the victim had a fatal organic disease.[104]

The exemption of the killer of a *terefah* from capital punishment is found in the Talmud. It is based upon the principle that the death penalty is administered only for the taking of a viable life. Since the death of the *terefah* is inevitable, the killer cannot be said to have taken a viable life, and he is exempt from capital punishment.[105] In the words of the commentators on the Talmud, 'the killer of a *terefah* has, in fact, killed a dead man'.[106]

At the same time, it is evident from Maimonides' careful choice of words that the killer remains liable to Divine punishment. The reason for the invocation of Divine sanctions is undoubtedly to close the apparent gap between the *halakhah* and the dictates of rational morality in this context. It must be morally wrong to kill a *terefah*, even if there is no penalty under human law for so doing! A similar problem arose in relation to abortion, and was discussed at length in Chapter 1. In that context, the creation of a prohibition on unjustified foeticide unsupported by any human sanction[107] was achieved by locating such a prohibition in the Noahide code.[108] This code, as explained in Chapter 1, is the expression of universal, rational morality in Judaism, providing a moral threshold below which positive *halakhah* may not fall.[109] The prohibition on foeticide relating to Noahides provides the basis for declaring foeticide to be a wrongful act for Israelites as well.[110] The link between killing a *terefah* and the Noahide prohibition on bloodshed is made by Maimonides, who rules that a Noahide who kills a *terefah* is liable to the death penalty.[111]

---

[104] *Hilkhot Rozeah*, 2:8. The Talmud also refers to someone who becomes a *goses* as a result of human action. On the one hand, such a person is in the last stage of life and as such, he fits into the *goses* category. On the other hand, as a victim of a specific physical injury, rather than 'natural death', such an individual would also appear to fit into the *terefah* category. The Talmud leaves this question unanswered but Maimonides rules that someone who becomes a *goses* as a result of human action is to be treated as a *terefah* and his killer is, therefore, exempt from capital punishment (*Hilkhot Rozeah*, 2:7).   [105] *Sanhedrin*, 78a.

[106] *Yad Remah*, *Sanhedrin*, 78a, *s.v. amar Rava*; *Shittah Mekubezet*, *Bava Kamma*, 26a, *s.v. vekhatav harav Yosef Halevy*; *Minhat Hinukh*, no. 34.

[107] R. Meir Simha Hacohen, *Mashekh Hokhmah*, Exodus 35:2. For a general treatment of the role of Divine penalties in Jewish law, see Elon (ed.), *Principles of Jewish law*, 522–4.

[108] See Ch. 1 nn. 124–5.   [109] See Ch. 1 s. 4.   [110] See Ch. 1 n. 124.

[111] *Hilkhot Melakhim*, 9:4. Foeticide and indirect homicide are also mentioned in this ruling.

R. Moses Feinstein infers a prohibition on the killing of a *terefah* as follows:

The prohibition on killing a *terefah* applies equally to a Jew and to a Noahide by virtue of the talmudic principle, 'There is nothing permitted to an Israelite yet forbidden to a Noahide'. Moreover, Maimonides explicitly provided that the killer of a *terefah* is exempt from human jurisdiction, implying that he is liable to Divine punishment in addition to having committed a transgression.[112]

R. Feinstein combines the elements of the Noahide prohibition on bloodshed with that of Divine punishment in order to ensure that the impression is not created that Jewish law permits the wanton killing of any *terefah*. That would be a forbidden act and must not be presented as anything else. As explained in Chapter 1, this combination of Noahide prohibition and Divine penalty also exists in other areas in which there is a gap between the positive provisions of Jewish law and the morality of preserving life, such as foeticide,[113] the killing of a non-Jew,[114] indirect homicide,[115] and all cases in which technical requirements prevent the execution of an established killer.[116] Jewish law thus closes the gap between law and morality with respect to the killing of a *terefah* by both prohibiting it under the Noahide code and invoking Divine sanctions against the killer.[117]

It was also pointed out in Chapter 1 that inclusion of a particular act in the Noahide prohibition on bloodshed does not merely provide a basis for declaring it prohibited, but it also clears the path in Jewish law for the exercise of monarchical jurisdiction against the perpetrator of the Noahide offence.[118] Maimonides is insistent that all those killers who escape the death penalty by virtue of the technicalities of the law of homicide are put to death by the king.[119] The basis for this monarchical

---

[112] *Resp. Iggrot Moshe, Yoreh Deah*, 3 no. 36. R. Feinstein also points out that Jews are always under a stricter obligation to be more moral than Noahides since 'they are sanctified by the commandments'. [113] See *Meshekh Hokhmah, Exodus* 35: 2.

[114] See *Sefer Ra'avan, Bava Kamma*, 113b; *Sefer Yereim*, 175; *Meshekh Hokhmah, Exodus* 21: 14.

[115] See nn. 34–5.

[116] *Hilkhot Rozeah*, 2: 2–3. It is also invoked in the case of suicide, see *Bava Kamma*, 91b; *Semahot*, 2 : 1; *Torah Temimah, Genesis*, 9 no. 8.

[117] See Elon (ed.), *Principles of Jewish Law*, 522. *Encyclopaedia Talmudit*, vii. 328; S. Federbusch, *Hamussar Vehamishpat Bevisrael* (Jerusalem, 1979), 140; H. Cohen (ed.), *Jewish Law in Ancient and Modern Israel* (New York, 1971), 12; B. Jackson, 'The Concept of Religious Law in Judaism', *Aufsteig und Niedergang der Romischen Welt*, 19 (1979), 33.

[118] See Ch. 1 nn. 129–130.

[119] *Hilkhot Rozeah*, 2: 4. This provision follows a number of cases of indirect homicide. It is, however, couched in much more general terms, i.e. 'all these killers and others like them'. The 'others' undoubtedly extends to those who are legally exempt as a result of evidentiary defects such as the lack of two witnesses to the entire crime or of a formal warning to the accused. Whether or not it also extends to the killer of a *terefah* is a moot point. It is unlikely that monarchical, capital jurisdiction would apply to foeticide or the killing of a non-Jew (*Hilkhot Rozeah*, 2: 11).

jurisdiction in the area of homicide is the royal mandate to preserve society at the very basic level of preventing bloodshed. R. Meir Simha Cohen, a commentator on Maimonides' code, defines this mandate by reference to the Noahide offence of bloodshed: 'The Israelite king is authorised by virtue of his role as the preserver of the social order to act in accordance with the Noahide Code, and this is a rational principle.'[120] In addition to locating the monarch's special jurisdiction with respect to established, but judicially unpunishable, homicides in the Noahide code, R. Cohen emphasizes the rational nature of that code and the king's obligation to enforce it. Thus, the rational morality of the Noahide code finds positive expression in Jewish law in the form of the king's jurisdiction to execute established but judicially unpunishable homicides.

It ought to be pointed out that the court is also empowered to bring about the death of an established murderer who, as a result of the technicalities of the rules of evidence in criminal trails, is exempt from punishment at human hands. Its jurisdiction is more limited than that of the king in terms of both the types of case within its scope, and the type of penalty it is authorized to mete out.[121] It is noteworthy that a similar situation developed under medieval Islamic law. In order to narrow the overly wide gap between those cases in which *sha'ariya* law mandated the death penalty for homicide and the need to establish the social order, the sovereign was empowered to punish proven murderers on a discretionary basis. Typical instances of the exercise of this discretion were cases in which there 'were no two upright witnesses' or in which the victim's family had received compensation money and were prepared to pardon the killer. This discretionary power eventually grew into an entire body of law known as the *siyasa sha'ariya*, which provides the basis for modern Islamic administrative law.[122]

Finally, it is important to point out that the rabbinic authorities are not unaware of the dangers posed by the granting of such wide powers to the king with respect to the punishment of established but judicially unpunishable homicides. In order to ensure that these powers are not abused, the king must, in accordance with a biblical commandment, be educated

---

[120] *Or Sameah, Hilkhot Melakhim*, 3: 10. This jurisdiction is extended by R. Meir Dan Plotzki to sexual crimes and theft, both of which threaten the basis of civilized society, see *Hemdat Yisrael*, 1, *Kuntres Ner Mitzvah*, no. 288, 75; J. D. Bleich, *Contemporary Halakhic Problems*, 4 vols. (New York, 1977–95), ii. 352 n. 11. See also Y. Blidstein, *Ikkronot Mediniim Bemishnat Harambam* (Bar Ilan, 1983), 124 nn. 18–19, 127.

[121] See I. Herzog, 'The King's Right to Pardon Offenders in Jewish Law' (Heb.), *Hatorah Vehamedinah*, 1 (1949), 18; J. Gershuni, *Mishpat Hamelukah*, 96; Blidstein, *Ikkronot Mediniim*, 124 n. 25.

[122] See N. Coulson, *A History of Islamic Law* (Edinburgh, 1964), 132; E. Rosenthal, 'Some Aspects of Islamic Political Thought', *Islamic Culture*, 22 (1948), 1; J. Schacht, 'The Law', in G. von Grunebaum (ed.), *Unity and Variety in Moslem Civilisation* (Chicago, 1985), 71.

in the rules and principles of the Torah, so that all his actions are guided solely by their spirit and content.[123] R. Nissim Gerondi also points out that the desire of the monarch to avoid any perceived abuse of power because of the danger such a development would pose to his authority is sufficient to ensure that the discretionary execution of murderers will not become a tool of royal terror.[124] Since there was no Jewish monarchy in the medieval period, this discussion is of a purely academic nature. The rabbis were not overtaxed by the spectre of royal tyranny on the part of a Jewish king, although they were aware of the problem and did attempt to suggest possible solutions.[125]

(c) The Practical Significance of Exempting the Killer of a *Terefah* from the Death Penalty in Tragic Choice Cases

The generally accepted position in *halakhah* with regard to the consequences of killing a *terefah* is that of Maimonides: the killer is morally culpable and subject to a Divine sanction, but is not subject to the jurisdiction of the human court. This exemption from human jurisdiction presumably counts for something. After all, the fact that there is no positive legal sanction on foeticide plays an important role in shaping the lenient approach of Jewish law towards therapeutic abortion.[126] Are there circumstances in which the exemption of the killer of a *terefah* from human punishment serves as a full or partial justification for bringing about the *terefah's* death? The answer to this question is that the legal exemption of the killer of a *terefah* from the death penalty does indeed play a role in tragic choice situations, such as where the sacrifice of one life is necessary for the saving of many lives, and also in some modern medical dilemmas.

A classical tragic choice case is that of a group of defenceless travellers who are surrounded by armed brigands and offered a grim choice: either they hand over one member of the group to the slaughter, or they will all die.[127] The unanimous decision in that case is that it is forbidden to pick an individual and hand him over.[128] However, a difference of opinion

---

[123] Deut. 17: 18–20; *Derashot Haran*, no. 11.   [124] *Derashot Haran*, no. 11.

[125] On some of the aspects of Jewish political theory raised here, see Y. Blidstein, 'On Political Structures—Four Medieval Comments', *Jewish Journal of Social Studies*, 22 (1980), 54; 'Ideal and Real in Classical Jewish Political Theory', *Jewish Political Studies Review*, 2 (1990), 54.

[126] See Ch. 1 s. 1.

[127] *Yerushalmi, Terumot*, 8:4. Also see *Tosefta, Terumot*, 7: 20; *Tosefta Kifshutah, Terumot*, 7, 148; D. Daube, *Collaboration with Tyranny in Rabbinic Law* (London, 1965); S. Shilo, 'Sacrificing One Life for the Sake of Saving Many Others' (Heb.), *Hevra Vehistoria* (Jerusalem, 1980), 57.

[128] According to A. Enker, the underlying principle in Jewish law is that one life may be given up in order to save many lives, i.e. the numbers do count. However, the historical background to the case is the persecution of the Jews by the Romans, and in these circumstances, it would be too demeaning to pick a victim to be killed by the oppressors in order

exists in relation to a situation in which the brigands request a specific individual. According to one view, this formulation of the request makes all the difference, and the named person may be handed over in order to save the whole group. This is based upon a biblical precedent,[129] and, presumably, also upon the moral intuition that it is more heinous to pick a victim and then proceed to hand him over to the slaughter, than to hand over a marked man. According to another view, the named person may only be given up if he is also guilty of a capital criminal offence.[130] Maimonides rules in accordance with the latter view,[131] and his position is adopted by the majority of halakhic authorities.[132] There is yet another opinion according to which the basic issue is whether the named individual has a chance to escape or not. If there is no such chance and the whole group, including the marked man, will die together, it is permitted to hand him over in order to save the rest of the company, even if he is not guilty of any capital offence.[133]

to save the skins of the rest of the group (*Hekhreah Vezorekh Bamishpat Haivri* (Tel-Aviv, 1977), 202–3). The debate as to the moral justification of sacrificing one person in order to save a whole group is also an open one in general moral philosophy. According to J. Harris, sacrificing one life in order to save two is morally correct, since failing to do so is, in effect, tantamount to killing two people (*Violence and Responsibility* (London, 1980), 18). J. Glover, on the other hand, disagrees, and points out the side effects of putting Harris's position into practice would be truly awful. One example Glover gives is the terror that would be induced in society by a policy such as the forcible removal of organs from one individual in order to save a number of lives. According to Glover, there are strong grounds for refusing to make the numbers issue into the dominant moral consideration in problems of this nature (*Causing Death and Saving Lives* (London, 1981)). Also see J. Taurek, 'Should the Numbers Count?', *Philosophy and Public Affairs*, 6 (1977), 293.

[129] See 2 Sam. 20, in which a named individual, Sheva ben Bikhri, was killed in order to save an entire city from death.

[130] This view is also based upon 2 Sam. 20. Sheva ben Bikhri was, in fact, a rebel against king David, and the siege had been laid by Joab, David's general. He was, therefore, guilty of a capital crime under Jewish law. See *Resp. Habah Hayeshanot*, no. 43, for a discussion of the nature of the capital offence in question, and its extension to offences against universal, rational morality.

[131] *Hilkhot Yesodei Hatorah*, 5: 5.

[132] *Bayit Hadash, Yoreh Deah*, 153; *Turei Zahav, Yoreh Deah*, 157: 7; cf. *Hagahot Hagra, Yoreh Deah*, 157: 7.

[133] This approach is implicit in the *Tosefta* cited in n. 127. It was applied in a rather dramatic form in a Holocaust *responsum* dealing with the culpability of a father who stuffed rag into the throat of his infant child in order to prevent him crying and thereby attracting the attention of the SS in the street above to the presence of the Jews hiding in an underground bunker. When the danger had passed and the rag was removed, it was discovered that the baby had suffocated to death. In his *responsum*, R. Simon Efrati ruled that the father was not culpable under Jewish law since the baby was a named individual, in the sense that he constituted an objective threat to the survival of the whole group, and had no way of avoiding the fate of the group should it be discovered by the Nazis. R. Efrati reconciles this explanation with Maimonides' ruling that the named individual must also be liable to the death penalty by distinguishing between judicial and objective death penalties, and reading that distinction into the texts of the Jerusalem Talmud (Terumot 8: 4) and Maimonides' ruling

One of the medieval commentators on the Talmud, R. Menahem Meiri, raises the issue of giving up a *terefah* in order to save the group: 'And it seems quite clear that in the travellers' case, if one of them was a *terefah* then he may be given up in order to save the lives of the rest, since the killer of a *terefah* is exempt from the death penalty.'[134] *Tarfut*, according to R. Meiri, also produces the 'marked man effect'. The life of the *terefah* is clearly of an inferior status to that of a viable individual, since there is no death penalty for his murder. The travellers' dilemma is one in which there is a morally arguable case for giving up one person to save a whole group. *Tarfut* is the extra factor, just like the naming of a particular individual, that tips the scale in favour of giving up the *terefah* in order to save the whole group. Hence, we have an example of how the exemption of the killer of a *terefah* from capital punishment, becomes an operative factor in a tragic choice case.

R. Meiri's position is further explicated by R. Joseph Babad in terms of the talmudic dictum upon which the principle of the inviolability of individual human lives is based, i.e. 'How do you know that your blood is redder? Perhaps the blood of the other person is redder?'[135] R. Babad argues that the blood of a *terefah* is 'less red' than that of a viable individual; consequently, he may be sacrificed in order to save the rest of the group. R. Babad explains the permission to give up a named individual along similar lines: the fact that he has committed a capital crime, and would have already been sentenced to death had he not fled and joined the travellers, means that his blood is 'less red', in the sense that he is less physically viable than a person who has not committed such a crime.[136]

Not all authorities are in agreement with R. Meiri's conclusion. R. Ezekiel Landau, for example, states quite categorically that 'the very idea that a *terefah* might be killed for the sake of preserving a viable life is unheard of'.[137] R. Landau's statement, however, must be read in its context. It was made in response to a suggestion that the mere fact that foeticide does not carry any legal penalty ought to mean that it is a permitted act under Jewish law. In the course of his refutation of this suggestion, R. Landau makes the above-mentioned statement regarding the killing of a *terefah* in order to establish the principle that absence of a positive sanction does not constitute a licence to kill. His point is that just as the exemption of the killer of a *terefah* from capital punishment does not allow any

---

(*Hilkhot Yesodei Hatorah*), 5: 5. On R. Efrati's reading, Maimonides implies that even if the named individual is innocent of any crime, but he will die with the rest of the group because he has no way of escaping their fate, he is considered to be under the sentence of death and may, therefore, be given up (*Resp. Migei Haharigah*, no. 1).

[134] *Bet Habehirah, Sanhedrin*, 74a, s.v. *venireh li pashut.*   [135] *Sanhedrin*, 74a.
[136] *Minhat Hinukh*, no. 296.   [137] *Resp. Noda Biyehuda*, 2, *Hoshen Mishpat*, no. 59.

terefah to be killed on sight, similarly, the absence of a definitive legal penalty for foeticide does not justify the destruction of the nearest available foetus. In this light, it is not too difficult to deflect the full force of R. Landau's criticism. First, the expression 'unheard of' is a rhetorical rather than legal expression, and R. Landau cites no source for this objection. Secondly, the context of his critique is the direct destruction of a foetus, and it is arguable that had the suggestion been made in terms of indirect foeticide for a valid moral reason, the answer may well have been different, and the point about the *terefah* made in far less forceful terms.[138]

The question of giving up a *terefah* to save a group, or even one viable person,[139] remains an open one, with no definitive ruling either way.[140] In practice, R. Meiri's view has been applied in more than one tragic choice case in recent times. One example from the Holocaust period concerns the throwing of the bodies of the victims of Nazi gas chambers into crematoria, even though they still exhibited some faint signs of life. In the course of a *responsum* on this issue, it was suggested that the clearly established *tarfut* of the victims, together with the threat of certain death hanging over those ordered to dispose of the corpses should they refuse to do so, may justify a halakhic decision that Jewish *kapos* who carried out this horrendous task were not culpable murderers under the *halakhah*.[141]

The modern period has witnessed the application of R. Meiri's approach to more than one medical dilemma. A good example is the surgical separation of Siamese twins which took place in Philadelphia in 1977. In that case, female Siamese twins with joined hearts were born to an orthodox Jewish couple living in Lakewood, New Jersey. One of the twins had a normal four-chamber heart, whereas her sister's heart consisted of two chambers only.[142] In effect, one heart was sustaining two babies, and without the separation and sacrifice of the weaker sibling, neither twin would survive for longer than nine months. The physician in charge of the case was Dr Everett Koop, who was later to become the Surgeon General of the United States. He recommended separation, and assembled a large team of experts for a highly complex, and in many ways uncertain, surgical procedure. The operation was due to be performed at the Children's Hospital in Philadelphia. The parents, however, would not consent to the separation without halakhic approval, and the medical team had to wait until

---

[138] R. Landau's argument is, in fact, dealt with by later authorities, some of whom criticize it whilst others accept it in a modified form, see *Resp. Beth Yizhak*, 2, *Yoreh Deah*, no. 162; *Resp. Yabia Omer*, 4, *Even Haezer*, no. 1.   [139] See *Minhat Hinukh*, no. 296.

[140] See A. Steinberg, *Encyclopaedia of Jewish Medical Ethics*, iii. 14–15.

[141] E. Ben-Zimra, 'Halakhic Decisions Relating to the Sanctity of Life and Martyrdom in the Holocaust Period' (Heb.), *Sinai*, 80 (1977), 151.

[142] For purposes of the decision it was assumed that the defective heart could be assigned to one twin and the defective one to the other and there was no question of one common organ shared by two individuals.

R. Moses Feinstein, the leading halakhic authority in North America at the time, issued a ruling. After several very lengthy consultations with the medical team, R. Feinstein gave his approval, ruling that the procedure was halakhically permitted. The major halakhic source upon which his ruling was based was, by all accounts, the above-mentioned case of the travellers faced with the choice of surrendering one of the group members or being killed. The weaker twin was the equivalent of the named individual in that case, and it was therefore permitted to sacrifice her life in order to save that of her sister. The operation was a success in the sense that the stronger twin did survive; unfortunately, she died some two months after the separation from hepatitis contracted from a blood transfusion.[143]

R. Feinstein did not actually pen a written *responsum* detailing his decision, but the halakhic precedents upon which his decision was based were widely reported at the time,[144] and his son-in-law, R. Moses Tendler, published his own reconstruction of his father-in-law's reasoning.[145] Other scholars have also attempted to reconstruct R. Feinstein's reasoning in that case.[146] In our view, it is based upon the application of the law of the *terefah* to the travellers' case along the lines described above. As already observed, most authorities accept Maimonides' ruling that in order to qualify for sacrifice as a named individual under the travellers' case precedent, it is necessary for that individual to be also guilty of a capital crime. Clearly, the weaker twin was not guilty of any capital offence, rendering the relevance of the travellers' case questionable. However, the fact that she had a heart with two chambers meant that under Jewish law, she was a *terefah*. Her condition definitely falls into the category of a fatal organic defect, since had she been born a singleton, she would have died at birth. If we apply R. Meiri's argument that a *terefah* may be sacrificed for the sake of a group, or, in accordance with R. Babad's gloss, for the sake of another potentially viable individual, then the weaker twin may be given up for the sake of saving the stronger, potentially viable one. The English phrase used by the academic commentators who wrote on the case at the time it took place, in order to express the halakhic basis for sacrificing the life of the weaker twin, was that she was 'designated for death'.[147] This phrase indicates that the essence of R. Feinstein's ruling lay in the fact that the weaker twin was physically incapable of surviving on her own: in other words, she was a *terefah*. Since both sisters would die unless the weaker one was disconnected

---

[143] See D. Drake, 'The Twins Decision: One Must Die So One Can Live', *Philadelphia Inquirer*, 6 October 1977.

[144] See ibid.; G. Annas, 'Siamese Twins: Killing One to Save the Other', *Hastings Centre Report*, 17 (1987), 27–8.   [145] See *Letorah Ulehora'ah: Sefer Zikkaron* (New York, 1979), 114.

[146] See J. D. Bleich, *Bioethical Dilemmas* (Hoboken NJ, 1998), 292.

[147] See the sources cited in nn. 143–4.

from her stronger sibling, the separation was justified on the basis of the law of the *terefah*.

The phrase 'designated for death' used in relation to the 1977 case was influential in a more recent decision of the English Court of Appeal in a case involving the separation of Siamese twins whose Catholic parents objected to separation on religious grounds. This case will be discussed at length in section 6, which deals with the defence of necessity in the common law.

Before leaving the 1977 case, it is worthwhile paying attention to the second argument attributed to R. Feinstein in reaching his decision on the separation. This argument involves a pilot ejecting from a burning plane and successfully opening his parachute. As he is sailing to the ground, a second pilot, whose parachute failed to open, passes him and grabs hold of his leg. The parachute is only capable of bringing one person safely to the ground, and if both of them maintain their grip, neither one will survive. According to R. Feinstein, the first pilot is permitted to dislodge the second one, and send him hurtling to certain death in order to save his own life. In halakhic terminology, the second pilot in that case is a pursuer (*rodef*), and under Jewish law, it is permitted to kill any person who is pursuing another person with intent to kill, provided that the threat to the pursued person is direct and immediate, and all other means of preventing the killing have been tried without success.[148]

There are, however, situations in which the law of the pursuer applies even though the pursuer does not actually intend to kill the person being pursued, but merely constitutes an objective threat to his life. The prime example of this type of objective pursuer is the killing of a foetus for the sake of saving the mother.[149] In Maimonides' opinion, the foetus threatening its mother's life comes within the ambit of the law of the pursuer, even though it has no intention whatsoever of doing her any harm, much less of killing her. The same goes for the second pilot and the weaker Siamese twin. They are both considered pursuers, even though they do not intend the death of the person being pursued.

R. Feinstein may have felt the need to turn to the pursuer principle as well as the travellers' case because the latter deals only with the giving up of a named individual to others who will do the actual killing, and not with the killing of the pursuer in a direct fashion. The separation of the Siamese twins involves a direct act of killing the twin 'designated for death'. The instant the surgeon's scalpel severs the connection between the weaker twin's heart and the aorta of the stronger one, the former must die. In order to strengthen the case for carrying out the surgery, therefore,

---

[148] See Maimonides, *Hilkhot Rozeah*, 1: 6, 9; Deut. 25: 12; *Sanhedrin*, 8: 7; 72b; Elon (ed.), *Principles of Jewish Law*, 474.   [149] See *Hiddushei R. Hayyim Halevi, Hilkhot Rozeah*, 1: 9.

R. Feinstein cites the objective pursuer precedent in addition to the case of the travellers.

Yet another modern medical illustration of the use of R. Meiri's approach in relation to the overriding of the life of a *terefah* for the sake of saving viable life is found in the halakhic literature dating from the early years of heart transplant surgery. In order for a heart transplant to be of any use, the heart must be transplanted while it is still beating; once the donor's heart has ceased to beat, the heart is useless for transplant purposes. The main halakhic problem here is that if the cessation of heartbeat constitutes the definition of death in Jewish law—and there are a number of authorities who support this position[150]—then the act of removing a living heart from a donor is murder. In order to deal with this problem, R. Judah Gershuni suggested that a cardiac transplant may be permitted in the case of a *terefah* donor. Since the killer of a *terefah* is exempt from the death penalty, R. Gershuni opined that in R. Meiri's view, it would be permitted to sacrifice the *terefah* donor in order to save the life of the recipient of his heart, in the same way that it is permitted to allow a *terefah* to be given up in order to save the life of the travellers. In both cases, there is a valid moral justification for using the fact of the exemption of the killer of a *terefah* from the death penalty in order to justify a course of action leading to his death.[151] In fact, as we will explain at length in Chapter 6, the Israeli Chief Rabbinate's decision on the definition of death in 1989 solved the problem by extending the definition of death to the irreversible dysfunction of the brain-stem. This stage precedes the cessation of heartbeat and, as a result, the donor is legally dead before his heart is removed. Although R. Gershuni's argument was never used in practice as the primary basis for permitting cardiac transplants, it finds some degree of expression in the Chief Rabbinate's provision that the cardiac donor should be an accident victim in addition to being brain-stem dead. The point about the accident victim is that such a person readily falls into the category of a *terefah*, since it may be assumed that as an accident victim, he is, by definition, suffering from a fatal organic defect. In this way, the law of the *terefah* provides a small but significant contribution to the halakhic permission for removing the still beating heart for the sake of saving another life.[152]

The final example of the use of the law of the *terefah* in a medical context is the ruling that it is permitted to give a non-*terefah* priority in relation to

---

[150] See Ch. 6 s. 1.

[151] *Kol Zofayikh*, 376. Also see M. Halperin, 'Heart Transplants in Jewish Law' (Heb.), *Sefer Assia*, 5 (1986), 68.

[152] See M. Halperin, 'The Legal Implications of the Chief Rabbinate's Decision Regarding Heart Transplants in Israel' (Heb.), *Assia*, 47–9 (1990), 112. The decision will be discussed at length in the following chapter.

scarce medical resources in a situation in which a choice must be made between saving his life and that of a *terefah*.[153]

What is the relevance, if any, of the law of the *terefah* for the issue of withdrawing life-support from a terminally ill patient when no other life is at stake? At first sight, the answer is none at all. In all the tragic choice cases and medical dilemmas cited above, the law of the human *terefah* is applied in order to strike a balance between competing claims to life. The conclusion in each case is that the non-*terefah* takes precedence over the *terefah*. However, in none of these cases is the law governing the killing of a *terefah* applied to a situation in which the sole result is the death of the *terefah*. In each and every case, it is for the sake of saving viable life that the law of the *terefah* swings into operation.

On the other hand, the fact that the *terefah* is suffering may tip the scales in favour of putting the exemption rule into practice and ruling leniently in terms of the prohibition on removing life-support prior to the establishment of death. There is some halakhic support in both Orthodox[154] and Conservative[155] writings for removing life-support from a *terefah* in cases of great suffering, and this position is strengthened—at least under the Orthodox view—if the life-support is removed in an indirect manner.[156] The use of the *terefah* category in this context is a very recent step, and although the issue is still a matter of debate, it holds out the prospect of new and fresh ways of thinking about one of the major dilemmas in modern bioethics and biomedical law.

6. THE EXEMPTION OF THE KILLER OF A *TEREFAH* FROM CAPITAL PUNISHMENT, THE PREROGATIVE OF MERCY, AND THE DEFENCE OF NECESSITY IN THE COMMON LAW

In the year 1412, a Spanish Jewish physician by the name of Joshua Lorki converted to Catholicism. He had contemplated such a step for some years, but it was the fiery sermons of the famous Dominican preacher, Vicente Ferrer, that finally convinced him to become a Catholic. He

---

[153] *Resp. Ziz Eliezer*, 17 nos. 10, 72.

[154] N. Goldberg, 'Terminating Artificial Respiration in the Case of a Fatally Ill Patient in Order to Save a Potentially Viable Individual' (Heb.), *Emek Halakhah Assia*, 1 (1986), 83. The somewhat controversial nature of this position is reflected by the fact that R. Goldberg's article is presented together with numerous critical notes by R. Levi Yizhak Halperin who is of the opinion that the law of the *terefah* has absolutely no relevance for the treatment of the terminally ill in Jewish law.

[155] E. Dorff, 'A Jewish Approach to End-Stage Medical Care', *Conservative Judaism*, 43 (1991), 32. See especially n. 66. See also D. Sinclair, 'The Terminal Patient in Jewish Law', *Tel-Aviv University Studies in Law*, 12 (1994), 300 n. 84, and the *Encyclopaedia of Jewish Medical Ethics*, iv. 408.   [156] See *Encyclopaedia of Jewish Medical Ethics*, iv. 408.

assumed the name of Geronimo de Santa Fé and became an implacable enemy of Judaism. Immediately after his conversion, he instigated a public disputation in Tortosa, in which the Jewish side was treated in a particularly humiliating manner. He also published a polemical pamphlet seeking to demonstrate that the Talmud was a morally offensive work. One of the doctrines cited in this pamphlet was the exemption of the killer of a *terefah* from the death penalty, which Lorki claimed was thoroughly immoral; he also pointed out that non-Jewish law recognized no such exception to criminal liability in the law of homicide.[157]

The Jewish response was not slow to arrive. It appeared in the form of a work entitled *Milkhemet Miztvah* by R. Solomon b. Simon Duran, whose father, R. Simon b. Zemah Duran, was one of the outstanding rabbinic authorities of the period. R. Solomon was head of the Talmudic Academy in Algiers, and eventually succeeded his father as rabbi of the whole community. In addition to attacking the lax morals of the Christian clergy, R. Duran also dealt with the specific points raised by Lorki. R. Duran observed that the legal exemption of the killer of a *terefah* is not a blanket permission to kill any *terefah* in sight, but rather, a means of making the law of homicide, and particularly the mandatory death sentence, more flexible in hard cases. The very same result, observed R. Duran, is achieved in non-Jewish law by means of royal clemency. Indeed, R. Duran went even further and suggested that the approach of Jewish law is preferable, since it does not give the impression that the course of justice is being perverted. Pardoning a convicted killer creates the impression—particularly in the minds of the victim's family—that a legally culpable individual has escaped without any penalty. In Jewish law, by contrast, exemption from the death penalty is an integral part of the law, and consequently, its application is not perceived as a departure from the idea of justice.[158]

The point here is not to decide which approach is superior, but merely to observe that both Jewish and non-Jewish law possess mechanisms for dealing with the tension between the need to protect the value of human life by executing every killer in society, and the need to temper the strict demands of law and justice in morally challenging situations. The dispute between Jewish law and non-Jewish law over this issue is not as to whether the tension exists or not; it is over the means to be adopted in order to overcome this tension.

---

[157] *De Judaeis Erroribus Ex Talmuth*, published in *Biblioethera Maxima Veterum Patrum*, 3 (Frankfurt, 1602). On Joshua Lorki, see *Encyclopaedia Judaica*, xi. 494–5.

[158] *Milkhemet Miztva*, 32b, *s.v. od heshiv*.

It is fascinating to note the use of the mechanism of the royal pardon in order to deal with this tension in the famous nineteenth-century case of *R. v. Dudley and Stephens.*[159] In this case, the captain and first mate of a ship that capsized at sea on the way from England to Australia killed and ate the cabin boy in order to survive. The deed was done after eighteen days in an open boat, during which the supplies of food and water had run out and all the survivors were in poor physical shape. The cabin boy was in worse physical shape than any of the other sailors. Four days after the cabin boy had been killed and eaten, the survivors of the shipwreck were rescued. The accused were indicted for murder on the basis of the testimony of another mariner who had turned Queen's evidence. They were found guilty of murder and sentenced to be 'hanged by the neck until dead', but they were promptly pardoned by Queen Victoria, who commuted their death sentences to six months' imprisonment.[160]

The court was not prepared to accept a defence of necessity,[161] even in the form of the well-established 'custom of the sea', according to which lots would be drawn in order to select a mariner who would be sacrificed in order to save the lives of the rest of the crew.[162] This has remained the mainstream position in the common law until very recently: despite attempts by eminent jurists to use the doctrine of necessity in the context of medical euthanasia, it is not available as a defence to murder in English courts.[163] This position was concisely summed up by Cardozo J., the

---

[159] (1884) 14 QBD 273.

[160] For a detailed account of the facts, the trial, and the aftermath, see B. Simpson, *Cannibalism and the Common Law* (Chicago, 1984).

[161] For a recent analysis of this doctrine in the context of the criminal law, see F. McAuley and J. McCutcheon, *Criminal Liability* (Dublin, 2000), ch. 17.

[162] See Simpson, *Cannibalism*, 249. The practice of drawing lots has a biblical precedent, see Jonah 1:7. This practice was, apparently, fully condoned by the Admiralty and the Board of Trade prior to the case, and it is noteworthy that Dudley and Stephens made no attempt to conceal their cannibalism. It would appear that the main reason for the case coming to court was to discourage a practice that did not sit well with Victorian moral sensibilities.

[163] See *AG v. Whelan* [1934] IR 518; L. Fuller, 'The Speluncean Explorers', *Harvard Law Review*, 62 (1948-9), 616; G. Williams, *The Sanctity of Life and the Criminal Law* (London, 1956), 286, 290; *Textbook of Criminal Law* (London, 1978), 559; *R v. Howe* [1987] 1 All ER 771; J. Smith and D. Hogan, *Criminal Law* (London, 1999), 249-50; M. Otlowski, *Voluntary Euthanasia and the Common Law* (Oxford, 1997), 173-4. See, however, *R v. Adams* [1957], Cr. LR 365, in which Devlin J. used the necessity principle in order to justify the administration of life-shortening analgesics to a terminally ill patient. It has also been used to justify the classical decision to permit therapeutic abortion in English law (*R v. Bourne* [1938] 3 All ER 615; Smith and Hogan, *Criminal Law*, 245 n. 17). It is important to distinguish necessity from the emerging defence of duress of circumstances. This defence relates to actions done under threat, e.g. driving on the pavement in order to escape a threatening gang of youths, or a husband who drove his stepson, who had overslept, to work even though he was disqualified from driving. He did so because his wife feared that the boy would lose his job if he were late, and threatened to commit suicide if he would not drive the lad to his place of employment, (Smith and Hogan, ibid. 242). This defence always involves a threat from other people,

famous American judge who wrote that there is no 'principle of human jettison' in the common law.[164]

The court in the shipwrecked mariners case was not prepared to make any concession to the necessity argument on the basis of the fact that the boy's physical condition was much worse than that of the grown men on board, and that he was the closest one to death.[165] Now it is arguable that under Jewish law, the cabin boy was a *terefah*. However, in this case, there would appear to be little justification for using the law of the *terefah* to justify his death. This is because there was absolutely no certainty that killing him would save the lives of the remaining crew members. The fact that the mariners' victim was a *terefah* is only relevant to their punishment. The killing of a *terefah* carries a Divine not a human sanction.

The refusal of the common law to recognize necessity as a defence to a murder charge, while relying on the royal prerogative of mercy or its modern equivalents to remove the moral sting from this refusal, has been characterized as lacking in intellectual force: 'When, however, all is said and done, probably the most persistent English attitude to the problem raised by the necessity plea—intellectually unsatisfying though it may be—is that hard cases are best dealt with by the prerogative of mercy.'[166] The contemporary equivalent of the prerogative of mercy in the area of euthanasia include policy decisions not to prosecute physicians who carry out acts of mercy-killing; unconvincing findings by juries that such physicians did not intend the deaths of the deceased; the return by the jury of verdicts of manslaughter or other lesser offences, and extremely light sentences handed out by judges to those doctors actually found guilty of murder. These equivalents, which open up a wide gap between the law in theory and its practical application, clearly fall into the category of the 'intellectually unsatisfying', especially in the context of the modern euthanasia debate. Indeed, it is the dissatisfaction with the existence of this gap that, *inter alia*, underlies much of the contemporary criticism of the application of the criminal law to cases of medical euthanasia.[167]

The first step towards changing this unsatisfactory state of affairs, and recognizing the relevance of the doctrine of necessity for biomedical law was taken in the recent decision of the English Court of Appeals to permit the separation of Siamese twins with conjoined hearts.[168] The facts of the

whereas the necessity doctrine under consideration here applies in situations where there is no immediate human threat. It is objective circumstances, in the strictly objective sense of the word, that constitute the basis of this defence.

[164] *Law and Literature and Other Essays and Addresses* (Colorado, 1931), 113.

[165] See Simpson, *Cannibalism*, 60–2.

[166] P. Glazebrook, 'The Necessity Plea in English Criminal Law', *Cambridge Law Journal* (1972), 118–19.   [167] See Otlowski, *Voluntary Euthanasia*, 185–6.

[168] *Re A (Children)* (2001) 2 WLR 480.

case are as follows: Mary and Jodie were born connected to each other in the lower abdominal region, in St. Mary's Hospital, Manchester, on 8 August 2001. Each child possessed a complete set of limbs and organs. Mary's heart, however, was much weaker than that of Jodie, and the medical view was that Mary was being kept alive by Jodie's heart. Had Mary been born a singleton, she would not have survived. Mary's lungs were also much weaker than Jodie's, and there was some evidence to the effect that her brain was less developed than that of her sister. Without surgical intervention to separate the two children, both would die within a period of about six months. The physicians did not wish to wait for a complication to occur before doing surgery, since that would make the chances of success much smaller. As it is, the separation of this type of Siamese twins is a long and complex procedure, entailing a considerable amount of follow-up surgery and other treatments. The considered medical opinion, therefore, was to perform the operation as soon as possible.

Separating Mary and Jodie meant that Mary would die as a direct result of the operation. Her own heart was far too weak to maintain a proper blood supply, and within seconds of severing the connection between her circulatory system and Jodie's aorta, Mary would be dead. In effect, the doctors would be killing Mary in order to allow Jodie a chance to survive. This was not acceptable in terms of the religious convictions of the twins' parents, both practicing Catholics from a small island near Malta, who refused to consent to the separation on the grounds that it conflicted with their religious beliefs. It was because of their opposition to the doctors' decision to separate that the case came to court.[169]

The first court to hear the case was the Family Division of the High Court, which overruled the wishes of the parents and permitted the surgery. The court began by reiterating the well-established principle in both family and medical law, that the proper basis for resolving conflicts between parents and doctors over the treatment of a child is that of the child's best interests.[170] In this case, the court found that it was in the best interests of Jodie to live and, somewhat surprisingly, that it was in the best interests of Mary to die. Amongst the arguments used in order to downgrade Mary's interest in life was that her retarded development would cause her to suffer as a result of being attached to her normal sister. Jodie would pull her around in order to expand her contact with the world. Mary's world would always be much narrower and she would become a mere appendage of Jodie, lacking any capacity for the realization of her

---

[169] See Ch. 4 n. 106 and the body of the text there for a discussion of the attitudes of English courts to disputes between physicians and parents regarding the medical treatment of their children.
[170] See Children Act, 1989, Chapter 1, section 1; *Re B (A minor)* (1981) 1 WLR, 1424.

own, much more passive, will. This would result in distress and frustration on Mary's part and, as result, it was in her best interests to die.

In terms of the issue of directly causing the death of one innocent twin in order to save the life of the other, the Judge made an analogy with a person being kept alive through artificial nutrition. The withdrawal of artificial nutrition from a patient in a persistent vegetative state was permitted in English law,[171] provided that this course was in his best interests.[172] Since it was not in Mary's best interests to remain connected to Jodie, the separation was permitted.

The parents appealed to the Court of Appeal, which upheld the decision of the Family Division, although on entirely different grounds. Indeed, the Court specifically rejected the grounds offered by the Family Division for its decision. In relation to the application of the criterion of the child's best interests, the Court of Appeal held that it was not up to a court of law to decide that a particular life was not worth living and that death was in that person's best interests. The only question that may legitimately be answered by a court in this type of case is whether or not the treatment being proposed is for the benefit of the patient.[173] Killing Mary was certainly not of any benefit to her. On the other hand, it was in Jodie's best interests to be separated, since that was the only way in which she would be able to achieve the prospect of long-term survival. The only way of resolving this clash of interests between the two children was to 'choose the lesser of the two evils and so find the least detrimental alternative'.[174] In this case, the lesser of the two evils was to sacrifice Mary for the sake of Jodie, since she alone was capable of long-term survival, and without the separation, both twins would die. It is noteworthy that the Court used the phrase 'designated for death' in order to characterize Mary, and attributed it to 'the words of the rabbinical scholars involved in the 1977 case in Philadelphia'.

In terms of the criminal issue of murder, the Court of Appeal found that the Judge in the Family Division was wrong in comparing the situation to that of a patient attached to an artificial respirator. There is no analogy. Artificial respiration is a medical procedure, governed by medical law according to which it may be removed once it has been established that the procedure is no longer in the patient's best interests. In the present

---

[171] This term is used to denote someone who has lost all brain function with the exception of the brain stem, which controls the so-called vegetative functions, i.e. breathing, regulation of heartbeat, the sleep cycle, digestion, and the reactions to light.

[172] *Airedale NHS* v. *Bland* (1993) 1 All ER 821.

[173] 'The question is always whether the treatment would be worthwhile, not whether the patient's life would be worthwhile. Were one to engage in judgments of the latter sort, and to conclude that certain lives were not worth living, one would forfeit any principled basis for objecting to intentional killing' (J. Keown, 'Restoring Moral and Intellectual Shape to the Law After Bland', 113 *Law Quarterly Review* (1997), 485.

[174] *Re A (Children)* (2001) 2 WLR 480, 525.

case, however, it was nature that joined Mary and Jodie and made their lives interdependent. The issue is not that of medical law alone but impinges upon regular criminal law since, in effect, Mary is being killed in order to save Jodie's life.

In order to justify the Court of Appeal's ruling that the surgical separation of the twins did not impinge upon the criminal law and involve the surgeons in an act of murder, Brookes L.J. turned to the doctrine of necessity as a defence under the criminal law. In his view, the fact that Mary alone was 'designated to die' as a result of her physical condition meant that her death was justified by necessity. The separation of Jodie and Mary did not, therefore, constitute an act of murder. Brookes L.J. pointed out that the position in the common law had not always been the one adopted in R v. *Dudley and Stephens* and the later case of R v. *Howe*.[175] The use of the necessity defence to justify the killing of one innocent person in order to save the life of another innocent individual is found in the older works on the common law of England, and it is to be found in Francis Bacon's *Elements of the Common Laws of England*.[176] It was also recommended by various Law Commissions as a defence in special circumstances, e.g. where many lives could be saved by killing one individual, or in a medical situation of the type under discussion in the Siamese twins case.[177] Brookes L.J. also referred to academic writers and in particular, to the discussion of a case in which a ferry capsized in the North Sea and a group of survivors was waiting in the water to climb a ladder to safety. A young man froze halfway up the ladder, probably as a result of a combination of cold and fear, and no one was able to continue climbing to safety. Realizing that they could not last much longer in the icy waters, one of the survivors, an ex-soldier, pushed the unfortunate youth off the ladder and to certain death. As a result of his action, the rest of the group survived. In the opinion of the academic writers, the ex-soldier's action did not constitute murder under the common law, since it was justifiable in terms of the defence of necessity.[178] Following these writers, Brookes L.J. distinguished the case of the Siamese twins from R v. *Dudley and Stephens*. In the latter case, Lord Justice Coleridge had based his opposition to the necessity defence on two main arguments. The first was that there was no objective reason necessitating the choosing of the cabin boy rather than another sailor. The second was the threat to the principle of the value of

---

[175] [1987] 1 All ER 771.

[176] Originally published in 1630, this work is included in Montague (ed.), *Works* (London, 1831), xiii. 160.

[177] See *A Criminal Code for England and Wales* (1989), Law Commission no. 177, 1, 4(4), 45c; *Offences Against the Person and General Principles* (1993), Law Commission, no. 218, 35: 6.

[178] See J. Smith, *Justification and Excuse in the Criminal Law* (London, 1989), 77–8; A. Ashworth, *Principles of Criminal Law* (Oxford, 1999), 153–4.

human life posed by a lenient decision.[179] Neither of these arguments applied in the present case. Since Mary was 'designated for death' because of her physical state, there was a very clear reason for sacrificing her in order to save her sister. Her death was, therefore, an objectively justifiable necessity. As far as the issue of upholding the value of human life was concerned, Brookes J. relied upon the highly unusual nature of the case in order to deflect any charge that his decision would have an adverse effect upon social morality.

Ward L.J. chose a different line of argument in order to justify the separation. In his view, not intervening in order to save Jodie's life may be just as much a matter of murder as cutting the aorta that provided Mary's life-blood. Murder may, after all, be effected by omission as well as commission. This approach led him to the ineluctable conclusion that if, in a hypothetical case, parents at the gates of a concentration camp were offered the possibility of saving one of their two children, they would be guilty of murder if they refused to choose, and entered the gates with both their offspring. The Judge immediately pointed out that the parents would not actually be prosecuted, but in terms of strict legal logic, they would still be murderers. This is rather harsh, and Ward L.J.'s reference to the non-prosecution of such parents indicates that he himself is aware of the harshness of his position. In this respect, Lord Justice Brooke's necessity-based approach is more appealing.

The Siamese twins case marks an important change in the approach of the common law to the doctrine of necessity. It rejects the older Victorian view that morally challenging cases affecting human life are best dealt with indirectly at the level of royal pardon, executive clemency, or any of the other procedural devices available for that purpose. In its path-breaking decision, the Court of Appeal has, to a certain extent, restored the intellectual force that was lacking in the older attitude to the necessity doctrine, with the result that from now on, the moral tension generated by these tragic choice cases in the medical area may be tackled in open court rather than at the level of prosecution, jury trial, or sentencing policies. This is in line with R. Solomon Duran who emphasizes the need to deal with the moral tension in the law of the *terefah* in open court rather than by an act of executive clemency.[180] The Court of Appeal also used the phrase 'designated for death' in order to explain its decision to sacrifice Mary for the sake of Jodie. This phrase comes from the report of R. Feinstein's decision in the 1977 Philadelphia case, and as explained above, indicates the significant role played by the law of the *terefah* in his

---

[179] In the words of the Home Secretary, Sir William Harcourt, 'We cannot give *carte blanche* to every ship's captain, when he runs low on provisions, to eat his cabin boy.'
[180] *Milkhemet Miztva*, 32b, *s.v. od heshiv.*

decision. Both the phrase itself, and the concept that medically proven non-viability constitutes a valid basis for preferring one innocent life to another, helped the Lord Justices in crafting their decision in this morally challenging case. In this respect, Jewish law made an important contribution to the restoration of a doctrine last encountered in the writings of Bacon to the bosom of the common law.

7. *GOSES, TEREFAH*, AND THE HUMANIZING OF THE DYING PROCESS IN THE *HALAKHAH*

The starting point of the *goses* category in the *halakhah* is that 'the *goses* is a living person in all respects', and the killer of a *goses* is liable to the death penalty.[181] As the law unfolds, this starting point becomes less compelling, and the combination of the permission to remove impediments to death, together with the principle of the prevention of suffering, militates towards allowing the *goses* to die. Starting points are important since they affect the course of the entire argument; in the present context, the notion that the '*goses* is a living person in all respects' clearly acts as a constraint upon morally unsound arguments in favour of terminating life-support. The likelihood is, therefore, that a decision in favour of such a step will be carefully thought out and closely argued before it is reached. The tendency will be to err on the side of life in making decisions with regard to its termination. Nevertheless, there will be cases in which the better course, both legally and morally, is not to impede death. In relation to such cases there is a sufficiently wide range of concepts and principles available for the amelioration of the primary life-preserving thrust of the *goses* category and its replacement with a more individualized form of treatment. The case-law over the centuries amply demonstrates the humanizing trend of the *halakhah* in this area. The combination of strict starting points and a complex grid for justified exceptions is the halakhic model for this highly morally sensitive area of the law.[182]

At this stage, it is necessary to point out that the law of the *goses* is aimed primarily at caregivers, ranging from the family to the physicians. Indeed, the bulk of Jewish law is aimed at private citizens rather than at courts of law. The thrust of Jewish law is educational almost as much as it is legal; accordingly, the law of the *goses* deals mainly with directives for

---

[181] *Semahot*, 1: 1; *Encyclopaedia Talmudit*, v. 393; *Sanhedrin*, 78a; Maimonides, *Hilkhot Rozeah*, 2: 7.

[182] In this sense, the *halakhah* is a casuistic system. Casuistry, in its best rather than its abused form, has recently been suggested as a model for an intellectually rigorous approach to modern bioethical issues, see A. Jonsen and S. Toulmin, *The Abuse of Casuistry* (University of California, 1988).

treatment rather than with sanctions for misdeeds. The emphasis on how to deal with the dying rather than on the penalties involved in precipitating their death also serves as a bulwark against the erosion of the principle of the primacy of human life. The alienation of much of modern Western society from the realities of death and dying,[183] and the adoption of an almost exclusively criminal law-based approach to this area, do not necessarily bode well for the humane treatment of the terminally ill. A law that brings people into contact with the dying, in practical as well as theoretical terms, is likely to contribute more to respect for human life than one that casts the entire issue in terms of criminal liability. It is important also to bear this aspect of the humanization of the dying process in mind when considering the law of the *goses*.

At the same time, the criminal law side of dealing with the terminally ill is not ignored by the *halakhah*. The *terefah* category represents the view that in morally justifiable circumstances of the type described above, it may be permitted to bring about the death of a *terefah*. The individuals concerned are not treated as regular murderers, but are subject to Divine or extra-legal jurisdiction. In practice, it would be necessary to set up special bodies to deal with such cases, many of which arise in our hospitals on a daily basis. These bodies would apply moral as well as legal criteria in their decisions. This is not an idea that is easily applicable in a society subscribing to a wide range of different moral values, but even in such a society, it is not totally without merit. The basis for such an institution is undoubtedly the hospital ethics committee, which in many countries has become a feature of modern medical reality. The forum for applying the moral dimension inherent in the law of the *terefah* would, however, need to be closer to a court than the current hospital ethics committee; it would be midway between a court of law and a hospital ethics committee.

8. THE TREATMENT OF THE TERMINALLY ILL IN MODERN *HALAKHAH*

Limited autonomy, the law of the *goses*, the principle of preventing suffering, and the *terefah* category are the four major elements in relation to the treatment of the terminally ill that emerge from this and the previous chapter. In this section, the role of each of these elements in relation to the treatment of the terminally ill will be summarized briefly.

R. Feinstein extends the doctrine of limited autonomy to a competent adult who refuses basic life-support such as artificial nutrition, even after

---

[183] See E. Kubler-Ross, *On Death and Dying* (New York, 1969).

every effort has been made to get him to change his mind.[184] Historically, autonomy is the most recent arrival on the halakhic scene, but it is definitely on the map.[185] This is probably a result of the inevitable influence of general ideas upon halakhic thinking. Patient autonomy is, after all, a major contribution to modern bioethics, and constitutes a sea change in bioethical thinking in the decades since the Second World War. Searching for ways to promote autonomous decisions in relation to both competent and incompetent terminal patients is the face of the future in both general and Jewish law. Amongst the major methods for cultivating such autonomy are documents designed with a view to making personal wishes about the end of life into legally valid instruments. This is a task that will presumably preoccupy halakhists in the twenty-first century.

The basic distinction in modern *halakhah* relating to the *goses* is between therapy, which may be discontinued, and the maintenance of basic functions, i.e. respiration, feeding, and the supply of liquids, which must not be discontinued until the establishment of death. This distinction was explained at length in section 2. In relation to the maintenance of basic functions, it is worthwhile pointing out a further distinction between respiration on the one hand and food and liquids on the other. As will be explained in the next chapter, the ability to breathe independently is the classical halakhic definition of life. It is, therefore, permissible to attempt to wean a patient from an oxygen-rich respirator, since the inability to breathe normal air is, in fact, an indication that the patient is dead.[186] Nutrition and hydration, on the other hand, have no role to play other than the maintenance of basic life, and must, presumably, be maintained until death. There are two new developments regarding nutrition and hydration. The first is the possibility that they be classified as therapy rather than maintenance because of their highly medical nature. The second is the possible application of the prevention of suffering principle to a PVS patient in such a way that it overrides the prohibition on precipitating his death. Both of these developments figure in the recent Israeli draft law on the terminally ill patient outlined in the Appendix. This law is based mainly upon halakhic principles.

The mandate to prevent suffering in the dying process underlies the permission both to remove an impediment to death and to give painkillers to a *goses*, even though they will precipitate his death over a period of time. R. Feinstein's emphasis on trauma-prevention in the context of the dying patient is also an application of the principle of preventing suffering in this area of the *halakhah*. One of the problematic aspects of this principle is in its application to a PVS patient. On the one hand,

---

[184] *Resp. Iggrot Moshe, Hoshen Mishpat*, 2 no. 73.   [185] See Ch. 4 s. 3.
[186] See Ch. 6 s. 1.

easing suffering is a justification for removing basic life-support from such a patient. On the other hand, it is difficult to justify applying the principle to a comatose individual who apparently feels no pain. This point was made by Lord Mustill in the English case of *Bland*, in his observation that the difficult thing about applying the best interests of the patient criterion to a PVS patient is the fact that he seems to have no interests at all.[187] The one suggestion made with regard to this issue was that the principle of suffering-prevention might be extended to the family of the individual concerned. This is a risky approach, however, and may create more problems than it solves.

The relevance of the *terefah* category for the terminally ill is in the area of criminal liability. Killing a *terefah* does not carry the death penalty in Jewish law, and the exemption from the death penalty has been applied to various medical dilemmas in which the life of a viable person is saved at the cost of the life of the *terefah*. The possibility of applying this exemption to the termination of a *terefah*'s life-support is problematic, because there is no viable life to be saved. Be that as it may, the significance of the *terefah* law in this area is in relation to the establishment of a forum other than a regular criminal court for dealing with cases involving the mercy-killing of a human *terefah*.

---

[187] Note the comment of Lord Mustill in the English case of *Airedale NHS Trust* v. *Bland* to the effect that what makes it so difficult to decide on the best interests of a PVS patient is the fact that he or she does not, in fact, have any interests at all!

6

Science, Halakhah, and Public Health Policy: The Definition of Death, Heart Transplants, Organ Donation, and the Allocation of Scarce Medical Resources

1. THE DEFINITION OF DEATH

The principle source for the halakhic definition of death is the talmudic discussion of the mounting of a rescue mission on the Sabbath day on behalf of people who may be trapped under the rubble of a fallen building. The possibility that all those trapped in the debris are already dead gives rise to a question with regard to the permissibility of the mission. As already observed, the Sabbath is always overridden by the saving of human life.[1] In the case of the fallen building, however, it is not clear that life will be saved, as the accident victims may already be dead. If that is so, the mission ought not to be undertaken, since removing debris—unless for the sake of saving life—is forbidden on the Sabbath. The Talmud, nevertheless, rules in favour of the rescue, on the grounds that even a chance of saving life is sufficient to justify breaking the Sabbath laws.[2]

The question of defining death becomes relevant once the bodies are unearthed, because of the prohibition on handling a corpse on the Sabbath. Once it is established that the rescue party is dealing with a corpse, it must leave it and move on to other trapped bodies or to the next pile of rubble. The Talmud records two views with regard to the definition of death in this context.[3] According to the first, absence of breath in the nostrils is the definitive test. According to the other, it is the absence of activity in the heart[4] that establishes the victim's demise. The Talmud

---

[1] See Ch. 4 nn. 61–3.   [2] *Yoma*, 8: 7.   [3] *Yoma*, 85a.

[4] Some manuscript texts substitute 'navel' for 'heart'. This is also the reading found in the Jerusalem Talmud (*Yoma*, 8: 5) and in several medieval commentaries on the Talmud. Rashi, however, maintains the 'heart' version (*Yoma*, 85a, *s.v. hakhi garsinan*) as does R. Menahem Meiri, *Yoma*, 85a. The 'heart' version is the one relied upon in all later halakhic works (*Resp. Haham Zvi*, no. 77; *Resp. Imrei Yosher*, 2 no. 2; *Resp. Levush Mordekhai*, no. 124; *Resp. Divrei Hayyim*, 2 no. 64; *Resp. Shoel Umeshiv*, pt. 2, 1 no. 100). It is noteworthy that in the light of the fact that the navel is the site of the diaphragm, the 'navel' version could be

proceeds to find biblical support for the first view in the verse, 'in whose nostrils was the breath of life',[5] and on this basis, the major halakhic codes adopt the breath test, ruling that death is established by the absence of breath in the nostrils, not by the absence of cardiac activity.[6]

It is noteworthy that from his commentary both here and elsewhere in the Talmud,[7] it may be inferred that according to Rashi, the heart receives air directly from the nostrils and sends it via the arteries to the brain. In the Sabbath rescue mission case, Rashi may be understood as saying that the heart is the source of breathing, and the nostril test is simply the most effective way of determining that the heart is still maintaining its vital functions. In effect, this approach requires cessation of both respiration and heartbeat before the person may be declared dead. Rashi's understanding of the role of the heart is that of Galen, the classical Roman physician, and it was the accepted theory during Medieval and Renaissance times.[8] There is no basis for it in the talmudic text, however, and Rashi's apparent incorporation of Galen's theory into his commentary would appear to reflect a desire to bring the talmudic definition of death into line with the regnant scientific theory of the Middle Ages. Galen's idea that the heart plays a role in breathing was eventually discredited by William Harvey in the early seventeenth century, and it is now accepted that the cardiac and the respiratory systems are separate.

The discrediting of the Galenic theory notwithstanding, some halakhists continued to use this inference from Rashi as a basis for defining death in terms of the heart rather than the breath.[9] The question that then arises is the validity of legal inferences based upon obsolete science.[10] Do such developments carry halakhic weight, and to what extent can they be used in order to deviate from long-standing halakhic decisions? These and related questions will be discussed in relation to heart transplants at the end of section 2.

---

understood as simply another way of testing for absence of breath, with the result that respiration would be the sole test for death in the Talmud. On this reading, there is simply no talmudic reference to any cardiac criterion for defining death. Such a conclusion would be in line with the more liberal respiration-based approach to the definition of death in the modern debate over heart transplants (see s. 2).

[5] Gen. 7: 22. It is noteworthy that the Hebrew word for breath, *neshimah*, has the same root as the word for soul, *neshamah*.

[6] Maimonides, *Hilkhot Shabbat*, 2: 19; *Tur, Orah Hayyim*, no. 329; *Shulhan Arukh, Orah Hayyim*, 329: 4.

[7] *Yoma*, 85a, *s.v. hakhi garsinan*. See also *Shabbat*, 134a, *s.v. delo menashti*.

[8] See C. Singer, *A Short History of Medicine* (Oxford, 1928), 56–8.

[9] See *Resp. Hakham Zevi*, no. 77; *Resp. Hatam Sofer, Yoreh Deah*, no. 338.

[10] In this context, it is noteworthy that Maimonides indicates in no uncertain terms that the sages were children of their times as far as scientific matters are concerned, and there is no doctrine of rabbinic infallibility in this area (*Guide for the Perplexed*, bk. 2: 4).

Another important talmudic source relating to the definition of death is a passage dealing with the ritual consequences of decapitation. Under Jewish law, death results in ritual impurity and according to the Mishnah, decapitated animals are ritually impure, even though their bodies are still moving in a spasmodic manner, presumably indicating some cardiac activity.[11] One way of understanding this mishnah is that decapitated animals are dead for purposes of ritual law because their heads have been severed from their bodies. In the absence of actual decapitation, the animal is not considered dead for purposes of ritual impurity.[12] Another way of understanding the mishnah is to focus on the function of the head as the seat of the brain, and to understand decapitation as the destruction of all brain function, including that of breathing. On this understanding of the mishnah, the irreversible cessation of all brain function, including the brain stem which controls breathing, is conceptually synonymous to decapitation, and a totally brain-dead animal is halakhically dead even though its head is still physically attached to its body.[13]

The decapitation mishnah expands the definition of death in two ways. First, it indicates that death may be established in Jewish law even if the heart continues to beat, since heartbeat always continues for a brief interval following physical decapitation. The same applies in relation to irreversible brain-stem death: the heart continues beating for a short period after the brain stem has become irreversibly dysfunctional.[14] Second, this mishnah demonstrates that lack of movement is not a necessary element in the definition of death, since decapitated creatures often move in a violent and jerky fashion.[15]

The *halakhah* on defining death was consolidated in the early nineteenth century by R. Moses Sofer, who concludes that cessation of breath, rather than cardiac activity, is the definitive definition of death in Jewish law. R. Sofer argues that since the breath test is found in the account of the creation of humankind at the beginning of the book of Genesis,[16] it predates the rest of Jewish law both historically and in terms of its scope, i.e. it is binding upon both Noahides and Israelites.[17] This means that it cannot be confined to a particular area of Jewish law, which is a possibility in relation to the other tests discussed in the Talmud,[18] all of which may be

---

[11] *Ohaloth*, 1: 6.
[12] J. D. Bleich, 'Of Cerebral, Respiratory and Cardiac Death', *Tradition*, 24 (1989), 46–7.
[13] A. Steinberg, 'Establishing the Time of Death' (Heb.), *Assia*, 53–4 (1994), 13 n. 1.
[14] See A. Steinberg, *Encyclopaedia of Jewish Medical Ethics* (Heb.) (Jerusalem, 1988–98), vi. 36.
[15] Maimonides, *Commentary to the Mishnah, Ohaloth*, 1: 6.   [16] Gen. 7: 22.
[17] See the discussion of Noahide laws and the relationship between that system and Jewish law in Ch. 1 s. 4.
[18] The definition of death is also discussed in other talmudic contexts, notably family law and the treatment of the *goses*, see *Encyclopaedia of Jewish Medical Ethics*, vi. 29.

explained as being applicable only to the specific area of the *halakhah* in which they are cited. According to R. Sofer, the biblical origin of the breath test, together with its wide scope, ensures its normative primacy over all other tests mentioned in the halakhic tradition.[19]

R. Sofer proceeds to add certain safeguards to the breath test, which may be explained in light of the historical background to his *responsum*. As early as the eighteenth century people were aware that premature burials were not an infrequent occurrence, since most people died at home, and the average family member was not an expert in determining death. Moreover, even the most highly qualified physicians of that period were not always able to establish death beyond all doubt. In those days individuals suffering from asphyxia, concussion, hysteria, apoplexy, and narcotic overdose were all in danger of undergoing premature burial. As awareness of premature burial became widespread, several European states and principalities took measures to try and prevent it. The most widespread of these measures was the requirement that a period of two to three days elapse between death and burial. 'Waiting mortuaries' were set up all over Europe, specifically for the purpose of accommodating the bodies during this period.[20] Now the *halakhah*, with only very limited exceptions, requires burial to take place on the day of death.[21] Any attempt by a secular authority to impose a waiting period upon the Jews was likely to encounter serious opposition. In May 1772 Duke Frederick of Mecklenburg ordered all citizens living in his Duchy to wait three days between the establishment of death and burial. The local Jewish community turned to Moses Mendelssohn, the famous Enlightenment philosopher and leader of German Jewry, with a request that he use his influence in order to persuade the Duke to exempt them from the decree. Mendelssohn, who was a progressive modernist, initially attempted to persuade the community to accept the edict on halakhic grounds, including the argument that weighty prohibitions on Sabbath labour are suspended in order to save life, even in cases in which the life-saving element is of a doubtful nature.[22] Mendelssohn's view was opposed by the rabbis of the period, particularly R. Jacob Emden, who refuted most of his arguments on halakhic grounds. It is interesting to note that the rabbinical response to Mendelssohn reflects policy considerations as well as purely legal ones. It is evident that the rabbis' approach to the question of delayed burial was also informed by their fear that religious tradition

---

[19] *Resp. Hatam Sofer, Yoreh Deah*, no. 338. From R. Sofer's argument it is evident that there are instances in which the definition of death will change in accordance with the halakhic context and the circumstances of the case.

[20] See K. Iserson, *Death to Dust* (Tuscon, 1994), 28–38.

[21] Deut. 21: 23; *Sanhedrin*, 46a; *Encyclopaedia Talmudit*, ix. 434–44.

[22] *Yoma*, 8: 7.

in general would be weakened if acceptance of secular legislation in matters affecting religious observance became an accepted norm in the Jewish community. The debate between Mendelssohn and the rabbis remained an internal one and, in the end, the letter he wrote to the Duke pressed the latter to exempt the Jews from the three-day waiting period on the grounds, *inter alia*, that the Jewish dead were handled solely by experienced burial society members, who were well trained in recognizing the signs of death, and could be relied upon to avoid live burials. The Duke did indeed, accede to the request, and the Jews were allowed to maintain their traditional burial practices.[23]

In the course of a very short period of time, this issue became a touchstone for the tension within the Jewish community between traditionalists and modernists, and remained so for a long period of time. It is against this background that R. Sofer wrote his landmark *responsum*. As already mentioned, R. Sofer emphasizes that the core element in any halakhic definition of death is the cessation of breathing. However, as a staunch defender of the tradition, he was presumably also aware of the need to convince the observant community that its traditional definition was above all suspicion with regard to premature burial. In order to build a sufficiently convincing case, R. Sofer surmised that there must have been traditional tests of a practical nature for the establishment of death above and beyond the general requirement of the cessation of breathing. These tests would have been communicated orally by one generation to the next, and would have been carried out by the burial society members of the past. At some stage, however, they were forgotten.[24] R. Sofer recommends that the loss of these traditional tests be compensated for by adding two contemporary criteria, i.e. lack of pulse and the total absence of any movement, to the mainstream halakhic criterion of lack of breath. This step would satisfy the demands of both tradition and modern medical science. R. Sofer acknowledges that even this threefold test—breath, pulse, and movement—might not catch every single case of mistaken death, but the chance of someone satisfying all three elements and still being alive was so slim as to be no longer significant.

---

[23] See *Bikkurei Haitim* (1822–23), 209; M. Samet, 'Delaying Burial' (Heb.), *Assufot*, 3 (1989), 417–23.

[24] The existence of an oral tradition regarding tests for death is also mentioned by R. Mose Isserles some two centuries earlier. According to R. Isserles, this tradition has been lost and 'we are no longer sufficiently expert in order to be able to determine accurately the moment at which death occurs' (*Orah Hayyim*, 330: 8). The context of R. Isserles' comment is the talmudic rule permitting the surgical removal of a foetus from the womb of a dead mother on the Sabbath day. R. Isserles is hesitant to recommend the practical application of this rule on the grounds that the mother may not be dead and the operation will bring about her demise. This is an interesting illustration of the tension between traditional halakhic norms and the medical knowledge and sensitivities of the day; the very issue which R. Sofer is attempting to resolve. R. Isserles's ruling is also referred to in Ch. 1 nn. 24, 157–8.

In R. Sofer's conclusion, therefore, the definition of death is threefold: no breath, no pulse (cardiac activity), and absolutely no movement.[25] There is, however, an important distinction that must be made between the absence of breath and the lack of pulse and movement. Only the first is absolutely binding, since it alone carries a fully fledged talmudic pedigree. The other two merely act as supporting evidence and, as such, may be displaced by superior legal sources or by better medical science. For example, the lack of movement test does not apply to decapitated but still moving creatures, since the Mishnah treats them as corpses. If lack of movement was a fully fledged halakhically normative sign of death, such creatures would have to be treated as living beings incapable of imparting the ritual impurity associated with a corpse. In the light of this distinction between lack of breath and absence of pulse and movement, it may also be assumed that in the course of time, the tests relating to lack of pulse and of movement may be changed in accordance with new medical insights. Absence of breath, on the other hand, will always remain a legally binding criterion for establishing death in the *halakhah*.

A salient feature of R. Sofer's *responsum* is the way in which he resolves the tension between the halakhic tradition and the medical knowledge and moral sensibilities of his time in a manner entirely compatible with his highly traditional outlook and temperament. Sensing that the breath test alone will not pass muster either medically or morally, he posits an oral tradition that would have been acceptable had it not been lost. Thus, the strength of the tradition is not undermined by the new reality: having been lost, the tradition can never be consulted and subjected to a critical examination. At the same time, a substitute can be offered that follows in the footsteps of that tradition, i.e. the criteria of pulse loss and lack of movement. This approach allows halakhic authorities to remain both true to *halakhah* and flexible in applying the law to changing medical and scientific realities. Such flexibility is vital, if the tradition is to retain its relevance in contemporary times.[26]

At the time of its writing, R. Sofer's *responsum* was not especially noteworthy within halakhic circles, since there was no significant practical difference between the breath test and the other two criteria. The burial societies used all three tests to the best of their ability, and even in medical circles, nothing of any practical significance turned on the difference between loss of breathing and lack of pulse as a definition of death. In recent times, however, R. Sofer's definition has become the starting point for a heated halakhic debate over heart transplants. Those who permit such transplants adopt the view that the total and irreversible loss of all independent capacity to breathe (brain-stem death) is the definitive

[25] *Resp. Hayam Sofer, Yoreh Deah*, no. 338.   [26] See Ch. 5 s. 2.

definition of death, even if the heart is still beating. Those who prohibit cardiac transplantation define death in terms of cardiac failure, and rely upon the opinion of Rashi and the other authorities mentioned above, as well as the element of loss of pulse referred to in R. Sofer's *responsum.*

The use of R. Sofer's definition as a precedent for prohibiting heart transplants is open to the objection that R. Sofer himself draws a distinction between absence of breath, which is the test based upon the Bible, Talmud, and the major codes, and lack of pulse, which is a substitute for one of the lost tests of the oral tradition. It seems unlikely that R. Sofer would reject a rigorous medical test for death based upon lack of breath simply because it did not accord with his cardiac criterion. Since the latter was introduced in order to close any gap that might have arisen between the tradition and modern medicine, it is reasonable to assume that a test that meets with full medical approval would be acceptable, even if its sole basis was the absence of independent respiratory capacity.

As far as Rashi and the scholars who follow his explanation of the role of the heart are concerned, it has already been pointed out that this approach is derived from the Galenic idea that the heart is the seat of breathing, an idea that is not true in terms of modern medical science. In this context, it is important to note that even R. Sofer states that 'we do not deny empirical reality'.[27]

Finally, it ought to be observed that those authorities who define death in terms of the cessation of both respiration and heartbeat tend to marshal aggadic, philosophical, and kabbalistic sources in order to bolster their case for including lack of cardiac activity in their definition. The high incidence of such sources indicates that the strictly legal basis for the dual requirement for defining death may not be that strong.[28]

2. HEART TRANSPLANTS

Cardiac transplantation can only be done with a live, still-beating heart. Clearly, it is incompatible with a definition of death based upon the cessation of cardiac function. If death is defined by the loss of heartbeat, and a still-beating heart is removed from a donor, an act of murder will have been committed. In order to accommodate human heart transplants, which began in earnest in the 1960s, the Harvard Ad Hoc Committee of 1968 recommended that the definition of death be based upon the

---

[27] *Resp. Hatam Sofer, Yoreh Deah,* no. 167.

[28] See the famous case of the heartless chicken, in which R. Zevi Ashkenazi proves that all chickens have hearts and there can be no such thing as a heartless chicken for the purposes of the dietary laws using numerous extra-halakhic sources (*Resp. Haham Zvi,* no. 77). Also see Bleich, 'Of Cerebral...Death', 46–7.

irreversible cessation of brain-stem function, which occurs a short time before the termination of cardiac activity. Under this definition, the still-beating heart is removed from a dead donor, not a live one. The brain stem is that part of the brain which governs a person's vegetative functions, including breathing, swallowing, yawning, responses to light, and the sleep/wake cycle. As far as breathing is concerned, the brain stem sends neural impulses to the diaphragm and chest muscles, and these in turn expand and allow the lungs to fill with air. The result is breathing. Once the brain stem ceases to function, there is no longer any capacity for independent breathing. Brain-stem dysfunction may be established neurologically, electrically, and chemically. The loss of brain-stem breathing function may be compensated for by the use of an artificial respirator, thereby enabling the heart of a legally dead individual to be kept alive until it is needed for a transplant.[29]

The halakhic position on brain-stem death is in dispute. It seems fairly clear that R. Moses Feinstein accepts that death may be established on the sole basis of the irreversible loss of the capacity to breathe independently, 'even if the heart is still capable of functioning'. There are those who dispute this understanding of his position, arguing that R. Feinstein does not recognize loss of brain-stem function as death if the heart is still beating.[30] R. Moses Tendler, a son-in-law of R. Feinstein, strongly advocates the view that his father-in-law accepted loss of brain-stem function as the definition of death, and supports it on the basis, *inter alia*, of the

---

[29] See 'A Definition of Irreversible Coma: Report of the Ad Hoc Committee of the Harvard Medical School to Examine the Definition of Brain Death', *Journal of the American Medical Association*, 205 (1968), 337–40; President's Commission for the Study of Ethical Problems in Medicine and Biomedical and Behavioral Research, *Medical, Legal and Ethical Issues in the Determination of Death* (Washington, DC, 1981), 62–84.

[30] *Resp. Iggrot Moshe, Yoreh Deah*, 3 no. 132. Also see 'Concerning Brain Death' (Heb.), *Assia* 53–4 (1994), 24–5 for additional correspondence by R. Feinstein on this matter. The doubt concerning his position arises because his *responsa* can be read in more than one way. Whereas it seems fairly clear that in *Resp. Iggrot Moshe, Yoreh, Deah*, 3 no. 132, he maintains that death is determined solely by lack of breath, there are two other *responsa* in which he seems to reject the concept of brain death as a legitimate halakhic method for defining death (*Resp. Iggrot Moshe, Yoreh Deah*, 2 no. 146 and *Hoshen Mishpat*, 2 no. 72). It is, however, arguable that the reference to brain death in the two last-mentioned *responsa* is to the destruction of areas of the brain other than the brain stem. Since a patient with a functional brain stem can still breathe independently, he is halakhically alive, and removing his heart would, indeed, constitute an act of murder. In the first *responsum* mentioned above, however, he is dealing with the cessation of brain-stem activity; the patient in this case is completely incapable of breathing independently. A ruling that such a person is dead fits in well with the classical breath test for the establishment of death. Those who oppose loss of brain-stem capacity as a halakhic method of determining death argue that R. Feinstein totally rejects any form of brain death, and in the one *responsum* in which he appears to accept it, he does so only after the heart has already ceased to beat (Bleich, 'Of Cerebral…Death', 59–60). This argument is, however, difficult to accept since the tests described by R. Feinstein make little medical sense if the heart has, indeed, stopped beating (see Steinberg, *Encyclopaedia of Jewish Medical Ethics*, vi. 5–8).

mishnaic law regarding decapitated animals. In his *responsum*, R. Feinstein refers to lack of blood flow to the brain as evidence of cessation of brain-stem activity. Adopting the functional decapitation interpretation of the Mishnah described above, R. Tendler sees a precise analogy between the establishment of the lack of blood flow to the brain and functional decap-itation. In both cases, death is defined in terms of loss of brain function. R. Tendler also cites anecdotal evidence to the effect that his father-in-law encouraged cardiac transplantation.[31]

In 1986, the Israeli Chief Rabbinate issued a decision permitting heart transplants and laying down the tests required for the establishment of the irreversible destruction of brain-stem function.[32] The Chief Rabbinate based its decision upon the criterion of lack of breath in the Sabbath rescue case, and the position of R. Sofer with regard to the dominant role of that criterion in his *responsum* on the definition of death. R. Feinstein's ruling in support of the brain-stem approach also provided important support for this decision. An important medical factor in the Chief Rabbinate's decision was the tremendous improvement in the success rate of cardiac transplantation due to the highly successful anti-rejection drug, cyclosporine. In the light of the excellent recovery statistics resulting from the use of this drug, as opposed to those of the early days of cardiac trans-plants in which the success rate was virtually nil, the Chief Rabbinate was confidant that its decision would lead to the saving of many lives, thereby helping to fulfil the paramount *mitzvah* of preserving human life.

An entirely opposing view is adopted by R. David Bleich.[33] He takes issue with R. Tendler's understanding of R. Feinstein's position, contend-ing that the latter rejected any form of brain death, including cessation of brain-stem function, for halakhic purposes. R. Bleich also rejects any anal-ogy between decapitation and loss of brain-stem function. As far as he is concerned, there is a world of difference between the physical severing of a limb or organ from the body, and loss of function in that limb or organ. One may not, therefore, argue that the lack of blood flow to the brain stem, which is an indication of loss of functional ability, is equivalent to physical decapitation.[34] According to R. Bleich, R. Sofer's threefold defini-tion of death must be accepted as fully binding, regardless of the differ-ence in normative ranking between the three elements of breath, heart function, and movement; in practice, R. Sofer clearly intended that they

---

[31] 'Jewish Law and the Time of Death', *Journal of the American Medical Association*, 240 (1978), 109; 'Determining Death and Transplanting Organs' (Heb.), *Emek Halakha Assia*, 2 (1990), 213–16.

[32] See Y. Jakobovits, 'Brain Death and Heart Transplants: The Israeli Chief Rabbinate's Directives', *Tradition*, 24 (1989), 1–14.   [33] See Bleich, 'Of Cerebral... Death', 46–7.

[34] See *Ohaloth*, 1: 6; Bleich, 'Of Cerebral... Death', 46–7; Steinberg, 'Establishing Time of Death', 13 n. 1.

all be part of the definition of death. Finally, R. Bleich argues that the techniques currently employed for determining irreversible loss of brain-stem function are not sufficiently refined for the purpose of achieving the level of certainty required for the establishment of death according to Jewish law.

A similar view is held by R. Shlomo Zalman Auerbach, who accepts in theory that irreversible cessation of the brain stem establishes death, but is not prepared to apply this criterion in practice. In his view, the fact that the heart is still beating raises the possibility that despite medical evidence to the contrary, a part of the brain stem might still be alive. As a result, R. Auerbach is only prepared to declare a person dead if his heart has ceased to beat for at least thirty seconds after the establishment of irreversible loss of brain-stem function. During the time between the conventional medical determination of brain-stem death and the absence of heartbeat for at least thirty seconds, the individual is 'doubtfully dead' and as such, the laws of the *goses*[35] apply. It is certainly an act of homicide to transplant the heart of a *goses*.[36] R. Auerbach also indicates that once the tests such as blood-flow studies or neurological examinations for brain-stem dysfunction have taken place, and the results indicate death, all life-support may be discontinued, although actual death may not be declared until thirty seconds after loss of heartbeat.[37]

Both R. Bleich and R. Auerbach are sceptical with regard to the conclusiveness of the latest medical tests for the termination of brain-stem activity. R. Tendler, on the other hand, is adamant in his defence of scientific evidence, and, for example, includes slides of nuclide scans of the brain stem in his articles in order to convince his rabbinic colleagues of the correctness of his view.[38] Leaving aside the question of who is right in this debate, the underlying issue of the weight to be assigned to empirically sound and scientifically proven evidence in the shaping of halakhic decisions is a highly significant one, and merits further discussion.

The leading exponent of the view that science and *halakhah* ought to be reconciled whenever possible is Maimonides. In general, he assigns a high value to 'empirical and rational'[39] evidence in the shaping of halakhic decisions and concepts. Now, the quest for harmony between rationality and the tradition is often associated with Maimonides the

---

[35] See Ch. 5 ss. 1–2.

[36] 'Organ Transplants From Cadavers to the Dangerously Ill' (Heb.), *Assia*, 53–4 (1994), 26–8. [37] See Steinberg, *Encyclopaedia of Jewish Medical Ethics*, vi. 15.

[38] See his 'To Guide the Perplexed on the Halakhah of Brain Stem Death', *Rabbinical Council of America Publication* (August 1991), 2.

[39] This phrase is found in his *Iggrot Harambam*, ed. Y. Kafah (Jerusalem, 1972), 134–5. For a list of sources in which Maimonides deals with the nature of valid scientific evidence, see Ch. 4 n. 29.

philosopher,[40] but not always with Maimonides the jurist. In fact, this quest is a pervasive feature of his halakhic writings, even though he does not spell out his methodology for achieving it in the same way that he does in his philosophical works. One illustration of Maimonides' desire to syntheize science and *halakhah* is his strongly rational approach to the theological value of human healing, and his unqualified ranking of human healing as a *mitzvah*, both of which were discussed in Chapter 4. The law of the *terefah* provides two additional illustrations of the quest for unity between science and *halakhah* in Maimonides' legal writings. In the previous chapter, the definition of a human *terefah*—someone suffering from a fatal defect or disease—was outlined, together with its ramifications for modern medical dilemmas, including the question of heart transplants.[41] In his definition of the human *terefah*, Rashi relies upon the extensive body of halakhic literature dealing with the closed list of defects and diseases constituting the definition of an animal *terefah*. Maimonides, however, avoids the well-established animal precedents, and opts instead for a purely medical definition. The fact that the Talmud itself does not explicitly apply the definition of *terefah* found in relation to animals to humans provides him with the methodological leeway to ignore the traditional list of *terefot* in the animal context, and opt instead for a purely medical definition. Presumably, his reason for doing so is because the talmudic tests for animal *tarfut* are limited to a fixed list that reflects the veterinary science of the time. Maimonides, ever the rationalist, is fully aware that what is fatal in one generation may not be fatal in the next. In order to avoid a conflict between *halakhah* and science in relation to the application of the law of the human *terefah*, he chooses a definition based upon science rather than tradition. Rashi, on the other hand, defines human *tarfut* on the basis of the animal criteria set out in the Talmud, because this is the safer course from the standpoint of both tradition and the inner consistency of the law. He is not bothered by the possibility of a contradiction between empirical science and *halakhah* which might arise as a result of the changing nature of fatal illness over time. Maimonides,

---

[40] In one of the most oft-quoted passages in the *Guide for the Perplexed*, 2: 25, Maimonides professes his readiness to interpret any biblical verse that conflicts with rationally proven truths in such a way that the conflict disappears. In his *Letter on Astrology*, he states that any empirical or rational proposition must stand up to the test of rational examination and, therefore, God gave people 'eyes in their front and not at their back' in order to teach them to assess empirically based evidence in an objective way, and to reject it if it does not accord with the evidence of their senses. In the same letter, he sharply criticizes those who do not test out their ideas in terms of logical and empirical truth, but instead rely upon the fact that they found them in books, even if those works were penned by venerable and respected individuals.
[41] See Ch. 5 s. 5. For the role of the *terefah* category in relation to heart transplants, see Ch. 5, nn. 150–2.

on the other hand, is concerned by the possibility of such a conflict, and in order to avoid it, he adopts a purely medical definition of human *tarfut*.

The second illustration of Maimonides' harmonization of science and *halakhah* in relation to the law of the *terefah* is his deviation from the fixed list of animal *terefot* in relation to the loss of an upper jaw. The Talmud rules that only the loss of an animal's lower jaw renders it a *terefah*.[42] In his codification of the *halakhah*, however, Maimonides includes the upper jaw in the list of *terefot* that make an animal unfit for consumption.[43] The rabbis of Lunel wrote to Maimonides expressing surprise that he had added something to a specifically closed talmudic list. Surely this was a deviation from accepted legal methodology and an error on his part! In his reply, Maimonides makes clear that there is no methodological bar to adding a related item to a closed list: it would be wrong to remove one of the talmudic defects, but the option of adding is always present.[44] Having crossed this methodological hurdle, Maimonides explains at length that the likelihood of dying from the loss of an upper jaw is much higher than in the case of the loss of the lower jaw, since the upper jaw plays a vital role in warming the air breathed in by the animal. In its absence, the air is cold, and the animal is almost certain to die as a result of respiratory illness. From a scientific perspective, therefore, such an animal is a *terefah* and should be included in the list of *terefot* on the basis of an a fortiori argument from the lower jaw. Maimonides agrees that the meat from an animal that has lost its upper jaw is not prohibited 'in the other halakhic works', but he ventures to suggest that this is only because the other codifiers did 'not set their minds to these [scientific] matters and had they done so, they would have reached a similar conclusion'.[45]

Maimonides is a particularly strong advocate of synthesizing *halakhah* and science; other authorities are much less perturbed by the existence of a gap between the two disciplines, and generally tend to give pride of place to the least controversial halakhic solution, even if it is out of step with scientific developments.[46]

One way of viewing the contemporary debate over cardiac transplants is from the perspective of this difference between Maimonides and other halakhic authorities over the question of the synthesis of science and *halakhah*. Those tending to adopt irreversible dysfunction of the brain stem as a definitive sign of death are closer to the position adopted by

---

[42] *Hullin* 3: 2; *Hullin* 55b.   [43] *Hilkhot Shehitah*, 10: 12–13.

[44] It is, for example, forbidden to add or to subtract from the laws of the *Torah* (Deut. 4: 2; 13: 1). It is, nevertheless, permitted to add personal stringencies in the area of ritual law without falling foul of this prohibition (Maimonides, *Hilkhot Shvitat Asor*, 3: 3).

[45] *Teshuvot Harambam*, ed. J. Blau, no. 315.

[46] See Ch. 4 n. 30 for a number of illustrations of Maimonides' tendency to rely on science in the shaping of the *halakhah* and some instances in which Nahmanides adopts a non-scientific but halakhically more consistent course.

Maimonides. Those who reject this test are closer to the position adopted by those authorities who do not regard the harmonization of science and *halakhah* as an important value in Jewish law, and prefer, instead, to maintain as much consistency with as broad a range of halakhic precedents as possible. In this respect, the underlying issue is, indeed, the weight to be assigned to accepted scientific methods in the halakhic process.

In terms of popular practice, it would appear that halakhically observant Jews exercise choice in this area. Some follow those authorities who permit heart transplants and cardiac donation, whereas others follow the prohibitionist school and refrain from cardiac donation. Indeed, two rabbinically approved consent forms to post-mortem organ donation are available to Orthodox Jews in the United States. One includes the heart and follows the position adopted by R. Tendler. The other excludes the heart and reflects the view of R. Bleich.

It is noteworthy that even those authorities who forbid heart transplants do not raise any halakhic objection to the use of a heart once it has been removed from the donor's body.[47] The existence of a group of people who are unwilling to donate hearts but are willing to accept them raises the question of reciprocity in relation to the allocation of organs available for transplant, which is a strong moral, if not halakhic, issue. On moral grounds, such a position is problematic and surely requires serious consideration by authorities who oppose transplants.

A final reflection on this topic from a scientific rather than a legal perspective, is that there is always the possibility that scientific and technical developments may make debates such as the one over heart transplants into purely academic disagreements. Scientists are currently attempting to create and perfect techniques for the regeneration of damaged tissue and organs, including the heart.[48] If they are successful, organ transplantation and with it, the debate, will become relics of the past. At the present time, however, it is still necessary to grapple with the definition of death in relation to the law and ethics of cardiac transplantation.

3. ORGAN DONATIONS

(a) Live Donors

Jewish law requires personal intervention in order to save life, based on the biblical injunction 'not to stand idly by your neighbour's

---

[47] See A. Steinberg, *Encyclopaedia of Jewish Medical Ethics*, ii. 232–4. As will be observed below, it is halakhically permitted to use the fruits of unethical research results or materials for life-saving purposes: J. D. Bleich, 'Fetal Tissue Research', *Tradition*, 24 (1989), 71–7.

[48] See D. Mooney and A. Mikos, 'Growing New Organs', *Scientific American*, 280 (April 1999), 38–44.

blood'.[49] At the same time, there is a biblical prohibition on risk-taking, and self-injury is halakhically prohibited.[50] The question that then arises is the extent to which people are required to risk their lives in order to save someone else from certain death. The answer to this question would appear to be a point of dispute between the Babylonian Talmud and the Jerusalem Talmud. The Babylonian Talmud consistently adopts the view that individuals are not required to risk their lives in order to save others from certain death.[51] The Jerusalem Talmud, on the other hand, seems to indicate that the right course of action is to attempt to save a fellow human being from certain death, even if this involves a risk to one's life.[52] In his formulation of the *halakhah*, Maimonides indicates that he follows the opinion of the Babylonian Talmud, ruling that the obligation to save life applies only in the absence of risk to the rescuer's life.[53] This is the position adopted by the vast majority of halakhic authorities from the medieval period until the present day.[54] Nevertheless, the opinion expressed in the Jerusalem Talmud surfaces in a wide range of halakhic sources, indicating that despite its lack of normative clout, there is something morally and spiritually compelling about the argument that in certain cases, it is the right thing to risk one's life in order to save that of another person.[55]

The differing views of the two Talmuds were combined in a ruling by R. David b. Zimra (Radbaz) in the fifteenth century. In a case involving a threat to kill one individual if the other would not consent to losing a limb, Radbaz distinguishes between carrying out a legal obligation and adopting the 'way of the pious' by going beyond the requirements of the law. The individual faced with the loss of a limb is under no halakhic

[49] Lev. 19: 16; *Sanhedrin*, 73a. For a general discussion of this obligation, see A. Kirschenbaum, 'The Good Samaritan and Jewish Law', *Dine Israel*, 7 (1976), 7–85. It is noteworthy that an Israeli law bearing this verse as its title was passed in 1998. Under this law, a person is obliged to attempt to save anyone whose life is subject to a direct and immediate threat, provided that they are capable of doing so without endangering themselves or other people. Non-compliance with this law is punishable by a fine (M. Halperin, 'The "You Shall Not Stand Idly by the Blood of Your Neighbour" Law' (Heb.), *Assia*, 65–6 (1999), 5–8). This obligation is part of a cluster of injunctions dealing with the need to save and preserve human life in Jewish law, see Ch. 4 s. 4.

[50] Deut. 4: 9; Maimonides, *Hilkhot Hovel Umazzik*, 5: 1.

[51] *Bava Metzia*, 62a; *Niddah*, 61a; *Nedarim*, 81a; *Tiferet Yisrael*, *Yoma*, 8: 7.

[52] *Terumot*, 8: 4.

[53] *Hilkhot Rozeah*, 1: 14. In his formulation of the obligation, Maimonides adds the rider 'and he is capable of rescuing'. This phrase provides the basis for the claim that Maimonides restricts the obligation to rescue to situations in which the rescuer's life does not come under threat (*Resp. Radbaz*, 5, *Leshonot Harambam* no. 618; *Minhat Hinukh*, no. 296).

[54] *Beth Yosef*, *Hoshen Mishpat*, 426; *Sefer Meirat Einaim*, *Hoshen Mishpat*, 426: 2; *Resp. Yehave Daat*, no. 84; M. Hirshler, 'Kidney Donation from an Incompetent and Brain Damaged Donor' (Heb.), *Halakhah Urefuah*, 2 (1981), 122 n. 5.

[55] *Beth Yosef*, *Hoshen Mishpat*, 426; *Resp. Havat Yair*, no. 146.

obligation to undergo the amputation for the sake of saving his fellow from certain death, since the amputation involves a definite risk to his life. Amputations in the fifteenth century were highly dangerous affairs, and the likelihood of post-operative survival was small. Nevertheless, since there was no direct threat to the amputee's life, there was no bar to him choosing to act in a pious manner by agreeing to lose a limb in order to save someone from certain death. Indeed, such a course of action is praiseworthy. Radbaz introduces a positive element of personal discretion into the *halakhah* by allowing individuals to make up their own minds with regard to risk-taking for the sake of saving life. Later authorities emphasize the virtue of such a course of action, and advise people not to be too zealous in protecting their own lives when taking a risk could save another person from certain death.[56] However, if the risk is a direct threat to life itself, then any person who undertakes it is a 'pious fool' and his action is contrary to the *halakhah*.[57]

Modern halakhic authorities base their approach to live organ donations on the Radbaz scheme. There is a minority view that since any invasive operation is a potential threat to life, there is no obligation to donate an organ, even to an individual who will certainly die without it, and anyone who donates a live organ is acting contrary to the *halakhah*.[58] The majority of authorities adopt a more realistic approach to the evaluation of risk, and rule that since modern medicine has significantly reduced the risks involved in live organ transplantation, donors are considered pious individuals whose acts are fully endorsed by the *halakhah*, although there is no obligation to donate.[59] A small but growing group of authorities is prepared to rule that in extremely low-risk cases such as blood donations, bone-marrow transplants, and even some kidney transplants, donation by compatible live donors is even halakhically obligated.[60] Modern *halakhah* turns on the question of risk to the donor. In the case of a significant risk to life the donation is forbidden. If the risk is not to one's life, the donor is permitted to act piously and to donate. A decision that the donation is halakhically obligatory may be made in a case in which the risk to the donor is minimal.

The issue of legally incompetent donors has also been addressed by halakhic authorities. Since minors are exempt from all halakhic

---

[56] *Arukh Hashulhan, Hoshen Mishpat*, 426: 4.　　　[57] *Resp. Radbaz*, 3 no. 627.

[58] *Resp. Ziz Eliezer*, 9 no. 45. Blood donation is also prohibited since the Bible calls blood 'the soul' (Deut. 12: 23) and a donation is, therefore, potentially life-threatening.

[59] *Resp. Iggrot Moshe, Yoreh Deah*, 2 no. 174; *Nishmat Avraham, Yoreh Deah*, 157: 4; Hirshler, 'Kidney Donation', 122–8.

[60] *Resp. Shevet Halevi*, 5 no. 219; N. Bar-Ilan, 'Halakhic Aspects of Bone-Marrow Transplants' (Heb.), *Assia*, 51–2 (1992), 59–71; *Resp. Yehave Daat*, 3 no. 84; *Nishmat Avraham, Yoreh Deah*, 349: 3.

obligations, there is no basis upon which to compel a minor to donate an organ, even in a case of negligible risk. In this context, parental wishes are irrelevant.[61] Organ donations from the mentally incompetent are permitted only for the direct benefit of the ward.[62] There is a minority view, which is based upon the principles governing charitable gifts made on behalf of mentally incompetent wards,[63] that it is permitted to authorize an organ donation by a ward if it can be established that the vast majority of competent individuals would donate in similar circumstances.[64] In an Israeli Supreme Court decision on a kidney transplant from a mentally ill son to his father, Elon J. held that the appropriate halakhic criterion was that of direct benefit. He distinguished between the law governing charitable gifts, which is a purely financial matter, and the giving up of an organ, which is a matter of the ward's physical health and welfare. In his view, Jewish law does not apply the principles governing charitable bequests on behalf of a ward to the donation of their organs. The physical risks involved in organ donation militate against the use of criteria applicable to financial matters.[65]

As far as the issue of organ sales is concerned, it would appear that there is no principled objection in Jewish civil law to the sale of regenerative organic material, such as hair[66] or blood.[67] In this respect, Jewish law is more liberal than American law, although the position in the United States may be changing in favour of recognizing people's rights to legal title in their body parts and any organic products derived from those parts.[68] In relation to organs, however, a halakhic problem arises, since the element of risk involved in their transplantation and its aftermath may constitute a breach of the prohibition on self-injury.[69] As already explained, this prohibition is overridden by the obligation to save life, provided that the risk to the donor is not excessive.[70] The significance of this point for organ sales is that the sale must be made for the purpose of saving life in order for it to survive a charge of illegal self-injury. This requirement would need to be translated into practical law, both in terms of the price of the organ and its direct and immediate therapeutic use.

[61] Y. Zilberstein, 'Kidney Transplantation' (Heb.), *Halakhah Urefuah*, 4 (Jerusalem, 1985), 156–7.   [62] Hirshler, 'Kidney Donation', 122.

[63] See D. Sinclair, 'Kidney Donations from the Legally Incompetent in Jewish and Comparative Law', *Israel Law Review*, 27 (1989), 588.

[64] M. Meiselman, 'Halakhic Problems Relating to Kidney Transplants', *Halakhah Urefuah*, 1 (Jerusalem, 1981), 114.   [65] *Attorney-General* v. *A*, CA 698/86, PD 42 (2) 57–9.

[66] *Nedarim*, 4: 4.   [67] Resp. *Iggrot Moshe, Hoshen Mishpat*, 1 no. 103.

[68] See *Moore* v. *Regents of the University of California*, 793 P. 2d. 479 (Cal. 1990), and *Hecht* v. *Superior Court*, 20 Cal. Rept. 2d. 275 (Ct. App. 1993) in relation to the ownership of a dead man's sperm.   [69] Deut. 4: 9: Maimonides, *Hilkhot Hovel Umazzik*, 5: 1.

[70] The overriding of the prohibition on self-injury by the need to save life is dealt with in *Tosafot, Bava Kamma*, 91b, *s.v. elah* and the commentary of the *Pnei Yehoshua, ad. loc.*

Such practical arrangements would certainly militate against any purely commercial enterprise in organs from live donors, since the therapeutic goal of the sale would need to be extremely well-defined to overcome the halakhic prohibition on self-endangerment.

There is also a policy dimension to the sale of organs, which generally manifests itself in the argument that the legalization of organ sales will result in the wealthy exploiting the poor in order to get all the organs they need, whereas the poor will be unable to afford organs should they find themselves on the buying rather than the selling end of the trade in human spare parts. Leaving aside the ethical and economic logic of this argument, which is debatable,[71] it is clear that Jewish law is sensitive to the need to prevent this type of exploitation.[72] According to R. Judah the Pious, the reason for the biblical prohibition on remarrying one's divorced wife after she was subsequently married and divorced by another man[73] is to prevent wealthy men paying the poor husbands of attractive women to divorce them so that they can marry them for a short period, divorce them once their charms have worn off, and then send them back to their now less poor but still needy husbands, who will dutifully remarry their ex-wives as part of the deal.[74] R. Judah considers the economic exploitation of the poor by the rich to be so reprehensible that it deserves to be nipped in the bud by a preventative biblical law.

In terms of law as opposed to policy, however, the legitimacy of organ sales in the *halakhah* turns on the requirement that in order for the sale to be halakhically valid, it must be clearly directed to the saving of life and not to any other goal, including pure commercial gain.

(b) Cadaver Transplants

Under Jewish law, it is prohibited to leave a corpse unburied overnight,[75] to derive any benefit from a cadaver,[76] and to disfigure the dead.[77] Jewish law also imposes a positive obligation to bury a dead body.[78] In the eighteenth century, R. Ezekiel Landau was asked whether an autopsy could be performed on the victim of a particular disease in order to obtain the knowledge necessary to prevent others dying from that very malady.

---

[71] See N. Zohar, 'Toward Justice in the Organ Trade', *Israel Law Review*, 27 (1993), 541–5.

[72] See Y. Lau, 'The Sale of Organs for Transplantation' (Heb.), *Tehumin*, 18 (1998), 125–36.

[73] Deut. 24: 1–4.

[74] *Commentary on the Torah*, end of *Parashat Ki Teze*: M. Halperin, 'Halakhic Aspects of Live Organ Transplantation' (Heb.), *Assia*, 45–6 (1989), 57–9.

[75] Deut. 21: 23; *Sanhedrin*, 46a. There is some doubt as to the normative status of all these rules, and disputes as to whether or not they are biblical or merely rabbinic are endemic to this field of *halakhah*.   [76] *Sanhedrin*, 47b.

[77] Ibid. 47a.   [78] Ibid. 46b.

R. Landau replied that the above-mentioned halakhic norms are all suspended in a case in which there is 'a sick individual at hand', whose life may be saved as a result of the post-mortem.[79]

In addition to this general principle, halakhic authorities have restricted the scope of each of these norms. The prohibition on leaving a corpse unburied overnight is suspended in a case in which the delay is for the purpose of honouring the deceased, e.g. waiting for close relatives to arrive and participate in the funeral. The same exception applies in relation to the obligation to bury a corpse: it is suspended where the honour of the deceased is at stake.[80] The prohibitions on deriving benefit from or disgracing a corpse are both limited to non-therapeutic procedures of a degrading nature.[81]

Both the general principle enunciated by R. Landau and the limitations imposed upon the norms relating to the treatment of corpses in Jewish law militate in favour of cadaver organ donations. Organs obtained from cadavers are designated for direct and immediate life-saving, especially in the current era of few organs and long donor waiting lists. Transplanting an organ from a cadaver in order to save another person is certainly not a degrading activity: on the contrary, it is a highly dignified act.[82] Indeed, the giving of life is the most honourable of all deeds,[83] and the rules regarding autopsies would not appear to constitute a serious obstacle to cadaver donations. In fact, the majority of modern authorities permit the transplanting of corneas, skin, kidneys, and livers from corpses to living recipients.

An interesting and original approach to the question of cadaver organs was developed by R. Isser Yehudah Unterman, according to whom the fact that a transplanted organ is capable of living and functioning in the recipient's body means that these organs are not actually dead. Hence, the prohibition on leaving a corpse unburied, and the obligation to bury it, do not apply; neither do the prohibitions on deriving benefit from a corpse and disfiguring it. Since the transplanted organ is not a dead body-part, the regulations applying to corpses are irrelevant.[84]

---

[79] *Resp. Noda Biyehuda*, 2, *Yoreh Deah*, no. 210.   [80] Maimonides, *Hilkhot Avel*, 4: 8.

[81] *Resp. Mishpetei Uziel*, *Yoreh Deah*, nos. 28–9; *Resp. Yabia Omer*, 3, *Yoreh Deah*, no. 23. An interesting problem is posed in relation to the consumption of flesh from a corpse for therapeutic purposes (*Pithei Teshuvah*, *Yoreh Deah*, 349: 1). It is noteworthy that Radbaz permits the consumption of mummy parts for medicinal reasons on the grounds that the flesh is completely dry, and its consumption does not fall into the normal category of 'benefit' that would apply to the eating of fresh corpse flesh (*Resp. Radbaz*, 3 no. 979). Similar reasoning underlies the view that dissecting and studying corpses does not involve the prohibition on deriving benefit from a cadaver.

[82] A. Steinberg, *Encyclopaedia of Jewish Medical Ethics*, iv. 560–2.

[83] *Nishmat Avraham*, *Yoreh Deah*, 349: 3.

[84] *Shevet Miyehuda*, 313–25. R. Unterman does insist that the family's consent be obtained before the transplant is carried out.

The common factor in all the modern decisions on autopsies is that the therapeutic justification must be direct and immediate. In the absence of such justification, the above-mentioned halakhic rules remain in force, and no part of a corpse may be left unburied. It goes without saying that even in permitted cadaver transplant situations, any parts that are not actually used must be given a proper burial.

Foetal tissue transplantation is associated with possible cures for Parkinson's disease and nerve damage,[85] including broken spinal cords.[86] The tissue is obtained from dead foetuses or from foetuses especially grown for the purpose of harvesting their stem cells. There is little hard scientific evidence of significant therapeutic value in any of these areas, and 'foetal tissue transplantation is far from confirmed as an effective therapy'.[87] The halakhic requirements regarding the burial of foetuses, however, are less rigorous than those applying to adults, and it is not at all clear that foetal remains are subject to the prohibitions on deriving benefit from or disfiguring a corpse.[88] From this perspective, there would not appear to be a serious problem with foetal tissue transplantation under Jewish law, even if the tissue was not intended for the direct and immediate saving of life. There is, however, a strong and influential negative argument of a policy nature in this area, i.e. the legalization of foetal transplants will encourage unjustified abortions and ought to be banned. The subject of abortion in Jewish law was dealt with in Chapter 1, and nothing more need be said in the present context than that it involves a complex balance between legal and moral elements, and the halakhic approach is more lenient than the approach encountered in Catholic sources.[89] At the same time, there is every reason to believe that any halakhic response to the use of foetal tissue would take the abortion policy argument into account and would actively seek to minimize the risk of encouraging illegal and unjustified abortions, especially in the absence of direct and immediate therapeutic benefit.[90]

(c) The Gap Between the *Halakhah* and Modern Organ Transplant Policy

The harvesting and transplantation of organs on both national and international levels is a uniquely modern phenomenon, making it something of a challenge to craft a normative legal response using halakhic sources

---

[85] See 'Cures from the Womb', *Newsweek*, 22 February 1993, 49–51.

[86] J. McDonald and the Research Consortium of the Christopher Reeve Paralysis Foundation, 'Repairing the Damaged Spinal Chord', *Scientific American* (September 1999), 61–2.   [87] See 'When Abortions Save Lives', *Time*, 13 April 1992, 60.

[88] See Bleich, 'Fetal Tissue Research', 71–7.   [89] See Ch. 1 pp. 24–25.

[90] See Bleich, 'Fetal Tissue Research', 71–7.

that go back several centuries and reflect an entirely different medical background. As already explained, the major doctrines developed by halakhic authorities are the principle of risk-prevention in the case of live donors, and the rule limiting cadaver donations to cases in which the organs will be of immediate and direct use in saving life. These doctrines are the product of certain realities, some of which are no longer relevant; they are often out of line with current social and medical policy, which is keen to increase the number of organs available for donation and to use legal arrangements in order to further that goal.[91] For example, in the context of live organ donations, it would seem that the halakhic emphasis on minimizing risk, rather than on the virtue of giving an organ to save another person's life, is not particularly conducive to the expansion of the number of organs available for transplantation in general. Also, the emphasis on the direct and immediate saving of life is likely to deter the establishment of organ banks that store organs for use worldwide, and in relation to which it may not be said with certainty that each organ is destined for an immediate and direct life-saving purpose.

In terms of the realities underlying the *halakhah* in this area, many of the talmudic cases that provide the basis for the principle of risk-avoidance deal with situations in which people are forced to decide between risking death at the hands of a tyrant, or standing by while a fellow Jew is executed, ostensibly as a result of their unwillingness to take a risk.[92] This is the context of Radbaz's case described above. In all these cases, the tyrant is in control, and there is no guarantee that the sacrifice of a limb will ensure the removal of the death threat to the other person. A capricious tyrant is as likely to kill all those involved as he is to keep his promise. In such circumstances, the best course may be to avoid co-operating with the tyrant and not to play his game. There is also the possibility that he will become tired of dealing with unco-operative victims and simply let everybody go free. There is a significant difference between the ethos in these persecution cases, and that of organ transplantation in the modern era. Perhaps that difference ought to have an effect upon the way in which these precedents are applied. After all, in relation to transplants, the risk-taking is self-imposed for the best of possible motives, namely,

[91] See H. Schwartz, 'Bioethical and Legal Considerations in Increasing the Supply of Transplantable Organs', *American Journal of Law and Medicine,* 10 (1985), 397; M. Defever, 'The Policies of Organ Transplantation in Europe: Issues and Problems', *Health Policy,* 16 (1990), 95; T. Randall, 'Too Few Human Organs for Transplantation, Too Many in Need... and the Gap Widens', *Journal of the American Medical Association,* 265 (1991), 1223; M. Kramer, 'The Shortage of Organs for Transplantation in Israel: Have We Given Up?' (Heb.), *Harefuah,* 124 (1993), 24.

[92] See the sources referred to in nn. 50–1, 56. See also the sources cited in Ch. 5, nn. 127–8.

the altruistic saving of human life. In such a context, the better course is surely to take the risk and to save the other person. It may be argued that, in contemporary halakhic discourse, the balance should be shifted away from the risk principle to that of noble altruism, and potential donors ought to be encouraged to be generous rather than grudging in their approach to organ donation.

A case for fostering a more generous approach to live organ transplants may also be made in doctrinal terms. The basis for such an approach may be found in the halakhic notion of limited autonomy, outlined in detail in Chapter 4. It will be recalled that the claim that the *halakhah* expresses itself exclusively in terms of obligation and leaves no room for individual choice is too strong, and that in certain life-and-death situations, a person is allowed to choose a course of action that is not halakhically optimal, but is justified in moral and life-enhancing terms. In these cases, individual choice is the correct halakhic response. The autonomy in this type of case is 'limited' because it is not, per se, a high value in the halakhic system, but merely serves as a means for providing a solution for a hard case. The two examples given in Chapter 4 were chronically ill people undergoing high-risk operations for the sake of dramatically improving their quality of life, and the taking of life-threatening risks for the sake of earning a living. In both cases, morally justifiable and life-enhancing desires clash with the most consistent halakhic analysis of the correct course of action for the individual concerned.[93]

The notion of limited autonomy may also be applied to live organ transplants. In dealing with the determination of risk, an individual may feel that the *halakhah* requires him to err on the side of self-preservation. At the same time, he may also feel strongly that it would be the right thing to donate a live organ, even if a certain amount of risk is involved. Such an individual might legitimately be encouraged to exercise limited autonomy in favour of donation, rather than to adopt the attitude that since the *halakhah* in this area is based upon the risk principle, any error should be made in favour of self-preservation. Emphasizing the halakhic legitimacy of limited autonomy with respect to a valid choice, i.e. one which is compatible with the halakhic value of saving life, even if it is not entirely consistent with halakhic doctrine, would be an important step towards encouraging donations in these circumstances. Spelling out the fact that the exercise of limited autonomy, even at the expense of strict halakhic consistency, is legitimate, and possibly even desirable, would undoubtedly be an important contribution not only to the field of live organ transplant policy, but also to halakhic creativity as a whole.

---

[93] See Ch. 4 s. 3.

The way forward so far as furthering modern cadaver organ donation policy is concerned is to emphasize the obligation to save life at the expense of the obligation to respect the bodies of the dead. The problem of striking the correct balance between these two obligations in the modern era is the core of contemporary autopsy *halakhah*. As already mentioned, the eighteenth-century halakhic response to the tension between these two obligations was to permit autopsies only if their purpose was the direct and immediate saving of human life.[94] Twentieth-century authorities have attempted to meet the challenge of applying this criterion in an era in which a particular piece of information may not be of any immediate and direct therapeutic value, but may, as a result of being shared with the universal research community, prove invaluable for producing a cure for a widespread and serious disease. R. Abraham Isaiah Karelitz points out that according to the Talmud, an alarm may be sounded on the Sabbath to warn of an impending plague, even though it has not yet reached the town in question. The same principle would justify making military preparations on the Sabbath for an impending war. R. Karelitz insists upon the presence of some 'present danger' before permitting these breaches of the Sabbath laws. He does not, for example, allow epidemic alarms when there is no plague anywhere in the vicinity, nor does he permit military preparations during a period of complete peace.[95] Applying R. Karelitz's approach to autopsies would mean that autopsy would have to fall into the category of an 'impending cure' before it became halakhically permissible. This, presumably, would depend upon the stage of scientific progress with regard to the disease that the autopsy is intended to investigate. Not all medical research has reached the level of an impending cure by the time the first autopsy is requested, and the possibility that important scientific information necessary for reaching that level may be lost as a result of not doing the post-mortem is very real. In these terms, R. Karelitz's approach is not satisfactory.

An entirely different approach is adopted by R. Feinstein, who concludes that the criterion of direct and immediate saving of life ought to be adhered to in as strict a manner as possible, since it is much too difficult in contemporary times to define the point at which the results of an autopsy cease to be of therapeutic significance. In the light of this difficulty, R. Feinstein retreats to a narrow interpretation of the saving of life, and bans all procedures except for those that are absolutely guaranteed to save life. In response to the objection that this approach will result in the

---

[94] *Resp. Noda Biyehuda*, 2, *Yoreh Deah*, no. 210.

[95] *Hazon Ish*, *Ohaloth*, 22: 32. The talmudic discussion on sounding plague alarms on the Sabbath is located in *Eruvin*, 45a, and *Ta'anit*, 21b.

stifling of medical progress, R. Feinstein points out that there is no halakhic obligation to study medicine. An already-trained physician is obliged to practise life-saving therapy, but there is no obligation to study medicine in the first place.[96]

Adopting R. Feinstein's position would mean, in effect, that observant Jews would not study or practise medicine, at least not in the way in which it is studied and practised in the modern world, but would still, presumably, take advantage of medical services offered by others. This is clearly an unsatisfactory situation, both in terms of the powerful mandate to save life in Jewish tradition, and the moral discomfort engendered by a situation in which Jews may only receive medical attention but not give it to others. At the same time, R. Feinstein defends his basic position in powerful and emotive terms. In his view, a more liberal approach to the autopsy issue may well 'result in the sweeping aside of all limits and the consequent nullification of the entire body of Divine commandments'. If the needs of science override all aspects of the law governing the treatment of the dead, society as a whole has a serious moral problem, and R. Feinstein's reluctance to go along with the permissive approach to autopsies is understandable.

R. Ben Zion Uziel goes to the other extreme. He begins his *responsum* by declaring that we are now living in a new reality, in which science assures us that 'if the beneficiary of research is unknown to us at the present time, he will certainly become known to us tomorrow'. R. Uziel points out that each and every autopsy may hold the key to the future understanding of a serious disease, and if it is not performed, 'this knowledge will remain hidden for ever and many people may eventually die as a result'.[97] He is, therefore, prepared to permit all autopsies on the basis of a purely medical justification. This view is not entirely satisfactory either, since it ultimately fails to deal with the issue of placing limits on non-therapeutic medical procedures, the resolution of which is necessary on the moral as well as the theological level. Very few moralists would be happy with an answer to the problem of finding the right balance between respect for the dead and medical therapy that simply said, 'leave it all to the scientists'. Moreover, this completely open approach can hardly be justified in the light of either the halakhic rules governing the treatment of the dead, or the above misgivings regarding the fate of the *halakhah* in general articulated by R. Feinstein.

Clearly, finding the right balance between medical progress and the preservation of halakhic norms regarding the dead is a knotty problem.

---

[96] *Responsa Iggrot Moshe, Yoreh Deah,* 3, no. 155. See also Ch. 4 s. 4 on the halakhic status of medical practice in Jewish law.

[97] *Responsa Mishpetei Uziel, Yoreh Deah,* no. 28; N. Zohar, *Alternatives in Jewish Bioethics* (New York 1997), 127–35.

At the end of the day, the only option is to continue struggling with the tension between conflicting views, and to attempt to establish guidelines aimed at ensuring that the claims of both medical science and Jewish law are properly respected. There can be little doubt that the growing awareness of the life-saving options available as a result of increasing global communications will help move halakhic discourse in the area of cadaver transplantation towards a more generous approach to donation.

Our discussion thus far has been anchored in the *halakhah,* and the views of halakhic authorities on the right balance between saving life and the proper treatment of dead bodies. There is, however, more to life than law, and cadaver transplantation is an area in which this observation is surely borne out by reality. There are a whole host of Jewish beliefs concerning dead bodies and the afterlife that seem to be incompatible with donation, and in the minds of many Jews, these beliefs often override clearly articulated legal doctrines.[98] Not donating cadaver organs for reasons of lore is apparently much more widespread than refraining from donation for reasons of law. As a result, education for cadaver donation cannot be limited to halakhic discourse; it must also include the living tradition and provide for its adjustment to a more spiritualized understanding of death and of life after death.

To sum up, the two recommendations for bridging the gap between *halakhah* and the modern policy of encouraging organ donation are the adoption of a personal-choice approach (limited autonomy) to live organ donations rather than the full-blown risk-avoidance doctrine of traditional *halakhah,* and the adaptation of the direct and immediate life-saving justification for cadaver donations to the realities of modern medicine. At the same time, it is important not to lose sight of the moral imperative to treat dead bodies with dignity, and any developments in this area of the law must take that imperative into account.

4. THE RATIONING OF SCARCE MEDICAL RESOURCES

Rationing is an issue in any area in which an economic argument can be made for limiting individual access to a particular resource, for the purposes of regulating its distribution, either in the present or in the future. It arises in relation to all forms of public expenditure, but is particularly controversial in the field of public medicine, since this is an area in which rationing may condemn certain members of the public to

---

[98] See E. Dorff, 'Jewish Law and Lore: The Case of Organ Transplantation', *Jewish Law Annual,* 12 (1997), 65. One of the major beliefs militating against organ donation is that of the resurrection of the dead (see L. Jacobs, *Principles of the Jewish Faith* (London, 1964), 398.

death. The growing expense of sophisticated medical treatment makes it impossible to ignore its economic ramifications, and even the most caring of contemporary physicians finds it difficult to avoid the issue of rationing as long as he continues to work in publicly funded medical practice.

The basic talmudic source for the question of rationing in this context is the mishnah, which discusses the extent to which the public purse must be depleted in order to save individual lives in relation to the rescue of captives.[99] The rule is that if Jews are taken captive, they must be redeemed by any Jewish community that learns of their plight, and their redemption takes precedence over every other charitable deed. However, they are to be redeemed at a fair price only. The community is not required to pay an exorbitant fee for the release of Jewish captives.[100] The Talmud seeks to clarify the reason for this rule, and one of its suggestions is that there is no obligation to pay ransoms that are so excessive that the community will be left without sufficient funds for its own upkeep.[101] Now the obligation to ransom captives overrides all other charities, because captives are considered to be in mortal danger every minute they remain in captivity; their release, as pointed out by Maimonides, also constitutes the fulfilment of the biblical commandment 'not to stand idly by your neighbour's blood'.[102] From the rule that the community is not required to impoverish itself in order to rescue captives, it may be concluded that in principle, the public is permitted to ration its resources even in situations in which some individuals are likely to lose their lives. According to R. Sofer, the rationale behind this conclusion is that the lack of adequate funding constitutes a threat to the physical, as well as to the financial welfare of the community as a whole, and the avoidance of such a threat, even if it is not as imminent as the threat to the captives themselves, must take precedence. Saving the lives of a whole community is superior to saving the lives of individuals.[103] Rationing life-saving resources with a view to benefiting the majority would thus appear to be legitimate under Jewish law.[104]

In another talmudic passage, the conflict between the saving of an individual's life and the welfare of the community as a whole comes into even sharper focus. Under rabbinic legislation, it is forbidden to keep small livestock such as sheep and goats in parts of the Land of Israel used for

---

[99] The obligation to ransom captives overrides almost all other forms of communal expenditure including the purchase of a synagogue (*Bava Bathra*, 8a–b; Maimonides, *Hilkhot Matnot Aniyim*, 8: 10–12).   [100] *Gittin* 4: 6.

[101] Ibid. 45a; *Yam Shel Shlomo, Gittin*, ch. 4 no. 66.

[102] See n. 49 and Maimonides, *Hilkhot Matnot Aniyim*, 8: 10.

[103] *Resp. Hatam Sofer, Hoshen Mishpat*, no. 177.

[104] See M. Hirshler, 'The Obligation to Save the Lives of the Dangerously Ill' (Heb.), *Halakhah Urefuah*, 2 (1971), 48.

agriculture, because these animals graze in such a way that the soil is eventually incapable of being used for agricultural purposes.[105] This prohibition was extended to keeping an animal in one's home in an agricultural area for any length of time. The Talmud relates that a certain pious man became sick and was told by his physician that he would only recover if he drank freshly obtained goat's milk every morning. A goat was brought into his house and it provided the milk, but the sages disapproved of his action and refused to enter his house in order to pay a sick visit.[106] R. Menahem Hameiri explains that even though the milk was necessary to save the man's life, he should not have kept the goat in his home in defiance of a rabbinic decree designed to save the population as whole from economic catastrophe and eventual starvation.[107] This approach fits in with the principle established in the law regarding the rescue of captives, that the long-term physical welfare of the community as a whole overrides that of individuals and their immediate needs.[108] Rationing medical resources for the sake of the common good would, therefore, appear to be a defensible position under Jewish law, although the specifics of any particular rationing scheme and the hierarchy of values it reflects will undoubtedly differ in certain respects from those currently under discussion in secular law.

Finally, it is the view of some modern authorities that rationing ought not to be introduced in the case of patients who have already commenced life-saving treatment. Such patients are in direct and immediate need of the treatment, and their need overrides the future needs of even a large majority. Mass rationing may be introduced once there are no patients who are presently receiving the rationed treatment.[109]

---

[105] *Bava Kamma*, 7: 7; *Tosefta, Shevi'it*, 3: 13.   [106] *Bava Kamma*, 80a.

[107] Ibid. *s.v. ma'aseh*. Other commentators come to a less forceful conclusion. According to Maharsha, the disease was not, in fact, life-threatening (ibid. *s.v. ma'aseh*). R. Shalom Shwadron maintains that the pious man was held blameworthy solely because of his own especially high standards of piety; regular individuals would be justified in keeping the goat in their homes notwithstanding the future threat to the community at large (*Resp. Maharsham*, 5 no. 54).

[108] It would also appear that the long-term preservation of the health of community A overrides the immediate life-saving needs of community B. The Talmud rules that spring water which is used for hygienic purposes by one village need not be diverted for the use of another village, the inhabitants of which do not have enough to drink. Since ignoring hygiene will eventually threaten the lives of the inhabitants of the first village, they are not under any obligation to forfeit their water in order to save the lives of the others (*Nedarim*, 80b).

[109] See *Encyclopaedia of Jewish Medical Ethics*, iv. 263–4.

Conclusion

1. LAW, MORALITY, AND CASUISTRY

Biomedical *halakhah* is a fundamentally legal enterprise. The rules and principles applied by the *halakhah* to biomedical matters are derived using typically legal reasoning from the normative texts of Jewish law. They are rooted in the Talmud, its commentaries and super-commentaries, halakhic codes and commentaries, super-commentaries on these codes, and in the *responsa* literature. These rules and principles have developed over a long period of time, and they provide a complex and richly textured framework for dealing with modern biomedical problems ranging from the challenges of the new genetics to the thorny legal and moral issues raised by the treatment of the terminally ill. The starting point for biomedical *halakhah* is legal rather than moral: morality influences the *halakhah* but it does not provide its foundation.

The legal rules and principles underlying Jewish biomedical *halakhah* are open to both wide and narrow interpretations. This is particularly evident in areas such as abortion and assisted reproduction. As a result, contemporary biomedical *halakhah* in these areas recognizes many diverse and competing views. Since broad moral principles such as the sanctity of life,[1] and natural reproduction,[2] do not trump legal doctrines in halakhic reasoning, the resulting discourse is pluralist in nature, although it may be complemented by a more definitive moral stance. The preservation of a fundamental distinction between law and morality in biomedical *halakhah* is an important factor in stimulating wide-ranging legal development even with regard to the most morally challenging issues in modern bioethics.

An interesting illustration of the constraining effect of broad moral principles upon legal development in relation to morally challenging questions is the recent decision of the English Court of Appeal on the surgical separation of the Siamese twins discussed in Chapter 5 section 6. Here the broad moral principle, whereby necessity can never be a defence to a murder charge, threatened to cut off the development of an equally morally justifiable legal doctrine permitting the separation. It will be recalled that one of the twins was born with a seriously

---

[1] See E. Keyserlingk, *Sanctity of Life or Quality of Life* (Ottawa, 1979), 19–20 for a discussion of the different forms of this principle in moral thought.   [2] See Ch. 2.

underdeveloped heart, and remained alive solely due to the blood supply generated by the heart of her stronger sister. The medical prognosis was that without the separation, both twins would die within the year; separation also meant that the weaker twin would die on the operating table. The twins' parents were practising Catholics who objected on religious grounds to the separation and, in effect, to the deliberate killing of one daughter. In order to help it justify its ruling permitting the separation, the court referred to the halakhic permission to sacrifice one fundamentally innocent life for the sake of another such life. Jewish law was invoked by the court because the common law, from the English Civil War onwards, had steadfastly refused to recognize the defence of necessity in relation to homicide, rendering it unable to provide any legal leeway for deferring to medical opinion in the present case. This refusal was based upon the adherence of the common law to a broad sanctity of life principle, which on moral grounds absolutely forbade giving up one innocent life for the sake of saving another. Whereas in most cases this broad approach is morally justifiable, the moral justification for adhering to it in the present case is much weaker, since killing the non-viable twin is the only way in which the life of the viable twin might possibly be saved. However, the acceptance of the broad principle by the common law was absolute, and the Court found itself without the necessary flexibility for dealing with the morally equivocal situation of the Siamese twins. The Court took a not insignificant interest in the complex approach of the *halakhah* to this type of situation and, together with the views and arguments of Law Commissioners and academic writers and its own reasoning, reached a decision that it felt was both morally sound—although not necessarily compelling—and legally correct. At the end of the day, the separation was ordered.

Now the above remarks relating to the fundamentally legal approach to this area must not be understood to mean that morality does not play any role in biomedical *halakhah*. As we have seen throughout the previous chapters, moral principles exert a significant influence on this field,[3] albeit not exerted in a direct fashion: morality plays out its role within the interstices of the law. Moral principles do not feature either as starting points for halakhic arguments or as norms that compete with or override those derived from legal doctrine. The influence of morality makes itself felt in an indirect and often unarticulated fashion. The relationship between the legal doctrine and the moral dimension is subtle, and often needs to be

---

[3] See e.g. the situation with regard to non-therapeutic foeticide (Ch. 1 s. 3); the issue of killing a human *terefah* (Ch. 5 s. 5), and the moral misgivings with respect to the use of assisted reproduction (Ch. 2 s. 4).

read between the lines or under the surface. More will be said on this topic in section 2 below.

An important feature of biomedical *halakhah* is the use of casuistic, or case-based, reasoning. The idea that a significant part of the legal decision-making process is taking into account the impact of a decision upon the lives of the people involved in the case and society at large is a pervasive feature of this field. Particularly good examples are to be found in relation to abortion,[4] artificial reproductive techniques,[5] and patient autonomy.[6] Now, the extreme form of casuistry, according to which the facts of the case are the sole motivating factor behind the decision, has often been identified with lack of moral foundation. In the halakhic context, however, the facts of the case do not constitute the sole factor in the decision-making process, with the result that the moral weightiness of the issues at stake is not diminished by the casuistic approach. On the contrary, the use of casuistry, in the positive sense of the term, helps to avoid the reduction of serious moral issues such as abortion to a superficial debate between holders of competing moral positions, who do not distinguish between the circumstances of different cases. Precisely because it is able to make subtle distinctions between very similar cases, based, *inter alia*, upon the effects of a particular decision upon the parties or on society in general, the *halakhah* is able to retain its moral integrity and provide a principled basis for decision-making in a wide range of circumstances. The value of this approach for contemporary bioethics in general has not gone unnoticed,[7] and in this respect too, Jewish law provides a valuable source for modern comparative biomedical law.

2. LAW, MORALITY, AND RATIONALITY

The influence of universal, rational morality upon Jewish biomedical law is a pervasive theme in the present work. As pointed out in Chapters 1 and 5, it is anchored in the need to preserve the fundamental moral fabric of society, a need that underlies the Noahide prohibition on bloodshed. This prohibition provides the formal justification for incorporating universal, rational morality into the halakhic system as a benchmark for testing the moral standard of halakhic rules. Universal, rational morality underlies the moral condemnation of non-therapeutic foeticide and the

---

[4] See e.g. the opinion of R. Waldenberg regarding the abortion of a Tay-Sachs foetus (Ch. 1 nn. 142–3.   [5] See e.g. R. Nebenzhal's opinion in relation to IVF (Ch. 2, n. 107).
[6] See Ch. 4.
[7] See A. Jonsen and S. Toulmin, *The Abuse of Casuistry* (University of California, 1988), ch. 17, for a general discussion of the potential benefit of the case-based method for modern bioethics.

killing of a human *terefah*, neither of which are subject to any definitive legal bar or positive human sanction. It also manifests itself in the halakhic responses to new technologies in the areas of human reproduction and genetic manipulation, as described in Chapter 3. In all these areas, a cautionary note is introduced into the purely legal discussion as a result of considerations of a fundamentally moral nature. Since issues affecting life and death, including the ways in which we reproduce life and tinker with its structure, affect the fundamental moral basis of all society, it is entirely fitting that their legal treatment be influenced by principles of a moral nature.

This moral input into biomedical *halakhah* is also necessary in the light of its casuistic nature. It was the trenchant criticism of the Catholic casuists by Blaise Pascal in the mid-seventeenth century that eventually lead to their downfall. Pascal focused on the existence of an intolerably wide gap between the largely case-driven legal framework established by the casuists, and the moral principles that were meant to be guiding them in their decisions. As a result he succeeded in bringing the entire casuistic enterprise into disrepute.[8] The *halakhah* avoids this pitfall by using broad moral principles as a means of restoring moral shape to any legal doctrine that seems to be seriously missing the moral mark as a result of its case-based orientation.

It is important to observe that the relationship between the legal and the moral elements in biomedical *halakhah* is a dynamic one in the sense that the former is never entirely displaced by the latter. Hence, even in a case in which the moral influence is present, the legal solution is still an option, and it may be applied if the circumstances indicate that the appropriate moral course of action is, in fact, to act in accordance with the strictly legal position. The discussion of non-life-saving abortions in relation to defective foetuses in Chapter 1, and of the sacrificing of a *terefah* to save viable life in Chapter 5, provide good illustrations of this interplay between law and morality. In both instances, the original legal position is complemented by a moral one that provides ample scope for a decision that deviates from the original legal doctrine. However, the moral position may in turn be displaced by the legal one in circumstances in which there are specific moral grounds for so doing. A case-specific moral justification is strong enough to justify retreating from the general moral position and deciding in accordance with pure law. The moral dimension never entirely supplants the legal dimension: it merely suspends it in certain cases, with the option that if it is morally justifiable, the legal position may well provide the solution at the end of the day.

---

[8] Ibid. ch. 12.

We have seen that the influence of the universal, rational morality of the Noahide prohibition on bloodshed on biomedical *halakhah* is expressed in a number of different forms in the literature. One form consists of expressions of moral wrongfulness, ranging from the most general, e.g. 'not allowed',[9] as in the case of non-therapeutic abortion, to the more specific, e.g. 'the abominations of Egypt' in the context of AID.[10] Included in this form is the labelling of non-therapeutic abortion 'a profanation of God's Name',[11] and the rejection of AID on the grounds that it poses a threat to the traditional Jewish value of the unity of the family.[12] Another form of moral condemnation is the invocation of Divine punishment and the extra-legal jurisdiction of the monarch, both of which figure in relation to non-therapeutic foeticide and the killing of a *terefah*. Finally, the moral dimension may make itself felt in a specific reference to non-Jewish morality, as in the case of R. Yair Bachrach's use of non-Jewish morality as an argument against the abortion of foetuses born to adulterous and promiscuous parents,[13] and the references in the *responsa* of R. Moses Zweig and R. Jacob Breisch to the Catholic position in their stringent rulings on the abortion of thalidomide foetuses, and AID, respectively.[14]

There references to the Catholic position on abortion raise an important issue with regard to the moral element in biomedical *halakhah*. It was explained at length in Chapter 1 that the moral dimension that operates in this area of the *halakhah* is of a universal, rational nature. Its basis lies in the Noahide laws, which, in theory at least, apply to all non-Jews to this very day. While it is possible that some religions of the world embrace the Noahide laws, they are not synonymous with any one religious system. These laws, and the morality they engender, retain their own special quality, which is their universal, rational nature. It is important to preserve this moral quality of Noahide law in its role as the moral benchmark of biomedical *halakhah*. Clearly, the content of any moral system is open to debate, and it has already been observed that the scope of the morality referred to in the context of the *halakhah* is the minimum necessary for the preservation of civilized society. Now, while it is to be expected that there will always be some controversy with regard to the content of this morality, it ought not to embrace moral principles that go well beyond the rational notion of the preservation of society and enter into the realm of ideology. In other words, the mandate provided by the Noahide laws to incorporate general moral principles is not an

---

[9] See Ch. 1 nn. 91–2.
[10] See Ch. 1 nn. 87–93.
[11] See Ch. 1 n. 138 and ch. 2 n. 91.
[12] See Ch. 2 n. 99.
[13] See Ch. 1 n. 132.
[14] See the sources cited in n. 11.

open-ended one. It is confined to the preservation of the basic morality required for the purpose of ensuring the survival of civilized society, and ought not to extend beyond that mandate.

It is particularly appropriate that the moral benchmark of halakhic bio-medical law is characterized by the feature of rationality. This is because the strictly legal basis for one of the fundamental legal principles in Jewish biomedical law, namely, that one innocent life may not be given up for the sake of preserving another, is pure reason. In seeking to find a legal basis for this principle, the Talmud eschews biblical proof-texts in favour of the rational argument: 'How do you know that your blood is redder? Perhaps the blood of the other person is redder?'[15] Reason *(sevarah)* constitutes a legal source of Jewish law, and it is characterized by 'an appreciation of the characteristics of human beings in their social relationships, and a careful study of the real world and its manifestations'.[16] Not only is the principle that one life may not be given up for the sake of saving another one based upon reason, but the exceptions to it are also derived on the basis of ration-ality alone. These exceptions were discussed extensively in Chapter 5, and are exemplified in the view of R. Menahem Hameiri, according to whom 'it seems quite clear' that the life of a *terefah* (someone suffering from a fatal condition) may be sacrificed in order to save an entire group of viable people.[17] The rationally compelling force of the argument that the life of a fatally ill person may be given up for the sake of saving a number of viable lives is sufficient to provide R. Hameiri with a halakhically valid conclu-sion. According to another commentator, the talmudic statement that 'the blood of one person is not redder than that of another' includes the poten-tial inference that if it can be shown that there is a basis for downgrading the blood of one individual in favour of another, the principle of treating all lives equally no longer applies.[18] Rationality is an important part of the legal aspect of biomedical *halakhah*, and in this respect, the application of rational morality is an extension of the existing law rather than the impo-sition of an external feature upon it. This point was made in Chapter 1, in which it was pointed out that the moral concepts are naturally applicable to abortion law by virtue of the moral significance of foetal life and its destruction, as opposed to the Sabbath laws which are essentially theolog-ical in nature and to which such principles are not naturally relevant.

The above-mentioned forms of expressing the moral influence on the *halakhah* in this area share a common feature, namely, the preservation of the boundary between law and morality. There are however, exceptions to

---

[15] *Sanhedrin*, 74a.   [16] M. Elon, *Jewish Law* (Philadelphia, 1994), 987.
[17] *Bet Habehirah, Sanhedrin*, 74a, s.v. *Venireh li pashut.*   [18] *Minhat Hinukh*, no. 296.

this rule, the most prominent of which is in the case of abortion. In that context, the boundary is often extremely unclear, and the moral element drives an attempt to found a firm legal prohibition on acts that are essentially free of any legal bar in Jewish law. A classic example of this form of moral influence is R. Feinstein's reasoning in the Tay-Sachs foetus debate, discussed at length in Chapter 1. This blurring raises serious concerns. Boundaries serve not only to keep things apart: their establishment is necessary in order to appreciate how different things influence each other. Boundaries cannot be crossed unless they exist. Halakhic authorities in the area of abortion have traditionally taken care to preserve the boundary between law and morality, even as they apply both elements to the case at hand. A good example is R. Yair Bachrach's *responsum* on the abortion of a *mamzer* foetus.[19] R. Bachrach states quite categorically that under 'the law of the Torah', abortion in the case of a *mamzer* foetus is 'perfectly permissible'. He nevertheless proceeds to rule against it on moral grounds, and explains that permission to abort would undermine the universally recognized necessity in both Jewish and non-Jewish society to deter immoral and promiscuous behaviour by prohibiting the abortion of the fruits of sin. Other authorities, such as R. Joseph Hayyim[20] and R. Yehiel Weinberg,[21] indicate—albeit far less explicitly—that it is important to preserve the existence of a boundary between law and morality with regard to halakhic decisions on abortion. The same applies to those authorities who make explicit reference to non-Jewish morality in the course of their halakhic decisions regarding biomedical matters.[22] Leaving aside the question of whether the particular moral principles they use accord with the moral tradition in this area of the *halakhah*, the fact that they give expression, however modest, to the moral dimension is significant. In the absence of any articulation of moral premises, it is easily assumed that only the purely legal aspects are relevant, and that there is no role for universal, rational morality in biomedical *halakhah*. In order to prevent this assumption from being made, the role of morality must be articulated. This can only be done if the boundary between legal and moral elements in this area of *halakhah* is properly preserved.

The issue of boundary preservation is a pervasive feature of general halakhic discourse, particularly in relation to the classical rubrics of biblical and rabbinic law.[23] A striking illustration of the motivation for blurring normative boundaries, and of the dangers involved in such a step, is the debate between two eminent European halakhic authorities in the early

---

[19] See Ch. 1 n. 132.   [20] See Ch. 1 n. 139.
[21] See Ch. 1 n. 76.
[22] See Ch. 1 n. 132 and n. 138.
[23] See Introduction, s. 4(c).

part of the nineteenth century. R. Moses Sofer, the staunchly Orthodox leader of Hungarian Jewry,[24] suggested that the distinction between biblical and rabbinic law be deliberately blurred in order to maintain mass observance of the *halakhah*. The specific context of this suggestion is the issue of delayed burial, which was a major debate between traditionalists and modernists, including the growing Reform movement, from the late eighteenth century onwards.[25] The normative status of the halakhic prohibition on delaying burial is unclear, and there are differing views as to whether it is biblical or rabbinic. There is also a debate as to whether it is a purely negative commandment, or a combination of both positive and negative injunctions. R. Sofer wrote that the prohibition was biblical as well as consisting of negative and positive injunctions, which makes it into a very formidable prohibition indeed.[26] An objection to this approach was raised by R. Zvi Hirsch Hayyes, a younger contemporary of R. Sofer, who had an unusually wide secular education for a traditional halakhic authority of the period. According to R. Hayyes, R. Sofer's legal categorization of the prohibition on delayed burial is not universally accepted in halakhic sources,[27] and R. Sofer ought, at least, to have given expression to the fact that there were different views on this matter. In his reply to this objection, R. Sofer explains that he does not feel bound to tell the whole truth regarding the legal pedigree of laws that are contested by reformers, such as that prohibiting delayed burial. In relation to such laws, the better course is to upgrade their normative status to that of biblical law, since that is the only way to ensure their observance amongst the community at large. R. Sofer proceeds to elucidate the dangers of telling the whole halakhic truth and its deleterious effects upon public observance, with an illustration drawn from the area of the Sabbath laws. R. Ezekiel Landau, one of the most prominent halakhic authorities at the end of the eighteenth century, dealt with the issue of Jewish-owned factories running on the Sabbath, and suggested various ways in which this could be done, if the result of Sabbath closure would be economic ruin for an entire community. In one of his *responsa* on this matter, R. Landau cited the view that the biblical prohibition on writing on the Sabbath only applies to Hebrew. Writing in any other language is prohibited at the

---

[24] Much has been written about R. Sofer and his important contribution to Orthodox ideology in Post-Emancipation times. An important essay is J. Katz, *Halakhah Vekabbalah* (Jerusalem, 1984), 353–86.

[25] See *Bikkurei Haitim* (1822–3), 209; M. Samet, 'Delaying Burial' (Heb.), *Assufot*, 3 (1989), 417–23.

[26] R. Sofer's *responsum*, together with R. Hayyes's reply, is found in *Kol Sifrei Maharatz Hayyes* 1, *Darkhei Hora'ah*, no. 6, 269–70.

[27] *Resp. Havvat Yair*, no. 139; R. Aaron of Worms, *Meorei Or*, Notes to *Sanhedrin*, 15a.

rabbinic level only.[28] R. Sofer is critical of R. Landau for articulating this view in his *responsum*. According to R. Sofer, it ought to have been suppressed, 'since it is now used by the wicked in order to justify writing in languages other than Hebrew on the Sabbath'. R. Hayyes takes issue with R. Sofer's approach and argues for normative purity and the preservation of the distinction between biblical and rabbinic law, even at the expense of possible mass transgression of the latter. He relies upon Maimonides' constant emphasis in his halakhic writings on the need to preserve the distinction between biblical and rabbinic law as an independent value,[29] and also on the biblical injunction 'to keep afar from a false matter'.[30] The obligation to tell the truth is a fundamental moral principle, and should not be displaced by the need to encourage religious observance.

It is worthwhile dwelling on the time-conditioned aspect of R. Sofer's approach. Clearly, in a generation in which the Reform movement was only beginning to make serious inroads into the traditional community, there may have been some pastoral wisdom in closing ranks against the modern world, and shoring up every aspect of traditional practice with as much support as possible, even at the expense of the normative purity of the *halakhah*. The efficacy of this approach, however, must be called into question with regard to a generation in which choices have been made, and there is no longer a large group of waverers for whose souls a genuine war may be waged. R. Abraham Kook raised this point in Mandatory Palestine at the beginning of the twentieth century in relation to a strict decision of R. Sofer regarding the use of legume oil on the Passover.[31] According to R. Kook, the social conditions under which R. Sofer's decision was made had changed, and it was doubtful if the stringency of his ruling was still justified in the light of the new circumstances. The decision in question turned on R. Sofer's staunch defence of all Jewish customs, despite the dubious normative grounds on which some of them were based. According to R. Kook, the reason for R. Sofer's approach lay in 'the need of the hour', i.e. the vital struggle against the Reform movement in the early nineteenth century. R. Sofer ruled stringently on matters of custom in order to uphold the old order in its entirety. In R. Kook's day, there was no longer a large group of waverers who might be swayed by R. Sofer's tactics: the vast majority of Jews had already made up their minds and had thrown in their lot with either the traditionalists or the modernists. The appropriate course of action in R. Kook's period was,

---

[28] *Resp. Noda Biyehuda*, pt. 2, *Orah Hayyim*, nos. 29, 33. In general, see J. Katz, *The 'Shabbes Goy'* (Philadelphia, 1989), 121–30.

[29] *Hilkhot Mamrim*, 2: 9.   [30] Exod. 23: 7.

[31] Ashkenazi Jews customarily refrain from using legumes (*kitniyot*) on Passover, except in emergency situations. The case dealt with by R. Kook involved oil derived from legumes, which is also subject to the customary bar. R. Sofer adopted a particularly stringent approach to the preservation of this custom, in all its forms (*Resp. Hatam Sofer, Orah Hayyim*, no. 122).

therefore, to draw a clear line between that which is absolutely prohibited, and that which is permitted, so that there is no doubt that any halakhic pronouncement must be taken seriously, and not regarded as a mere tactical device.[32]

This debate illustrates the reasons for the blurring of normative boundaries in the *halakhah*, and the dangers inherent in such a step. In the light of R. Kook's observations, the best course for contemporary *halakhah* is to prefer normative purity over possible pastoral benefits. The boundary between law and morality in modern biomedical *halakhah* is no exception to this recommendation. Clarifying the distinction between the legal and the moral in this area is the best way of encouraging interaction between them. Such interaction is vitally necessary for the continued development of contemporary biomedical *halakhah*. It would be a mistake if the distinction between morality and law was abandoned, and biomedical *halakhah* was presented in purely legal terms.

3. MEDICAL SCIENCE AND *HALAKHAH*

Halakhah is constantly being challenged by new developments in medical science. The ability to identify a genetically defective foetus, the use of artificial reproductive techniques, the knowledge that enables us to clone human beings, and the definition of brain-stem death are all examples of these challenges, and the bulk of this book is devoted to the halakhic responses to them. In each case it is evident that Jewish law strives to meet the challenges posed by scientific progress in a sophisticated manner. By its nature, law is slow in fashioning a definitive response to new discoveries in medical science. This is to be expected, since it would be unwise to attempt to forge a legal consensus in relation to a fresh scientific discovery without slow and careful deliberation regarding the effects of any new decision upon both the internal coherence of the legal system and upon society at large. The formulation of a response at the moral level takes even longer, since it is even more complex than the purely legal response, and is expressed in more subtle and indirect ways. Nevertheless, the time does eventually arrive for a legal system to set out a definitive response to new scientific and medical discoveries and techniques, and the *halakhah* has to decide whether to embrace the new developments wholly or only in part, or to maintain the old law without change. By virtue of its novelty, much of contemporary biomedical

---

[32] *Orakh Mishpat* (Jerusalem, 1977), no. 112. See H. Ben-Menahem, 'The Judicial Process and the Nature of Jewish Law', in N. Hecht, B. Jackson, S. Passamaneck, D. Piatelli, and A. Rabello (eds.), *An Introduction to the History and Sources of Jewish Law* (Oxford, 1996), 433–4.

halakhah is at the former slower and more speculative stage. Some insight into the process of developing a definitive approach in this area may be gained from the halakhic treatment of abortion. This topic, which was addressed in detail in Chapter 1, is one of the few in the area of biomedical *halakhah* that has a long and rich halakhic history. This history demonstrates that *halakhah* does eventually develop a definitive response to biomedical matters, and that that response often takes the form of a complex interplay between legal and moral elements in relation to a particular process or development.

In terms of the theoretical issue of the relationship between science and *halakhah*, it was observed in the second section of Chapter 6 that there are conflicting views with regard to the degree of enthusiasm with which fresh scientific discoveries ought to be incorporated into the *halakhah*. Maimonides, in his defence of additions to the list of fatal defects that render an animal unfit for consumption, makes it very clear that in his view it is necessary to adopt well-founded scientific discoveries, provided they do not come into conflict with existing halakhic norms and do not breach any of the systemic rules of Jewish law.[33] Maimonides' approach to the impact of science upon *halakhah* is undoubtedly informed by his rational view of knowledge and his belief in the need to synthesize all valid human understanding.[34] Not all halakhic authorities are of the same mind as Maimonides, and many are not prepared to adopt new and rationally compelling scientific insights as a matter of course. In their view, there is no need to be overzealous in incorporating new scientific knowledge into the *halakhah*, especially if it is in conflict with existing halakhic doctrines. There is no definitive position on this issue, although the ongoing engagement of Jewish law with new technologies, especially in the areas of assisted reproduction and genetics, indicates that the balance tilts in favour of Maimonides rather than his opponents.

More specifically, the issue of the incorporation of science into halakhic decisions arises in relation to cadaver donations for research purposes, a subject dealt with in the third section of Chapter 6. In this context, much turns on the question of whether halakhic authorities are prepared to recognize scientific progress as a value, and incorporate it into their decisions. Some authorities are keener than others to accept the halakhic relevance of the need to use cadavers for research, and the debate continues.

---

[33] Ch. 6, text at nn. 42–6. In adding to the closed list of fatal defects, Maimonides is accused of a breach of a systemic rather than a substantive rule of Jewish law. His response is to argue that the correct understanding of the closed nature of the list is that it may not be detracted from; additions, which are also logically related to existing defects, are acceptable.

[34] Ch. 4 n. 30.

Another important issue in relation to scientific input into the halakhic process is boundary preservation. In order to achieve a Maimonidean type of synthesis between science and *halakhah*, it is vital to define the exact boundaries of both disciplines, and to have a very clear idea of what constitutes sound science on the one hand, and valid *halakhah* on the other. In order that biomedical *halakhah* rise to the challenge of this synthesis, halakhists committed to it must cultivate expertise in both medical science and the systemic structure of Jewish law. This approach is particularly important for the halakhic analysis of very new issues such as genetics, discussed above in Chapter 3. In this field, it is vital to distinguish between sound science and mere speculation, and to define very clearly the halakhic stand on any particular issue. Systemic considerations are often as important as substantive ones, and just as it is necessary to establish whether genetically modified foods constitute a breach of the biblical ban on mixing species, it is necessary to establish the normative status, if any, of the idea that in general, humans should not alter the patterns of God's creation.[35] Clear and precise thinking is the key to the matching of science and religion in the halakhic context.

4. LIMITED PATIENT AUTONOMY

The roots of the concept of limited patient autonomy with respect to the termination of life-support, discussed at length in Chapter 4, lie both in the traditional concept of spiritual healing, and in the idea that in certain circumstances the patient's wishes are the correct answer to a biomedical problem in the *halakhah*. Autonomy in the strong form, i.e. the notion that respecting a person's wishes is a value that stands at the apex of the legal system as a whole, is not recognized in Jewish law. The concept of patient autonomy in biomedical *halakhah* is based upon the idea that patient preference is the appropriate response in a case in which there are strongly competing halakhic and moral norms. In particular, this notion applies to a terminal patient for whom the question is one of delaying death rather than of choosing a cure. In such a case, both precedent and rationality support factoring the patient's wishes into the halakhic decision, not because autonomy overrides the *halakhah*, but because it now has a role to play within the system. Also, the patient is not left with the feeling that *halakhah* simply ran out of answers at a critical point in his life. It is the *halakhah* itself that mandates patient preference in this type of case. It is important for rabbis dealing with the fatally ill and the dying to understand this point, and to be sufficiently open to the wishes of the patient,

[35] See Ch. 3 n. 88.

and the halakhic role those wishes may play, in order to provide complete halakhic guidance at the end of life.

Organ donation is another field in which the concept of respecting the donor's wishes may have a useful role to play in the *halakhah*. In Chapter 6 section 3, it was argued that the traditional halakhic criterion for permitting such transplants, namely, a favourable evaluation of the risk to the donor, ought to be broadened to include the donor's wishes. In a case in which the donor wishes to give the organ, but the objective assessment is evenly balanced, the donor's wishes should tip the scales in favour of transplantation.

The concept of limited autonomy is an important one for the relationship between *halakhah* and democracy. It demonstrates that modified democratic values are compatible with *halakhah*, provided that neither *halakhah* nor democracy insist on retaining their full blown forms. This issue was explored at length in Chapter 4 in relation to coercive life-saving medical therapy.

From a modern comparative perspective, limited autonomy is a useful concept, since few patients possess the medical knowledge necessary for making a truly informed decision regarding their treatment. The average patient operates within the parameters provided by his physician, and his own ethical and spiritual systems. Limited autonomy is a good way of describing what actually takes place at the level of the doctor–patient relationship. The situation at this level is quite different to the one suggested by strong autonomy and patients' rights discourse. Acknowledging the dependence of the patient upon the physician in determining the course of the former's medical treatment is likely to encourage a more realistic legal approach to the whole question of patient decision-making and informed consent.

5. LEGAL AND EXTRA-LEGAL DIMENSIONS

As indicated in the subtitle, this book explores some of the extra-legal dimensions of Jewish biomedical law, i.e. the relationship between morality and law, the influence of science upon the *halakhah*, and the growing awareness and implementation of patient autonomy. It is worthwhile noting that whereas the moral dimension has long been recognized as a part of the *halakhah* in this area, the influence of science upon the law has only become a major issue in modern times, and concern with the role of autonomy in Jewish medical law is a very recent development indeed. The legal sources we have sought to illuminate in the light of these extra-legal dimensions are, therefore, both ancient and contemporary, and range from the Talmud to the most recent *responsa*. By examining the broader picture, we have attempted to gain a richer understanding of these sources, and a fuller appreciation of the underlying theories governing the relationship between the legal and the extra-legal in biomedical *halakhah*. We have also invoked the extra-legal dimension in order to explain the not insignificant number of conflicting rulings issued by halakhic authorities in relation to issues such as abortion and assisted reproduction.

In our view, this approach to biomedical law is particularly appropriate for a legal topic that requires us to engage in an analysis of the most basic moral issues encountered by human society. A purely legal perspective would not do justice to the complexity of this topic, and this is true for both general biomedical law, and the *halakhah*. This is an area in which the law cannot be fully understood without an appreciation of its extra-legal dimensions.

At the same time, sight must not be lost of those settled principles of law that have governed the field of biomedical law since ancient times. The legal foundations of biomedical *halakhah* are a vital source of stability in a highly complex and morally controversial world. In order to grapple successfully with the growing challenge of biomedical law, therefore, the contemporary jurist needs to be true to settled legal doctrine and sensitive to its broader implications. In the biomedical sphere, the quest for a synthesis between the legal and the extra-legal is undoubtedly the face of the future.

Appendix: The Israeli Draft Law: The Terminally Ill Patient, 5762-2002

1. The Public Committee Concerning the Terminally Ill Patient[1]

In February 2000, the Minister of Health established a Public Committee for the purpose of drawing up draft legislation regarding the medical treatment of the terminally ill in Israel. Prof. A. Steinberg, a pediatric neurologist, professor of medical ethics, and author of *The Encyclopaedia of Jewish Medical Ethics* was appointed chair of the Committee. The Committee was eventually divided into four subcommittees in the following areas of specialization: medicine, law, philosophy, and *halakhah*. Each subcommittee was headed by a noted authority in its area of responsibility, and consisted of a number of experts in that area. The full Committee consisted of fifty-nine members.

The Committee was asked to produce a draft law as quickly as possible, and it did so in January 2002. The draft law was accompanied by a short report, the brevity of which was the result of the need to formulate the proposed law with a minimum of delay. In its report, the Committee pointed out that it intended, at some time in the future, to publish a lengthy volume containing written contributions by the individual members, and important source material upon which the Committee relied.

The first part of this appendix provides a summary of the report. The second part outlines the major features of the draft law, and comments on the background to some of its provisions. The third part is a brief comment on the draft law in the light of the discussion of the terminally ill in the present volume.

The report begins with a list of reasons for the emergence of the treatment of the terminally ill patient as one of the most pressing bioethical issues in recent times. These reasons include the existence of medical technology capable of keeping people alive even though their physical and mental quality of life is negligible, the rejection of medical paternalism together with the rise of patient autonomy, the wide divergence of moral positions with regard to the treatment of the terminally ill amongst both society at large and the medical profession, the growing public awareness of, and involvement in, the treatment of this type of patient, and, finally, the problem of allocating scarce medical resources to terminal individuals.

The next section of the report deals very briefly with the medical and legal background to the terminally ill and their treatment in Israel. Notwithstanding the absence of any definitive documented evidence, it is clear that in the medical context, there is no uniform approach to this issue. The treatment of these patients varies from medical centre to medical centre, from department to department within the same centre, and, on occasion, from doctor to doctor within the same

---

[1] A. Steinberg, 'The Report of the Public Committee on the Terminally Ill Patient' (Heb.), *Assia* 69–70 (April, 2002) 5–23.

department. This is not a satisfactory state of affairs, and the development of a uniform medical approach to this area was a major factor in the Minister of Health's decision to convene the Committee.

In relation to the case-law, it was noted that there was only one Supreme Court decision expressing an opinion on this issue, and it tended to favour the sanctity of life principle over that of patient autonomy.[2] There have been a number of decisions in this area at the District Court level, and they generally tend to favour patient autonomy over the sanctity of life principle.[3] The feature common to all the legal decisions in this area is the struggle with the problem of finding the right balance between the principles of human dignity and freedom, and the values of Judaism, including that of human life, upon which the State of Israel is based.[4] The search for this balance also underlies the provisions of the proposed draft law.

As far as legislation is concerned, a draft law on the issue of advance medical directives is currently before the Law and Constitution Committee of the Knesset. This draft law, however, is still in the very earliest stage of discussion by the Committee, and it is much narrower in scope than the draft law under discussion.

It is noteworthy that a section stating that 'a terminal patient has a right to die with dignity, and is entitled, whenever possible, to medical support in order to help him realize that right', was deleted from the final version of the Israeli Patient's Rights Law, 1996, on the grounds that it did not offer any definition of the terminal condition, or specify the type of treatment that could be withheld or withdrawn. Clearly, there is a pressing need for comprehensive and detailed legislation based upon the notion of a balance between sanctity of life and patient autonomy in this area.

The Committee's goal in the legal area was to achieve as broad a consensus as possible between opposing views in Israeli society regarding the treatment of the terminally ill, and to produce a draft law tailored to the special needs of the State of Israel. The Committee did not neglect the comparative aspect, and reviewed the legal arrangements adopted in this area by a number of different countries. It also considered the positions of the major non-Jewish religious groups in Israel, i.e. Catholic, Moslem, and Druze. In the final analysis, the Committee strove to forge its consensus within the legislative framework of the basic values of the State of Israel—Judaism and democracy, and the draft law reflects this uniquely Israeli approach to the issues raised by the treatment of the terminally ill patient.

In terms of moral issues, the report mentioned that the Committee concentrated on the value of human life, the quality of life, patients' rights, the principle of beneficence, avoidance of harm, and the just allocation of scarce medical resources. Secondary issues included the slippery slope argument in this area of the law, the

---

[2] *Yael Sheffer* v. *State of Israel*, CA 506/88, PD 48 (1) 87. This case was discussed in Ch. 4 s. 7, and again at the end of Ch. 5 s. 2. See also D. Sinclair, 'Jewish Law in the State of Israel', *Jewish Law Annual*, 12 (1997), 259.

[3] See the cases mentioned in Ch. 4 nn. 137–8. See also *Arad* v. *General Health Fund*, PM 2349/95, PM 55 (2) 253; *Gilad* v. *Soroka*, PM 1030/95, PM 56 (1) 441. There are approximately twenty District Court decisions in this area, but most of the recent ones are still unpublished. See also Sinclair, 'Jewish Law', 263.

[4] See Human Dignity and Freedom Act, 1992, section 8, and Sinclair, 'Jewish Law', 260.

question of who should make the definitive decision with regard to the withholding or withdrawing of treatment, the issue of decision-making in cases where the medical outcome is an uncertain one, and the physician's role with respect to terminal patients. Detailed discussion of these issues was reserved for the forthcoming volume.

2. Draft Law: The Terminally Ill Patient, 5762-2002[5]

Under this draft law, there is a presumption that every person wishes to live. The presumption of life may, however, be rebutted in the case of a terminal patient, who is defined as a person suffering from an incurable medical condition, and whose life expectancy does not exceed six months.[6] If the terminal patient is competent, then the presumption of life may be rebutted by his most recent statement to the effect that he wishes to die. In relation to an incompetent patient, the presumption may be rebutted by valid advance medical directives, or on the instructions of a duly-appointed medical surrogate. In addition, the physician responsible for the incompetent terminal patient may conclude, on the basis of clear evidence given by family or friends, or the view of the patient's guardian, that there is no longer any presumption in favour of continued survival.

Any doubts as to the rebuttal of the presumption are to be resolved in favour of the preservation of life. In a case in which there is a disparity between any of the above-mentioned methods for rebutting the presumption, or if the treating physician finds himself in disagreement with any of them, the matter is to be resolved by the hospital ethics committee.

Every person over the age of 17 years is presumed competent, unless there is a qualified and documented medical opinion to the contrary. If the patient is unwilling to accept the treating physician's decision regarding his lack of competence, the issue is to be resolved by the hospital ethics committee. The ethics committee is also empowered to resolve disputes between parents and physicians with regard to the medical treatment of terminal minors.

The draft law provides that a competent terminal patient's request to have life-prolonging medical treatment beyond that offered by the medical staff must be honoured. The only exceptions are procedures which, from a medical point of view, will not, in fact, prolong the patient's life, or are likely to do him damage.

---

[5] *Assia*, 69–70 (April 2002), 24–58.

[6] Six months is also the time-factor in the definition of a terminally ill person in Oregon's Death With Dignity Act, 1997. As pointed out in Ch. 5 s. 2, contemporary halakhists do not define the dying individual (*goses*) in quantitative terms. In terms of Jewish law, therefore, the Committee was certainly free to adopt any reasonable quantification of the terminal condition for the purposes of the draft law. One may, however, ask why the twelve-month limit used in relation to the *terefah* (Ch. 5 s. 5) was not adopted in order to define this condition. Presumably, the answer is that the Committee thought that this was too long a period for defining the terminal condition in a modern context.

In the absence of a presumption of life, no medical treatment may be administered to a competent terminal patient without his informed consent.[7] At the same time, the draft law provides that the medical staff is obliged to make every effort in order to encourage such a patient to agree to receive medically indicated oxygen, nutrition, hydration, standard medication, and palliative care. This provision is presented in the notes to the draft law as the result of a balance between the halakhic obligation to maintain all basic life-support, and the democratic right to refuse all forms of medical treatment, including procedures aimed at maintaining basic physical functions. The halakhic justification for this concession is that although coercive life-preserving treatment is in principle mandated by Jewish law, there is a view that it does not apply to the terminally ill on the grounds that the trauma induced by physical coercion is itself likely to hasten that person's death.[8] The use of physical force in this context is also undignified and impractical. A directive to the medical staff strongly to encourage the patient to accept basic life-preserving procedures is, therefore, the appropriate halakhic response to a competent terminal patient who no longer wishes to live. The democratic right to refuse treatment in this context is entirely compatible with a strong medical recommendation to accept such basic necessities as oxygen and nutrition.

The withholding of treatment from an incompetent terminal patient is governed by the provisions relating to the rebuttal of the presumption in favour of life outlined above. In addition, a physician is permitted to withhold extraordinary medical treatment in the case of an end-stage incompetent patient, i.e. a person suffering from the failure of more than one vital physical system, who has less than two weeks to live. Extraordinary medical treatment is defined by the draft law as any procedure with a low success rate, or experimental in nature, or likely to cause suffering to the patient or significant damage to his health.

Thus far on the issue of withholding treatment. In relation to the withdrawing of medical treatment from both the competent and the incompetent patient, the draft law makes a basic distinction between continuous medical treatment, which is not designed to be administered at intervals nor to be stopped in order that the patient may be examined between treatment cycles, and periodic treatment that is designed to be administered at separate intervals and renewed on the basis of diagnostic evaluation between cycles. It is forbidden to withdraw continuous medical treatment in circumstances in which such withdrawal is likely to lead to the patient's death, unless the withdrawal is justified on grounds of a purely medical nature. On the other hand, periodic treatment aimed at treating the patient's terminal condition may be withdrawn in order to prevent significant suffering.

---

[7] In the case of a non-terminal patient, coercive life-saving therapy may be administered under section 15 (2) of the Patients' Rights Law, 1996. As pointed out at the end of Ch. 4 s. 7, the conditions for the administration of such therapy are approval by the hospital ethics committee, full disclosure to the patient of the medical situation and proposed treatment, unanimous medical opinion as to the need to carry out the proposed procedure, and a reasonable basis for assuming that the patient will, in fact, consent retroactively to the procedure.

[8] The holder of this view is, of course, R. Feinstein, whose *responsa* on this issue (*Resp. Iggrot Moshe, Hoshen Mishpat*, 2 nos. 73–4) were cited in the context of our discussion of limited patient autonomy in Jewish law at the end of Ch. 4 s. 5.

In the notes to the draft law, it is pointed out that continuous treatment is basically confined to artificial respiration, and that periodic treatment includes most of the other procedures commonly carried out with respect to terminally ill patients, e.g. chemotherapy, radiotherapy, and dialysis. Resuscitation is also regarded as a periodic treatment. Mention is also made in the notes of the possibility that an appropriately designed 'time-clock' may be used in order to transform continuous treatment into the periodic form.[9] This possibility is currently being investigated by experts in *halakhah* and technology.

The sections dealing with this distinction and its application to the terminally ill were the most controversial aspect of the draft law. On the one hand, strong supporters of the halakhic approach and of the sanctity of life principle rejected any distinction between different types of treatment, and insisted that it was forbidden to discontinue any life-maintaining procedure until the establishment of death. On the other hand, committed adherents of patient autonomy rejected the above-mentioned distinction on the grounds that the autonomy principle ought to be the dominant one, and the fact that the treatment was continuous ought not to stand in the way of it being terminated should the patient so desire. The overwhelming majority of the Committee, however, felt that the distinction between continuous and periodic treatment was the best way of balancing the two competing principles, and of fulfilling the requirements of both Judaism and democracy in this highly controversial area of contemporary law and bioethics.

It ought, however, to be pointed out that the national ethics committee is empowered to make specific recommendations with regard to such cases.

The draft law also deals with the administration of analgesics, and provides that life-shortening palliative treatment is to be provided to all terminal patients, provided that the degree of danger posed by the treatment to the patient's life is not unduly serious. The basis for this provision, cited in the notes to the draft law, is the double-effect doctrine, according to which it is permitted to perform an act leading to both a morally virtuous result and a morally deleterious one, provided that the sole intention of the person performing the act is to achieve the morally virtuous effect.[10]

The draft law explicitly forbids both active euthanasia by physicians and physician-assisted suicide.

The draft law also deals with a number of procedural issues including the documentation of decisions regarding the treatment of terminal patients, the drawing up and implementation of advance medical directives, the appointment and

---

[9] This possibility was raised by R. Eliezer Waldenberg in his leading *responsum* on the treatment of the terminally ill in Jewish law (*Resp. Ziz Eliezer*, 13 no. 89) cited in Ch. 5 s. 2(b).

[10] See J. Mason and R. McCall Smith, *Law and Medical Ethics* (London, 1999), 437–8. This doctrine does not figure in halakhic sources. The reason given for administering life-shortening analgesics under Jewish law relates to the issue of causation, i.e. no one dose is sufficient to cause death, and in such circumstances, the paramount value is the prevention of suffering, see Ch. 5 nn. 78–9.

powers of a health proxy, the procedure for appealing the proxy's decision, combining advance directives and a health proxy, cancelling and amending advance directives, and the exemption of physicians and ethics committee members from legal liability for acts performed or omitted in accordance with this draft law.[11]

Noteworthy amongst these procedural issues are the membership, appointment, powers, and procedures of ethics committees. All institutional committees are to include medical experts, a rabbi (or in the case of a non-Jew, an appropriate religious authority), and a lawyer. A novel feature of the draft law is the provision for a national ethics committee for the purpose of resolving disputes between institutional ethics committees, hearing appeals, and dealing with exceptional cases. The national committee is to include an ethicist, a nursing sister, and a social worker or clinical psychologist, in addition to the standard combination of medical specialists, rabbi or other religious authority, and lawyer. All members of the national committee are to be senior personnel in their respective areas of specialization. Appeals from the national committee go to a three-judge bench of the District Court.

The final section of the draft law deals with physicians who object, on grounds of conscience, values, or medical discretion, to providing or withholding treatment under this law. In such circumstances, the physician may refer the patient to another doctor, in accordance with hospital regulations.

In conclusion, it ought to be pointed out that the draft law received the unqualified approval of forty-eight members of the Committee. This is certainly a significant majority—81 per cent—and it indicates the general feeling amongst the members of the Committee that the draft proposal was the best balance that could be achieved at the present time between the demands of Judaism and democracy in this area. The dissenting opinions attached to the report were mainly in relation to the distinctions between withholding and withdrawing of treatment, and between continuous and periodic procedures. Only one Committee member rejected the absolute prohibition on physician-assisted suicide. There was no support whatsoever amongst the dissenting opinions for active euthanasia by physicians.

3. Comment

In the light of our discussion in Chapters 4 and 5 above, it is evident that the major analytical concepts codified in the draft law are based upon contemporary Israeli halakhic thinking in this area. The draft law's major contribution is the development of methods and procedures for the application of these concepts in a medical context, and the creation of mechanisms for dealing with hard cases, which have a tendency to arise fairly frequently in relation to the terminally ill. A number of halakhic concepts raised in the above-mentioned chapters do not appear to have been taken into account

---

[11] The legal liabilities of physicians are dealt with under the Patients' Rights Law, 1996. The proposed law will not affect these liabilities, nor those of ethics committee members under that law.

by the Committee. Amongst these are the law governing the *terefah*,[12] and the tentative distinction made between natural and artificial means of life-support.[13]

Nevertheless, the provisions laid down in the draft constitute a significant attempt to bridge the gap between contemporary *halakhah* and modern bioethical trends in a practical medical context and, as such, they represent an important contribution to Jewish biomedical law in relation to the terminally ill patient.

[12] Ch. 5 s. 5.   [13] Ch. 5 nn. 61–3.

Select Bibliography

AMSEL, M., 'Further Important Details Regarding Artificial Insemination' (Heb.), *Hamaor*, 16 (1965), 147.

ANNAS, G., 'Siamese Twins: Killing One to Save the Other', *Hastings Centre Report*, 17 (1987), 27.

APTOWITZER, A., 'The Status of the Embryo in Jewish Law', *Jewish Quarterly Review*, 15 (1924), 85.

ARIES, P., *Western Attitudes Toward Death: From the Middle Ages to the Present* (Johns Hopkins University Press, Baltimore, 1974).

ASHWORTH, A., *Principles of Criminal Law* (Oxford University Press, Oxford, 1999).

ATLAS, S., *Netivim Bemishpat Ivri* (American Academy for Jewish Research, New York, 1978).

AUERBACH, S., 'Artificial Insemination' (Heb.), *Noam*, 1 (1958), 145.

—— 'Organ Transplants From Cadavers to the Dangerously Ill' (Heb.), *Assia*, 53–4 (1994), 26.

AVINER, S., 'Genetic Engineering, Free Will and Hazardous Experiments on Human Beings' (Heb.), *Assia*, 61–2 (1998), 43.

BAER, I., 'The Religious-Social Tendency of *Sefer Hasidim*' (Heb.), *Zion*, 1 (1948), 3.

BAR-ILAN, N., 'Halakhic Aspects of Bone-Marrow Transplants' (Heb.), *Assia*, 51–2 (1992), 59.

BAZAK, J. 'Caesarian Section After Brain Death' (Heb.), *Assia*, 65–6 (1999), 13.

BELKIN, S., *Philo and the Oral Law* (Harvard University Press, Cambridge, Mass., 1940).

BENAMOZEGH, E. *Israël et l'humanité* (Ernest Leroux, Paris, 1914).

BEN-MEIR, Y., 'The Lineage of a Child Born to A Surrogate Mother and an Egg Donor' (Heb.), *Assia*, 41 (1986), 25.

BEN-OR, G., 'Cloning and Artificial Reproduction Techniques' (Heb.), *Assia*, 61–2 (1998), 10.

BEN-SHLOMO, E., 'Rejecting Medical Therapy on Grounds of Piety' (Heb.), *Assia*, 49–50 (1990), 73.

BEN-ZIMRA, E., 'Halakhic Decisions Relating to the Sanctity of Life and Martyrdom in the Holocaust Period' (Heb.), *Sinai*, 80 (1977), 151.

BICK, E., 'Foetal Implants' (Heb.), *Tehumin*, 7 (1986), 266.

—— 'Ovum Donations: A Rabbinic Conceptual Model of Maternity', *Tradition*, 28 (1993), 28.

Biomedical Legal Decisions (Heb.) (Israel Medical Association, Tel Aviv, 1989).

BLEICH, J. D., 'Maternal Identity', *Tradition*, 19 (1981), 359.

—— 'Natural Law', *Jewish Law Annual*, 7 (1988), 5.

—— 'Of Cerebral, Respiratory and Cardiac Death', *Tradition*, 24 (1989), 44.

—— 'Fetal Tissue Research', *Tradition*, 24 (1989), 69.

—— 'Maternal Identity Revisited', *Tradition*, 28 (1993), 51.

—— *Contemporary Halakhic Problems*, i (Ktav Publishing House, New York, 1977); iv (1995).

—— *Bioethical Dilemmas* (Ktav Publishing House, Hoboken, NJ, 1998).

BLEICH, J. D., 'Cloning: Homologous Reproduction in Jewish Law', *Tradition*, 32 (1998), 47.

—— 'Genetic Screening', *Tradition*, 34 (2000), 63.

BLIDSTEIN, Y., 'On Political Structures—Four Medieval Comments', *Jewish Journal of Social Studies*, 22 (1980), 54.

—— *Ikkronot Mediniim Bemishnat Harambam* (Bar Ilan University Press, Ramat Gan, 1983).

—— 'Ideal and Real in Classical Jewish Political Theory', *Jewish Political Studies Review*, 2 (1990), 54.

BROYDE, M., 'The Establishment of Maternity and Paternity in Jewish and American Law', *National Jewish Law Review*, 3 (1988), 117.

—— 'Cloning People: A Jewish Law Analysis of the Issues', *Connecticut Law Review*, 30 (1998), 503.

BURNS, C. (ed.), *Legacies in Ethics and Medicine* (Science History Publications, New York, 1977).

CANTOR, N., 'A Patient's Decision to Decline Life-Saving Medical Treatment', *Rutgers Law Review*, 26 (1973), 228.

—— *Legal Frontiers of Death and Dying* (Indiana University Press, Bloomington, 1987).

—— *Advance Directives and the Pursuit of Death with Dignity* (Indiana University Press, Bloomington, 1993).

CARDOZO, B., *Law and Literature and Other Addresses* (F. B. Rothman, Littleton, Colo., 1986).

CORINALDI, M., "The Legal Status of a Child Born Using Donor Sperm on Eggs", (Heb.), *Sheratan Hanishpat Haiwri*, 18–19 (1992–1994), 295.

CAULFIELD, T. 'Clones, Controversy, and Criminal Law', *Alberta Law Review*, 39 (2001), 341.

CHAJES, Z. H., *The Student's Guide Through the Talmud*, trans. J. Shachter (Feldheim Publishers, New York, 1960).

CHURCH, F. (trans.), *The Trial and Death of Socrates* (Macmillan, London, 1910).

COGGAN, D., 'On Dying and Dying Well', *Proceedings of the Royal Society of Medicine*, 70 (1977), 75.

Congregation for the Doctrine of the Faith, 1980, Declaration on Euthanasia, *Origins* 10 (1980), 154.

CORNS, C., 'Deciding the Fate of Frozen Embryos', *Law Institute Journal*, 64 (1990), 273.

COULSON, N., *A History of Islamic Law* (Edinburgh University Press, 1964).

COVER, R., *Justice Accused* (Yale University Press, New Haven, Conn., 1975).

D'ENTRÈVES, A., *Natural Law* (Hutchinson, London, 1970).

DAUBE, D., *Collaboration With Tyranny in Rabbinic Law* (Oxford University Press, London 1965).

DEFEVER, M., 'The Policies of Organ Transplantation in Europe: Issues and Problems', *Health Policy*, 16 (1990), 95.

DIENSTAG, J., 'Natural Law in Maimonidean Thought and Scholarship', *Jewish Law Annual*, 6 (1987), 75.

DORFF, E., *Matters of Life and Death: A Jewish Approach to Medical Ethics* (Jewish Publication Society, Philadelphia, 1988).

—— 'A Jewish Approach to End-Stage Medical Care', *Conservative Judaism*, 43 (1991), 3.

—— 'Jewish Law and Lore: The Case of Organ Transplantation', *Jewish Law Annual*, 12 (1997), 65.

DORFF, E., and NEWMAN, L. (eds.), *Contemporary Jewish Ethics and Morality* (Oxford University Press, Oxford, 1995).

DRAKE, D. 'The Twins Decision: One Must Die So One Can Live', *Philadelphia Inquirer*, 6 October 1977.

DRESSER, R. 'Ethical and Legal Issues in Patenting New Animal Life', *Journal of Jurimetrics*, 28 (1998), 399.

DWORKIN, G., *The Theory and Practice of Autonomy* (Cambridge University Press, Cambridge, 1988).

DWORKIN, R., *Life's Dominion* (Harper Collins, London, 1993).

DWORKIN, R., *Limits: The Role of Law in Bioethical Decision Making* (Indiana University Press, Bloomington, 1996).

DYSON, A., and HARRIS, J. (eds.), *Experiments on Embryos* (Routledge, London, 1990).

EDELSTEIN, L., *Ancient Medicine* (Johns Hopkins University Press, Baltimore, 1987).

ELIYAHU, M., 'Discarding Fertilised Eggs and Foetal Reduction' (Heb.), *Tehumin*, 11 (1991), 272.

ELLINSON, G., 'The Foetus in the *Halakhah*' (Heb.), *Sinai*, 66 (1970), 20.

ELON, M. (ed.), *The Principles of Jewish Law* (Keter Publishing House, Jerusalem, 1974).

—— *Jewish Law: History, Sources, Principles* (Jewish Publication Society, Philadelphia, 1994).

ENKER, A., *Hekhreah Vezorekh Bamishpat Haivri* (Bar Ilan University Press, Ramat Gan, 1977).

ETKIN, W., 'Jacob's Cattle and Modern Genetics', *Tradition*, 7 (1965), 5.

FAUR, J., *Iyyunim Bemishneh Torah* (Mossad Harav Kook, Jerusalem, 1978).

FEDERBUSCH, S., *Hamussar Vehamishpat Bevisrael* (Mossad Harav Kook, Jerusalem, 1979).

FEINSTEIN, M. 'Endangering Transient Life for the Sake of a Doubtful Recovery' (Heb.), *Halakhah Urefuah*, 1 (1980), 131.

—— 'Concerning Brain Death' (Heb.), *Assia*, 53–4 (1994), 24.

FELDMAN, D., *Marital Relations, Birth Control and Abortion in Jewish Law* (Schocken, New York, 1974).

FELGNER, P., 'Non-Viral Strategies for Gene Therapy', *Scientific American*, 276 (1997), 86.

FINNIS, J., *Natural Law and Natural Rights* (Oxford University Press, Oxford, 1980).

FIRRER, B., 'Regarding Artificial Procreation' (Heb.), *Noam*, 6 (1964), 295.

FOX, M., 'Maimonides and Aquinas on Natural Law', *Dine Israel*, 5 (1972), 1.

FRIMER, D., 'On the Element of Intention in the Law of the Pursuer' (Heb.), *Or Hamizrah*, 22 (1984), 309.

—— 'Israel, the Noahide Laws and Maimonides', *Jewish Law Association Studies*, 2 (1986), 89.

—— 'Jewish Law and Science in the Writings of R. Isaac Halevy Herzog', *Jewish Law Association Studies*, 5 (1991), 33.

FULLER, L., 'The Speluncean Explorers', *Harvard Law Review*, 62 (1948–9), 616.

FULLER, L., *The Morality of Law* (Yale University Press, New Haven, Conn., rev. edn., 1969).

GANZ, C., 'The Frozen Embryos of the Nahmani Couple' (Heb.), *Iyyunei Mishpat*, 18 (1994), 83.

GLAZEBROOK, P., 'The Necessity Plea in English Criminal Law', *Cambridge Law Journal* (1972), 118–19.

GLOVER, J., *Causing Death and Saving Lives* (Penguin Books, London, 1981).

GOLDBERG, N., 'Establishing Maternity in the Case of Foetal Implants' (Heb.), *Tehumin*, 5 (1984), 249.

—— 'Terminating Artificial Respiration in the Case of a Fatally Ill Patient in Order to Save a Potentially Viable Individual' (Heb.), *Emek Halakhah Assia*, 1 (1986), 83.

GOODMAN, M., COHEN, J., and SORKIN, D. (eds.), *The Oxford Handbook of Jewish Studies* (Oxford University Press, Oxford, 2002).

GOREN, S., 'Embroyo Transplantation According to the Halakhah' (Heb.), *Hazofeh*, 17 December 1984.

GRAZI, R. (ed.), *Be Fruitful and Multiply* (Genesis Press, Jerusalem, 1994).

GRISEZ, G., 'Should Nutrition and Hydration be Provided to Permanently Comatose and Other Mentally Disabled Patients?' *Linacre Quarterly*, 57 (1990), 31.

HALEVY, H. D., 'Removing a Patient With No Chance of Recovery from an Artificial Respirator' (Heb.), *Tehumin*, 2 (1981), 304.

—— 'On Foetal Reduction' (Heb.), *Assia*, 47–8 (1989), 14.

—— 'Non-Consensual Medical Treatment' (Heb.), *Hazofeh*, 18 July 1991.

HALPERIN, M., 'Heart Transplants in Jewish Law' (Heb.), *Sefer Assia*, 5 (1986), 68.

—— 'Halakhic Aspects of Live Organ Transplantation' (Heb.), *Assia*, 45–6 (1989), 57–9.

—— 'Organ Transplants From Living Donors in Jewish Law' (Heb.), *Assia*, 45–6 (1989), 34.

—— 'The Legal Implications of the Chief Rabbinate's Decision Regarding Heart Transplants in Israel' (Heb.), *Assia*, 47–8 (1989), 111.

—— 'The "You Shall Not Stand Idly by The Blood of Your Neighbour" Law' (Heb.), *Assia*, 65–6 (1999), 5.

HANNAM, P., 'In Vitro Fertilisation', *Irish Theological Quarterly*, 55 (1989), 14.

HARRIS, J., *Violence and Responsibility* (Routledge, Kegan & Paul, London, 1980).

HART, H., *The Concept of Law* (Oxford University Press, Oxford, 1964).

HECHT, N., JACKSON, B., PASSAMANECK, S., PIATELLI, D., and RABELLO, A. (eds.), *An Introduction to the History and Sources of Jewish Law* (Oxford University Press, Oxford, 1996).

HERZOG, I., 'The King's Right to Pardon Offenders in Jewish Law' (Heb.), *Hatorah Vehamedinah*, 1 (1949), 18.

—— *The Main Institutes of Jewish Law* (Soncino Press, London, 1965).

HIRSHLER, M., 'Test Tube Babies According to the Halakhah' (Heb.), *Halakhah Urefah*, 1 (1980), 313.

—— 'Kidney Donation from an Incompetent and Brain Damaged Donor' (Heb.), *Halakhah Urefuah*, 2 (1981), 122.

—— 'The Obligation to Save the Lives of Sick and Dangerously Ill Individuals' (Heb.), *Halakhah Urefuah*, 2 (1981), 35.

Human Genetics: The Science and its Consequences (Science and Technology Committee of the House of Commons, HMSO, London, 1995).

HUSIK, I., 'The Law of Nature, Hugo Grotius and the Bible', *Hebrew Union College Annual*, 2 (1925), 406.

ISERSON, K., *Death to Dust* (Galen Press, Tucson, Ariz., 1994).

JACKSON, B., *Essays in Jewish and Comparative Legal History* (E. J. Brill, Leiden, 1975).

—— 'The Concept of Religious Law in Judaism', *Aufsteig und Niedergang der Römischen Welt*, 19 (1979), 33.

—— 'The Jewish View of Natural Law', *Journal of Jewish Studies*, 52 (2001), 136.

—— '*Mishpat Ivri, Halakhah* and Legal Philosophy: *Agunah* and the Theory of Legal Sources', *Jewish Studies, an Internet Journal*, 1 (2002), 69, at http://www.biu.ac.il/JS/JSIJ/1-2002/Jackson.pdf, accessed 26 March 2003.

JACKSON, B., LIFSHITZ, B., GRAY, A., and SINCLAIR, D., 'Halakhah and Law', in M. Goodman, J. Cohen, and D. Sorkin (eds.), *The Oxford Handbook of Jewish Studies* (Oxford University Press, Oxford, 2002).

JAKOBOVITS, I., 'The Law Relating to the Precipitation of the Death of a Hopeless Patient Who is Undergoing Great Suffering' (Heb.), *Hapardes*, 31 (1957), pt. 1, 28; pt. 3, 16.

—— *Jewish Medical Ethics* (Bloch Publishing Co., New York 1975).

—— 'Some Modern *Responsa* on Medico-Legal Problems', *Jewish Medical Ethics*, 1 (1988), 6.

JAKOBOVITS, Y., 'Brain Death and Heart Transplants: The Israeli Chief Rabbinate's Directives', *Tradition*, 24 (1989), 1.

JONSEN, A., and TOULMIN, S., *The Abuse of Casuistry* (University of California Press, Berkeley, 1988).

KATZ, J., *Halakhah Vekabbalah* (Magnes Press, Jerusalem, 1984).

—— *The 'Shabbes Goy'* (Jewish Publication Society, Philadelphia, 1989).

KENNEDY, I., and GRUBB, A., *Medical Law* (Butterworths, London, 1994).

KEOWN, J. (ed.), *Euthanasia Examined* (Cambridge University Press, Cambridge, 1995).

—— 'Restoring Moral and Intellectual Shape to the Law After Bland', 113 *Law Quarterly Review* (1997), 485.

KEYSERLINGK, E., *Sanctity of Life or Quality of Life* (Law Reform Commission of Canada, Ottawa, 1979).

KILAV, A., 'Is Maternity Established by Conception or Birth?' (Heb.), *Tehumin*, 5 (1984), 260.

KIRSCHENBAUM, A., 'The Good Samaritan and Jewish Law', *Dine Israel*, 7 (1976), 7.

KOTTEK, S., 'The Best of Physicians are Destined for Purgatory' (Heb.), *Sefer Assia*, 2 (1981), 21.

KOTTEK, S., and GARCIA-BALLESTER, L. (eds.), *Medicine and Medical Ethics in Medieval and Early Modern Spain* (Magnes Press, Jerusalem, 1996).

KRAMER, M., 'The Shortage of Organs for Transplantation in Israel: Have We Given Up?' (Heb.), *Harefuah*, 124 (1993), 24.

KUBLER-ROSS, E., *On Death and Dying* (Macmillan, New York, 1969).

LAMM, N., and KIRSCHENBAUM, A., 'Freedom and Constraint in the Jewish Judicial Process', *Cardozo Law Review*, 1 (1979), 110.

LASKER, D., 'Kabbalah, Halakhah and Modern Medicine', *Modern Judaism*, 8 (1988), 1.

LAU, Y., 'The Sale of Organs for Transplantation' (Heb.), *Tehumin*, 18 (1998), 125.

LEAMAN, O., 'Maimonides and Natural Law', *Jewish Law Annual*, 6 (1987), 78.

LECKY, W., *History of the Rise and Influence of the Spirit of Rationalism in Europe* (London, 1870).

LEVIN, S., and BOYDEN, E., *The Kosher Code* (Hermon Press, New York, 1969).

LICHTENSTEIN, A., 'Does Jewish Tradition Recognize an Ethic Independent of *Halakhah*', in M. Kellner (ed.), *Contemporary Jewish Ethics* (Sanhedrin Press, New York, 1978), 102.

—— 'A Halakhic Perspective on Abortion' (Heb.), *Tehumin*, 21 (1991), 93.

LICHTENSTEIN, A., *The Seven Laws of Noah* (The Rabbi Jacob Joseph School Press, New York, 1981).

LOW, Z., 'Concerning the Children of Surrogate Mothers' (Heb.), *Or Hamizrach*, 133 (1989), 150.

MCAULEY, F., and MCCUTCHEON, J., *Criminal Liability* (Round Hall Sweet & Maxwell, Dublin, 2000).

MCDONALD, J., and the Research Consortium of the Christopher Reeve Paralysis Foundation, 'Repairing the Damaged Spinal Cord', *Scientific American* (September 1999), 61.

MCLEAN, S. (ed.), *Law Reform and Human Reproduction* (Dartmouth Publishers, Aldershot, 1992).

MANSPEIZER, D., 'Genetically Engineered Wonderland', *Rutgers Law Review* 543 (1991), 417.

MARITAIN, J., *Man and the State* (University of Chicago Press, 1951).

MASON, J., and MCCALL SMITH, R., *Law and Medical Ethics* (Butterworths, London, 1999).

MEISELMAN, M., 'Halakhic Problems Relating to Kidney Transplants', *Halakhah Urefuah*, 1 (Jerusalem, 1981), 114.

MENDELSON, D., 'Medical Confidentiality: Australian and Jewish Law', *Jewish Law Annual*, 12 (1997), 217.

MENSCH, E., and FREEMAN, A., *The Politics of Virtue* (Duke University Press, Duke, NC, 1995).

METZGER, Y., 'Is There an Obligation to Force a Patient to Receive Medical Treatment in Jewish Law?' (Heb.), *Hazofeh*, 5 July 1991.

MOONEY, D., and MIKOS, A., 'Growing New Organs', *Scientific American*, 280 (1999), 38.

MURPHY, T., and LAPPE, M. (eds.), *Justice and the Human Genome Project* (University of California Press, Berkeley, 1994).

NEBENZAHL, A., 'Observations on In Vitro Fertilization' (Heb.), *Sefer Assia*, 5 (1987), 92.

NOONAN, J. (ed.), *The Morality of Abortion* (Harvard University Press, Cambridge, Mass., 1971).

NOVAK, D., *The Image of the Non-Jew in Judaism* (D. Edward Mellon Press, New York, 1983).

—— *Natural Law in Judaism* (Cambridge University Press, Cambridge, 1998).

OTLOWSKI, M., *Voluntary Euthanasia and the Common Law* (Oxford University Press, Oxford, 1997).

Our Genetic Future (British Medical Association, Oxford University Press, 1992).

PELLEGRINO, E., and FADEN, A. (eds.), *Jewish and Catholic Bioethics: An Ecumenical Dialogue* (Georgetown University Press, Washington DC, 1999).

PHILLIPS, J., 'Wardship and Abortion Prevention', *Law Quarterly Review*, 95 (1979), 332.

POTOLSKY, M., 'The Rabbinic Rule "No Rules are Derived From Before Sinai"' (Heb.), *Dine Israel*, 6 (1967), 195.

President's Commission for the Study of Ethical Problems in Medicine and Biomedical and Behavioural Research, *Medical, Legal and Other Issues in the Determination of Death* (Washington, DC, United States Government Printing Office, 1981).

—— *Deciding to Forgo Life-Sustaining Treatments* (Washington, DC, United States Government Printing Office, 1983).

RABINOWITZ, G. 'Procedure for a Daughter who has Digressed from the Correct Way' (Heb.), *Halakhah Urefuah*, 1 (1980), 336.

—— 'A *Responsum* Regarding Homeopathy' (Heb.), *Halakhah Urefuah*, 3 (1983), 249.

—— 'The Dangerously Ill, the *Goses* and the Definition of the Time of Death' (Heb.), *Halakhah Urefuah*, 3 (1983), 114.

—— 'Selling Organs' (Heb.), *Assia*, 61–2 (1998), 58.

RAFAEL, S., 'Medical Confidentiality in a Halakhic Perspective' (Heb.), *Sefer Assia*, 3 (1983), 332–5.

—— 'Forcing Medical Therapy on a Patient' (Heb.), *Torah Shebal Peh*, 33 (1992), 74.

RAKOVER, N., 'Law as a Universal Value' (Heb.), *Sidrat Mehkarim Usekirot*, 58 (Ministry of Justice, Jerusalem, 1987).

—— *Gedol Kevod Habriyot* (Ministry of Justice, Jerusalem, 1998).

RANDALL, T., 'Too Few Human Organs for Transplantation, Too Many in Need . . . and the Gap Widens', *Journal of the American Medical Association*, 265 (1991), 1223.

RAPOPORT, S., 'Defining Danger to Life in the Context of Circumcision' (Heb.), *Halakhah Urefuah*, 1 (1980), 283.

RAZIEL, M., 'Forcing a Patient to Receive Medical Treatment' (Heb.), *Tehumin*, 2 (1981), 325.

REISNER, A., 'A Halakhic Ethic of Care for the Terminally Ill', *Conservative Judaism*, 43 (1991), 48.

RICHARDSON, C. (ed.), *Library of Christian Classics* (London, 1955).

RISPLER-CHAIM, V., *Islamic Medical Ethics in the Twentieth Century* (E. J. Brill, Leiden, 1993).

ROSNER, F., *Medicine in the Bible and the Talmud* (Ktav Publishing House, Hoboken, NJ, 1997).

ROSNER, F., and BLEICH, J. D. (eds.), *Jewish Bioethics* (Sanhedrin Press, New York, 1979).

ROTH, L., 'Moralization and Demoralization in Jewish Ethics', *Judaism*, 11 (1962), 294.

SAGI, A., 'Natural Law and *Halakhah*—A Critical Analysis', *Jewish Law Annual*, 13 (2000), 149.

SAMET, M., 'Delaying Burial' (Heb.), *Assufot*, 3 (1989), 417.

SCHOSTAK, Z., 'Ethical Guidelines for the Treatment of the Dying Elderly', *Journal of Halakhah and Contemporary Society*, 20 (1991), 62.

SCHWARTZ, H., 'Bioethical and Legal Considerations in Increasing the Supply of Transplantable Organs', *American Journal of Law and Medicine*, 10 (1985), 397.

SCHWARZSCHILD, S., 'Do Noahides Have to Believe in Revelation?', in M. Kellner (ed.), *The Pursuit of the Ideal: Jewish Writings of Steven Schwarzschild* (State University of New York Press, Albany, 1990), 29.

SCOTT, R., 'Autonomy and Connectedness: A Re-Evaluation of *Georgetown* and its Progeny', *The Journal of Law, Medicine and Ethics*, 28 (2000), 56.

SHAFRAN, Y., 'Genetic Cloning in the Light of the Halakhah' (Heb.), *Tehumin*, 18 (1998), 151.

SHALEV, C., 'A Man's Right to be Equal: The Abortion Issue', *Israel Law Review*, 18 (1984), 381.

SHANIN, E., 'International Responses to Human Cloning', *Chicago Journal of International Law*, 3 (2001), 255.

SHAPIRA, A., 'Informed Consent to Medical Procedures' (Heb.), *Iyyunei Mishpat*, 14 (1989), 225.

SHATZ, D., 'Concepts of Autonomy in Jewish Medical Ethics', *Jewish Law Annual*, 12 (1997), 3.

SHELUSH, S., 'The Use of Host Mothers' (Heb.), *Bitaon Hamoezah Hadati Haifa*, 39 (1992), 31.

SHERWIN, B., *In Partnership With God* (Syracuse University Press, Syracuse, NY, 1990).

SHILAT, Y., 'Genetic Cloning in the Light of the *Halakhah*' (Heb.), *Tehumin*, 18 (1998), 140.

SHILO, S., 'Sacrificing One Life for the Sake of Saving Many Others' (Heb.), *Hevra Vehistoria* (Ministry of Education and Culture, Jerusalem, 1980), 57.

—— 'Comments and Some New Light on the Foundations of Law Act' (Heb), *Shenaton Hamishpat Haivri*, 13 (1987), 351.

SILBERSTEIN, Y., 'Foetal Reduction' (Heb.), *Assia*, 45–6 (1989), 62.

SIMMONS, P., 'Religious Approaches to Abortion', in J.Butler and D. Walbert (eds.), *Abortion, Medicine and the Law* (New York, 1992), 713.

SIMPSON, B., *Cannibalism and the Common Law* (University of Chicago Press, 1984).

SINCLAIR, D., 'The Legal Basis for the Prohibition on Abortion in Jewish Law', *Israel Law Review*, 15 (1980), 109.

—— *Tradition and the Biological Revolution* (Edinburgh University Press, Edinburgh, 1989).

—— 'The Right to Life: Defending the Lives of the Terminally Ill, Foetuses and Non-Jews in Jewish Law' (Heb.), in G. Frishtik (ed.), *Human Rights in Jewish Law* (Sanhedrin Institute, Jerusalem, 1992), 33.

—— 'The Interaction between Law and Morality in Jewish Law', *Criminal Justice Ethics*, 11 (1992), 79.

—— 'Non-Consensual Medical Treatment of Competent Individuals in Jewish Law with some Comparative Reference to Anglo-American Law', *Tel-Aviv University Studies in Law*, 11 (1992), 227.

—— 'The Status of Human Healing and Coercive Medical Treatment in Jewish Law' (Heb.), *Shenaton Hamishpat Haivri*, 18–19 (1992–4), 270.

—— 'Kidney Donations from the Legally Incompetent in Jewish and Comparative Law', *Israel Law Review*, 27 (1993), 587.

—— 'The Terminal Patient in Jewish Law', *Tel-Aviv University Studies in Law*, 12 (1994), 283.

—— 'Jewish Law in the State of Israel', *Jewish Law Annual*, 6 (1987); 7 (1988); 11 (1994), 237.

—— 'Torah and Scientific Methodology in Rambam's Halakhic Writings', *Le'ela* (April 1995) 30.

SINCLAIR, D., 'Patient Self-Determination and Advance Directives', *Jewish Law Association Studies*, 8 (1996), 173.

—— 'Halakhic Methodology in the Post-Emancipation Period: Case Studies in the Responsa of R. Yechezkel Landau', *Le'ela* (April 1998), 16.

—— 'Medical Experiments on Human Beings in Jewish and Israeli Law', in *Israeli Reports to the 15th International Congress of Comparative Law*, ed. A. Rabello (The Harry and Michael Sacher Institute for Research and Comparative Law, Jerusalem, 1999), 129.

SINGER, C., *A Short History of Medicine* (Oxford University Press, Oxford, 1928).

SKEGG, P., *Law, Ethics and Medicine* (Oxford University Press, Oxford, 1984).

SKENE, L., 'When Can Doctors Treat Patients Who Cannot or Will Not Consent?', *Monash University Law Review*, 23 (1997), 77.

SMITH, J., *Justification and Excuse in the Criminal Law* (Stevens, London, 1989).

SMITH, J., and HOGAN, D., *Criminal Law* (Butterworths, London, 1999).

SOLOVEITCHIK, H., 'Three Themes in Sefer Hasidim', *Association of Jewish Studies Review*, 1 (1976), 311.

SOLOVEITCHIK, M., 'Test-Tube Baby' (Heb:), *Or Hamizrah*, 100 (1981), 127.

STEINBERG, A., *Encyclopaedia of Jewish Medical Ethics*, (Heb.), 6 vols. (Falk-Schlesinger Institute for Research in *Halakhah* and Medicine, Sha'arei Zedek Medical Centre, Jerusalem, 1988–98).

—— 'Establishing the Time of Death' (Heb.), *Assia*, 53–4 (1994), 5.

—— 'Human Cloning' (Heb.), *Assia*, 61–2 (1998).

STEINBOCK, B., 'Recovery from Persistent Vegetative State? The Case of Carrie Coons', *Hastings Centre Report*, 19 (1989), 14.

STERN, S., *Jewish Identity in Early Rabbinic Writings* (E. J. Brill, Leiden, 1994).

STERNBUCH, M., 'On Test Tube Babies' (Heb.), *Bishvilei Harefuah*, 8 (1978), 29.

STONE, S., 'Sinaitic and Noahide Law: Legal Pluralism in Jewish Law', *Cardozo Law Review*, 12 (1991), 1157.

SULMASY, D., 'Killing and Allowing to Die: Another Look', *Journal of Law, Medicine and Ethics*, 26 (1998), 55.

TABENKIN, H., 'Issues Relating to the Sale of a Kidney From a Live Donor' (Heb.), *Assia*, 63–4 (1998), 74.

TAUREK, J., 'Should the Numbers Count?', *Philosophy and Public Affairs*, 6 (1977), 293.

TENDLER, M., 'Jewish Law and the Time of Death', *Journal of the American Medical Association*, 240 (1978), 109.

—— 'Determining Death and Transplanting Organs' (Heb.), *Emek Halakha Assia*, 2 (1990), 213.

—— 'To Guide the Perplexed on the Halakhah of Brain Stem Death', *Rabbinical Council of America Publication* (August 1991), 2.

TRACHTENBERG, J., *Jewish Magic and Superstition* (Behrman's Jewish Book House, New York, 1939).

TWERSKY, I., *Introduction to the Code of Maimonides* (Yale University Press, New Haven, Conn., 1980).

—— 'Halakhah and Science: Perspectives on the Epistemology of Maimonides' (Heb.), *Shenaton Hamishpat Haivri*, 14–15 (1988–9), 121.

VEATCH, R., *Death, Dying and the Biological Revolution* (Yale University Press, New Haven, Conn., 1976).

WARHAFTIG, I., 'An Addendum to the Test Tube Babies Debate' (Heb.), *Tehumin*, 5 (1984), 268.

WEILER, Y., 'Surrogacy and Changes in the Concept of Parenthood' (Heb.), *Assia*, 57–8 (1966), 141.

WEINFELD, M., 'The Genuine Jewish Attitude Towards Abortion' (Heb.), *Zion*, 42 (1977), 129.

WEISS, I., *Dor Dor Vedorshav* (Platt & Minkus, Berlin, 1923).

WERNER, S., 'Mercy Killing in the Light of Jewish Law' (Heb.), *Torah Shebal Peh*, 18 (1976), 39.

WILGOOS, C., 'FDA Regulation: An Answer to the Questions of Human Cloning and Germline Therapy', *American Journal of Law and Medicine*, 27 (2001), 101.

WILKIE, T., *Perilous Knowledge* (Faber & Faber, London, 1994).

WILLIAMS, G., *The Sanctity of Life and the Criminal Law* (Knopf, New York, 1957).

WINFIELD, P., 'The Unborn Child', *Cambridge Law Journal*, 3 (1944), 76.

WOLFSON, H., *Philo* (Harvard University Press, Cambridge, Mass., 1962).

WOLNER, M., 'The Physician's Rights and Jurisdiction' (Heb.), *Hatorah Vehamedinah*, 7–8 (1956–7), 318.

YISRAELI, S., 'The Kibiyeh Incident in the Light of the *Halakhah*' (Heb.), *Hatorah Vehamedinah*, 4–6 (1953–4), 109.

——'The Ownership of Fertilized Embryos' (Heb.), in *Encyclopaedia of Jewish Medical Ethics*, iv. 22.

YOUNGER, J., and BARTLETT, E., 'Human Dignity and High Technology', *Annals of Internal Medicine*, 99 (1982), 252.

ZILBERSTEIN, Y., 'Kidney Transplantation' (Heb.), *Halakhah Urefuah*, 4 (1985), 156.

ZOHAR, N., 'Toward Justice in the Organ Trade', *Israel Law Review*, 27 (1993), 541.

——*Alternatives in Jewish Bioethics* (State University of New York Press, Albany, 1997).

ZWEIG, M., 'Regarding Abortion' (Heb.), *Noam*, 7 (1964), 45.

Index